The Platform Playbook

"*The Platform Playbook* brilliantly captures the shift from linear marketing to ecosystem-led growth. For marketers building strategy and operations in a platform world, it offers the frameworks and clarity needed to harness technology, scale effectively and thrive."

—Scott Brinker, Editor of *chiefmartec*

"A useful guide for B2B leaders navigating the shift from campaigns to ecosystems. With its mix of strategic insight and actionable frameworks, it's a valuable resource for CMOs and growth strategists looking to move from broadcast to co-creation, and from funnels to platforms."

—Sangeet Paul Choudary, Senior Fellow at the University of California, Berkeley, USA, and international best-selling author of *Platform Revolution* (2016) and *Reshuffle* (2025)

"*The Platform Playbook* presents a strategic roadmap for those leading organisational transformation, designing ecosystems and placing marketing at the centre of sustainable business growth. It empowers professionals to move beyond tactical delivery to strategic influence, shaping platforms that drive scale, collaboration, and innovation. Essential reading for leaders who view marketing as a catalyst for long-term organisational growth."

—Chris Daly, FCIM, Chartered Marketer and Chief Executive of the Chartered Institute of Marketing

Leeya Hendricks

The Platform Playbook

The Marketer's Guide to Designing, Scaling and Leading Platform Growth

Leeya Hendricks ⓘ
Hark Consultants
London, UK

ISBN 978-3-032-08030-1   ISBN 978-3-032-08031-8   (eBook)
https://doi.org/10.1007/978-3-032-08031-8

© The Editor(s) (if applicable) and The Author(s), under exclusive license to Springer Nature Switzerland AG 2026

This work is subject to copyright. All rights are solely and exclusively licensed by the Publisher, whether the whole or part of the material is concerned, specifically the rights of translation, reprinting, reuse of illustrations, recitation, broadcasting, reproduction on microfilms or in any other physical way, and transmission or information storage and retrieval, electronic adaptation, computer software, or by similar or dissimilar methodology now known or hereafter developed.
The use of general descriptive names, registered names, trademarks, service marks, etc. in this publication does not imply, even in the absence of a specific statement, that such names are exempt from the relevant protective laws and regulations and therefore free for general use.
The publisher, the authors and the editors are safe to assume that the advice and information in this book are believed to be true and accurate at the date of publication. Neither the publisher nor the authors or the editors give a warranty, expressed or implied, with respect to the material contained herein or for any errors or omissions that may have been made. The publisher remains neutral with regard to jurisdictional claims in published maps and institutional affiliations.

This Palgrave Macmillan imprint is published by the registered company Springer Nature Switzerland AG
The registered company address is: Gewerbestrasse 11, 6330 Cham, Switzerland

If disposing of this product, please recycle the paper.

Preface

The Platform Imperative

In the past, businesses competed by building moats—accumulating resources, assets, and advantages to fend off rivals.

Today, they win by building bridges.

We live in a platform economy: a world where value emerges not through isolated ownership but through connected collaboration. The companies that thrive are those that create ecosystems, nurture networks, and orchestrate collective growth.

This book was born from a realisation: that marketing itself must evolve. That traditional models—rooted in top-down messaging and passive consumption—no longer suffice in a world of empowered actors, open innovation, and value co-creation.

Over the course of this journey, you'll explore frameworks, case studies, and emerging technologies that redefine what it means to lead and grow in the platform era. Each chapter is a stepping stone towards a future where marketers become architects of engagement, facilitators of collaboration, and enablers of innovation.

Whether you are an executive, a strategist, an entrepreneur, or a marketer navigating digital transformation, my hope is that this book provides a roadmap—and a source of inspiration—for unlocking the immense potential of platform ecosystems.

London, UK   Dr. Leeya Hendricks

Acknowledgements

Collaborators in the Platform Journey

Writing about platform ecosystems naturally reminds me: nothing truly great is built alone.

I am deeply grateful to the communities of entrepreneurs, technologists, researchers, and strategists whose insights and innovations have shaped my thinking.

Special thanks to the pioneers who continue to reimagine marketing, not as a megaphone but as a conversation—and to the academics and business leaders whose research provided insights to shape the thinking for the foundations for many of the frameworks shared in this work.

Thank you to my colleagues, peers, and readers, who challenged assumptions, posed tough questions, and pushed this project towards greater clarity and relevance.

To my husband, my other half—thank you for walking alongside me on this journey of life and the writing of this book, from the very first day I dreamed of it. Your unwavering belief in me and your constant challenge to become a better version of myself every day made this work possible.

And to every platform builder—past, present, and future—this book is for you.

Competing Interests The author has no competing interests to declare that are relevant to the content of this manuscript.

Introduction

Leading Beyond the Funnel

With our fast-evolving business landscape, and a significant number of businesses driven by platforms, platforms are more than just digital channels—they are strategic ecosystems. They reshape how we create value, engage with customers, and ultimately, drive sustainable growth. This book is for those who don't just want to market, but lead. For those stepping beyond tactical execution into business transformation. For those who believe that success lies not in doing things right, but in choosing the right things to do.

My own journey began in the craft of marketing—audience insights, segmentation, campaign delivery, content calendars, demand generation. But as I stepped into broader business leadership roles, a clear truth emerged: vision matters more than mechanics. Commercial growth isn't just a by-product of good marketing; it's the result of strategic focus, bold decisions, and cohesive leadership across the organisation.

This book is for the value co-creators. The Chief Marketing Officer as business leader. The platform architect. The growth-focused strategist. If you've ever felt the pull between delivering short-term return on investment and enabling long-term strategic impact, this book is your blueprint.

You'll find that platforms, when designed with intention, enable collaboration, unlock innovation, and elevate the role of marketing to that of a strategic business function. Whether through data-enabled service delivery, actor engagement in B2B ecosystems, or creating communities around shared value—platforms create the conditions for scale.

The Platform Playbook is not a tactical manual—it's a strategic roadmap for leaders who see platforms as engines for transformation. This book is built for those shaping B2B organisations—from innovative startups and high-growth scale-ups to established enterprises and purpose-led institutions. Whether you operate in commercial markets or the non-profit space, this guide offers a lens to rethink business models, orchestrate ecosystems, and embed value creation at the core of your growth strategy.

It is a strategic playbook for building, leading, and scaling platform-centric businesses rooted in ecosystem thinking and value co-creation. This book is designed for leaders operating within B2B environments—from startups and scale-ups to mid-sized firms, enterprises, and mission-driven organisations. Whether commercial or non-profit, the unifying thread is a shared ambition: to unlock growth by architecting platforms that enable strategic collaboration, foster innovation, and embed marketing as a central lever of business leadership.

It's about how to build, lead, and evolve platform-centric businesses. As we witness the convergence of digital transformation, customer co-creation, and platform-enabled scale, we have a choice: to react or to lead. The leaders of tomorrow are not just optimising funnels; they are architecting ecosystems.

This book won't provide all the answers, but it will pose the right questions. It will help you identify the shifts required to lead with vision—to scale with purpose, and to build platforms that matter.

About This Book

The Platform Playbook was born from both boardroom experience and academic inquiry—and from a deep fascination with the evolving nature of B2B marketing. Unlike its B2C counterpart, B2B marketing is a complex, emotionally nuanced, and deeply strategic discipline. It sits at the intersection of relationships, revenue, and reputation—often invisible, yet always consequential.

This book reflects years of navigating that complexity across contexts. Having led marketing and growth strategies in startups, scale-ups, and large global enterprises, I've come to appreciate just how varied the role of the modern B2B marketer really is. It's not one job—it's many. It demands meta-agility: the ability to think strategically while acting tactically, to shift gears between speed and depth, to be both a lateral thinker and a domain expert.

In startups, it's about rapid execution, resourcefulness, and wearing multiple hats. In scale-ups, the focus shifts to codifying processes, aligning teams, and preparing for scale. And in large enterprises, the marketer must influence across silos, build executive credibility, and balance innovation with governance. Each stage demands a different type of marketer, and a different mindset.

Throughout my journey, from Chief Marketing Officer roles in high-growth tech companies like Prytek, Delta Capita, and Rimm, to executive positions in global giants such as Accenture, Gartner, IBM, and Oracle, I've observed one unifying truth: the marketers who thrive are not just communicators. They are systems thinkers. Business leaders. Platform builders.

The Platform Playbook reflects that insight. It's not a manual on marketing tactics. It's a strategic lens—one that equips you to design, lead, and scale platform-centric businesses in the interconnected, fast-moving B2B landscape we operate in today. It's a step, but one that affirms the growing relevance of the work I've been passionate about: reimagining B2B strategy through ecosystems, platforms, and value creation. These ideas are no longer abstract concepts—they're becoming central to how businesses compete, collaborate, and create lasting impact.

These pages are informed by ongoing conversations happening at the intersection of industry and academia—conversations about navigating complexity, co-creating meaningful value, and building resilient, scalable systems that move beyond theory into practice. From how platform models are transforming B2B markets, to the role of actor engagement in shaping innovation, this space continues to evolve in powerful and exciting ways.

This book is for those who don't fit neatly into job descriptions—those who are both specialists and generalists, who operate across strategy and execution, who build with both speed and substance. It's for the leaders building not just brands, but ecosystems. If that sounds like you—welcome. You're in the right place.

Contents

Part I Foundations of Platform Ecosystems and Value Co-Creation

1	The Evolution of Marketing in Platform Ecosystems	3
2	Marketing Leaders as Drivers of Co-Creation	13
3	Foundations of Platform Ecosystem	21
4	Bridging the Gap—Aligning CMOs and CEOs for Platform Growth	31
5	The Power of Ecosystems in Value Co-Creation	41

Part II Core Mechanics of Value Creation and Engagement

6	Key Players in Platform Ecosystems	55
7	Building Partnerships—The Role of Complementors	65
8	Overcoming Barriers in Institutionalised Markets	77
9	Leveraging Actor Engagement in the Digital Era	89
10	Building Trust and Collaboration in Digital Ecosystems	99

Part III Strategic Frameworks for Platform Growth

11	Stimulating Engagement through Platforms as a Service	113
12	Community-Building Strategies for Marketers	127
13	Using Engagement to Drive Value Co-Creation	139
14	Value Co-Creation—The New Marketing Currency	151
15	Reciprocal Resource Integration in Ecosystems	159

Part IV Technology as a Catalyst

16	Using Technology to Foster Co-Innovation	173
17	Case Studies—Successful Value Co-Creation in Fintech	185
18	Challenges and Opportunities for Marketers	197
19	Understanding Institutional Barriers to Innovation	207
20	Strategies to Overcome Resistance in Marketing for Ecosystems	217

Part V Scaling and Structuring for Regional and Global Growth

21	Platforms as a Disruptor: Insights from Asset Management	229
22	Plug-and-Play Solutions for Agility and Scalability	241
23	The Role of Leadership to Drive Change	251
24	Scaling Platforms with Complementors	261
25	Collaboration Strategies for Platform Growth	273
26	Regional Strategies for Legitimacy and Expansion	281

Part VI Future-Ready Platform Strategies

27	Using Resource Integration to Amplify Scale	293
28	Unlocking Future Marketing Potential: The Interplay of Actor Engagement and Co-Creation	303
29	Advanced Marketing Strategies for Platform Ecosystems	313

30	Emerging Trends in AI, IoT, and Cloud Computing for Marketers	323
31	Designing a Scalable Platform-Driven Marketing Strategy	333

Conclusion	341
Consolidated References	343
Index	365

About the Author

Dr. Leeya Hendricks is a strategic business leader, platform architect, and marketing visionary with a career that bridges practice, academia, and governance. Having started her journey deep in the mechanics of marketing—from data-driven campaigns and brand transformation to commercial performance—Leeya's path has evolved into one of executive influence, cross-sector leadership, and systemic change.

She is an internationally recognised executive and academic whose career spans the intersection of strategic marketing, platform innovation, and business transformation. With over two decades of experience leading in both enterprise and growth-stage environments, Leeya brings a rare perspective—combining practical leadership with academic rigour and board-level insight.

She has served as Chief Marketing Officer at pioneering firms such as Prytek, Delta Capita, and Rimm, where she architected platform-led growth strategies, shaped global brand identities, and delivered measurable commercial impact. Prior to that, Leeya held senior executive roles at global powerhouses including Accenture, Gartner, IBM, and Oracle, where she led transformative initiatives in technology, consulting, and data-driven innovation.

Her career reflects deep fluency in both established systems and emerging models—from navigating institutional complexity to designing agile, co-creative ecosystems. Leeya is particularly known for her ability to translate strategic vision into executable growth, combining the discipline of enterprise leadership with the dynamism of scale-up innovation.

Today, Dr. Hendricks serves as a board advisor, executive mentor, lecturer, speaker, and serves on a number of boards. She is a non-executive director and Board member of the Chartered Institute of Marketing and is an established Fellow and Chartered Marketer. Her work continues to influence how organisations think about marketing, not as a function, but as a force for ecosystem-led growth.

As a former Chief Marketing Officer turned Managing Director and board advisor, she brings a rare blend of executional expertise and strategic foresight. Her experience spans global enterprises, high-growth scale-ups, and platform-centric ventures—always with a focus on driving growth through ecosystem thinking and co-creation.

Her academic work, including a PhD focused on B2B platform ecosystem development and published papers, builds on a foundation of real-world impact. She has lectured at a number of universities; and is recognised for her contributions to platform strategy, ecosystems and value creation in institutionalised industries, and the evolution of marketing from functional silo to organisational growth engine. She currently serves as a visiting lecturer to post-graduate and masters students for International Business and Law at the MCI, Management Centre Innsbruck.

Whether advising boards, leading transformation programmes, lecturing, or mentoring the next generation of leaders, Leeya champions a single idea: that sustainable growth is a result of alignment—between people, purpose, and platforms.

The Platform Playbook is a culmination of that journey—blending insight and experience into a roadmap for those who don't just want to grow their business but redefine its impact.

Abbreviations

Ad	Advert
AI	Artificial Intelligence
AML	Anti-Money-Laundering
API	Application Programming Interface
App	Application
AR	Augmented Reality
B2B	Business to Business
B2C	Business to Consumer
BaaS	Banking-as-a-Service
CaaS	Compliance-as-a-Service
CAC	Customer Acquisition Cost
CCPA	California Consumer Privacy Act
CEO	Chief Executive Officer
CMO	Chief Marketing Officer
CRM	Customer Relationship Management
CX	Customer Experience
ERP	Enterprise Resource Planning
ETF	Exchange Traded Fund
ESG	Environmental Social Governance
EV	Electrical Vehicle
EVP	Ecosystem Value Proposition
Fintech	Financial Technology
GDPR	General Data Protection Regulation
HIPAA	Health Insurance Portability Accountability Act
ID	Identification Document

iOS	iPhone Operating Systems
IOT	Internet of Things
IT	Information Technology
ISV	Independent Software Vendor
KPI	Key Performance Indicator
KYC	Know-your-Customer
LMS	Learning Management System
M&A	Merger and Acquisition
ML	Machine Learning
MVP	Minimum Viable Product
NGO	Non-governmental Organisation
NPS	Net Promoter Score
PaaS	Platform-as-a-Service
PR	Public Relations
Q&A	Question and Answer
R&D	Research and Development
Regtech	Regulatory Technology
ROI	Return on Investment
SaaS	Software-as-a-Service
SDK	Software Development Kit
SDL	Service-Dominant Logic
UGC	User Generated Content
UI	User Interface
UX	User Experience

List of Figures

Fig. 1.1	Marketing's Platform Value Engine Model	10
Fig. 2.1	Co-Creation Engine in Platform Ecosystems Model	17
Fig. 3.1	Structure of a Platform Ecosystem Hub	28
Fig. 4.1	Alignment Loop Between CEO and CMO in Platform Growth	37
Fig. 5.1	Ecosystem Value Co-Creation Model	48
Fig. 6.1	Roles in a Platform Ecosystems Model	61
Fig. 7.1	Complementor Engagement in Platform Ecosystems Model	73
Fig. 8.1	Navigating Barriers in Institutional Ecosystems Model	86
Fig. 9.1	Actor Engagement Lifecycle Model	95
Fig. 10.1	Trust and Collaboration Stack Model	107
Fig. 11.1	PaaS Engagement Engine Model	123
Fig. 12.1	Community Engagement Flywheel Model	135
Fig. 13.1	Engagement Co-Creation Value Loop	147
Fig. 14.1	Co-Creation Spiral Model	156
Fig. 15.1	Reciprocal Resource Integration Cycle	168
Fig. 16.1	Co-Innovation Technology Stack	180
Fig. 17.1	Fintech Value Co-Creation Ecosystem	192
Fig. 18.1	Co-Creation Challenge-Opportunity Balance	204
Fig. 19.1	Barrier Mapping Model	214
Fig. 20.1	Ecosystem Resistance Navigation Model	223
Fig. 21.1	Paas Transformation Journey Model	237
Fig. 22.1	Plug-and-Play Advantage Cycle	248
Fig. 23.1	Leadership-Driven Change Ecosystem Model	258
Fig. 24.1	Scaling Platforms Through Complementor Networks	268

Fig. 25.1	Strategic Alliances Driving Platform Growth Model	277
Fig. 26.1	Strategic Pillars for Regional Platform Success	287
Fig. 27.1	Scaling Through Ecosystem Resource Integration Model	300
Fig. 28.1	Self-Reinforcing Cycle of Actor Engagement and Co-Creation	309
Fig. 29.1	Self-Perpetuating Growth Model	320
Fig. 30.1	AI-IoT-Cloud Integration Model for Marketers	329
Fig. 31.1	Scalable Platform Marketing Model	339

List of Tables

Table 15.1	Resource Reciprocity Map	169
Table 16.1	Co-Innovation Opportunity Canvas—Template Grid	181
Table 18.1	The Co-Creation Tension Matrix	205
Table 19.1	Barrier Transformation Map—Template Grid	215
Table 20.1	The Ecosystem Resistance Audit—Template Grid	225
Table 21.1	PaaS Transformation Opportunity Canvas—Template Grid	238
Table 22.1	Plug-and-Play Adoption Canvas—Template Grid	249
Table 23.1	Leadership for Change Canvas—Template Grid	259
Table 24.1	Complementor Strategy Canvas—Template Grid	269
Table 26.1	Regional Strategy Canvas—Template Grid	288
Table 27.1	Resource Integration Strategy Canvas—Template Grid	301
Table 28.1	Engagement—Co-Creation Alignment Map—Template Grid	310
Table 29.1	Platform Marketing Strategy Alignment Grid—Template Grid	321
Table 30.1	Emerging Technology Adoption Readiness Audit—Template Grid	330
Table 31.1	Platform-Driven Marketing Readiness Blueprint—Template Grid	340

Part I

Foundations of Platform Ecosystems and Value Co-Creation

1

The Evolution of Marketing in Platform Ecosystems

Marketing has always been about connection, reaching the right audience with the right message to drive action. But as the rules of business evolve, so too must the role of marketing. No longer confined to linear campaigns and product push, today's marketing leaders are navigating a more complex, decentralised, and dynamic environment, the platform ecosystem.

In traditional models, marketing focused on transactional exchanges between producers and consumers. The aim was clear: position a product, capture attention, and convert leads into sales. But in a platform economy, this producer–consumer dichotomy no longer defines the landscape. Instead, platforms operate as ecosystems where value is co-created by many, businesses, customers, partners, developers, and even competitors (Gawer & Cusumano, 2014).

Platforms such as **Amazon**, **Salesforce**, and **Alibaba** exemplify this shift. They do not merely facilitate transactions, they orchestrate interactions. Every actor within the ecosystem contributes to and benefits from shared infrastructure, data, and services. The result is a fluid, scalable model of growth that thrives on inclusivity, decentralised participation, and shared outcomes.

From Control to Collaboration

In a platform world, control is no longer the lever—collaboration is. The most successful platform marketers today are those who can architect ecosystems, engage diverse actors, and build strategies that foster co-creation

(Mancuso et al., 2024). The focus is no longer on owning every component, but on enabling connections that create value for all participants.

This demands a fundamental mindset shift. Rather than pushing a message to an audience, platform marketers must design systems where value is exchanged continuously—where customers also become contributors, where partners expand the offer, and where engagement is incentivised through network dynamics.

The Engine Room: Core Concepts in Platform Marketing

To understand the dynamics of platform ecosystems, we must examine the interconnected mechanics that drive their scalability and sustained value. At the core of this model lie three foundational concepts that, together, define how platforms function and flourish. First, network effects—the powerful phenomenon where a platform's value grows exponentially as more participants engage with it (Katz & Shapiro, 1985).

Every additional user, partner, or developer doesn't just add value—they multiply it, enriching the data landscape, expanding functionality, and enhancing the innovation capacity of the ecosystem (Parker & Van Alstyne, 2023). This creates a self-reinforcing cycle of growth where scale itself becomes a strategic advantage. Equally critical is actor engagement. In a platform context, engagement transcends metrics—it becomes the lifeblood of the ecosystem. From user-generated content and peer validation to collaborative feature development and API integrations, every touchpoint is an opportunity for co-creation.

Platforms that cultivate active, contributive engagement tap into deeper loyalty and unlock higher-order value that goes far beyond simple transactions (Lusch & Nambisan, 2015). Finally, resource integration underpins the entire system. Value in a platform economy is not generated in isolation—it emerges through the seamless blending of external capabilities.

Whether it's integrating logistics partners, leveraging analytics tools, or embedding personalisation engines, marketers in platform businesses must operate as orchestrators—designing connected experiences that transcend organisational boundaries and deliver impact no single entity could achieve alone. This shift redefines the marketer's role as one of strategic ecosystem leadership, where success is measured not by outputs alone, but by the collaborative value created and sustained over time.

To understand this new terrain, we must look at the mechanics behind platform ecosystems. Three foundational concepts define this model:

- **Network Effects**: The value of the platform increases as more actors participate. Each new user, partner, or developer enhances the platform's utility, data richness, and innovation potential (McIntyre & Srinivasan, 2017). This creates a self-reinforcing loop of growth—a virtuous cycle where scale amplifies impact.
- **Actor Engagement**: Engagement is no longer a metric—it's the currency of the ecosystem. From peer reviews to API integrations, content contributions to co-developed features, engaged actors are what give a platform its edge (Aarikka-Stenroos & Ritala, 2017). When marketers shift their focus to enable and amplify this engagement, they unlock deeper loyalty, richer insights, and more meaningful impact.
- **Resource Integration**: Value is no longer created in silos. In a platform, growth is powered by the seamless integration of third-party capabilities (Ceccagnoli et al., 2012)—from logistics to analytics, payments to personalisation engines. Marketers become orchestrators of value chains, shaping collaborative experiences that deliver more than any one actor could alone.

Technology as a Catalyst, Not a Crutch

The evolution of marketing is not just philosophical—it's technological. Artificial intelligence (AI), cloud infrastructure, and connected devices have made platform ecosystems viable and scalable. AI enables real-time decisioning, hyper-personalisation, and behavioural insight. Cloud platforms facilitate integration, collaboration, and speed. IoT provides continuous feedback loops from the physical world, while blockchain introduces trust and traceability at scale.

The evolution of marketing in today's economy isn't solely a philosophical shift—it's a technological revolution. AI, cloud infrastructure, connected devices, and emerging digital ledgers have not only made platform ecosystems possible—they have made them scalable, dynamic, and enduring. Yet, while these technologies empower, they also elevate our responsibility: no longer can marketers lean on tech as a spare part—they must instil it with purpose, strategy, and collaboration.

AI: The Intelligent Backbone AI does more than automate tasks—it injects empathy, foresight, and agility into marketing. AI-powered systems can analyse behavioural patterns in real time, enabling hyper-personalisation at scale (Kumar et al., 2021). Imagine dynamic landing pages that change based on user intent, or chatbots that interpret tone and sentiment to offer empathic, context-aware assistance. True value emerges when AI isn't just used to predict behaviour—but to collaborate: inviting users to co-create experiences, feed back into the system, and participate in shaping the narrative.

Cloud: The Shared Nervous System Cloud technology offers the connective tissue for modern ecosystems. By providing flexible, scalable infrastructure, it enables brands, developers, and partners to work together seamlessly (Vaska et al., 2021)—without the friction of heavy IT deployments or stovepipe architectures. Cloud environments host APIs, shared data lakes, analytics dashboards, and collaboration portals, underpinning new modes of interaction. Marketers can tap into these tools to prototype, test, iterate—and most importantly, share access to co-creation spaces with their ecosystem.

IoT: The Real-World Feedback Loop Internet-of-Things (IoT) devices bridge the divide between digital and physical worlds, generating a continuous flow of real-world usage and sentiment data (Ng & Wakenshaw, 2017). Be it smart wearables, connected home devices, or in-store sensors, IoT offers marketers direct lines to observe value in action—and the freedom to adapt offerings in near real time. Think of a fitness platform that recognises stress patterns through wearables and adjusts workout suggestions accordingly—closing the loop between physical experience, emotional wellbeing, and platform engagement.

Blockchain: The Backbone of Trust In ecosystems growing bigger and more diverse, trust doesn't scale on reputation alone—it needs anchoring. Blockchain brings transparency, traceability, and immutability to every transaction, from a co-designed product release to data-sharing agreements or loyalty rewards (Treiblmaier, 2018). This fosters collaboration because every actor—user, partner, regulator—can rely on verified records of contribution, consent, and value exchange. For marketers, blockchain isn't just a buzzword—it's a promise of integrity.

Together, these technologies have transformed what's possible. But they've also raised the bar. Today's marketer is not just a storyteller or analyst—they are a systems thinker, a data strategist, a catalyst for co-creation.

In *The Platform Playbook*, we explore how these roles converge. The platform marketer is no longer a service function—they are a growth leader, a commercial architect, and a visionary who sees the whole game board, not just their piece of it.

Beyond the Toolbox: A Systems-Centred Mindset

Individually, these technologies bring remarkable possibilities. Yet when combined, they form the digital commons—shared infrastructure that allows interaction, insight, and innovation to converge in real time. However, their real value is not in automation alone. When treated merely as operational supports or short-term fixes, they risk becoming crutches—leading to tactical gains but long-term fragmentation. When embraced as catalysts, however, they fundamentally reshape the marketing function into something more strategic, collaborative, and resilient.

Platforms are no longer static stacks of technology. They are living, breathing ecosystems (de Reuver et al., 2018). In this context, marketers must shift from thinking in linear funnels to designing interconnected feedback loops. For instance, when a new feature is introduced on a platform, it doesn't simply enhance functionality—it often prompts behavioural change. That behavioural change, in turn, generates fresh insights that influence how future features are designed, how campaigns are crafted, and how messages are delivered. This is the essence of systems symbiosis.

At the same time, creativity is not replaced by data—it is refined by it. AI-driven tools allow marketers to infuse emotional intelligence into their storytelling, using behavioural signals and context-aware cues to shape narratives that resonate on a personal level. Whether it's a developer navigating APIs or a consumer shopping across a platform's marketplace, this level of tailored communication elevates creative strategy to a new plane of relevance.

Technology also unlocks co-creation at scale (Ramaswamy & Ozcan, 2018). Marketers no longer have to speak on behalf of the customer—they can create with them. Collaborative design platforms, shared dashboards, and open contribution models powered by the cloud and blockchain transform users and partners into contributors. The marketer's role becomes one of facilitation—curating spaces where innovation and feedback are ongoing, participatory processes.

Crucially, this evolution demands a new kind of leadership. Marketers today are not simply message managers—they are collaboration architects. They must integrate tools and strategies that bridge functions and disciplines, from engineering and legal to product and partner relations. It is their orchestration that makes co-creation not just aspirational, but operational.

In sum, these technologies do not define marketing's future on their own. It is how they are applied—with vision, purpose, and empathy—that will shape the next generation of ecosystem-driven growth.

The Platform Marketer: Growth Architect and Game-Changer

In *The Platform Playbook* we trace how these technological layers coalesce into a new marketing paradigm: the marketer as growth architect, ecosystem orchestrator, and visionary. They look at the board—and see connections, not just campaigns; relationships, not just reach. Their north star isn't a sales target—it's an engagement ecosystem that scales, renews, and sustains itself.

Technology isn't the answer—it's the amplifier. What matters most is what we design it to enable. Real-time insights, adaptive experimentation, equitable participation, trustworthy blueprints—these are what turn a platform from a showcase to a movement.

Because in the end, platforms thrive not by what they own, but by what they connect. And marketers who understand this—and shape the technology they use to fuel collaboration—will lead businesses into a future where value isn't just created—it's co-created, together.

From Transaction to Transformation

This chapter marks the beginning of a strategic shift—one where marketers step into a new mandate. It's not about being louder. It's about being more connected. It's about recognising that real value is no longer generated at the edge of the business—it's created in the middle, where relationships, data, services, and communities converge.

In traditional models, marketing was often tethered to a single point of interaction: the transaction. Campaigns aimed to convert attention into sales, measure success through clicks and conversions, and optimise for funnel velocity. But as industries digitise and customer expectations evolve, such linear models fall short. Value today is emergent—shaped over time, across touchpoints, and through multi-directional interaction (Chandler & Lusch, 2015).

This transformation shifts marketing from a communication function to a coordination function. The modern marketer is not just a messenger but an integrator—orchestrating between internal teams, external partners, technology layers, and customer communities. They are not merely driving demand; they are facilitating discovery, dialogue, and design. Every engagement becomes an opportunity to co-create, not just to convince.

Ecosystems are the new battlegrounds of business, and platforms are the arenas where value is contested and created (Jacobides et al., 2018). Whether in fintech, healthcare, education, or enterprise software, the companies that win will be those that enable participation—that unlock the creativity, capability, and contribution of their networks. And in this context, marketing becomes central to platform growth.

To succeed in this new role, marketers must master systems thinking (Meadows, 2008). They must understand not just audiences, but actors—developers, regulators, influencers, and integrators—and how each contributes to the whole (Parker et al., 2016). They must read signals from multiple directions and build strategies that are iterative, inclusive, and informed.

In the chapters ahead, we'll explore how to lead in this space, how to design platform strategies that scale, how to measure what matters, and how to turn ecosystems into engines of sustained competitive advantage. We'll go beyond the buzzwords to examine practical tools, visual frameworks and real-world examples that explain this shift.

Welcome to the evolution. You're not just marketing anymore. You're building a value engine—one that runs on trust, powered by participation, and designed to scale (Cennamo, 2021). This is not a trend—it's a transformation. And it's already underway.

Visual Framework: Marketing's Platform Value Engine Model

Figure 1.1 presents a framework designed to reflect marketing's evolving role within platform ecosystems. It captures the shift from traditional linear marketing to ecosystem-led dynamics, highlighting the key components that drive value creation, scalability, and sustained engagement in B2B platform businesses.

You can visualise the *Marketing's Platform Value Engine* model as a transformation from a flat line into a circular, interconnected system—where every actor, action, and integration contributes to the platform's ongoing momentum.

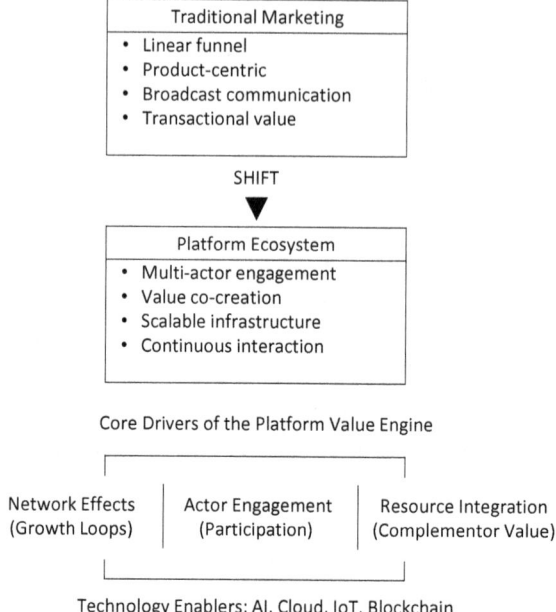

Fig. 1.1 Marketing's Platform Value Engine Model

Reflective Prompt: From Marketer to Ecosystem Leader

Take a moment to reflect on your current organisation's approach to marketing and business growth:

1. Are you still primarily operating within a campaign mindset—focused on reach, clicks, and conversions?
2. Where in your organisation are there opportunities to shift from communication to co-creation?
3. Who are the "complementors" in your business ecosystem that could unlock new value through collaboration?
4. How could you better structure your data, partnerships, or technologies to serve a broader ecosystem?

Exercise: Mapping Your Platform Potential

1. **Identify Three Key Ecosystem Actors**
    - Who outside your organisation—partners, clients, developers, suppliers—could play a role in co-creating value with you?
2. **List Your Current Marketing Channels**

- For each channel (e.g. website, content, CRM, events), ask:
- Is this channel enabling engagement, or just broadcasting?
- What could I do to make it more collaborative?

3. **Pinpoint Opportunities for Integration**

    - What tools, platforms, or services could you integrate to enhance user experience or scale more effectively?

This chapter helps you map out and begin rethinking your marketing function not as a standalone department, but as the architect of a platform—a value engine built to scale with others.

References

Aarikka-Stenroos, L., & Ritala, P. (2017). Network management in the era of ecosystems: Systematic review and management framework. *Industrial Marketing Management, 67*, 23–36. https://doi.org/10.1016/j.indmarman.2017.08.010

Ceccagnoli, M., Forman, C., Huang, P., & Wu, D. J. (2012). Cocreation of value in a platform ecosystem: The case of enterprise software. *MIS Quarterly, 36*(1), 263–290. https://www.jstor.org/stable/41410417

Cennamo, C. (2021). Competing in digital markets: A platform-based perspective. *Academy of Management Perspectives, 35*(2), 265–291. https://doi.org/10.5465/amp.2016.0048

Chandler, J. D., & Lusch, R. F. (2015). Service systems: A broadened framework and research agenda on value propositions, engagement, and service experience. *Journal of Service Research, 18*(1), 6–22. https://doi.org/10.1177/1094670514537

de Reuver, M., Sørensen, C., & Basole, R. C. (2018). The digital platform: A research agenda. *Journal of Information Technology, 33*(2), 124–135. https://doi.org/10.1057/s41265-016-0033-3

Gawer, A., & Cusumano, M. A. (2014). Industry platforms and ecosystem innovation. *Journal of Product Innovation Management, 31*(3), 417–433. https://onlinelibrary.wiley.com/doi/10.1111/jpim.12105

Jacobides, M. G., Cennamo, C., & Gawer, A. (2018). Towards a theory of ecosystems. *Strategic Management Journal, 39*(8), 2255–2276. https://doi.org/10.1002/smj.2904

Katz, M. L., & Shapiro, C. (1985). Network externalities, competition, and compatibility. *The American Economic Review, 75*(3), 424–440. https://www.jstor.org/stable/1814809

Kumar, V., Dixit, A., Javalgi, R. G., & Dass, M. (2021). Digital transformation of business-to-business marketing: Framework and research agenda. *Journal of*

Business & Industrial Marketing, 36(5), 849–867. https://doi.org/10.1016/j.indmarman.2021.03.008

Lusch, R. F., & Nambisan, S. (2015). Service innovation: A service-dominant logic perspective. *MIS Quarterly, 39*(1), 155–175. https://doi.org/10.25300/MISQ/2015/39.1.07

Mancuso, I., Petruzzelli, A. M., & Panniello, U. (2024). Value creation in data-centric B2B platforms: A model based on multiple case studies. *Industrial Marketing Management, 119*, 1–14. https://doi.org/10.1016/j.indmarman.2024.04.001

McIntyre, D. P., & Srinivasan, A. (2017). Networks, platforms, and strategy: Emerging views and next steps. *Strategic Management Journal, 38*(1), 141–160. https://doi.org/10.1002/smj.2596

Meadows, D. H. (2008). *Thinking in systems: A primer*. Chelsea Green Publishing.

Ng, I. C. L., & Wakenshaw, S. Y. L. (2017). The internet-of-things: Review and research directions. *International Journal of Research in Marketing, 34*(1), 3–21. https://doi.org/10.1016/j.ijresmar.2016.11.003

Parker, G., & Van Alstyne, M. (2023). Platforms: Their structure, benefits, and challenges. In *Handbook of digital enterprise* (pp. 763–780). Springer. https://doi.org/10.1007/978-3-031-45304-5_33

Parker, G. G., Van Alstyne, M. W., & Choudary, S. P. (2016). *Platform revolution: How networked markets are transforming the economy and how to make them work for you*. W. W. Norton.

Ramaswamy, V., & Ozcan, K. (2018). *The co-creation paradigm*. Stanford University Press.

Treiblmaier, H. (2018). The impact of blockchain on the supply chain: A theory-based research framework and a call for action. *Supply Chain Management: An International Journal, 23*(6), 545–559. https://doi.org/10.1108/SCM-01-2018-0029

Vaska, S., Massaro, M., Bagarotto, E. M., & Dal Mas, F. (2021). The digital transformation of business model innovation: A structured literature review. *Frontiers in Psychology, 11*, Article 539363. https://doi.org/10.3389/fpsyg.2020.539363

2

Marketing Leaders as Drivers of Co-Creation

In platform ecosystems, value isn't delivered—it's co-created. This is a profound shift from the traditional marketing playbook where the goal was to move a customer through a linear journey towards purchase. Today, in multi-actor environments, the marketer's role is no longer to simply convert, it's to catalyse.

The most effective marketing leaders now operate as architects of co-creation. They're not just running campaigns—they're building infrastructure for interaction, shaping how businesses engage with customers, partners, and complementors across the ecosystem. They sit at the intersection of insight and influence—using data, storytelling, and strategy to connect value creators and value receivers in powerful, scalable ways.

The Strategic Position of Marketing in the Platform Economy

Marketing has always been a boundary-spanning discipline, connecting internal teams with the market. But in the context of platforms, that bridging function becomes central to the business model itself. The marketer becomes the orchestrator—designing engagement systems, facilitating knowledge flows, and creating conditions for trust and participation.

Marketing leaders are often the first to detect emerging signals—shifting customer expectations, behavioural trends, and opportunities for innovation. This sensitivity to context, combined with their ability to frame, communicate, and activate responses, positions them as key enablers of co-creation.

Crucially, co-creation is not about extracting value from customers. It's about creating environments in which value can be exchanged, enhanced, and multiplied (Lemon & Verhoef, 2016)—often in ways that neither the business nor the customer could achieve alone.

How Marketers Activate Co-Creation in Ecosystems

At its core, co-creation is about tapping into collective energy and expertise. And marketers, far from being bystanders, are the active catalysts of this collaborative dynamism. Here's how they turn latent potential into co-creative momentum:

Strategic Community Building At the heart of co-creation lies community—not just in the casual, social sense, but as an intentionally curated ecosystem of contributors (Nambisan & Baron, 2009). Marketers build and nurture these networks with purpose. They design content that sparks conversation, develop forums and digital spaces for exploration, and deploy recognition systems that reward contributors. Through leaderboards, visibility schemes for top contributors, or simple yet sincere acknowledgements, marketers transform passive audiences into active co-architects, shaping both platform narrative and experience.

Leveraging Data and Artificial Intelligence In a platform ecosystem, data isn't just a by-product—it's a raw material for innovation (Hagiu & Wright, 2020). Marketers harness AI and analytics not to chase vanity metrics, but to detect trends, personalise engagement, and anticipate emerging opportunities. For instance, a surge of questions around a new feature triggers a rapid tutorial or prompts a virtual co-design session. By translating real-time signals into action, marketers breathe life into the feedback loop—converting data into adaptive, evolving engagement strategies.

Facilitating Multi-Actor Collaboration Co-creation happens in an environment designed to bring actors together—developers, designers, end-users, partners, even regulators (Lusch & Nambisan, 2015). Marketing leaders choreograph this interaction: hosting ideation sessions, setting up reward systems, and sequencing contributions so that each actor's strengths align. Think hackathons with dual goals—problem-solving and content creation—or partner campaigns where user feedback shapes the final product. These are not add-on activities—they're woven into the platform strategy, turning interaction into genuine co-creation.

Feedback Loops and Adaptive Marketing Traditional marketing responded to feedback on a quarterly or annual cycle. In a platform ecosystem, feedback is live, flowing through every component (Wiersema, 2013; Ritala et al., 2024). Marketers set up systems to capture sentiment, usage patterns, and behavioural shifts—and then design Agile responses. Maybe an unexpected usage spike leads to a new tutorial or an interactive webinar. Maybe a partner's feature prompts co-branded content. The result is a living platform—one that learns, adapts, and grows with its contributors (Rust & Huang, 2014).

Marketing Leadership as Ecosystem Strategy The CMO's role has expanded. No longer confined to campaigns and brand management, today's marketing leader is part strategist, part ecosystem architect. They help design business models alongside product leaders, structure growth frameworks, and ensure that platform value isn't siloed—it's shared. They align messaging with co-creation, positioning the platform not just as a utility, but as a space for collective innovation (Budde et al., 2024). In every conversation—whether with internal teams, partners, or users—they hold the connective tissue of the ecosystem together.

This shift demands a new mindset: from broadcasting to enabling; from persuasion to participation; from messaging to facilitation. The marketer becomes a storyteller one moment, a strategist the next, and a systems designer shortly after—all within the same hour. They act as conduits, turning audience insights into contributions, and contributions into new experiences. They build platforms that don't just deliver products—they evolve through the collective ingenuity of their participants.

Towards Sustainable, Scalable Co-Creation

Marketing leaders have the ability, and the responsibility, to shape platform ecosystems that are resilient, adaptive, and human-centred. Their work doesn't just drive revenue. It builds trust, unlocks innovation, and sustains engagement over time.

Marketing leaders are no longer just revenue drivers—they are architects of sustained, scalable co-creation. In the shifting landscape of platform ecosystems, their influence reaches far beyond promotional campaigns. By fostering environments rooted in resonance and reciprocity, they embed trust into the core of the platform, ignite collaborative innovation, and instil engagement that endures long after the flash of initial launch.

To build such ecosystems, co-creation strategies must be both human-centred and structurally sound (Ramaswamy & Ozcan, 2016). First, marketers must adopt orchestration mindsets—identifying the unique motivations of users, partners, and complementors, and crafting mechanisms like shared analytics dashboards, co-design workshops, or recognition programmes that align contributions with meaningful reward. This promotes more than interaction—it nurtures investment, loyalty, and purpose-driven participation.

Next, they must embed adaptive governance (Tiwana, 2014). Dynamic ecosystems require flexible rules that evolve as the platform grows, while maintaining clarity and fairness. By bringing transparency to decision-making and value-share mechanisms, marketing leaders reduce friction and establish the credibility necessary for deeper stakeholder investment.

A third pillar lies in systemic measurement (Möller, Nenonen & Storbacka, 2020). Beyond traditional metrics like click-throughs or downloads, platform marketers track co-creation indicators such as collaborative contributions, multi-actor conversions, and repeat engagements. These measures help pivot strategies, allocate resources, and signal when to double down—or double back.

Finally, they foster a culture of experimentation (Thomke, 2020). By treating co-creation as a living laboratory, teams pilot small, cross-functional initiatives, measure results, and iterate. This approach both lowers the barrier for new partners to join and demonstrates to the broader ecosystem that innovation is intentional, organised, and rewarded.

In doing so, marketing leaders help shift the platform from a transactional venue into a thriving ecosystem of continuous co-creation and mutual growth (Ramaswamy & Ozcan, 2018). They elevate the platform's purpose—from building markets to building meaning—where every participant knows their voice matters and their effort benefits the collective.

When marketing leadership embraces this mandate, they earn a rightful seat at the leadership table—not merely to promote what the business is, but to help define what it could become. In markets shaped by connection and collaboration, that role may be the single most strategic distinction between the transient and the transformative.

As platform business models continue to evolve, one thing is clear: the marketer's seat at the leadership table is not optional, it's essential. Not because they promote the business, but because they help shape what the business becomes.

Visual Framework: The Co-Creation Engine in Platform Ecosystems

Figure 2.1 presents a framework that captures the evolving role of marketing leaders within platform ecosystems. It highlights how marketing leaders act as orchestrators of engagement and enablers of sustained, multi-actor value creation.

The *Co-Creation Engine in Platform Ecosystems* model frames the marketing leader as a central driver in building a responsive, inclusive, and innovative platform—not through control, but through facilitation and orchestration.

> **Reflective Prompt: Are You Creating, or Just Communicating?**
>
> Consider your current role in your organisation's platform ecosystem:
>
> 1. Are you enabling co-creation, or merely broadcasting messages?
> 2. How often are your customers and partners shaping what your business becomes?
> 3. Where in your platform experience is engagement passive, and how might you invite contribution?
> 4. Do your current data and feedback mechanisms feed into strategy, or remain operational?
> 5. As a marketing leader, your greatest leverage isn't just in communication—it's in creating the conditions for others to participate, innovate, and scale value with you.

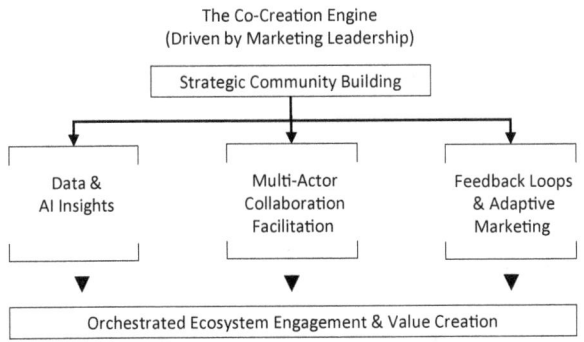

Fig. 2.1 Co-Creation Engine in Platform Ecosystems Model

> **Exercise: Mapping Your Co-Creation Levers**
>
> 1. **Identify 3 Stakeholder Groups**
>   List three actor types in your ecosystem (e.g. customers, developers, partners). For each:
>   - How do they currently engage?
>   - What more could they contribute if given the right tools or incentives?
>
> 2. **Evaluate Your Feedback Infrastructure**
>   - What mechanisms do you currently have in place to gather feedback (e.g. surveys, NPS, analytics)?
>   - Are these loops real-time? Do they result in visible changes or iterations?
>
> 3. **Design One Participation Touchpoint**
>   - Create a low-friction way for actors to contribute to your platform—a community challenge, beta test group, insight forum, or content collaboration. Ask: *What would make this valuable and rewarding for them?*

This chapter helps you assess and activate *the* marketing levers available to you, repositioning your function from message delivery to ecosystem design—from marketing manager to co-creation leader.

References

Budde, L., Haenggi, R., Laglia, L., & Friedli, T. (2024). Leading the transition to multi-sided platforms (MSPs) in a B2B context–the case of a recycling SME. *Industrial Marketing Management, 116*, 106–119. https://doi.org/10.1016/j.indmarman.2023.12.002

Hagiu, A., & Wright, J. (2020). Data-enabled learning in digital platforms. *American Economic Review, 110*(3), 889–917. https://doi.org/10.1111/1756-2171.12453

Lemon, K. N., & Verhoef, P. C. (2016). Understanding customer experience throughout the customer journey. *Journal of Marketing, 80*(6), 69–96. https://doi.org/10.1509/jm.15.0420

Lusch, R. F., & Nambisan, S. (2015). Service innovation: A service-dominant logic perspective. *MIS Quarterly, 39*(1), 155–175. https://doi.org/10.25300/MISQ/2015/39.1.07

Möller, K., Nenonen, S., & Storbacka, K. (2020). Networks, ecosystems, fields, market systems? Making sense of the business environment. *Industrial Marketing Management, 90*, 380–399. https://doi.org/10.1016/j.indmarman.2020.07.013. https://doi.org/10.1016/j.indmarman.2020.08.008

Nambisan, S., & Baron, R. A. (2009). Virtual customer environments: Testing a model of voluntary participation in value co-creation activities. *Journal of Product Innovation Management, 26*(4), 388–406. https://doi.org/10.1111/j.1540-5885.2009.00667.x

Ramaswamy, V., & Ozcan, K. (2018). *The co-creation paradigm*. Stanford University Press.

Ramaswamy, V., & Ozcan, K. (2016). Brand value co-creation in a digitalized world: An integrative framework and research implications. *International Journal of Research in Marketing, 33*(1), 93–106. https://doi.org/10.1016/j.ijresmar.2015.07.001

Ritala, P., Keränen, J., Fishburn, J., & Ruokonen, M. (2024). Selling and monetizing data in B2B markets: Four data-driven value propositions. *Technovation, 130*, 102935. https://doi.org/10.1016/j.technovation.2023.102935

Rust, R. T., & Huang, M.-H. (2014). The service revolution and the transformation of marketing science. *Marketing Science, 33*(2), 206–221. https://doi.org/10.1287/mksc.2013.0836

Thomke, S. (2020). *Experimentation works: The surprising power of business experiments*. Harvard Business Review Press.

Tiwana, A. (2014). *Platform ecosystems: Aligning architecture, governance, and strategy*. Morgan Kaufmann.

Wiersema, F. (2013). The B2B agenda: The current state of B2B marketing and a look ahead. *Journal of Business & Industrial Marketing, 28*(8), 638–642. https://doi.org/10.1016/j.indmarman.2013.02.015

3

Foundations of Platform Ecosystem

In the new economy, platforms don't just support business—they are the business. At their core, platform ecosystems are more than just digital environments; they are living, evolving networks of interconnected actors co-creating value. Whether in fintech, health tech, education, or enterprise technology, the principle remains the same: the strength of the platform lies not in its product, but in the collaborative power of its ecosystem.

Understanding platform ecosystems is no longer optional for marketers—it's foundational. These ecosystems underpin much of the digital infrastructure we interact with every day. From **Amazon's** expansive marketplace to asset management platforms linking data, investors, and algorithms, platform ecosystems form the connective tissue of modern business.

Defining the Platform Ecosystem

A platform ecosystem is fundamentally a dynamic system of actors—consumers, producers, developers, partners—brought together by a central platform to interact, collaborate, and co-create value (de Reuver et al., 2018). Unlike linear or siloed business models, platform ecosystems thrive on openness, mutual benefit, and a shared purpose. Value is not pushed down a pipeline—it circulates, evolves, and scales.

This collaborative structure creates a self-reinforcing system. Each new participant doesn't just consume—they contribute. A new seller on a marketplace brings choice; a new app on a platform brings functionality; a new insight shared by a user enhances the experience for others. These small, cumulative inputs form the flywheel effect that drives ecosystem growth and differentiation.

A platform ecosystem is not merely a collection of interconnected services or users—it is a living, adaptive network of actors that collectively generate and sustain value (Constantinides et al., 2018). In contrast to traditional linear business models—where one entity produces and another consumes—platform ecosystems thrive on open architectures, shared incentives, and the continuous circulation of assets—whether those are data, applications, services, or insights. At its core, a platform ecosystem welcomes diversity: developers, partners, producers, consumers, regulators, and even competitors each bring unique contributions that interlock to form something greater than the sum of its parts (Parker et al., 2016).

Central to this model is the principle of mutual benefit (Lusch & Nambisan, 2015). Rather than imposing value top-down, the platform facilitates exchanges that empower participants to co-create. A new seller on a marketplace does more than sell—they expand variety and choice. A developer creating an app adds new functionality, enriching the user experience for all. A customer sharing behavioural data prompts refinements that can optimise everything from navigation to personalisation. Importantly, each of these contributions doesn't merely serve individual needs—it triggers positive externalities that ripple through the ecosystem.

This reciprocal architecture generates what we call a flywheel effect (Cennamo, 2021). Unlike staged processes that demand repeated push effort, ecosystems accumulate momentum. One contribution attracts another, new features invite further adoption, and growing participation cements trust and utility. Over time, the platform evolves—its contours shift in tandem with emergent behaviour, newly formed partnerships, or innovative use cases (Kim & Parker, 2020). The platform is not set and forget—it is shaped, sustained, and improved by its community.

Openness is the lifeblood of this structure. By exposing APIs, documentation, and governance frameworks, platform owners allow others to build, integrate, and innovate upon their foundation. This openness breeds variety—products, services, and value constellations that the platform itself may never have envisioned (Boudreau, 2010). Yet openness must be purposeful—too much without guardrails can degrade quality or fragment identity, too little can stifle innovation and deter participation. Platform architects balance inclusion with direction, ensuring that shared purpose remains clear.

Purpose itself unifies the ecosystem. It is the implicit contract that binds participants in a shared trajectory—whether that is democratising finance, transforming healthcare delivery, or accelerating sustainable commerce. Purpose roots members in a larger mission, strengthens relational bonds, and animates engagement beyond transactional logic.

Governance too is both mechanism and signal. Fair, transparent rules around revenue-share, quality standards, data use, and platform access define what is permissible. They also act as scaffolding—safeguarding trust, aligning incentives, and guiding collaboration. Good governance is visible and comprehensible; it encourages contributions by reducing uncertainty and articulating how input translates into collective value.

A mature ecosystem displays emergent properties—decentralised innovation, adaptive resilience, and co-created identity. Veteran participants become mentors, newcomers quickly find their niche, and platform-wide interventions can be trialled and adopted with agility. Ecosystems breathe—they expand, contract, diversify, and renew, responding dynamically to shifts in demand, technology, or regulatory context.

Defining a platform ecosystem, then, requires us to see beyond products and services—to recognise the relational architecture that binds actors together into a co-creative system (Evans & Schmalensee, 2016). It's not about what a platform offers, but what it enables: connections, collaborations, and compound value—endlessly iterated and collectively owned. In the chapters ahead, we'll explore how to design, nurture, govern, measure, and lead such systems—turning ecosystems into sources of sustained competitive advantage and platforms into places where everyone wins.

The Architecture of a Platform Ecosystem

Effective ecosystems are built on thoughtful architecture—not merely lines of code, but structures, relationships, and intentional design that support scale, agility, and resilience. This architecture typically comprises three foundational layers: infrastructure, interaction, and innovation. Each layer plays a distinct but interconnected role in enabling platforms to thrive in a dynamic digital landscape. There are three essential layers:

Infrastructure Layer: This is the foundation—the technology stack that enables secure, scalable operations. Cloud computing, APIs, data standards, and emerging technologies like blockchain all fall within this domain. For marketers, understanding this layer matters not for its technical details, but for what it enables: flexibility, responsiveness, and integration at scale (Brinker, 2020). It includes cloud technologies, APIs, secure data environments, and distributed ledger technologies like blockchain.

These elements underpin the operational capacity of a platform—ensuring scalability, security, and seamless integration. This layer will matter less for marketers as it relates to its technical specifics and more for its strategic potential. It enables rapid deployment of campaigns, real-time analytics, and collaborative integrations across internal and external actors. The growing availability of AI-enhanced cloud environments further accelerates this, offering marketers flexible tools to personalise, automate, and optimise at scale.

Interaction Layer: This is the engagement engine. Matchmaking algorithms, User Experience (UX) design, personalisation tools, and collaboration features define how ecosystem actors interact (Tiwana, 2014). It's here that marketers work to build meaningful relationships, foster feedback, and design moments of value that build trust and loyalty. This is where UX design, personalisation engines, matchmaking algorithms, and feedback mechanisms converge. It defines how users, partners, and developers engage with the platform. AI plays a critical role here, interpreting behavioural signals to shape adaptive, real-time experiences (Kumar et al., 2021). Marketers work closely within this layer to craft journeys that are immersive, relevant, and emotionally resonant—turning routine interactions into value-rich moments that foster trust and loyalty.

Innovation Layer: The true differentiator. This is where external contributors—developers, partners, users—are empowered to innovate *on* the platform, not just *within* it. It's the app store, the data plug-in, the community-generated insight. Ecosystems that embrace this layer become self-renewing, turning engagement into invention. This is where ecosystems become regenerative (Cennamo & Santalo, 2019). This layer empowers external contributors—developers, partners, users—to build on top of the platform rather than just use it.

Tools such as open APIs, modular design frameworks, and community portals enable co-creation and third-party development (Ghazawneh & Henfridsson, 2013). Here, marketers can nurture grassroots innovation, support the launch of partner-created features, and amplify community-led growth. The integration of AI into this layer further unlocks creative capacity, allowing for smarter design, faster prototyping, and collaborative experimentation.

Across all layers, AI acts as the unifying force. It enhances the performance of infrastructure, deepens engagement in the interaction layer, and accelerates innovation by supporting ideation, testing, and iteration. As ecosystems evolve, AI enables platforms to operate not as static environments, but as adaptive systems capable of learning, evolving, and responding to the needs of their actors in real time.

As such, a platform's architecture isn't just its technical foundation—it's the strategic scaffolding that enables sustainable growth (Grewal et al., 2021). Infrastructure provides the backbone, interaction drives connection, and innovation ensures renewal. Together, they form the engine of modern, co-creative ecosystems.

Governing the Ecosystem

With openness comes complexity. Governance is what holds the ecosystem together—a combination of rules, systems, and cultural norms that shape behaviour. In platform ecosystems, governance must strike a delicate balance: open enough to invite participation, structured enough to protect integrity.

From eligibility criteria (who can join) to data policies (how information is shared), to value distribution (how benefits are allocated), governance frameworks shape the very dynamics of the ecosystem (Wareham et al., 2014). In regulated industries, this is especially critical. Financial platforms, for instance, must meet strict compliance standards while still enabling innovation. Strong governance isn't a barrier to growth—it's what makes sustainable growth possible.

Network Effects: The Growth Engine

Network effects are the heartbeat of platform ecosystems. The concept is simple: as more participants join and engage, the value of the ecosystem increases—for everyone. But realising network effects isn't automatic. It takes strategy.

Early-stage platforms often struggle with the cold-start problem: too few users to attract others. Marketing plays a key role in overcoming this hurdle—through incentives, partnerships, and targeted engagement. Once network effects begin to take hold, growth becomes exponential, not linear. A well-orchestrated ecosystem compounds its value over time.

Co-Creation and Value Innovation

In traditional businesses, innovation often happens behind closed doors. In platform ecosystems, it happens out in the open—through co-creation. When customers, partners, and developers actively shape the products and services they use, something powerful happens relevance, loyalty, and innovation align (Parker et al., 2016).

Value innovation occurs when ecosystems not only improve what exists but invent what didn't. AI-driven insights in financial platforms, user-generated product customisations, or entirely new services emerging from developer communities—these are the outputs of ecosystems that embrace openness and creativity.

Challenges on the Path to Ecosystem Maturity

Despite their promise, platform ecosystems are not easy to build—particularly in institutionalised or heavily regulated sectors (Hendricks and Matthyssens (2022). Traditional mindsets, compliance requirements, and cultural inertia can create resistance. Misalignment among ecosystem actors, uneven capabilities, and unclear value propositions can slow momentum. Technological infrastructure, too, must be built with scalability in mind. As platforms grow, they must maintain security, reliability, and performance—all while evolving to meet changing needs. This demands foresight, investment, and cross-functional leadership.

Frameworks for Understanding Ecosystems

Two useful lenses help us navigate this complexity:

1. **The Platform Governance Framework** identifies three forms of control: participation (who can join), interaction (how they behave), and distribution (how value is shared). Previous work describe similar dimensions of governance across dynamic platform ecosystems (Tiwana et al., 2010; Wareham et al., 2014), this framework helps leaders design systems that are inclusive, fair, and sustainable with three forms of control.

2. **The Service Ecosystem Framework** views platforms as networks of co-creation—a shift from linear value chains to relational webs (Vargo & Lusch, 2016). Here, marketers and strategists focus not just on delivering value but enabling it to emerge through actor interaction.

Marketing's Role in Ecosystem Strategy

Ecosystems aren't just a backdrop for marketing—they *are* the context in which modern marketing happens. They offer marketers access to networks of contributors, rich data sources, and feedback loops that can drive hyper-relevance and innovation.

But this also redefines the marketer's role. It's no longer about pushing a brand message. It's about shaping how the brand *interacts* within the ecosystem—how it enables, empowers, and evolves alongside its community. In this landscape, marketing isn't a function. It's a capability embedded in the architecture of growth.

Visual Framework: The Structure of a Platform Ecosystem

Figure 3.1 presents a framework outlining the three core architectural layers of a platform ecosystem and how they interact with governance and network effects to enable co-creation and sustainable growth.

The *Structure of a Platform Ecosystem Hub* model demonstrates how these layers interact with governance structures and network effects to enable co-creation, resilience, and sustainable growth across the ecosystem.

> **Reflective Prompt: Are you Building the Ecosystem or Just Participating in One?**
>
> As a leader, ask yourself:
>
> 1. Is your business intentionally designing its ecosystem, or simply reacting to market dynamics?
> 2. Do you know which layer of the ecosystem you influence most—infrastructure, interaction, or innovation?
> 3. Are your governance frameworks enabling trust and collaboration, or creating friction?

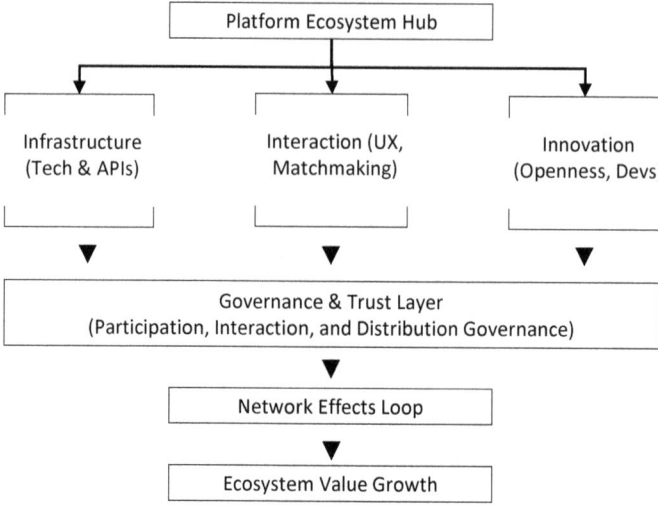

Fig. 3.1 Structure of a Platform Ecosystem Hub

4. How are you measuring network effects? Are you actively nurturing them or waiting for them to happen?
5. The strength of a platform lies not in its individual components, but in how intentionally those components are orchestrated to enable scalable, shared value.

Exercise: Audit and Architect Your Ecosystem

1. **Map Your Current Ecosystem Architecture**
   - Identify what sits within your infrastructure (e.g. platforms, tools, APIs)
   - List interaction channels and mechanisms (e.g. UI/UX, feedback systems)
   - Highlight innovation enablers (e.g. partner programmes, developer access)

2. **Evaluate Governance Maturity**
   - Do you have clear rules for who can participate and how?
   - Are value exchanges (rewards, recognition, monetisation) transparent and fair?
   - Are there friction points that prevent collaboration or innovation?

3. **Diagnose Your Network Effects**
   - Where do network effects currently occur?

- What actions can you take to accelerate them (e.g. referrals, integrations, co-marketing)?

4. **Design One Experiment to Strengthen the Ecosystem**
   - This could be a new API release, a co-creation challenge, or a content partner programme.
   - Ask: How does this reinforce one or more layers of the ecosystem?

This chapter helps you step back and see your business not just as a player within the market, but as an ecosystem architect—someone who can shape interactions, drive collaboration, and build the conditions for exponential growth.

References

Boudreau, K. J. (2010). Open platform strategies and innovation: Granting access vs. devolving control. *Management Science, 56*(10), 1849–1872. https://doi.org/10.1287/mnsc.1100.1215

Brinker, S. (2020). *The rise of the platform ecosystem: Martech's shift toward composability*. Chiefmartec Blog. https://chiefmartec.com

Cennamo, C. (2021). Competing in digital markets: A platform-based perspective. *Academy of Management Perspectives, 35*(2), 265–291. https://doi.org/10.5465/amp.2016.0048

Cennamo, C., & Santalo, J. (2019). Generativity tension and value creation in platform ecosystems. *Organization Science, 30*(3), 617–641. https://doi.org/10.1287/orsc.2018.1270

Constantinides, P., Henfridsson, O., & Parker, G. G. (2018). Introduction—Platforms and infrastructures in the digital age. *Information Systems Research, 29*(2), 381–400. https://doi.org/10.1287/isre.2018.0794

de Reuver, M., Sørensen, C., & Basole, R. C. (2018). The digital platform: A research agenda. *Journal of Information Technology, 33*(2), 124–135. https://doi.org/10.1057/s41265-016-0033-3

Evans, D. S., & Schmalensee, R. (2016). *Matchmakers: The new economics of multisided platforms*. Harvard Business Review Press.

Ghazawneh, A., & Henfridsson, O. (2013). Balancing platform control and external contribution in third-party development: The boundary resources model. *Information Systems Journal, 23*(2), 173–192. https://doi.org/10.1111/j.1365-2575.2012.00406.x

Grewal, D., Guha, A., Satornino, C. B., & Schweiger, E. B. (2021). Artificial intelligence: The light and the darkness. *Journal of Business Research, 136*, 229–236. https://doi.org/10.1016/j.jbusres.2021.07.043

Hendricks, L., & Matthyssens, P. (2022). Platform ecosystem development in an institutionalized business market: the case of the asset management industry. *Journal of Business & Industrial Marketing, 38*(2), 395–413. https://doi.org/10.1108/JBIM-04-2021-0193

Kim, J. Y., & Parker, G. G. (2020). Platform strategy. *Harvard Business Review, 98*(1), 94–101.

Kumar, V., Ramachandran, D., & Kumar, B. (2021). Influence of new-age technologies on marketing: A research agenda. *Journal of Business Research, 125*, 864–877. https://doi.org/10.1016/j.jbusres.2020.01.007

Lusch, R. F., & Nambisan, S. (2015). Service innovation: A service-dominant logic perspective. *MIS Quarterly, 39*(1), 155–175. https://doi.org/10.25300/MISQ/2015/39.1.07

Parker, G. G., Van Alstyne, M. W., & Choudary, S. P. (2016). *Platform revolution: How networked markets are transforming the economy—and how to make them work for you*. W. W. Norton & Company.

Tiwana, A. (2014). *Platform ecosystems: Aligning architecture, governance, and strategy*. Morgan Kaufmann.

Tiwana, A., Konsynski, B., & Bush, A. A. (2010). Research commentary—Platform evolution: Coevolution of platform architecture, governance, and environmental dynamics. *Information Systems Research, 21*(4), 675–687. https://doi.org/10.1287/isre.1100.0323

Vargo, S. L., & Lusch, R. F. (2016). Institutions and axioms: An extension and update of service-dominant logic. *Journal of the Academy of Marketing Science, 44*(1), 5–23. https://doi.org/10.1007/s11747-015-0456-3

Wareham, J., Fox, P. B., & Cano Giner, J. L. (2014). Technology ecosystem governance. *Organization Science, 25*(4), 1195–1215. https://doi.org/10.1287/orsc.2014.0895

4

Bridging the Gap—Aligning CMOs and CEOs for Platform Growth

In a platform-centric business, marketing is not a support function; it is a growth engine. And yet, in many organisations, the relationship between the Chief Marketing Officer (CMO) and the Chief Executive Officer (CEO) remains one of the most misaligned and under-leveraged in the leadership team. This disconnect is not just unfortunate; in platform ecosystems, it is strategically dangerous.

When the CEO and CMO operate in silos, platform growth stalls. Engagement loops weaken, innovation is delayed, and market messaging loses relevance. In contrast, when these two leaders are aligned strategically, operationally and narratively, they create the conditions for ecosystems to scale, co-create, and evolve with agility. This chapter explores how that alignment is achieved and why it is now a prerequisite for any platform business seeking sustainable growth.

The Divide: Legacy Playbooks Versus Platform Realities

At the heart of the tension lies a divergence in orientation. CEOs, particularly in platform businesses, are growth-driven, data-led, and strategically impatient. They think in metrics such as user acquisition, customer acquisition (CAC), return on investment (ROI) and platform monetisation (Hirt & Willmott, 2020). Many CMOs, by contrast, remain anchored to legacy branding models, prioritising awareness, sentiment, and creative campaigns

(Day, 2020). These are valuable but often disconnected from the CEO's immediate agenda.

This mismatch is compounded when CMOs resist transformation. Every modern CEO is leading some form of organisational shift, whether digitalisation, M&A, or ecosystem expansion. When marketing appears hesitant or disconnected from these efforts, credibility quickly erodes. In a platform world where speed and alignment matter more than perfection, CMOs must be growth partners rather than guardians of outdated processes.

In traditional businesses, marketing and leadership walk somewhat parallel—but in platform-driven enterprises, success demands alignment. At the heart of this tension lies a divergence in orientation. CEOs in platform businesses are typically growth-driven, data-led, and strategically impatient. They focus on metrics such as user acquisition, CAC, ROI, and platform monetisation (Day, 2020). Every quarter, every month, often every week, they chase signals that show traction, scalability, and competitive momentum. Growth is not aspiration—it is expectation.

Many CMOs, by contrast, continue to focus on legacy branding models. They prioritise awareness, sentiment, share-of-voice, and creatively sparkling campaigns. These are valuable—but often disconnected from the CEO's agenda, which demands real-time relevance, rapid iteration, and quantifiable outcomes (Day, 2020; Wirtz & Lovelock, 2022). Campaign rallies, advertising awards, and brand resonance can feel remote when compared with active daily growth metrics. This cultural dissonance becomes obvious when CMOs resist transformation.

Silence in the seat of influence becomes collusion; where the divide isn't merely about output—it is about mindset. CEOs expect marketing to translate creative energy into ecosystem design. They want the CMO to understand not just storytelling but product design, not just channels but network dynamics. They want someone who sees the platform flywheel—acquisition leading to engagement, engagement driving monetisation, monetisation fuelling reinvestment and scale.

Bridging this divide requires marketers to embrace metrics that matter to CEOs. It means bringing forward data-driven insights that connect brand perception to acquisition velocity and lifetime value. It means running tests that show how community activation moves activation curves and lowers CAC. It means integrating with product roadmaps, not marketing calendars—ensuring credit is taken where credit is due and responsibility is shared when results are mixed.

This shift also requires adaptability (Wilden et al., 2016). Platforms operate in dynamic ecosystems where competitors can emerge overnight, and regulation can shift rapidly (Hänninen et al., 2018). The CMO must be as comfortable pivoting a messaging strategy mid-cycle while commissioning a creative shoot. The CMO would need to pilot micro-campaigns, embed analytics into every initiative, and be ready to repurpose brand assets in service of strategic advantage. When CEOs see CMOs operate at this level—fluidly, decisively, co-creatively with product and engineering peers—alignment emerges. Marketing becomes part of the engine, not just its decoration. The divide closes, and the enterprise moves as one.

In short, legacy playbooks won't win the platform race. What is needed is marketing that operates at the velocity, with the accountability and the ecosystem fluency expected from today's CEO. Only then can platform growth be fully realised—and only then can CMOs be the growth partners platforms need.

Reframing the Role: From Brand Custodian to Ecosystem Strategist

The modern CMO must step into a different role, not only defending the brand but also architecting the platform's narrative across stakeholders. This begins with aligning to the CEO's transformation agenda. That does not mean abandoning strategic marketing; it means sequencing it. Execution must come first, with influence following once trust is established.

Marketing must evolve from a standalone function to an embedded ecosystem capability, one that enables user acquisition, facilitates partner engagement, and accelerates innovation loops. In this model, the CMO becomes the platform's chief storyteller, connector, and enabler of growth.

In the growing platform economy, the Chief Marketing Officer cannot stay rooted in traditional brand stewardship—CMOs must evolve into ecosystem strategists. This transformation begins at the intersection of marketing and business strategy, aligning closely with the CEO's broader transformation agenda. Yet alignment is not abandonment. CMOs don't step back from strategic marketing; they simply reorder it. First comes execution—delivering measurable impact on acquisition, engagement, revenue, and partnerships. Once marketing proves its ability to drive momentum, influence naturally follows.

This sequence—execution before influence—is critical. CMOs who can show credible results early gain the trust and strategic space needed to shape long-term narrative and stakeholder perceptions (Wang & Jin, 2023). It shifts marketing from a promotional cost centre to a vital growth engine.

To succeed, marketing must become embedded deeply into the ecosystem's operations. Traditional siloes must dissolve. Instead of being a downstream receiver of features (Storbacka et al., 2016) and messages, marketing joins product, engineering, customer success, partnerships, and data teams as a connector. In this ecosystem model, the CMO plays three key roles:

1. **Chief Storyteller:** Rather than crafting ads, the CMO weaves a narrative that resonates across customers, developers, complementors, regulators, and internal stakeholders. They frame the platform's purpose, its mutual value exchange, and its place within broader social, technological, and market contexts. They shape how each actor perceives their role—and their reward—in the ecosystem.
2. **Strategic Connector:** Marketing bridges relationships and signals between ecosystem participants. Whether it's onboarding a banking partner, launching a developer accelerator programme, or activating a user advisory council, the CMO ensures seamless connections. They map roles, define responsibilities, and orchestrate collaborative moments that drive trust and mutual benefit.
3. **Innovation Enabler:** Marketing no longer stops at activation—it joins the innovation process itself. By identifying partner needs, user pain points, and behavioural patterns, the marketing function signals product opportunities. CMOs test proof-of-concepts, pilot co-created campaigns or features, and feed early learnings back into the roadmap. They enable a continuous cycle where innovation fuels marketing, and marketing fuels innovation.

Within this ecosystem strategist role, the CMO must shift severely: from controlling brand outputs to curating brand inputs. They become guardians not of a static identity, but of an evolving, shared narrative—one shaped by multiple actors contributing in real time (Iglesias et al., 2020). The narrative isn't just broadcast—it's co-created. The brand becomes a stage, and the audience becomes the cast.

This repositioning is not without challenges. Ecosystem strategies demand new skills, governance structures and cultural responses (Jovanovic et al., 2022). They require marketing leaders to balance brand consistency with local adaptation, to tolerate ambiguity, and to manage a multiplicity of stakeholder interests. They must champion shared vision while ensuring every actor sees their own value in participation.

Yet the prize is substantial. Ecosystem-driven platforms see higher engagement, stronger user retention, accelerated innovation, and richer data streams.

When marketing evolves into ecosystem strategy, it becomes an intrinsic part of core business architecture—not an auxiliary support.

In short, marketers who embrace this elevated role—connecting ecosystems, catalysing innovation, and weaving shared narrative—will redefine what it means to lead in a networked economy. The modern CMO is no longer just a custodian of perception; they are the architect of platform ecosystems—driving alignment, participation, and sustained growth.

Strategies to Align with the CEO

1. **Speak in Strategic and Financial Terms** Marketers must use the language of the boardroom. That means mapping marketing activities to revenue outcomes, demonstrating how campaigns influence monetisation, how engagement drives network effects, and how user journeys translate to lifetime value (Mintz, 2023). Use platform analytics to surface this impact. Track participation rates, referrals, content engagement, and ecosystem activation. Quantify contribution, not just visibility.
2. **Execute the Transformation Before Shaping It** Every platform business has a transformation narrative. Whether scaling globally, shifting business models, or onboarding ecosystem partners, marketing must begin by enabling that vision rather than reinterpreting it. Align early. Prove value. Then, once trust is built, co-shape the brand and growth story with influence and credibility.
3. **Use Narrative-Driven Marketing** We no longer operate in a single-brand-message world. Today's CMOs must run multiple narratives simultaneously (Torres Pena & Breidbach, 2021). This might include a growth narrative for investors, customer success stories for users, ecosystem messaging for partners and technical content for developers. These are not competing; they are complementary. Each narrative aligns to a different actor in the ecosystem and reflects the platform's multifaceted value.

How Alignment Accelerates Platform Growth

When the CEO and CMO move in unison, the effects ripple across the ecosystem:

1. **Stronger Engagement Loops**: Marketing can enhance user participation through initiatives such as user-generated content, gamified referrals, and co-creation campaigns. These strengthen network effects and deepen platform loyalty.
2. **Faster Monetisation**: Growth-oriented CMOs focus on driving conversion. By aligning content and lifecycle marketing with the CEO's goals, they reduce time to value and improve customer acquisition and retention.
3. **More Effective Ecosystem Partnerships**: Marketing can attract developers, suppliers, and service providers through B2B strategies that emphasise shared success and integration, helping to broaden the platform's offer.

From Fragmentation to Fusion: The Future of CEO-CMO Leadership

This is not a one-off alignment exercise. It requires an ongoing shift in mindset and operating model. The platform economy depends on collaborative leadership (Kartika, 2023). The CEO sets direction and scale, while the CMO activates narrative, participation, and partner engagement. When this relationship works, the business moves as one, with speed, agility, and a unified sense of purpose.

The CMO of the future is not just a marketing leader. They are an ecosystem leader. They understand growth levers, shape value exchanges, and operate as a strategic extension of the CEO. In a business landscape defined by platforms, this kind of leadership alignment is no longer optional. It is essential.

Visual Framework: The Alignment Loop Between CEO and CMO in Platform Growth

Figure 4.1 presents a strategic framework illustrating the alignment loop between the CEO and CMO within a platform ecosystem, highlighting how synergy between these roles drives co-creation, engagement, and scale.

The *Alignment Loop between CEO and CMO in Platform Growth* model underscores how CMOs translate the CEO's strategic vision into action by driving ecosystem engagement and platform co-creation, fuelling scalable, measurable growth.

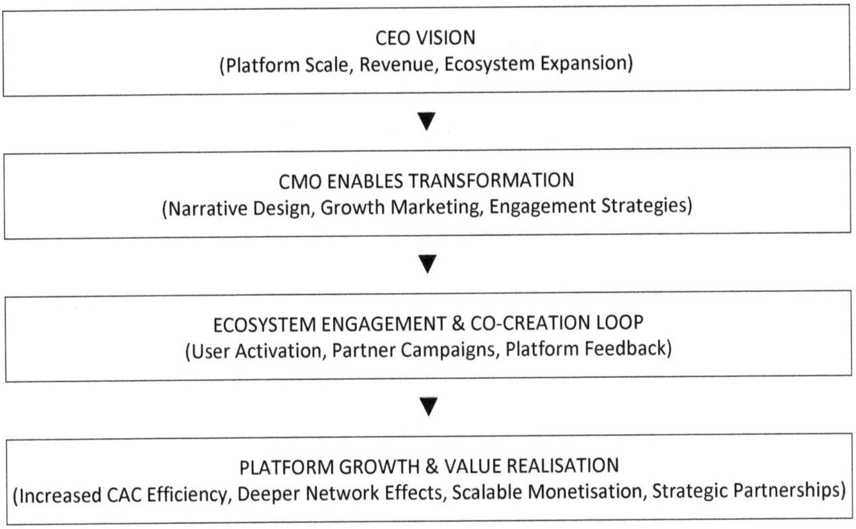

```
┌─────────────────────────────────────────────────────────────┐
│                        CEO VISION                            │
│      (Platform Scale, Revenue, Ecosystem Expansion)          │
└─────────────────────────────────────────────────────────────┘
                              ▼
┌─────────────────────────────────────────────────────────────┐
│                 CMO ENABLES TRANSFORMATION                   │
│    (Narrative Design, Growth Marketing, Engagement Strategies)│
└─────────────────────────────────────────────────────────────┘
                              ▼
┌─────────────────────────────────────────────────────────────┐
│           ECOSYSTEM ENGAGEMENT & CO-CREATION LOOP            │
│      (User Activation, Partner Campaigns, Platform Feedback) │
└─────────────────────────────────────────────────────────────┘
                              ▼
┌─────────────────────────────────────────────────────────────┐
│              PLATFORM GROWTH & VALUE REALISATION             │
│ (Increased CAC Efficiency, Deeper Network Effects, Scalable  │
│          Monetisation, Strategic Partnerships)               │
└─────────────────────────────────────────────────────────────┘
```

Fig. 4.1 Alignment Loop Between CEO and CMO in Platform Growth

---

Reflective Prompt: Are You Aligning with Strategy, or Running Parallel to It?

As a marketing leader, reflect on your current dynamic with the CEO and executive team:

1. Are your marketing objectives tightly aligned to the CEO's transformation plan?
2. Are you speaking in strategic, financial terms that connect with C-suite priorities?
3. Do your marketing efforts directly support platform engagement, partner activation, or monetisation goals?
4. Is your narrative evolving alongside the business strategy?

Alignment is not about compromise—it is about strategic synchronisation that creates momentum and shared ownership of growth.

> **Exercise: CEO-CMO Alignment Audit and Activation Plan**
>
> 1. **Assess Strategic Priorities**
>   - List the CEO's top three strategic goals this quarter.
>   - Map your marketing initiatives against these. Are they supporting, neutral, or misaligned?
> 2. **Translate Marketing into Business Value**
>   - Choose one active marketing initiative.
>   - Reframe it using business terms: What revenue driver or ecosystem engagement does it influence? Can you quantify its ROI?
> 3. **Design a Multi-Narrative Strategy**
>   - Develop three core narratives for your platform:
>   - A growth or scale narrative for stakeholders and investors
>   - A value narrative for customers or users
>   - An innovation or ecosystem narrative for partners and developers
> 4. **Create a CEO Sync Ritual**
>   - Propose a monthly or quarterly strategy sync with the CEO where marketing presents performance, impact, and ecosystem insights—not just campaigns.

This chapter helps you transition from marketing alignment to marketing leadership—demonstrating how your work not only supports the CEO's vision, but helps realise it through a platform-enabled, growth-first approach.

References

Day, G. S. (2020). Closing the marketing capabilities gap. *Journal of Marketing, 84*(4), 45–66.

Hänninen, M., Smedlund, A., & Mitronen, L. (2018). Digitalization in retailing: Multi-sided platforms as drivers of industry transformation. *Baltic Journal of Management, 13*(2), 152–168. https://doi.org/10.1108/BJM-04-2017-0109

Hirt, M., & Willmott, P. (2020). The CEO moment: Leadership for a new era. *McKinsey Quarterly.*. https://www.mckinsey.com/featured-insights/leadership/the-ceo-moment-leadership-for-a-new-era

Iglesias, O., Landgraf, P., Ind, N., Markovic, S., & Koporcic, N. (2020). Corporate brand identity co-creation in business-to-business contexts. *Industrial Marketing Management, 85*, 32–43. https://doi.org/10.1016/j.indmarman.2019.09.008

Jovanovic, M., Sjödin, D., & Parida, V. (2022). Co-evolution of platform architecture, platform services, and platform governance: Expanding the platform value of industrial digital platforms. *Technovation, 118*, Article 102218. https://doi.org/10.1016/j.technovation.2020.102218

Kartika, Levina. (2023). The role of strategic leadership and dynamic capabilities in the new reality of today's business WORLD 10.2991/978-94-6463-244-6_32. DOI:https://doi.org/10.2991/978-94-6463-244-6_32.

Mintz, O. (2023). Metrics for marketing decisions: Drivers and implications for performance. NIM marketing intelligence review. 15.18-23.10.2478/nimmir-2023-0003. https://doi.org/10.2478/nimmir-2023-0003

Storbacka, K., Brodie, R. J., Böhmann, T., Maglio, P. P., & Nenonen, S. (2016). Actor engagement as a microfoundation for value co-creation. *Journal of Business Research, 69*(8), 3008–3017. https://doi.org/10.1016/j.jbusres.2016.02.034

Torres Pena, M. V., & Breidbach, C. F. (2021). On emergence in service platforms: An application to P2P lending. *Journal of Business Research, 135*, 337–347. https://doi.org/10.1016/j.jbusres.2021.06.057

Wang, Y., & Jin, X. (2023). Exploring the role of shared leadership on job performance in IT industries: Testing the moderated mediation model. *Sustainability.* https://doi.org/10.3390/su152416767

Wilden, R., Devinney, T., & Dowling, G. (2016). The architecture of dynamic capability research identifying the building blocks of a Configurational approach. *Academy of Management Annals., 10*, 997–1076. https://doi.org/10.5465/19416520.2016.1161966

Wirtz, Jochen & Lovelock, Christopher. (2022). Services Marketing: People, Technology, Strategy, 9th edition. DOI:https://doi.org/10.1142/y0024.

5

The Power of Ecosystems in Value Co-Creation

We are no longer in an era defined solely by products or services. Instead, we are operating in a business landscape shaped by connectedness, collaboration, and shared value. In this world, ecosystems have emerged as powerful mechanisms for co-creation, enabling businesses to do more than just deliver value—they enable participants to create it together.

As we explored in earlier chapters, platform ecosystems are structured environments where value emerges not from single entities, but from networks of actors interacting and integrating their resources (Hein et al., 2023). In this chapter, we go deeper into what makes that value co-creation work, why it matters, and how marketers can harness it to unlock platform-driven growth.

We've moved far beyond a marketplace shaped by standalone products and services. Today's game is all about connectedness, collaboration, and shared value creation—and ecosystems are the engines that make it happen. In these environments, companies don't just *deliver* value—they *enable* it. Multiple actors—brands, users, developers, regulators—come together in purpose-built structures to co-create something bigger than the sum of its parts.

Platform ecosystems are more than technology. They are refreshed social systems where assets, ideas, norms, and trust circulate freely (Hendricks & Matthyssens, 2022). By integrating diverse resources—expertise from third-party developers, feedback from early adopters, distribution power from partners—platforms catalyse value that no single organisation could generate alone. Critically, this isn't serendipity; it's design. Intentional architectures, governance models, and incentives nurture ecosystems where contribution becomes a source of collective momentum.

For marketers, the power of ecosystems lies in their ability to unlock scalable co-creation. Instead of targeting users alone, marketers engage a web of stakeholders—partners who extend capability, customers who shape product experiences, developers who invent new use cases. These contributions not only accelerate innovation (Adner & Lieberman, 2021)—but they also embed loyalty, advocacy, and differentiation into the platform's DNA.

In doing so, value is no longer static—it becomes dynamic, perpetually renewed, and inherently shared. In this chapter, we will dissect the mechanisms that make value co-creation meaningful—and show how marketers can activate them to drive sustainable ecosystem growth.

Understanding Value Co-Creation in Ecosystems

At its core, value co-creation happens when multiple participants actively contribute knowledge, capability, and innovation to generate shared outcomes that are greater than the sum of individual inputs. This collaboration extends beyond simple transactions. It is about collective problem-solving, shared ownership, and long-term relevance. Value co-creation is a collaborative process where multiple participants actively contribute knowledge, capability, and innovation to build shared outcomes. Unlike simple transactions, co-creation is about collective problem-solving, shared ownership, and evolving relevance. It is the difference between selling a tool and growing a living system together.

In a high-functioning ecosystem, participants form an interdependent network of capabilities and insights. This might include customers who share lived experience, businesses with established infrastructure, developers possessing niche technical skills, suppliers contributing logistical strengths (Lusch & Nambisan, 2015)—and sometimes, yes, competitors with complementary assets. Each actor brings something unique, and the magic happens when their contributions intersect.

Take a financial ecosystem as an example. A traditional bank may provide stability, regulatory oversight, and trust. A fintech startup may bring agility, user-centric design, and cutting-edge payment technology. A data provider offers insights on behavioural trends, while a cybersecurity firm ensures protection against fraud and breaches.

Alone, each has value—but fragmented. Together, they build a next-generation payment solution that is secure, user-friendly, and adaptive to real-time market needs. Co-creation in practice. None of them could create this alone—but together, their shared input creates mutual value.

This collective process elevates outcomes in several ways:

1. **Depth of insight**—Customer input, developer creativity, and partner knowledge enrich the solution beyond any single view.
2. **Speed of iteration**—Multiple perspectives offer faster validation, tighter feedback loops, and accelerated refinement.
3. **Scalability of impact**—Shared ownership means shared promotion, trust-driven adoption, and wide distribution.
4. **Resilience in complexity**—Diverse contributions buffer against disruption; one participant's weakness is offset by another's strength.

This is the difference between working *in* a market and building an ecosystem: one is transactional, the other transformational.

Concretely, marketers play a pivotal role in activating this energy. They craft channels for participation—like ideation portals, hackathons, or beta programmes—and cultivate incentives that reward those who add value. They frame the narrative around how contributions weave into outcomes, ensuring each co-creator feels recognised and invested.

Crucially, co-creation must be intentional. It does not happen by accident. Platforms succeed when designed with structures that enable voluntary participation (Budde et al., 2024): open APIs, modular capabilities, feedback loops, and clear governance. For instance, a retail ecosystem might design a co-creation space where merchants can prioritise new features, customers can vote on product bundles, and fulfilment providers can offer flexible shipping models. Each input shifts the value chain—and each participant becomes a stakeholder in success.

Equally, co-creation thrives on cultural norms. Trust, transparency, and reciprocity must be baked into the ecosystem from day one. If participants sense hidden agendas or opaque reward structures, contribution dries up. Hence, some ecosystems employ gamification, peer review scoring, or shared revenue schemes—all designed to crystallise the link between input and recognition.

Let's consider the software environment. Developer communities around platforms like **GitHub** or **Salesforce** flourish because they are treated as authors, not anonymous users. Their code contributions are visible, credited, and often monetised through marketplace models (Ajimati et al., 2024). Marketers amplify this by showcasing top developers, sharing case studies, and supporting community events that spotlight innovation—reinforcing the belief that participant effort matters.

Finally, value co-creation reshapes performance metrics. Traditional ROI may not capture the ecosystem effect (Brodie et al., 2019). Instead, success is measured in co-innovated solutions launched, partner-led user growth, engagement depth, and shared revenue streams. These indicators reflect not only what the platform owns, but what it enables. Marketers must therefore evolve their dashboards to reflect ecosystem health—tracking metrics like active partner rates, joint campaign success, new co-created features, and recurring collaborative innovation.

In essence, value co-creation in ecosystems represents a shift from supply and demand (Ramaswamy & Ozcan, 2018) towards connection and contribution. It positions businesses as enablers of collective progress, rather than owners of discrete solutions. For marketers, understanding and enabling this shift is not optional—it is strategic. It means reframing the role from persuader to catalyst, from presenter to partner. It means building platforms where every voice, every capability, and every idea has the potential to shape value—and in doing so, building ecosystems that thrive.

The Foundations of Ecosystem-Based Co-Creation

There are three core principles that underpin effective co-creation within platform ecosystems:

1. **Orchestration Through a Platform Hub** At the centre of most ecosystems is a platform that acts as orchestrator (Jacobides et al., 2018). It connects the actors, sets interaction protocols, and provides the technological and operational foundation for collaboration. This orchestrator might not control everything—but it enables everything.
2. **Resource Integration** Every participant in the ecosystem brings their own assets—data, skills, infrastructure, or insight (Shen et al., 2024). When these are integrated intentionally, the result is synergy: the kind of outcome that none could have achieved alone. This integration also allows for rapid innovation, more agile responses, and stronger customer propositions.
3. **Trust and Transparency** Collaboration is only possible where trust exists. Participants must believe their contributions will be recognised, their data respected, and their rewards equitably shared (Laczko et al., 2023). This is

why governance—clear rules, open communication, aligned incentives—is so important. It creates the psychological and operational safety net needed for co-creation to thrive.

Frameworks for Ecosystem Co-Creation

Several frameworks can help us understand and lead in these environments. One is the **Service-Dominant Logic** (SDL), a model introduced by Vargo and Lusch (2004) which positions value not as something embedded in products, but something created through use and interaction. In this model, platforms act as facilitators—creating the conditions for actors to integrate resources and produce value collectively.

Another useful model is the **Ecosystem Value Chain**, which breaks down co-creation into three stages (Rawlins et al., 2018) and applies system dynamics modelling to analyse how ecosystem services are produced, delivered, and valued, emphasising the complex interactions within these systems. Here are the three stages:

1. **Resource Pooling**: Assembling complementary capabilities
2. **Collaborative Innovation**: Co-designing products, services, or experiences
3. **Shared Value Distribution**: Ensuring outcomes are distributed fairly and visibly among participants

These stages allow marketers and business leaders to track where their ecosystem sits on the co-creation journey, and where they can apply pressure to improve outcomes.

Technology as an Enabler of Co-Creation

Digital technologies are not just infrastructure—they are enablers of entirely new ways of working. Cloud computing supports real-time collaboration. APIs connect previously siloed systems. AI can uncover patterns and opportunities hidden in complex data. Blockchain offers decentralised trust models for transparency and accountability.

Together, these tools allow ecosystems to move faster, integrate more deeply, and scale with fewer constraints. They reduce friction while expanding reach.

For marketers, these technologies also offer richer data, more targeted activation strategies, and dynamic personalisation—not at the level of individual channels, but across entire ecosystems.

Real-World Examples of Ecosystem Co-Creation

Across industries, ecosystem-based innovation is already reshaping value creation:

1. **Healthcare**: Hospitals, med-tech providers and data analytics firms like **TeleTracking** co-create solutions that improve patient outcomes while reducing systemic costs.
2. **Finance**: Fintech ecosystems like **Cross River Bank**, empowers embedded financial services and combines traditional institutions, startups and regulatory tech to deliver faster, more secure, and more inclusive financial services.
3. **E-commerce**: Platforms like **Amazon** and **Alibaba** connect buyers, sellers, logistics, and cloud services to deliver not just products, but full-stack customer experiences.

In each case, the value is not delivered by a single player—it is orchestrated across many.

Challenges in Ecosystem Co-Creation

Despite their promise, ecosystems are not without complexity. Even the most promising ecosystems come with inherent complexity and potential friction. Four common hurdles that platform builders and marketers must navigate include:

1. **Misaligned Goals** Not every actor in the ecosystem will share the same objectives. Without a shared vision, even the best-resourced collaboration can flounder. Ecosystem participants often enter with different ambitions. One partner may seek rapid user growth—another may prioritise revenue per user or data insights. Without a shared vision and clear articulation of mutual outcomes, collaborations can stall or stray due to unresolved tensions.

2. **Complex Governance** Managing participation, ensuring accountability and resolving disputes at scale requires robust systems—often supported by both policy and technology. When actors span geographies, industries, or regulatory regimes, coordinating participation requires more than friendly cooperation. Platforms need defined policies, decision-making frameworks, and conflict-resolution mechanisms. These may be supported by role-based permissions, transparent audit trails, or governance councils—but implementing them is time-consuming and politically sensitive.
3. **Power Imbalances** Large players can dominate ecosystems, risking marginalisation of smaller actors. Inclusive governance and clear participation benefits are essential for balance and long-term trust. When dominant firms saturate a platform, smaller participants may feel overshadowed or discouraged. This can suppress innovation and erode trust. Inclusive design, fair benefit-sharing, and amplification of smaller voices are essential to preserve a healthy, dynamic ecosystem.
4. **Cultural and Operational Misfits**—Beyond systems, people and processes matter. Ecosystem actors often bring different operating styles, risk appetites, and time horizons. Integrating these cultures requires intentional onboarding, shared rituals, clear communication channels, and ongoing feedback mechanisms.

Implications for Marketing Leaders

This shift demands that marketers evolve from message-makers into ecosystem architects. No longer functioning on the periphery, they now actively shape value as it emerges within the network. To succeed, they must:

- Cultivate empathy for partner needs and ensure marketing efforts reinforce ecosystem goals.
- Create co-branding models that balance equity and brand integrity.
- Design campaigns that surface joint solutions or community milestones, reinforcing collective momentum.
- Champion structural mechanisms—like shared dashboards or contribution trackers—that reflect and reward co-creation in real time.

Marketers who build and enhance platforms through ecosystems do not simply promote offerings—they build relationships, integrate narratives, and create environments in which others want to participate (Hänninen et al., 2018). They must understand stakeholder incentives, navigate complex co-branding dynamics, and ensure that their work helps move the entire ecosystem forward.

This is a move from campaign design to value orchestration. From brand storytelling to shared story-building. Successful ecosystem marketing is not only about telling a story—it is about helping everyone in the ecosystem write it together.

Visual Framework: The Ecosystem Value Co-Creation Model

Figure 5.1 introduces a framework on how value is created within an ecosystem through structured collaboration, highlighting the key phases and enabling mechanisms that support sustainable, shared growth.

The *Ecosystem Value Co-Creation* model demonstrates how platform ecosystems become engines for innovation and growth by enabling co-creation through intentional infrastructure, aligned participation, and equitable distribution of value.

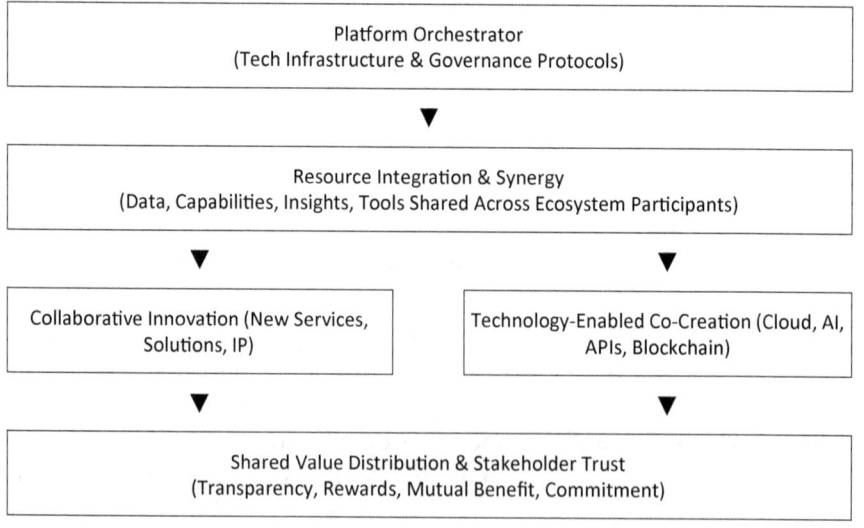

Fig. 5.1 Ecosystem Value Co-Creation Model

> **Reflective Prompt: Are You Co-Creating Value or Just Delivering It?**
>
> Reflect on your current business or platform strategy:
>
> 1. Are you working with other actors in a way that actively creates new value?
> 2. Do your users, partners, or customers contribute ideas, capabilities, or insight?
> 3. How is your organisation integrating resources from across its ecosystem?
> 4. What mechanisms do you have in place to distribute value fairly and visibly?
> 5. Shifting from a transactional mindset to a co-creative one opens new doors for growth—but it requires strategic intent and operational readiness.

> **Exercise: Designing Your Ecosystem Co-Creation Strategy**
>
> 1. **Map Your Ecosystem Stakeholders**
>   - List five different actor groups within your platform ecosystem. For each:
>   - What unique resources do they bring?
>   - How could they contribute to co-creation if invited?
>
> 2. **Audit Your Current Integration Mechanisms**
>   - How are you currently collaborating with stakeholders (e.g. co-marketing, co-development, feedback channels)?
>   - Where are the missed opportunities to deepen engagement?
>
> 3. **Define a New Co-Creation Initiative**
>
>   Choose one area where value could be enhanced through collaboration:
>   - What problem are you solving?
>   - Which actors would you engage?
>   - How would value be distributed fairly?
>
> 4. **Develop a Co-Creation Commitment Statement**
>   - Articulate how your organisation commits to building with others, not just for them. Share this internally or use it as a narrative anchor in your ecosystem communications.

This chapter helps you move from theoretical understanding to practical application—creating a foundation to make co-creation part of your strategic operating model.

References

Adner, R., & Lieberman, M. B. (2021). Disruption through complements. *Strategy. Science, 6*(1), 91–109. https://doi.org/10.1287/stsc.2021.0125

Ajimati, M. O., Carroll, N., & Maher, M. (2024). Adoption of low-code and no-code development: A systematic literature review and future research agenda. *Journal of Systems and Software, 222*, 112300. https://doi.org/10.1016/j.jss.2024.112300

Brodie, R. J., Fehrer, J. A., Jaakkola, E., & Conduit, J. (2019). Actor engagement in networks: Defining the conceptual domain. *Journal of Service Research, 22*(2), 173–188. https://doi.org/10.1177/1094670519827385

Budde, L., Haenggi, R., Laglia, L., & Friedli, T. (2024). Leading the transition to multi-sided platforms (MSPs) in a B2B context–the case of a recycling SME. *Industrial Marketing Management, 116*, 106–119. https://doi.org/10.1016/j.indmarman.2023.12.002

Hänninen, M., Smedlund, A., & Mitronen, L. (2018). Digitalization in retailing: Multi-sided platforms as drivers of industry transformation. *Baltic Journal of Management, 13*. https://doi.org/10.1108/BJM-04-2017-0109

Hein, A., Weking, J., Schreieck, M., Wiesche, M., Böhm, M., & Krcmar, H. (2023). Value co-creation in platform ecosystems: A structured literature review and future research directions. *Electronic Markets, 33*, 369–388. https://doi.org/10.1007/s12525-021-00473-9

Hendricks, L., & Matthyssens, P. (2022). Platform ecosystem development in an institutionalized business market: The case of the asset management industry. *Journal of Business & Industrial Marketing, 38*(2), 395–413. https://doi.org/10.1108/JBIM-04-2021-0193

Jacobides, M. G., Cennamo, C., & Gawer, A. (2018). Towards a theory of ecosystems. *Strategic Management Journal, 39*(8), 2255–2276. https://doi.org/10.1002/smj.2904

Laczko, C., Hullova, D., Needham, A., Ross, A., & Battisti, M. (2023). Building innovation ecosystems: Navigating tensions between trust and control. *California Management Review, 65*(4), 101–122. https://doi.org/10.1177/00081256231183209

Lusch, R. F., & Nambisan, S. (2015). Service innovation: A service-dominant logic perspective. *MIS Quarterly, 39*(1), 155–175. https://doi.org/10.25300/MISQ/2015/39.1.07

Ramaswamy, V., & Ozcan, K. (2018). *The co-creation paradigm*. Stanford University Press.

Rawlins, J. M., De Lange, W. J., & Fraser, G. C. G. (2018). An ecosystem service value chain analysis framework: A conceptual paper. *Ecological Economics, 147*, 84–95. https://doi.org/10.1016/j.ecolecon.2017.12.023

Shen, L., Shi, Q., Parida, V., & Jovanovic, M. (2024). *Ecosystem orchestration practices for industrial firms: A qualitative meta-analysis, framework development and research agenda.* Technological Forecasting and Social Change.

Vargo, S. L., & Lusch, R. F. (2004). Evolving to a new dominant logic for marketing. *Journal of Marketing, 68*(1), 1–17. https://doi.org/10.1509/jmkg.68.1.1.24036

Part II

Core Mechanics of Value Creation and Engagement

6

Key Players in Platform Ecosystems

Platform ecosystems are more than business models. They are networks of interdependent actors, each contributing unique capabilities, value, and perspective. These ecosystems are sustained not just by infrastructure or innovation, but by the collaboration of their participants—each playing a vital role in the co-creation of shared value.

Platform ecosystems have become one of the most powerful mechanisms for enabling scalable value creation. These ecosystems are not just collections of software and infrastructure. They are dynamic systems built around human, organisational, and technological collaboration (Thomas et al., 2024). Platforms succeed not solely through innovation or branding, but by curating an environment where diverse actors can interact, contribute, and grow together.

Unlike traditional linear business models, platform ecosystems are structured to facilitate exchange across a wide range of stakeholders (Fürstenau et al., 2023). They do not simply deliver a product or service—they enable a continuous flow of value through interactions, feedback, and innovation. The centre of gravity shifts from the organisation to the ecosystem—and marketers, product designers, developers, and users all become part of an integrated system of co-creation.

What makes these ecosystems function effectively is not just the technology or reach, but the deliberate architecture behind them. This includes governance mechanisms, incentive structures, communication pathways, and shared standards that coordinate behaviour and align interests. Platforms thrive when the design encourages engagement without overwhelming participants with friction or opacity.

However, ecosystems are not static. They are living entities that evolve over time. Each new feature, partner, or regulation changes the dynamics of the system (Kari et al., 2025). Each contribution—whether from a user, a developer, or a compliance partner—helps to refine the offering and influence its trajectory. This constant evolution introduces both opportunity and complexity, requiring organisations to maintain clarity of purpose while remaining adaptable.

To understand how ecosystems grow and sustain their momentum, it is essential to understand who participates in them. Ecosystems are composed of various actors—not merely as support functions, but as co-creators of value. Each actor brings different capabilities and perspectives (Hendricks, Matthyssens & Kowalkowski, 2024). Each role is essential to the ecosystem's function, its resilience, and its strategic potential.

To understand how ecosystems scale, sustain, and adapt, we must first understand their composition. From orchestrators and producers to end-users and regulators, each actor contributes to the ecosystem's function, resilience, and relevance (Heimburg & Wiesche, 2022). This chapter explores those roles in depth and examines how they interact to build value within the platform economy.

The next section explores those roles—not in isolation, but in context. How do they interact? Where do synergies arise? And what can marketers, leaders, and platform designers learn from understanding the full composition of a thriving ecosystem? The answers lie not in seeing actors as fixed entities, but as participants in a shared journey of mutual benefit and growth.

The Orchestrator: Strategic Architect and Enabler

At the centre of every platform ecosystem is the orchestrator—sometimes referred to as the platform owner. This role is far more than a technical facilitator. The orchestrator sets the strategic direction, builds the infrastructure, defines the governance model, and ensures the ecosystem is designed for growth.

Successful orchestrators are ecosystem enablers. They establish the rules of engagement, maintain trust, and balance openness with structure (Shen et al., 2024). In sectors like fintech, an orchestrator might coordinate among banks, startups, and regulators—ensuring not only that services work together technically, but that participants align around shared standards and goals. The orchestrator's value lies not in owning all activity, but in enabling it—shaping an environment where other actors can contribute meaningfully and scale collaboratively.

Producers and Service Providers: Driving the Core Offering

Producers and service providers create the tangible and intangible elements that give platforms their value. They supply the tools, services, applications, or products that attract users and generate engagement.

In digital ecosystems, producers may include software developers, content creators, or manufacturers. Service providers could range from logistics and data firms to customer support vendors or analytics specialists. What unites them is their role in enhancing the platform's utility—often by working in close collaboration with others in the ecosystem (Van Alstyne, Parker & Choudary, 2016). These players also play a critical role in innovation. When integrated well, they become co-creators—developing solutions alongside users, orchestrators, and complementors that evolve with market needs and technological capability.

End-Users: Consumers, Contributors, Co-Creators

While often seen as passive participants, end-users are fundamental to the health of an ecosystem. Their behaviours, feedback, and engagement drive platform dynamics (Wang, Zhao & Hong, 2024). In many cases, they also contribute content, insight, and advocacy—shifting from consumers to active co-creators. Their data helps inform product design, their participation builds network effects, and their loyalty sustains long-term platform viability. In user-centric ecosystems—from e-commerce to SaaS to community-based platforms—marketers must pay close attention to user voice, journey, and behaviour, not just as consumers, but as collaborators.

Complementors: Extending Reach and Deepening Value

Complementors add value by extending the platform's capability. These are the players that fill gaps, offer supplementary services, or open new markets. A cybersecurity firm in a fintech ecosystem, or a translation API in a learning platform, is a classic complementor—extending the value proposition without competing for core functionality. Complementors deepen engagement and help platforms stay relevant in more nuanced or specialist contexts (Gawer & Harracá, 2025). Managing these relationships effectively is key. Orchestrators benefit from complementor diversity and strength, while complementors gain access to user bases, data, and tools. When these dynamics are well-managed, the ecosystem becomes far greater than its individual parts.

Regulators and Policymakers: Shaping Trust and Compliance

In regulated industries, trust cannot be assumed—it must be designed. Regulators and policymakers play a critical role in shaping the boundaries of acceptable interaction within platform ecosystems (Fürstenau et al., 2023). They enforce rules around privacy, data security, ethics, and access, ensuring a fair and transparent operating environment. While sometimes perceived as constraints, these actors often enable innovation by creating legitimacy and protecting user rights. Platforms that engage regulators early and align with policy frameworks are better positioned to grow sustainably and earn public trust.

Interdependence as Ecosystem Strength

What sets ecosystems apart from traditional supply chains or partnerships is the interdependence between their participants. Producers rely on orchestrators for access and tools. Orchestrators rely on users and complementors for scale. Complementors rely on regulators for clarity (Chen & Tong, 2022). These relationships are fluid, dynamic, and collaborative. Building a strong ecosystem means more than having the right actors—it means managing their interactions effectively. That requires clarity in roles, incentives aligned to shared outcomes, and governance models that support long-term engagement and fairness.

Frameworks for Understanding Ecosystem Roles

Two models help illuminate the structure of platform ecosystems:

1. **The Ecosystem Actor Model** groups participants into core actors (such as orchestrators, producers, and complementors), enablers (like regulators and technology providers), and users. It provides a clear view of who is involved and how value is exchanged, earlier work (Carst & Hu, 2023; Shen et al., 2024) identifies critical roles—including orchestrators, complementors, and technology enablers—as part of a successful ecosystem orchestration toolkit.
2. **The Ecosystem Participation Framework** categorises engagement levels—from passive consumers to proactive contributors. This framework helps marketers identify opportunities to move users and partners up the engagement curve, strengthening the entire ecosystem in the process. Earlier work on ecosystem-level participation mapping and COBRAs model (Schivinski, Christodoulides & Dabrowski, 2016) provides further explanation.

Ecosystem-Aware Marketing Leadership

For marketers, understanding ecosystem roles is critical. Marketing no longer operates in isolation, targeting discrete segments with static campaigns. Instead, it takes place within an interconnected, multi-actor environment.

It unfolds within a vibrant, interconnected network of actors—producers, complementors, regulators, users—each playing an essential role in value co-creation. As such, the role of the marketing leader has shifted profoundly: no longer simply managing brand perception, the modern marketer must navigate and shape entire ecosystems.

Modern marketing requires ecosystem fluency. This includes knowing how to partner with producers, engage complementors, collaborate with regulators and empower users. It also means positioning the brand within a broader network of value creation—where reputation is not built by messaging alone, but by contribution, collaboration and shared success (Nim, Pedada, & Hewett, 2024). Understanding how producers innovate, how complementors enrich offerings, how regulators influence governance, and how users contribute feedback and advocacy is what it's about. Marketing leaders must grasp the levers and dynamics that tie these stakeholders together.

Marketers who excel in this space become natural facilitators of participation and co-creation. They design engagement strategies that deliberately connect actors across the value chain—whether through co-marketing initiatives, development accelerators, or community platforms. They curate partnerships, assess partner-fit, and align incentives so each participant stands to gain, encouraging deeper investment from contributors.

These leaders also serve as architects of collaborative experiences. They shape processes and channels that allow ecosystem partners to innovate together—be it joint product development, collaborative content creation, or data-sharing networks. Through this work, marketing transcends outbound campaigns. It becomes the glue that binds diverse actors into a cohesive, evolving system of mutual value (Agarwal & Kapoor, 2019).

Success in this role requires marketers to think in systems, not silos. They track measures that matter in these environments—such as partner contributions, co-created assets, ecosystem growth, and networked engagement—rather than simple reach or impressions (Schüler & Petrik, 2023). They invest in governance frameworks that define expectations, guardrails, and shared accountability.

Above all, ecosystem-aware marketing leadership is about trust and adaptability. It requires listening to partners, co-designing solutions, and evolving with the system. Leaders must cultivate an ethos of openness, reciprocity, and inclusivity—reinforcing the idea that the brand's success depends on the ecosystem's strength. In doing so, marketing becomes not just a function, but a force that orchestrates shared progress, resilience, and sustainable growth.

In this context, marketers become facilitators of participation, curators of partnerships, and architects of engagement strategies that connect actors across the value chain.

Visual Framework: Roles in a Platform Ecosystem

Figure 6.1 presents a framework of the core actors within a platform ecosystem and illustrates their interdependencies, highlighting how collaboration between roles contributes to platform scalability and value co-creation.

The *Roles in a Platform Ecosystems* model demonstrates how ecosystem health depends on clear roles, balanced contributions, and effective coordination across multiple actors—all centred around the orchestrator's role in enabling structure, trust, and innovation.

6 Key Players in Platform Ecosystems

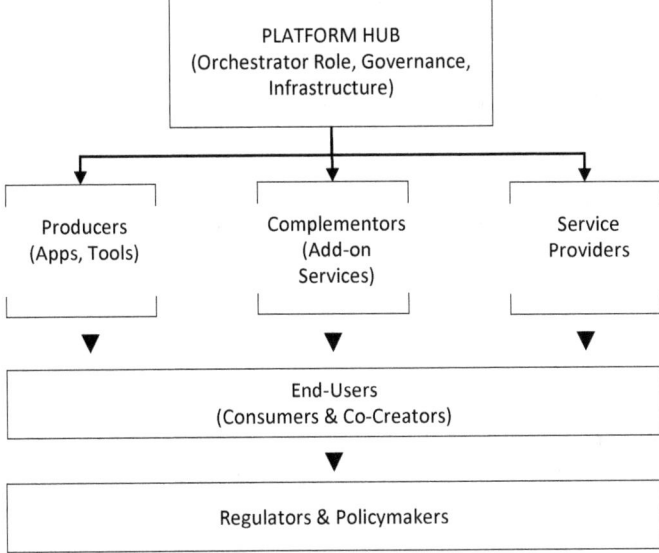

Fig. 6.1 Roles in a Platform Ecosystems Model

Reflective Prompt: Who Are Your Ecosystem Allies, and How Do You Engage Them?

Ask yourself:

1. Have you clearly identified the orchestrators, producers, complementors, and enablers within your platform ecosystem?
2. Which players are most critical to your growth right now, and how are you engaging them?
3. Are your marketing strategies designed to serve one group, or to orchestrate value across the whole ecosystem?
4. How might your approach to partnerships, user engagement, or regulatory collaboration shift if you reframe your business as part of an ecosystem?
5. Understanding your role in the ecosystem is not just strategic positioning—it is the foundation for collaborative growth.

Exercise: Stakeholder Engagement Mapping

1. **Identify Your Ecosystem Stakeholders**
   - Map out key actors within your ecosystem:
   - Who are your platform orchestrators?
   - Who contributes as producers or service providers?

- Which complementors expand your reach?
- Who regulates or enables your operations?

2. **Assess the Quality of Engagement**

   For each group:
   - How do you currently interact?
   - What value do they derive from the ecosystem?
   - What incentives could you offer to deepen collaboration?

3. **Design One Activation Strategy per Role**
   - For a complementor: Could you launch a joint service, bundle, or co-marketing campaign?
   - For a producer: Can you improve their development experience or monetisation?
   - For users: Could you invite them to contribute reviews, content, or feedback?
   - For regulators: Can you demonstrate proactive compliance or co-develop standards?

4. **Create a Relationship Health Check Framework**
   - Design a simple scorecard (e.g. trust, participation, alignment, impact) to track how strong your relationships are across key actors, and where investment is needed to strengthen the ecosystem overall.

This chapter helps with recognising that in ecosystems, no player wins alone—growth is mutual. When roles are well understood, and interactions are intentionally designed, platforms become more than scalable products. They become scalable communities of value.

References

Agarwal, S., & Kapoor, R. (2019). *Two faces of value creation in business ecosystems: Leveraging complementarities and managing interdependencies*. (Working paper). The Wharton School,. University of Pennsylvania.

Carst, A. E., & Hu, Y. (2023). Complementors as ecosystem actors: A systematic review. *Management Review Quarterly, 73*, 123–150. https://doi.org/10.1007/s11301-023-00368-y

Chen, L., Yi, J., Li, S., & Tong, T. W. (2022). Platform governance design in platform ecosystems: Implications for complementors' multihoming decision. *Journal of Management, 48*(3), 630–656. https://doi.org/10.1177/0149206320988337

Fürstenau, D., Baiyere, A., Schewina, K., Schulte-Althoff, M., & Rothe, H. (2023). Extended generativity theory on digital platforms. *Information Systems Research, 34*(4), 1686–1710. https://doi.org/10.1287/isre.2023.1209

Gawer, A., & Harracá, M. (2025). Inconsistent platform governance and social contagion of misconduct in digital ecosystems: A complementors perspective. *Research Policy, 54*(8), Article 104957. https://doi.org/10.2139/ssrn.5368760

Heimburg, V., & Wiesche, M. (2022). Relations between actors in digital platform ecosystems: A literature review. In *ECIS 2022 research papers (paper 93)*. Association for Information Systems. https://aisel.aisnet.org/ecis2022_rp/93

Hendricks, L., Matthyssens, P., & Kowalkowski, C. (2024). The co-evolution of actor engagement and value co-creation on digital platforms: Evidence from the asset management industry. *Journal of Business & Industrial Marketing. (Advance online publication)*. https://doi.org/10.1016/j.ijpe.2024.109467

Kari, A., Bellin, P., Matzner, M., & Gersch, M. (2025). Governing the emergence of network-driven platform ecosystems. *Electronic Markets, 35*. https://doi.org/10.1007/s12525-024-00745-9

Nim, N., Pedada, K., & Hewett, K. (2024). Digital marketing ecosystems and global market expansion: Current state and future research agenda. *International Marketing Review, 41*(5), 872–885. https://doi.org/10.1108/IMR-04-2024-0108

Schüler, F., & Petrik, D. (2023). Measuring network effects of digital industrial platforms: Towards a balanced platform performance management. *Information Systems and e-Business Management, 21*, 863–911. https://doi.org/10.1007/s10257-023-00655-x

Shen, L., Shi, Q., Parida, V., & Jovanovic, M. (2024). Ecosystem orchestration practices for industrial firms: A qualitative meta-analysis, framework development and research agenda. *Technological Forecasting and Social Change, 198*, 122171. https://doi.org/10.1016/j.jbusres.2023.114463

Thomas, L. D. W., Ritala, P., Karhu, K., & Heiskala, M. (2024). Vertical, horizontal, and collective complementarities in platform ecosystems. *Growth and Change, 55*(2), 350–371. https://doi.org/10.1080/14479338.2024.2303593

Van Alstyne, M. W., Parker, G. G., & Choudary, S. P. (2016). Pipelines, platforms, and the new rules of strategy. *Harvard Business Review, 94*(4), 54–62.

Wang, C., Zhao, X., & Hong, J. (2024). A meta-analysis of the effects of interaction on value co-creation in online collaborative innovation communities based on the service ecosystem framework. *Behavioral Sciences, 14*(12), 1177. https://doi.org/10.3390/bs14121177

7

Building Partnerships—The Role of Complementors

In a hyper-connected business world, partnerships have moved beyond being mere options—they have become strategic imperatives. Among these partnerships, complementors stand out as indispensable allies within platform ecosystems. The complementor is one of the most influential yet often underestimated actors. These entities enhance the value of the ecosystem by extending its reach, diversifying its offerings, and co-creating richer experiences for users. These collaborators do that and more, they don't just extend reach and diversify offerings; they actively shape richer, more dynamic user experiences. As markets grow more complex, platforms can no longer rely solely on internal innovation. They need a diverse ecosystem of partners to fuel growth, spark creativity, and tailor solutions to evolving needs.

Complementors play a crucial role in enabling platforms to innovate, scale, and respond to market needs (Gawer & Harracá, 2025). In this chapter, we explore who complementors are, the value they bring, and how to build partnerships that turn co-existence into co-creation.

Complementors come in many forms—app developers building specialised functionality, integration partners enhancing performance, agencies curating nuanced user experiences, or organisations from adjacent sectors unlocking fresh market potential. Each brings unique contributions: specialised tech, expanded distribution channels, and enhanced credibility. Imagine a fintech platform working with a complementary app to penetrate niche verticals or collaborating with a co-marketing partner to amplify brand awareness and establish trust far more efficiently than any solo campaign could.

When complementors are integrated thoughtfully, three critical advantages emerge. First is speed through specialisation—complementors often bring niche expertise, whether it's AI-driven analytics, regulatory compliance modules, or immersive training portals. This speed and focus are vital in fast-evolving markets where internal teams might struggle to keep pace. Next, their networks multiply reach and impact, transforming localised solutions into broader adoption through trust-based endorsements. Finally, their visible involvement builds co-created trust (FA et al., 2025). When end-users see partners contributing via certification programmes or joint support channels, the platform's credibility and openness become tangible.

Yet leveraging complementors is not just about forging agreements—it requires intentional partnership design rooted in mutual value. From the outset, both sides must clearly understand what each gains: revenue sharing, brand exposure, or joint go-to-market opportunities for partners; enhanced functionality, new users, or marketing support for the platform (Engert et al., 2021). Governance frameworks also play a crucial role. Co-authored roadmaps align feature development, while clearly defined API standards, certification protocols, and support tiers uphold technical consistency and quality (Hanafizadeh, 2025). Regular check-ins, ranging from quarterly business reviews to co-development hackathons, maintain alignment and surface innovative possibilities.

Sustaining these partnerships hinges on trust and transparency. By sharing performance metrics, usage analytics, and public recognition of partner contributions, platforms foster goodwill. When complementors see their efforts driving tangible platform growth, they remain committed—transforming one-off integrations into a virtuous cycle of co-creation.

It's also essential to be selective. Not every potential partner is a fit. Strong ecosystems prioritise depth over breadth, curating a focused group of complementors whose expertise, culture, market alignment, and long-term vision align with the platform. These high-potential collaborators elevate the overall quality and user experience. The most successful platform ecosystems don't just bring partners in—they evolve with them (Peng et al., 2023). Leading teams involve complementors in roadmap planning, support partner-led feature extensions, and treat them as co-innovators. Recognising that complementors—not just users—are primary architects of innovation ensures that the platform remains vibrant, adaptable, and ahead of disruption.

By shifting from co-existence to co-creation, platforms unlock their full potential—establishing ecosystems that are not only functional but forward-looking, collaborative, and scalable at their core.

Who Are Complementors?

Complementors are organisations or individuals whose products, services, or capabilities enhance a platform's core offering (Gawer & Harracá, 2025). They are not competitors, nor are they substitutes. Instead, they work in synergy with the platform, contributing additional value that makes the entire ecosystem more robust, attractive, and effective.

A classic example in fintech would be a payment platform that integrates with a cybersecurity partner to ensure transaction integrity. Another would be a data analytics provider that surfaces real-time financial insights from platform activity. These additions fill functionality gaps, address user-specific needs, and broaden the platform's application. What defines a complementor is not what they sell, but how their contribution strengthens the platform and supports its growth.

The Value of Complementors in Ecosystem Strategy

Complementors help platforms evolve from single-solution tools into expansive, adaptive systems. They add depth and breadth to platform capabilities by introducing specialist knowledge, technologies, and user propositions that the platform might not be able to develop in-house. They also serve as a bridge into new markets. By bringing their own customer bases, relationships and distribution networks, complementors help accelerate user acquisition, build credibility, and spark multi-directional engagement (Adner & Kapoor, 2010). This is especially powerful in B2B ecosystems, where complementors may operate in vertical markets or geographies the core platform is only beginning to enter.

Beyond utility, complementors can also be a key source of innovation. Many ecosystems have grown not through internal research and development (R&D) but through the ingenuity of third parties. App developers on mobile platforms, risk analytics tools in fintech, or wearable devices in health—these all originated from external players contributing to a shared infrastructure.

Building Effective Complementor Partnerships

Strategic partnerships with complementors do not happen by accident. They require deliberate planning, shared vision, and well-managed processes.

It begins with alignment—not only in product or service fit, but in values, user focus, and commercial ambition (Foss et al., 2022). Partners must understand and believe in the ecosystem's objectives. This helps avoid misalignment and reduces friction down the line.

Once alignment is established, platforms must create clear frameworks for interaction. These often include:

1. Defined onboarding processes
2. Transparent commercial agreements
3. API access or integration standards
4. Data-sharing rules
5. Ongoing performance measurement

Successful platforms also invest in relationship management. Regular communication, joint planning sessions, shared success metrics, and even co-branding initiatives all contribute to a more dynamic and engaged complementor base.

Frameworks for Understanding Complementor Roles

To work effectively with complementors, platform leaders and marketers must understand how these actors' function strategically. Two helpful frameworks include:

> **The Complementary Partner Model**, which focuses on three core dimensions:
>
> *Resource Alignment*—how well the complementor integrates with the platform. *Collaborative Innovation*—the potential to jointly create new solutions.
> *Shared Outcomes*—how benefits are distributed and mutual incentives maintained.
>
> **The Complementor Engagement Cycle**, which defines partnership development in three stages:
>
> - *Initiation*—identifying and attracting the right partners
> - *Integration*—embedding them into the ecosystem's workflows and infrastructure

- *Evolution*—iterating and expanding the partnership as user needs and technologies change

These frameworks help platform leaders avoid treating complementors as one-off vendors and instead nurture them as strategic contributors to the ecosystem's evolution.

Complementors in Action—Real-World Examples

Complementor impact is visible across industries:

Complementors are far more than supplementary partners—they are essential drivers of platform strength, innovation, and user trust. Their impact is seen across sectors where ecosystems flourish. Let's explore how they elevate platforms in technology, finance, and healthcare—and why they are foundational to sustained growth.

Technology

In the technology domain, platforms like **Salesforce**, **iOS**, and **Android** thrive as ecosystems precisely because of complementors. Independent app developers create extensions that are often more nimble, specialised, and responsive than platform owners could deliver alone. A single app, such as **Conga** on Salesforce, might enable advanced workflow automation, while another like **iTranslate** on iOS adds local language support or industry-specific compliance tools. These additions enhance the platform's core value and broaden its appeal to niche audiences. Complementors not only bring novel capabilities—they spark competition, set innovation benchmarks, and deepen user engagement by constantly enriching the experience.

Finance

Digital banking depends fundamentally on trust and security. Complementors in finance, such as **Socure** for identity verification, **Feedzai** for fraud detection, and **Nova Credit** for real-time credit scoring, add vital layers of reliability. Without them, platforms risk exposure to fraud and reputational damage. These partners also enable platforms to enter new markets quickly (Agyei-Boapeah et al., 2022). For example, a fintech can launch in a region leveraging a local know-your-customer (KYC) provider like **Onfido**, ensuring compliance with minimal overhead. Users instinctively trust platforms with familiar, third-party credentials integrated into everyday service—increasing adoption and retention.

Healthcare

Healthcare is another domain where complementors make a genuine difference. Telemedicine platforms integrate wearables, remote monitoring devices, and AI-driven symptom checkers that pull in nuanced patient data. For instance, **Amwell** integrates with devices from **Withings** for blood pressure and weight tracking, and platforms like **Wysa** for mental health support. This transforms care delivery from occasional consultations to continuous, personalised experiences. A telehealth solution that includes glucose monitors, blood pressure tracking, and mental health screening through third-party sensors can guide safer and more effective interventions (Paul et al., 2023). Clinicians gain real-time insights and predictive risk analytics, while patients receive proactive and personalised care pathways—none of which would be possible without complementary providers.

These sector-specific examples share a core truth: complementors amplify platform capability in areas that are too complex, specialised, or rapid-moving for a platform to handle alone. They bring domain expertise, regulatory knowledge, regional nuance, and innovative edge. They also leverage their own customer bases—creating an audience multiplier effect. When that happens, platform and complementors benefit symmetrically.

It's also worth noting how complementors influence brand perception. Users often credit platforms for solutions co-engineered with trusted partners. **Telehealth** users, for instance, may praise not only the convenience of on-demand consultations but also the seamless integration of their fitness tracker data—or the reliability of remote diagnostics. Each complementor subtly boosts credibility and trust in the core service.

Complementors also drive ecosystem innovation by acting as signals—rewarding successful providers with visibility, certifications, or preferential listings. This motivates others to innovate and keeps the platform fresh. Large platforms often host hackathons, developer days, and accelerator programmes targeting niche complementors. These initiatives surface new ideas—think novel payment options in finance or mental-wellbeing features in healthcare—that might never have emerged internally.

In short, complementors are the lifeblood of healthy, evolving ecosystems. They transform platforms into dynamic value zones—powering innovation, bolstering user trust, and reinforcing the perception that the platform is capable, resilient, and future-proof. Ignoring them isn't just a missed opportunity—it's strategic myopia.

Challenges in Managing Complementors

While complementors are vital, partnering with them comes with its own set of challenges. One of the most common issues is strategic misalignment, when a complementor's roadmap, corporate culture, or commercial objectives diverge from those of the platform. This may result in conflicting priorities, duplicated efforts, or incompatible solutions that ultimately detract from user experience. To prevent such misalignment, platforms must invest time in shared planning, establish clear alliance charters, and frequently check goals to ensure long-term alignment.

Quality control is another key concern. Because complementors operate independently, there is a risk that inconsistent standards or subpar performance could damage the platform's reputation (Yi et al., 2019). To uphold a seamless experience for users, platforms must implement rigorous vetting processes, certification programmes, and ongoing monitoring systems. Regular performance reviews, automated testing pipelines, and transparent SLAs (service level agreements) can help maintain quality across the ecosystem without stifling innovation.

Another challenge arises in the form of power imbalances. Larger or more established complementors may dominate influence within the ecosystem, shaping innovation agendas or negotiating favourable commercial terms. That can crowd out smaller players and limit the perceived openness of the platform (Jacobides et al., 2024). To safeguard fairness and diversity, platforms should introduce tiered governance structures, equitable revenue-sharing models, and participatory decision-making councils. Smaller complementors can then contribute meaningfully without being overshadowed.

Finally, the evolving nature of technology and user expectations can add complexity. Complementor readiness can sometimes lag behind platform upgrades, leading to compatibility issues. Platforms need to proactively communicate upcoming changes, offer sandbox environments, and support complementors through training, toolkits, and developer support (Liu et al., 2024). This kind of ecosystem stewardship not only prevents friction during transitions but also reinforces trust and shared ownership across actors.

By addressing misalignment, quality control, power imbalances, and technological coordination, platform leaders ensure that complementor relationships are not just strategic partnerships, but true engines of co-creation and growth.

Amplifying Growth Through Complementors

For marketers, complementors are growth accelerators. They offer access to new audiences, data, and value propositions that enhance brand relevance and customer experience.

By collaborating with complementors, marketers can run joint campaigns, co-create content and design solutions that reflect real-world use cases. They can also gain insight from complementor engagement data—helping refine personas, messaging, and product-market fit across the ecosystem. Marketing strategy should not view complementors simply as channels or support functions. They are partners in the storytelling and delivery of value (Parker et al., 2016). In many cases, they are also your best advocates—amplifying your platform's reach and credibility through their own networks.

Visual Framework: Complementor Engagement in Platform Ecosystems

Figure 7.1 presents a framework that outlines the flow of complementor value within the platform ecosystem, emphasising strategic integration, collaborative growth, and the mutual reinforcement of capabilities that drive sustained ecosystem success.

The *Complementor Engagement in Platform Ecosystems* model captures how complementors contribute strategically and operationally, enhancing the platform's utility and ecosystem-wide value.

7 Building Partnerships—The Role of Complementors

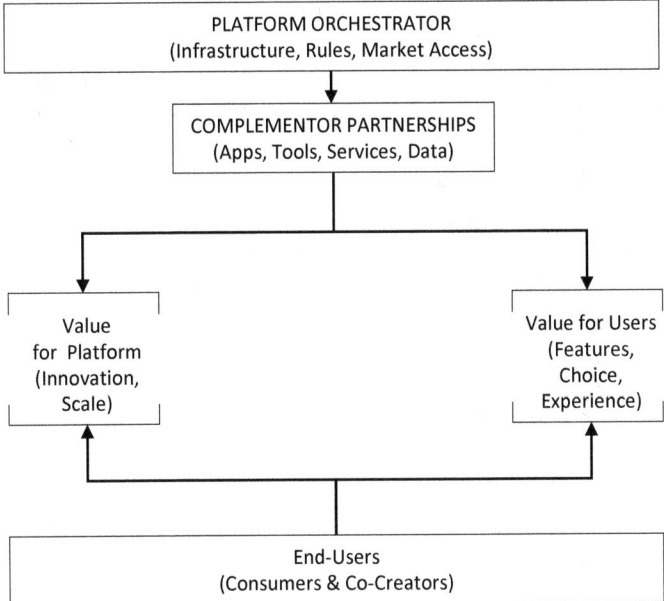

Fig. 7.1 Complementor Engagement in Platform Ecosystems Model

> **Reflective Prompt: Are You Leveraging Complementors as Partners or Providers?**
>
> Consider your current partnership strategy:
>
> 1. Are your complementors strategically aligned with your platform's goals?
> 2. Do you treat them as transactional vendors or collaborative partners?
> 3. How well are you integrating their offerings into your platform's user experience?
> 4. What shared outcomes are you pursuing, and how are they being measured?
> 5. Strong complementor partnerships can multiply value. But they require structure, trust, and shared ambition.

> **Exercise: Complementor Strategy Blueprint**
>
> 1. **List Your Current or Potential Complementors**
>   - Identify five partners or providers that could add value to your ecosystem.
>   - What do they offer that you do not?
>   - How would their inclusion enhance user experience or market reach?

2. **Assess the State of Engagement**
   - Are they integrated via APIs, referrals, co-branded offerings?
   - Are there blockers (technical, contractual, strategic) slowing integration?
   - What governance model is in place for the relationship?
3. **Design a Complementor Activation Plan**
   - Choose one complementor and develop a co-creation initiative (e.g. joint product, campaign, or community launch).
   - Define roles, benefits, and shared success metrics.
4. **Create a Communication Loop**
   - How will you and your complementor share feedback, performance data, and roadmap changes?
   - Schedule quarterly reviews or collaborative planning sessions.

This chapter helps operationalise complementor partnerships—moving from abstract value to tangible co-creation and sustained ecosystem growth.

References

Adner, R., & Kapoor, R. (2010). Value creation in innovation ecosystems: How the structure of technological interdependence affects firm performance in new technology generations. *Strategic Management Journal, 31*(3), 306–333. https://doi.org/10.1002/smj.821

Agyei-Boapeah, H., Evans, R., & Nisar, T. M. (2022). Disruptive innovation: Designing business platforms for new financial services. *Journal of Business Research, 150*, 134–146. https://doi.org/10.1016/j.jbusres.2022.05.066

Engert, M., Evers, J., Hein, A., & Krcmar, H. (2021). The engagement of complementors and the role of platform boundary resources in e-commerce platform ecosystems. *Information Systems Frontiers, 23*(3), 667–685. https://doi.org/10.1007/s10796-021-10236-3

FA, C., Ramezan Zadeh, M. T., Ozalp, H., & Volberda, H. W. (2025). The role of trust in a platform ecosystem: Exploring the impact of different trust dimensions on complementors' platform revenue. *Research Policy, 54*(8), 104957. https://doi.org/10.2139/ssrn.5180726

Foss, N. J., Schmidt, J., & Teece, D. J. (2022). Ecosystem leadership as a dynamic capability. *Long Range Planning, 56*(6), 102270. https://doi.org/10.1016/j.lrp.2022.102270

Gawer, A., & Harracá, M. (2025). Inconsistent platform governance and social contagion of misconduct in digital ecosystems: A complementors perspective. *Research Policy, 54*(8), 105300. https://doi.org/10.1016/j.respol.2025.105300

Hanafizadeh, P. (2025). *Governance system design model in platform ecosystems by a socio-technical systems theory*. Digital Policy, Regulation and Governance Advance online publication. https://doi.org/10.1108/DPRG-04-2025-0105

Jacobides, M. G., Cennamo, C., & Gawer, A. (2024). Externalities and complementarities in platforms and ecosystems: From structural solutions to endogenous failures. *Research Policy, 53*(1). https://doi.org/10.1016/j.respol.2023.104845

Liu, Z., Li, Z., Zhang, Y., Mutukumira, A. N., Feng, Y., Cui, Y., Wang, S., Wang, J., & Wang, S. (2024). Comparing business, innovation, and platform ecosystems: A systematic review of the literature. *Biomimetics, 9*(4), 216. https://doi.org/10.3390/biomimetics9040216

Parker, G. G., Van Alstyne, M. W., & Choudary, S. P. (2016). *Platform revolution: How networked markets are transforming the economy and how to make them work for you*. W. W. Norton & Company.

Paul, M., Maglaras, L., Ferrag, M. A., & Almomani, I. (2023). Digitization of healthcare sector: A study on privacy and security concerns. *ICT Express, 9*(4), 571–588. https://doi.org/10.1016/j.icte.2023.02.007

Peng, H., Lu, Y., & Gupta, S. (2023). Promoting value emergence through digital platform ecosystems: Perspectives on resource integration in China. *Technological Forecasting and Social Change, 189*, 122338. https://doi.org/10.1016/j.techfore.2022.122338

Yi, J., He, J., & Yang, L. (2019). Platform heterogeneity, platform governance and complementors' product performance: An empirical study of the mobile application industry. *Frontiers of Business Research in China, 13*(1), 13. https://doi.org/10.1186/s11782-019-0060-3

8

Overcoming Barriers in Institutionalised Markets

Institutionalised markets are known for their structure, stability, and predictability. They operate under longstanding regulatory frameworks, legacy systems, and cultural expectations that prize continuity over change. While this fosters reliability and consumer confidence, it can also resist innovation, making change not just an operational hurdle but a strategic challenge.

For businesses building platform ecosystems, these barriers are more than technical obstacles—they are systemic. Overcoming them is essential to enable co-creation, unlock collaboration, and drive sustainable growth. This chapter explores how ecosystem leaders can navigate institutional constraints while preserving the agility and innovation needed for success.

The challenge is to thread the needle: introduce new forms of value creation while respecting the frameworks that govern compliance and stakeholder trust. Leaders must reconcile the need to co-create with users and regulators with the responsibility to uphold institutional resilience.

In financial services, for example, compliance rules and internal risk protocols make change difficult. Direct-to-consumer fintech approaches often trigger regulatory concern. Leading players adopt hybrid strategies—developing modular innovations in controlled environments and scaling proven solutions. This iterative approach satisfies both institutional imperatives and ecosystem ambitions.

Healthcare is similarly complex. With its emphasis on data privacy, clinical accountability and interoperability, telehealth platforms often face inertia. Successful players create co-creation frameworks with clinicians and patients within established governance structures. By aligning development with policy review cycles, leaders enable structured evolution.

Across all institutionalised markets, legitimacy is key. Innovation must align with regulatory expectations and ethical standards. Marketers and platform leaders must communicate compliance, oversight and transparency—not just benefits (Fürstenau et al., 2023). Marketing becomes a tool for legitimacy as much as persuasion. Internal resistance is also common. Teams used to linear models may push back on open-ended ecosystems. Overcoming this requires engaging stakeholders in governance, involving them in shaping ecosystem policy and integrating co-creation into existing routines. Including platform metrics in board reports and compliance reviews embeds ecosystem work into corporate DNA.

Institutional markets don't reward moonshots. Instead, micro-pilots, regionally scoped rollouts, and joint ventures create low-risk paths to scale. Governance structures must balance institutional rigour with openness (Engert et al., 2025)—co-designed principles, partner access tiers, audit trails, and oversight boards build trust as an embedded feature.

Ultimately, institutionalised markets are not barriers to ecosystem growth—they are arenas where legitimacy becomes a lever for innovation. Leaders who master this balance will turn inertia into momentum and reframe what's possible within their industries.

Understanding Barriers in Institutionalised Markets

Markets such as finance, healthcare, insurance and education are examples of highly institutionalised environments. These sectors prioritise compliance, risk mitigation and stakeholder protection, often at the expense of rapid innovation (Hendricks & Matthyssens, 2022). Change in such settings is slow and incremental—and often met with resistance.

One key obstacle is structural inertia. This refers to the systems, processes, and hierarchies that have become fixed over time. These structures are designed to manage risk and enforce accountability, but they can also delay or dilute transformative initiatives (Dremel et al., 2021). Leaders within these markets may be cautious about adopting new models, fearing disruption to the reliability their stakeholders expect.

Another barrier is low inter-organisational trust. Many institutionalised sectors are dominated by incumbents with longstanding dominance (FA et al., 2025). These organisations are often wary of new entrants or collaborative frameworks. Concerns about data sharing, reputational risk, and regulatory scrutiny create an atmosphere of protectionism that inhibits ecosystem formation.

Navigating Institutional Resistance

To address these barriers, ecosystem strategists must understand the rules that govern institutional behaviour.

The **Institutional Logic Perspective** is one such framework. It explains how norms, values, and legal expectations shape what is considered legitimate within a market. In institutionalised environments, new platforms must align with this logic to be accepted (Thornton et al., 2012). Legitimacy often matters more than speed or novelty.

Another practical tool is the **Network Management Model**, which outlines six dimensions for overcoming ecosystem barriers:

1. Stakeholder alignment
2. Trust-building
3. Resource integration
4. Adaptive governance
5. Risk-sharing
6. Continuous innovation

These dimensions highlight that overcoming barriers is not about breaking rules—it is about building bridges.

Strategies for Ecosystem Entry and Growth

Success in institutionalised markets requires a blend of compliance and creativity. One powerful strategy is **proactive regulatory engagement**. Platforms that work closely with regulators—rather than treating them as obstacles—are better positioned to influence policy, gain early trust, and secure market credibility.

Another essential tactic is embedding trust into the ecosystem design. This includes creating governance models that ensure fairness, transparency, and data security. It also means establishing feedback loops so that ecosystem participants—including users, partners, and regulators—can raise concerns and see their input acted upon.

Navigating entry into institutionalised markets requires a nuanced combination of compliance and creative ecosystem design. One of the most effective approaches is proactive regulatory engagement. Rather than viewing regulators as adversaries, successful platforms position themselves as collaborative partners, involving regulators early in their product development cycles. This transparency fosters trust, helps shape relevant policy, and speeds up market acceptance. It also signals to other ecosystem actors—investors, customers, and partners—that the platform is both bold in innovation and rigorously compliant (Parker et al., 2016).

Equally critical is embedding trust structurally into the platform's architecture and governance model. At the outset, platform leaders must define clear principles of fairness, transparency, and data security—and ensure these values are reflected in each touchpoint (Reiners, 2022). This involves not only secure data handling and auditable processes, but also the creation of open feedback channels. By offering partners, users, and regulators opportunities to raise concerns, share insights, or suggest improvements, platforms demonstrate they value shared responsibility—and that ecosystem participation is a two-way conversation.

Technology enables much of this trust-building in practice. Blockchain, for instance, can deliver immutable audit trails that prove compliance and traceability to all stakeholders. AI can be harnessed to monitor for compliance anomalies, flagging potential risks in real time. Secure APIs and permissioned data access ensure only authorised actors receive the information they need—no more. These technical measures are not sidebar features—they form the credibility backbone of a regulated platform ecosystem.

To illustrate how these strategies work in the real world, consider two case studies.

Case Studies: Ecosystem Innovation in Established Markets

There are clear examples of platform businesses that have succeeded in difficult regulatory environments:

In finance, startups like **Starling Bank** and **TransferWise** have partnered with central banks, met capital requirements, and designed Compliance-as-a-Service (CaaS) capabilities into their products. Their legitimacy is a function of both innovation and alignment.

Rather than attempting to bypass legacy systems, these fintech pioneers integrated themselves deeply into the financial establishment. By engaging central banks and regulators early, they obtained full banking licences, met capital requirements, and embedded compliance tools directly into their services. For example, TransferWise (now Wise) integrates real-time compliance checks—screening transactions for fraud or money laundering before they're executed. This approach allowed them to operate at scale with legitimacy, while still offering faster and often cheaper services than traditional banks.

In **healthcare**, ecosystems have emerged that integrate electronic medical records, patient engagement apps and clinical diagnostics—all while respecting data privacy laws such as GDPR and HIPAA. These platforms did not bypass institutions—they collaborated with them.

Data privacy is sacrosanct. But some platform businesses have managed to thrive by building ecosystems around electronic medical records, diagnostic tools, and patient engagement solutions that respect GDPR, HIPAA, and other privacy standards (Paul et al., 2023). They do this not by sidestepping institutions, but by partnering with hospitals, insurers, and regulators to co-design governance frameworks. They then layer on secure data-sharing protocols, consent mechanisms, and audit trails—allowing multiple healthcare actors to collaborate safely and ethically.

Epic Systems' **MyChart** patient portal exemplifies a platform ecosystem that thrives on institutional partnerships. Beyond serving as an electronic medical record interface, MyChart integrates with providers, patient apps, and diagnostic tools—all while strictly adhering to GDPR, HIPAA, and other privacy regulations. Epic's partnerships with hospitals and patient-experience firms like **Press Ganey** allow deep integration of patient-reported insights into MyChart.

These cases show that platform ecosystems do not need to disrupt from the outside. They can succeed by innovating from within. By mapping regulation as a collaborator rather than a constraint, platforms can co-create legitimacy while delivering compelling value.

Looking forward, platform leaders must internalise compliance and trust-building as core pillars of strategy—not just box-ticking exercises (Reiners, 2022). Regulatory innovation labs, shared compliance sandboxes, and federated governance models (where partners and regulators sit at the same table) are likely to become industry standards. The platforms that master both creative collaboration and statutory obligation will shape the future of ecosystem-driven markets. In doing so, they will redefine what it means to grow—not just in scale, but in legitimacy, resilience, and shared success.

The Role of Adaptive Governance

Adaptive governance is the foundation of long-term ecosystem success in institutional markets. This approach balances structure with flexibility—allowing ecosystems to evolve as regulations, technologies, and user needs shift.

Key principles include:

1. **Stakeholder inclusion**—giving voice to all actors, including users, regulators, and complementors
2. **Responsive rule-making**—revising policies based on emerging risks or innovation
3. **Risk-sharing models**—joint ventures, pooled investments, and insurtech solutions that reduce individual exposure

These mechanisms reduce perceived risk, build consensus and keep the ecosystem relevant even as institutional landscapes evolve.

Leadership as a Catalyst for Change

In complex markets, leadership matters. It's far more than a title—it's a catalyst for progress. Visionary leaders articulate the case for transformation in language that resonates with regulators, boards, and end-users. They do not simply advocate for change—they build coalitions to realise it.

Ecosystem leadership is not the job of one person or firm. It is distributed across orchestrators, complementors and regulatory liaisons (Foss et al., 2022). These actors act as translators, innovators, and mediators—helping traditional stakeholders understand the value of new models without threatening the institutional order. By framing innovation as a shared journey rather than a unilateral ambition, these leaders invite participation from those who otherwise might resist.

Ecosystem leadership is inherently distributed. No single individual or organisation can steer the collective alone. Instead, a constellation of actors—platform orchestrators, complementors, industry insiders, and regulatory liaisons—must share responsibility (Tsytsyna & Valminen, 2024). These actors each play different yet complementary roles: some design the framework for collaboration, others supply the specialised capabilities, and still others translate new models into the language of compliance or institutional tradition.

Orchestrators set the vision and architecture—they decide who participates, by which rules, and how value is shared. Complementors amplify this vision through real-world application, demonstrating how modular solutions can be adapted to existing systems in ways that add value, not conflict. Regulatory liaisons act as bridges, interpreting the benefits of ecosystem models in terms of policy objectives, safeguards, and public interest (Hendricks & Matthyssens, 2022). Together, this trio—vision, implementation, and legitimacy—enables transformation on a scale that singular efforts cannot match.

The practical impact is profound. Take, for example, a fintech ecosystem entering a tightly regulated market. The orchestrator pitches the vision of a more efficient payments infrastructure. A complementor, such as a compliance-as-a-service provider, co-creates with the orchestrator to embed real-time audit trails and fraud detection. At the same time, a liaison maintains a continuous dialogue with regulators, presenting sandbox results and performance data transparently. The result is not a disruptive assault on the status quo—but rather an evolution that institutions can embrace.

This distributed leadership model extends beyond finance. In healthcare, an orchestrator may introduce a shared patient platform, while diagnostic partners supply medical device integrations, and oversight bodies endorse new data governance frameworks. Across sectors, the same pattern applies: bold vision, shared execution, and trusted compliance.

Ultimately, this is how ecosystems succeed in institutional contexts. Leadership that is inclusive and interconnected—not command-and-control—turns regulatory uncertainty into opportunity. It reframes institutional inertia as a platform for legitimacy. Most importantly, it unites traditional structures and emerging models into working systems that drive lasting, systemic change.

Marketing Where Trust Is Non-Negotiable

Marketing in institutionalised markets is not about hype—it is about clarity, credibility, and evidence. Marketing leaders must position their platforms as trustworthy, secure, and aligned with stakeholder values.

This means:

1. Highlighting compliance and security in all messaging
2. Demonstrating transparency in value propositions and pricing
3. Emphasising how innovation supports—rather than undermines—institutional goals

Marketers must also support ecosystem engagement through education, co-branded campaigns and content that showcases collaboration, not just competition. Trust is the most powerful asset in these environments—and marketers are the storytellers who help build it.

Marketing in institutionalised markets demands a level of trust that goes far beyond flashy slogans or clever visuals—it requires an unshakeable foundation rooted in transparency, credibility, and accountability. In environments shaped by regulation, legacy systems, and deeply held conventions, marketing becomes less about persuasion and more about reassurance (Hendricks & Matthyssens, 2022). This reassurance must come through consistently: every campaign, every piece of collateral, and every customer interaction needs to reflect unwavering integrity.

To convey that trust, marketing leaders must emphasise security and compliance at every step. This means clearly communicating how data is protected, how regulatory standards are met, and how systems are audited. It might mean dedicating sections of product pages to explain encryption protocols or including compliance badges in communications. Nothing should be left to assumption—every claim must be backed by evidence and independence.

Transparency must surface in value propositions and pricing, too. In institutional ecosystems, opaque fees or vague service descriptions erode confidence. Marketers must shift towards clear, modular pricing models that allow users to understand exactly what they're paying for and why (Liang et al., 2021). Case studies and usage reports clarifying ROI or efficiency gains further strengthen the narrative. By sharing real-world outcomes and performance metrics, marketing teams create credibility that resonates with institutional buyers, partners, and stakeholders.

Innovation is a non-negotiable—but only if it aligns with institutional values and priorities. Marketers must frame new features not as break-with-tradition, but as thoughtful enhancements to legacy systems and processes. Crafting messaging that emphasises evolution rather than revolution helps reduce institutional resistance. Innovation should feel familiar, reliable, and accountable.

Trust also grows through education and collaboration. Marketing must go beyond brand-centric messaging—creating co-branded campaigns, whitepapers, webinars, and training sessions that demonstrate joint effort and institutional endorsement. By hosting or sponsoring events alongside regulatory bodies or respected incumbent organisations, platforms can signal legitimacy. Educational content that demystifies complex areas—such as compliance frameworks or technical integrations—empowers users and shows respect for their sophistication.

This kind of marketing reframes the narrative. Instead of competing on hype or novelty, the emphasis moves to partnership, shared purpose, and mutual confidence (Roundy & Fayard, 2021). Marketers become steward-collaborators—a role that honours institutional history while enabling strategic evolution. In institutionalised markets more than any other, trust is the marketer's most powerful asset—and the storyteller is the architect of that trust.

Visual Framework: Navigating Barriers in Institutionalised Ecosystems

In Figure 8.1 introduces a framework illustrating the critical elements required to enter, build, and scale ecosystems within institutionalised markets. It highlights the importance of adaptive governance, regulatory navigation, and strategic alignment to overcome structural barriers and enable long-term ecosystem success.

The *Navigating Barriers in Institutional Ecosystems* model demonstrates that legitimacy, not disruption, is the route to ecosystem success in regulated environments. Trust and collaboration must be embedded at every level of strategy and operations.

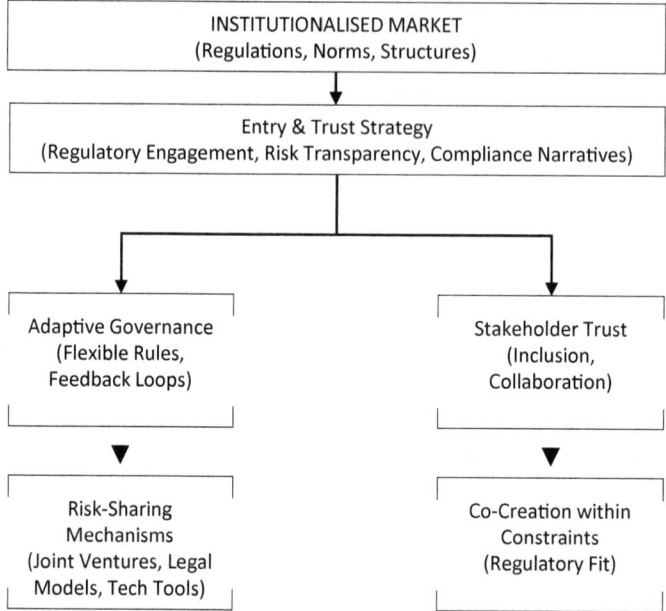

Fig. 8.1 Navigating Barriers in Institutional Ecosystems Model

---

Reflective Prompt: Are You Building for Trust or for Speed?

In your platform or ecosystem strategy:

1. Are you aligning your vision with the values and risk appetite of institutional stakeholders?
2. Have you mapped regulatory bodies as strategic partners rather than gatekeepers?
3. Are you building mechanisms that share risk and create accountability across the ecosystem?
4. Does your marketing narrative inspire confidence in cautious adopters?
5. In institutionalised markets, credibility is currency. It must be earned—and sustained.

Exercise: Ecosystem Readiness in Regulated Markets

1. **Identify Institutional Stakeholders**
    - List all actors whose approval, influence, or endorsement affects your ability to operate in the market (e.g. regulators, legal bodies, auditors, industry boards).
    - What are their core concerns, values, or red lines?

2. **Audit Your Governance Maturity**
   - Do you have documented, flexible governance policies?
   - How often are these policies reviewed or adapted?
   - Are users, partners, and regulators involved in shaping them?

3. **Assess Your Trust-Building Strategies**
   - What evidence are you providing that your platform is secure, compliant, and equitable?
   - How do you handle data access, consent, and transparency?
   - Are your marketing messages focused more on novelty or on reliability?

4. **Design a Collaborative Engagement Initiative**
   - Choose one high-stakes institutional actor and create a co-developed initiative (e.g. regulatory sandbox, public research partnership, compliance toolkit).
   - Define success metrics, roles, and communication cadence.

This chapter supports you in turning market resistance into a strategic advantage—by building legitimacy from the inside out, with trust, transparency, and value at the centre.

References

Dremel, C., Haskamp, T., Marx, C., & Uebernickel, F. (2021). Understanding inertia in digital transformation: A literature review and multilevel research framework. *Proceedings of the 42nd International Conference on Information Systems.*

Engert, M., Farchi, D., & Sayed, M. (2025). Self-organization and governance in digital platform ecosystems: Balancing top-down control and complementor coalitions. *MIS Quarterly, 49*(1), 85–112. https://doi.org/10.25300/MISQ/2024/18413

FA, C., Ramezan Zadeh, M. T., Ozalp, H., & Volberda, H. W. (2025). The role of trust in a platform ecosystem: Exploring the impact of different trust dimensions on complementors' platform revenue. *Research Policy, 54*(8), Article 104957. https://doi.org/10.2139/ssrn.5180726

Foss, N. J., Schmidt, J., & Teece, D. J. (2022). Ecosystem leadership as a dynamic capability. *Long Range Planning, 56*(6), Article 102270. https://doi.org/10.1016/j.lrp.2022.102270

Fürstenau, D., Baiyere, A., Schewina, K., Schulte-Althoff, M., & Rothe, H. (2023). Extended generativity theory on digital platforms. *Information Systems Research, 34*(4), 1686–1710. https://doi.org/10.1287/isre.2023.1209

Hendricks, L., & Matthyssens, P. (2022). Platform ecosystem development in an institutionalized business market: The case of the asset management industry. *Journal of Business & Industrial Marketing, 38*(2), 395–413. https://doi.org/10.1108/JBIM-04-2021-0193

Liang, L., Tian, L., Xie, J., Xu, J., & Zhang, W. (2021). Optimal pricing model of car-sharing: Market pricing or platform pricing. *Industrial Management & Data Systems, 121*(3), 594–612. https://doi.org/10.1108/IMDS-04-2020-0230

Parker, G. G., Van Alstyne, M. W., & Choudary, S. P. (2016). *Platform revolution: How networked markets are transforming the economy and how to make them work for you*. W. W. Norton & Company.

Paul, M., Maglaras, L., Ferrag, M. A., & Almomani, I. (2023). Digitization of healthcare sector: A study on privacy and security concerns. *ICT Express, 9*(4), 571–588. https://doi.org/10.1016/j.icte.2023.02.007

Reiners, S. (2022). Trust and its extensions in digital platform ecosystems: Key concepts and issues for future research. https://doi.org/10.1109/CBI54897.2022.10042.

Roundy, P. T., & Fayard, A.-L. (2021). Narratives in entrepreneurial ecosystems: Drivers of effectuation. *Small Business Economics, 57*(2), 467–483. https://doi.org/10.1007/s11187-021-00531-3

Thornton, P. H., Ocasio, W., & Lounsbury, M. (2012). *The institutional logics perspective: A new approach to culture, structure, and process*. Oxford University Press.

Tsytsyna, E., & Valminen, T. (2024). How are actor dynamics balanced in ecosystems? An in-depth case study of an autonomous maritime transportation ecosystem. *Review of Managerial Science, 18*, 2547–2582. https://doi.org/10.1007/s11846-023-00688-z

9

Leveraging Actor Engagement in the Digital Era

Actor engagement is no longer a peripheral concept in marketing. It is central to how value is created, sustained, and scaled within platform ecosystems. In a digital world defined by immediacy, interactivity, and iteration, enabling engagement is not just strategic—it is essential. This chapter explores how engagement fuels value co-creation and how marketing leaders can harness its power to strengthen relationships across diverse ecosystem actors.

Actor engagement has moved to the heart of modern marketing. Marketing is no longer about broadcasting messages or promoting products—it is about cultivating active relationships throughout the ecosystem. Engagement is the engine behind co-creation, innovation, and mutual value (Hendricks, Matthyssens & Kowalkowski, 2024). More than fleeting interactions, actor engagement means continuous, intentional exchanges. It's the difference between a single click and a feedback loop involving developers, users, and advocates. These loops build trust, insight, and relevance in real time.

In platform ecosystems, engagement cuts across traditional audience segments. Developers, customers, regulators, and partners all contribute unique value (Narvaiza et al., 2024). Marketing leaders must shift from managing campaigns to orchestrating conversations—designing systems, narratives, and touchpoints that empower actors to contribute and collaborate.

Consider a fintech platform co-developing a budgeting tool: the developer codes it, marketers promote it, users test it, and feedback leads to improvements. Regulatory advisors ensure compliance, and analytics track adoption (Hendricks, Matthyssens & Kowalkowski, 2024). What results is not a static product but a co-created, evolving service. This demands a new mindset in marketing leadership. Beyond personas and customer journeys, marketers must craft engagement journeys—encouraging contribution, advocacy, and long-term involvement. These are enabled through prompts, intuitive tools, recognition mechanisms, and shared goals.

Actors want to participate in something meaningful. Spotlighting contributors, hosting co-design sessions, and showcasing co-created outcomes deepen involvement.

Technology underpins this shift. Intuitive interfaces, feedback tools, and gamified experiences allow actors to see their impact. Real-time data helps marketers tailor engagement, invite collaboration early, and reward valuable participation.

But technology alone isn't enough (McKinsey Digital, 2024). Engagement thrives on human-centred leadership. Marketers must translate data into stories, resolve tensions between ecosystem actors, and design inclusive narratives that unite diverse goals.

Engagement must also be consistent. One-off campaigns fall short. Sustainable ecosystems require ongoing feedback loops, ideation, and permanent spaces for collaboration. Here, marketing becomes the connective tissue of the ecosystem.

When embedded into strategy, engagement becomes a multiplier. Each act of participation generates insights, loyalty, and new innovation pathways. Acting on those signals builds trust and drives adaptability at scale.

Ultimately, actor engagement turns marketing from message delivery into value orchestration (Hendricks, Matthyssens & Kowalkowski, 2024). It takes empathy, data fluency, and collaboration skills—but when done right, it transforms marketing from a function into a movement—and platforms from services into communities of innovation. The marketer's role in this shift is pivotal—it is foundational to the success of modern ecosystems.

Defining Actor Engagement in Ecosystems

In traditional marketing, stakeholders were often seen as passive recipients of brand messaging—recipients rather than participants. Actor engagement shifts this view, positioning individuals, groups, and institutions—users, developers, partners, influencers, and regulators—as active contributors in the value creation process. This shift in mindset carries profound implications.

Engagement is no longer confined to transactions. It encompasses feedback, advocacy, content contribution, service development, and real-time interaction. The term "actor" captures the diversity and agency of participants. They are not just buying or consuming—they are investing attention, insight, and creativity.

This reframes ecosystem roles. Actors are not just end-users who convert; they are co-creators and **amplifiers** (Van Dyck et al., 2024). A user submitting feedback, writing a review, or suggesting a feature transitions from observer to co-architect. Developers building integrations, agencies designing campaigns, and regulators co-shaping governance all play pivotal roles in directing platform growth. Recognising that every interaction is a chance for contribution reframes engagement as ongoing participation.

Actor engagement spans many behaviours. Feedback is a starting point. Advocacy builds when actors recommend the platform. Content contributions—like tutorials or use cases—enrich the ecosystem. Service development may appear as third-party tools or partner integrations. Real-time interactions, such as co-design sessions or live forums, reinforce dynamic relationships.

The power of this view lies in its recognition of varied motivations. Users seek connection and utility; developers pursue innovation; regulators want safety and fairness (Palmié et al., 2022). Embracing this diversity becomes a strategic advantage. Platforms channel it through product forums, developer APIs, and policy advisory groups.

This shift also redefines marketing—from monologue to collaboration. Marketers facilitate environments where valuable contributions emerge organically (Kowalkowski et al., 2012). They build developer toolkits, highlight user stories, and establish clear feedback loops. When actors see their input enacted, their commitment grows; participation becomes contagious.

A holistic engagement model enables richer metrics—beyond clicks to include contributions, retention, sentiment, and co-creation. Success becomes relational and generative. In this new role, marketers evolve into ecosystem enablers, embedding actor engagement into the core of strategy, innovation, and platform growth.

Key Traits of Actor Engagement

Actor engagement is:

1. **Relational**—based on trust, shared goals, and mutual contribution
2. **Multidimensional**—spanning behaviours, emotional connection, and community participation

3. **Iterative**—built over time through ongoing interaction, adaptation, and feedback

It encompasses both disposition (the motivation or readiness to engage) and behaviour (the visible actions taken in response). This means marketers must understand both the "why" and the "how" behind participation.

Frameworks for Mapping Engagement

Several models help leaders and marketers operationalise engagement. Two of the most useful are:

The Engagement Disposition-Behaviour Continuum, this continuum tracks the progression from passive awareness to active contribution—it draws on insights from the Psychological Continuum Model and the COBRAs behavioural taxonomy (Schivinski, Christodoulides, & Dabrowski, 2016)—mapping how evolving engagement mindsets (dispositions) lead to observable behaviours.

The stages typically include:

1. Awareness
2. Interest
3. Intention
4. Participation
5. Advocacy

By identifying where an actor sits, marketing teams can tailor engagement strategies that nudge them towards greater involvement.

The Actor Engagement Cycle This Framework Emphasises Engagement as a Process with Four Repeating Stages:

1. **Initiation**—capturing attention through relevance or need
2. **Interaction**—creating meaningful exchange
3. **Reflection**—helping actors assess the value of their engagement
4. **Adaptation**—evolving the experience based on feedback

These stages provide a roadmap for building durable, responsive relationships.

Digital Technologies as Enablers of Engagement

Technology has not only expanded the reach of marketing—it has transformed its role. In digital ecosystems, engagement happens in real time, often through channels that enable immediate response, customisation, and collaboration (Breidbach & Brodie, 2017).

AI and ML (machine learning) allow marketers to predict preferences and deliver highly targeted messages. Chatbots and conversational interfaces enable scalable, 24/7 engagement. Social platforms foster communities and content sharing that turn customers into advocates. Feedback mechanisms such as reviews, polls, and surveys help brands iterate offerings and deepen relevance.

More importantly, these technologies make engagement measurable. Platforms can track sentiment, participation frequency, churn risk, and behavioural shifts—then respond with speed and precision.

Value Exchange at the Centre of Engagement

Engagement thrives when actors perceive value—and when they contribute it in return. This reciprocal exchange might take many forms:

1. A personalised product recommendation in exchange for usage data
2. Exclusive access in return for content creation or advocacy
3. Meaningful connection in return for time and feedback

If the value is lopsided, actors disengage. If it is balanced and evolving, they stay involved and deepen their commitment. Marketers must carefully manage this exchange, constantly checking for relevance, fairness, and mutual gain.

Challenges in Actor Engagement

While the potential is vast, engaging actors in a platform ecosystem is not without friction.

Fragmentation is a key issue—actors engage across multiple devices, apps, and touchpoints, each with its own rules and formats (Gu & Li, 2022). Maintaining coherence across these experiences is difficult but necessary.

Expectation management is another challenge. As engagement deepens, so too does the demand for personalisation, responsiveness, and authenticity (Lemon & Verhoef, 2016). Delivering this at scale requires advanced tools and organisational agility.

Ethical considerations and data governance are also front and centre. Engaging actors without respecting privacy or transparency erodes trust—often irreversibly (Martin & Murphy, 2017). Platforms must lead with clarity, consent, and integrity in how data is used to personalise engagement.

Examples of Actor Engagement in Practice

Across industries, actor engagement is driving competitive advantage:

1. In **e-commerce**, platforms like **Amazon** use predictive algorithms and user reviews to personalise experiences and boost trust.
2. In **finance**, digital-first banks like **Monzo** use gamified dashboards and real-time spending insights to keep users engaged and informed.
3. In **entertainment**, services like **Spotify** and **Netflix** recommend content based on usage patterns, reinforcing stickiness and brand affinity.

Each example shows how actor engagement moves beyond acquisition—it sustains value creation and strengthens ecosystem bonds over time.

Marketing's Evolving Role

For marketers, actor engagement reframes the role from promotion to participation. The objective is no longer just visibility—it is involvement. Marketing teams must design experiences that invite collaboration, enable contribution, and reward commitment.

This means creating content loops, participatory journeys, and engagement incentives that reinforce actor motivation. It also involves listening more than broadcasting—tuning into what actors want, value, and expect.

In platform ecosystems, engaged actors become more than users—they become co-creators, ambassadors, and strategic assets. The challenge for marketers is to earn that engagement through empathy, value, and authenticity—and to use it wisely.

Visual Framework: The Actor Engagement Lifecycle

Figure 9.1 introduces a framework outlining the journey of actor engagement within platform ecosystems, tracing the progression from passive awareness to active co-creation. It highlights the key phases of engagement, supported by digital enablement, mutual value exchange, and platform-led interactions that deepen ecosystem participation over time.

The *Actor Engagement Lifecycle* model illustrates that actor engagement is not static—it evolves through participation and can be deepened with the right enablers and consistent value exchange.

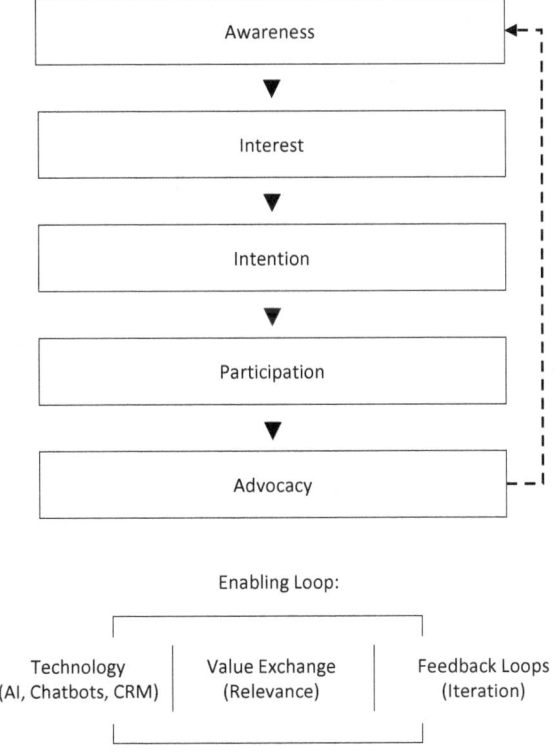

Fig. 9.1 Actor Engagement Lifecycle Model

> **Reflective Prompt: Are You Designing for Participation or Just Visibility?**
>
> As you evaluate your marketing and ecosystem strategy:
>
> 1. Are you inviting actors to engage or simply hoping they respond?
> 2. How are you measuring engagement beyond clicks and conversions?
> 3. Do your systems track the full journey from awareness to advocacy?
> 4. What value are you offering at each stage—and what are you asking in return?
>
> Actor engagement is not about gaining attention. It is about earning involvement.

> **Exercise: Actor Engagement Strategy Sprint**
>
> 1. **Map Your Actor Categories**
>   - Identify key ecosystem actors (e.g. users, partners, developers, influencers).
>   - For each, define what engagement looks like (e.g. co-creation, data sharing, advocacy).
>
> 2. **Plot the Engagement Journey**
>
>   Choose one actor group and map them across the five engagement stages:
>   - What triggers awareness?
>   - What builds interest or intention?
>   - What motivates participation?
>   - What encourages advocacy?
>
> 3. **Design Engagement Touchpoints**
>   - Identify one digital or real-world action you can take at each stage.
>   - Align these with technologies (e.g. automation, analytics, personalisation tools).
>
> 4. **Create a Value Exchange Scorecard**
>
>   For each engagement stage, assess:
>   - What value are we offering?
>   - What are we asking from the actor?
>   - Is the exchange fair and motivating?

This chapter helps you shift from transactional marketing towards relationship building—turning every interaction into an opportunity for mutual value creation.

References

Altschwager, T., Drennan, J., Winklhofer, H., & Jarvis, W. (2016). Actor engagement in the sharing economy: A life-cycle perspective. Proceedings of ANZMAC Conference Turning Visions into Reality.

Breidbach, C. F., & Brodie, R. J. (2017). Engagement platforms in the sharing economy: Conceptual foundations and research directions. *Journal of Service Theory and Practice, 27*(4), 761–777. https://doi.org/10.1108/JSTP-04-2016-0071

Digital, M. K. (2024). *September 13*. McKinsey & Company. https://www.mckinsey.com/capabilities/mckinsey-digital/our-insights/technology-alone-is-never-enough-for-true-productivity

Gu, G., & Li, Z. (2022). Technology fragmentation, platform investment, and complementary innovation. *SSRN*. https://doi.org/10.2139/ssrn.4061870

Hendricks, L., Matthyssens, P., & Kowalkowski, C. (2024). The co-evolution of actor engagement and value co-creation on digital platforms: Evidence from the asset management industry. *Journal of Business & Industrial Marketing. (Advance online publication)*. https://doi.org/10.1016/j.ijpe.2024.109467

Kowalkowski, C., Persson Ridell, O., Röndell, J., & Sörhammar, D. (2012). The co-creative practice of forming a value proposition. *Journal of Marketing Management, 28*(13–14), 1553–1570. https://doi.org/10.1080/0267257X.2012.736875

Lemon, K. N., & Verhoef, P. C. (2016). Understanding customer experience throughout the customer journey. *Journal of Marketing, 80*(6), 69–96. https://doi.org/10.1509/jm.15.0420

Martin, K. D., & Murphy, P. E. (2017). The role of data privacy in marketing. *Journal of the Academy of Marketing Science, 45*(2), 135–155. https://doi.org/10.1007/s11747-016-0495-4

Narvaiza, L., Campos, J. A., Martín-Peña, M. L., & Díaz-Garrido, E. (2024). Characterizing digital service innovation: Phases, actors, functions and interactions in the context of a digital service platform. *Journal of Service Management, 35*(2), 253–279. https://doi.org/10.1108/JOSM-12-2022-0401

Palmié, M., Miehé, L., Oghazi, P., Parida, V., & Wincent, J. (2022). The evolution of the digital service ecosystem and digital business model innovation in retail: The emergence of meta-ecosystems and the value of physical interactions. *Technological Forecasting and Social Change, 177*, 121496. https://doi.org/10.1016/j.techfore.2021.121496

Schivinski, B., Christodoulides, G., & Dabrowski, D. (2016). Measuring consumers' engagement with brand-related social-media content: Development and validation of the COBRAs scale. *Journal of Advertising Research, 56*(1), 64–80. https://doi.org/10.2501/JAR-2016-000

Van Dyck, M., Lüttgens, D., Diener, K., Piller, F. T., & Pollok, P. (2024). From product to platform: How incumbents' assumptions and choices shape their platform strategy. *Research Policy, 53*(1), Article 104904. https://doi.org/10.1016/j.respol.2023.104904

10

Building Trust and Collaboration in Digital Ecosystems

Trust and collaboration form the invisible architecture of successful digital ecosystems. They transform networks of connections into vibrant, dynamic environments—spaces where co-creation, innovation, and resilience thrive. Without trust, ecosystems remain brittle and transactional—a patchwork of interactions that lacks depth. But when trust is designed into the system and collaboration is carefully orchestrated, ecosystems flourish, scaling organically through aligned interests and collective energy.

In a digital ecosystem—where geography fades, participants are varied, and technology layers are dense—trust cannot be assumed (Reiners, 2022). It must be built systematically across multiple dimensions. Collaboration must be orchestrated through incentives, tools, and shared purpose. This chapter explores how businesses and marketers can embed both into the core of their ecosystem strategy.

First, transparency is essential. Participants must feel confident that data sharing is secure, intentions are clear, and actions are fair. This means publishing transparent data policies, using blockchain or other traceability tools to verify provenance, and implementing governance frameworks that let participants see how decisions are made (Cheong, 2025). Trust arises when partners, users, developers, and even regulators can observe the rules in operation and feel assured that the platform operates above board.

Second, consistency matters. A single security breach, unaddressed bug, or broken promise can corrode credibility. When platforms consistently uphold their standards (FA et al., 2025)—whether through compliance certifications, regular audits, rapid response to incidents, or consistent user experience—they reinforce confidence. Over time, participants come to expect reliability as a given, creating a foundation on which deeper collaboration can be built.

Third, reputation systems help surface trustworthy behaviour. Features like partner ratings, developer reviews, and success case highlights work as social proof. They reward dependable contributors and signal to newcomers that collaboration is both valued and visible. These systems visually embed trust in the ecosystem's infrastructure.

Collaboration, in turn, must be orchestrated—yet harmonised with participant motivation. It is not enough to provide portals; platforms need to make it easy, rewarding, and meaningful for participants to engage (Jacobides, Cennamo, & Gawer, 2018). Incentive mechanisms can include revenue-sharing models, visibility in marketing campaigns, co-branding opportunities, and early-access privileges. By aligning these incentives with participant goals—whether financial, professional, or mission-aligned—ecosystems encourage sustained contribution.

Technology plays a critical role in shaping collaboration. APIs need to be well-documented and stable; SDKs (Software Development Kit) must simplify integration; testing environments give confidence to experimenters. Collaboration tools—like shared dashboards, co-design platforms, or integrated community hubs (de Reuver, Sørensen, & Basole, 2018)—provide spaces where contributors can communicate, experiment, and build. And AI-driven matchmaking can connect participants with complementary needs or capabilities, shortening discovery cycles and igniting new projects.

Shared purpose binds trust and collaboration together. When platforms articulate why they exist and whom they serve—beyond mere profit—they create emotional resonance that encourages participation. Vision statements, community-driven missions, and success narratives remind actors that they are part of something bigger. When a developer sees a platform posting a case study about how their plug-in solved a real problem, or when a user engages not just with code but with the mission behind it, collaboration becomes more meaningful, and trust more emotional.

Embedding trust and collaboration requires leadership and governance. Orchestrators must design transparent accountability: who sets the rules, how disputes are resolved, what success means for all (FA et al., 2025). Advisory boards that include complementors, user champions, and industry partners—together with compliance liaisons—can build shared ownership. These structures distribute responsibility and reinforce that the platform is a co-owned ecosystem, not a gated kingdom.

Designing for trust and collaboration also means iterating over time. Ecosystems evolve, participants join and leave, and context shifts. Governance structures need flexibility (Hanafizadeh, 2025). Trust frameworks should be revisited in light of new regulations, new tech vulnerabilities or changes in participant demographics. Collaboration infrastructure—tools, incentives, narratives—must be refreshed to stay relevant and generous.

From a marketer's perspective, trust, and collaboration shape both brand image and business outcomes. Campaigns that celebrate community success, documentation that highlights transparent principles, and events that bring together stakeholders—these activities convert functional trust into deep relational credibility (Reiners, 2022). They show that the ecosystem isn't just a vendor—it's a community in motion.

Finally, consider the generative impact: as trust rises and collaboration deepens, ecosystems become self-sustaining. New participants are drawn in by visible benefits; existing actors double down on investment. The ecosystem's flywheel accelerates, creating innovation loops and reinforcing resilience (Thomas & Autio, 2019). In such environments, disruption becomes internal and continuous—they reinvent themselves rather than waiting for disruption to arrive.

In essence, digital ecosystems without trust and collaboration are empty shells. But with these attributes—built through design, nurtured with tools, aligned with purpose, and led strategically—they become living systems. Marketers and platform leaders who embed trust and design collaboration into the heart of their ecosystems hold not just the recipe for growth—they safeguard the future of value creation itself.

The Importance of Trust in Ecosystem Strategy

Trust is not an accessory in digital ecosystems—it is foundational. It is the confidence that participants have in the fairness, transparency, and reliability of the platform and its community. In sectors such as finance, health or education, where sensitive data and high-stakes decisions are involved, trust is not optional—it is critical.

In these contexts, trust is shaped by:

1. Data security
2. Compliance with regulation
3. Clarity of governance
4. Responsiveness to issues

5. Reputation and track record

Platforms that build trust at the structural level (policies, processes, protections) and at the relational level (consistency, clarity, empathy) are more likely to attract and retain committed actors.

The Trust Pyramid Framework

The **Trust Pyramid** helps conceptualise how trust is established in layers:

1. **Foundational Trust**—based on security, regulatory compliance, and functional integrity
2. **Relational Trust**—built through repeated positive interactions, transparency, and fairness
3. **Transformative Trust**—achieved when the platform helps actors succeed in ways they could not on their own

This progression shows that trust deepens over time, and that marketing and ecosystem design should address each layer with intention.

Fostering Collaboration Across the Ecosystem

Trust may enable participation, but collaboration drives value. In ecosystems, collaboration refers to the co-creation of products, services, campaigns, or solutions by multiple actors (Van Alstyne, Parker & Choudary, 2016)—from users and developers to partners and regulators.

Effective collaboration requires:

1. Shared goals
2. Aligned incentives
3. Open channels for dialogue
4. Tools for integration

When actors can contribute their expertise, data, or capabilities in a structured way, they feel ownership. That sense of investment leads to deeper engagement and greater innovation.

Barriers to Trust and Collaboration

Despite their importance, trust and collaboration face several challenges:

While trust and collaboration are foundational to the success of platform ecosystems, they are frequently undermined by systemic challenges that require careful navigation. A primary barrier is the lack of transparency—when participants are uncertain about how decisions are made, how their data is used, or how value is distributed, confidence in the platform begins to erode.

Compounding this issue is the frequent misalignment of incentives. Ecosystem participants often operate under differing business models or performance metrics. For example, a fintech startup may prioritise rapid user acquisition, while a regulatory body may focus on compliance and long-term risk mitigation—objectives that can come into conflict without a shared framework for alignment.

Technology adds another layer of complexity. Advanced tools like AI and blockchain offer significant value but also introduce a degree of opacity that can alienate non-technical stakeholders. Without clear communication about how these technologies function and how they impact outcomes, the trust they are meant to foster can be undermined.

Moreover, power imbalances within the ecosystem can distort collaboration. Dominant actors—by virtue of capital (Brodie et al., 2019), data access, or network effects—may inadvertently crowd out smaller or emerging voices. This not only limits innovation but can destabilise the ecosystem's long-term health.

These challenges can be summarised as follows:

1. **Lack of transparency:** Erodes confidence when processes and data usage remain unclear.
2. **Misaligned incentives:** Different KPIs or goals create conflicting priorities across stakeholders.
3. **Technological opacity:** Sophisticated tech like AI or blockchain requires active explanation and education.
4. **Power imbalances:** Risk marginalising smaller actors and diluting ecosystem diversity.

Addressing these issues demands a multidimensional approach—blending governance, inclusive design, and empathetic leadership—to ensure that trust and collaboration are not just aspirational values, but operating principles embedded in the fabric of the platform.

Strategies for Building Trust and Collaboration

1. **Transparent Governance**

    Platforms should establish clear rules of engagement, including:
    (a) Participation criteria
    (b) Conflict-resolution processes
    (c) Data usage policies
    (d) Reward distribution mechanisms

    These structures build trust and reduce ambiguity.

2. **Technological Enablement**

    (a) Tools like blockchain can provide immutable, shared ledgers of transactions.
    (b) AI can surface opportunities for collaboration by identifying shared interests or complementary capabilities. APIs enable seamless integration between actors.

3. **Aligned Incentive Models**

    Co-creation must be worthwhile. Platforms should:

    (a) Share revenues or recognition with contributors
    (b) Offer tiered access or exclusive resources
    (c) Celebrate ecosystem success stories

    These incentives motivate actors to invest in the platform's success.

4. **Active Communication and Community Management**

    Engagement deepens through dialogue. Ecosystems should:

    (a) Host regular forums, Q&A sessions, or workshops
    (b) Use social tools to foster peer-to-peer support
    (c) Collect and act on feedback visibly

    This builds both connection and credibility.

Examples in Practice

PayPal has built a payment ecosystem trusted by buyers and sellers globally. Its buyer protection policies, transparent pricing, and conflict-resolution tools help maintain confidence.

PayPal's Trusted Ecosystem.

PayPal has earned its place as one of the most reliable payment ecosystems worldwide by layering transparency and protective mechanisms into its core. The company's buyer protection policies act as a safety net, allowing users to transact with confidence, knowing there is recourse in case of fraud or unresolved issues. Transparent pricing—detailing fees upfront—ensures that both buyers and sellers understand transactional costs, reducing friction and suspicion (Choudary, 2021). Their conflict-resolution toolkit further demonstrates a commitment to fairness, reinforcing the platform's role as a trusted intermediary rather than a silent processor. Over time, these trust-building design choices have created a flywheel effect: the more secure and transparent the system feels, the more users, merchants, and developers choose to stay—and to build upon it.

Teladoc Health build trust through encryption, compliance with health regulations, and strong user interfaces. They also foster collaboration between doctors, insurers, and patients.

Teladoc's Health Secure Collaboration

In healthcare, trust is non-negotiable—and telemedicine and virtual healthcare platforms are acutely aware of this reality. They safeguard sensitive medical data through end-to-end encryption, secure access controls, and robust compliance with regulations like HIPAA and GDPR. Such technical rigour ensures that patients feel confident sharing personal health information. But securing data is only part of the story. These platforms also foster collaboration by balancing the needs of multiple stakeholders (Aanestad, Vassilakopoulou & Øvrelid, 2019)—doctors, insurers, tech partners, and patients—through intuitive interfaces and streamlined workflows. Virtual consultations, shared records, and dynamic referral tools all serve to bring traditionally siloed actors together around a shared therapeutic purpose. Trust here hinges not only on regulatory compliance but on smooth and meaningful collaboration.

Amazon's seller programmes encourage third-party providers to participate in joint campaigns, use performance analytics, and integrate their logistics, creating a virtuous cycle of mutual benefit.

Amazon's Ecosystem Advantage

Few platforms rival **Amazon** in orchestrating an ecosystem that thrives on mutual success. Their seller programmes include joint campaigns like Prime Day and lightning deals that align incentives between Amazon and third-party merchants. Integrated logistics simplifies fulfilment for sellers, freeing them to focus on growth rather than hardware or warehouse investments (Van Alstyne, Parker & Choudary, 2016). Performance analytics introduce transparency, allowing partners to track sales, optimise pricing, and fine-tune offers in real time. This feedback not only empowers sellers but reinforces their commitment—and links their success directly to the platform's. Amazon's ecosystem operates on a multiplier effect: as partners grow and innovate, the marketplace becomes richer, attracting more customers—and more partners.

Marketing Implications in Ecosystems

In ecosystems, marketing must do more than attract attention—it must earn trust and support collaboration. This means:

- **Leading with transparency**—around data, policies, and value
- **Designing inclusive campaigns**—that feature partners and contributors
- **Promoting ethical use of technology**—as part of the brand narrative
- **Celebrating ecosystem achievements**—rather than just platform milestones

When marketers step into ecosystem-driven platforms, their role expands far beyond brand awareness—they become custodians of both trust and collaboration.

Lead with Transparency Communicating openly about data use, pricing, and user rights isn't just ethical—it's strategic. Transparency builds credibility and lowers the barrier to participation (Cusumano, 2022), making users feel safer and stakeholders more anchored.

Design Inclusive Campaigns Featuring partners and providers in marketing campaigns shifts the narrative from "our platform" to "our network." Co-branded stories, partner spotlight campaigns, and joint PR efforts reinforce the message that success is a shared journey.

Champion Ethical Technology Technology should serve, not supplant (Agyei-Boapeah, Evans, & Nisar, 2022). Marketers must foreground how AI, encryption, and data tracking are used responsibly—framing them as tools that protect and enable rather than intrude or exploit.

Celebrate Ecosystem Wins Rather than focusing on internal milestones like feature launches, marketing should elevate stories of mutual success. Customer testimonials, partner case studies, and developer showcases highlight the real-world impact of collaboration.

Trust and collaboration are not just operational enablers—they are strategic differentiators. Marketers who understand this will not only build better campaigns, but more meaningful, resilient brands. These applied examples show that in ecosystems, marketing must earn attention through authenticity and support collaboration through design. It must act as an ecosystem steward—ensuring trust is tangibly felt and collaborative energy is tangibly rewarded. That's how a platform becomes more than a product—it becomes a movement.

Visual Framework: The Trust and Collaboration Stack

Figure 10.1 presents a framework that illustrates the progressive layers of trust and the enabling mechanisms for collaboration within digital ecosystems, demonstrating how structural and behavioural elements combine to drive sustained engagement and innovation.

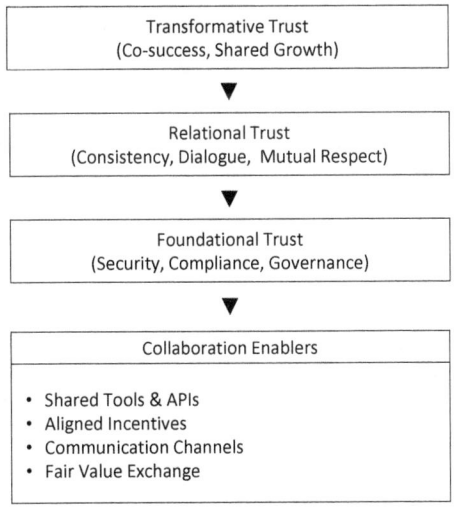

Fig. 10.1 Trust and Collaboration Stack Model

The *Trust and Collaboration Stack* layered model shows that collaboration is most effective when trust is established progressively—and maintained through operational clarity and shared value.

> **Reflective Prompt: Are You Earning Trust or Expecting It?**
>
> As you assess your platform or marketing strategy:
>
> 1. Have you invested in the systems that build trust from the ground up?
> 2. Are your governance structures visible, consistent, and fair?
> 3. How are you aligning actor incentives to encourage collaboration?
> 4. Are your communications inclusive, responsive, and value-driven?
>
> Trust and collaboration are not built once—they are renewed with every interaction.

> **Exercise: Ecosystem Trust and Collaboration Health Check**
>
> 1. **Assess Your Trust Infrastructure**
>   - Do you have clear governance policies? How visible are they to participants?
>   - Are your security, data, and compliance measures regularly reviewed and explained?
> 2. **Map Trust Across Layers**
>   - Use the Trust Pyramid model:
>   - What builds foundational trust in your ecosystem?
>   - What enables relational trust between actors?
>   - Where can you create transformative value?
> 3. **Review Your Collaboration Mechanics**
>   - Do you offer tools for partners or users to contribute (e.g. APIs, dashboards, forums)?
>   - Are there reward systems for contributions (revenue share, promotion, data access)?
> 4. **Design One New Trust-Building Initiative**
>   - Choose one weak point in the trust-collaboration stack.
>   - Develop an initiative (e.g. trust badge, ethical data use pledge, co-creation challenge).
>   - Define how you will communicate, measure, and evolve it.

This chapter helps ensure your platform does not just function efficiently but earns the trust and engagement of its most valuable asset—its ecosystem of participants.

References

Aanestad, M., Vassilakopoulou, P. & Øvrelid, E. (2019). Collaborative innovation in healthcare: Boundary resources for peripheral actors. https://aisel.aisnet.org/icis2019/is_health/is_health/24

Agyei-Boapeah, H., Evans, R., & Nisar, T. M. (2022). Disruptive innovation: Designing business platforms for new financial services. *Journal of Business Research*, 150, 134–146. https://doi.org/10.1016/j.jbusres.2022.05.066

Brodie, R. J., Fehrer, J. A., Jaakkola, E., & Conduit, J. (2019). Actor engagement in networks: Defining the conceptual domain. *Journal of Service Research*, 22(2), 173–188. https://doi.org/10.1177/1094670519827385

Cheong, B. C. (2025). Leveraging blockchain for enhanced transparency and traceability in sustainable supply chains. *Discover Analytics*, 3, 6. https://doi.org/10.1007/s44257-025-00032-7

Choudary, S. P. (2021). *Platform scale: How an emerging business model helps startups build large empires with minimum investment.* Second Edition.

Cusumano, M. A. (2022). The evolution of research on industry platforms. *Academy of Management Discoveries*, 8(1), 7–14. https://doi.org/10.5465/amd.2020.0091

de Reuver, M., Sørensen, C., & Basole, R. C. (2018). The digital platform: A research agenda. *Journal of Information Technology*, 33(2), 124–135. https://doi.org/10.1057/s41265-016-0033-3

FA, C., Ramezan Zadeh, M. T., Ozalp, H., & Volberda, H. W. (2025). The role of trust in a platform ecosystem: Exploring the impact of different trust dimensions on complementors' platform revenue. *Research Policy*, 54(8), Article 104957. https://doi.org/10.2139/ssrn.5180726

Hanafizadeh, P. (2025). *Governance system design model in platform ecosystems by a socio-technical systems theory.* Advance online publication. https://doi.org/10.1108/DPRG-04-2025-0105

Jacobides, M. G., Cennamo, C., & Gawer, A. (2018). Towards a theory of ecosystems. *Strategic Management Journal*, 39(8), 2255–2276. https://doi.org/10.1002/smj.2904

Reiners, S. (2022). *Trust and its extensions in digital platform.* Key Concepts and Issues for Future Research. https://doi.org/10.1109/CBI54897.2022.10042

Thomas, L. D. W., & Autio, E. (2019). Innovation ecosystems. *SSRN Electronic Journal.* https://doi.org/10.2139/ssrn.3476925

Van Alstyne, M. W., Parker, G. G., & Choudary, S. P. (2016). Pipelines, platforms, and the new rules of strategy. *Harvard Business Review*, 94(4), 54–62.

Part III

Strategic Frameworks for Platform Growth

11

Stimulating Engagement through Platforms as a Service

As we continue to operate in the digital ecosystem economy, engagement is not a linear act of consumption but an active, collaborative process between platforms and their participants. Platform-as-a-Service (PaaS) models are a good example at the heart of this transformation. By offering scalable infrastructure and open environments for co-creation, PaaS platforms have become powerful enablers of engagement, innovation, and mutual value exchange.

This chapter explores the mechanics of engagement through PaaS, the frameworks that underpin it, and how marketers and platform leaders can harness this model to drive growth and participation.

At their core, PaaS platforms are built to facilitate interaction on a fundamental level. They offer developers a sandbox—a secure, flexible environment in which they can build and test new applications (Giessmann, 2012). They give businesses plug-and-play tools to tailor offerings quickly. And they empower customers to shape the user experience through data, feedback, and usage patterns. This creates a symbiotic relationship where every participant—be it a developer, marketer, or end-user—contributes to and benefits from collective advancement. The result is an ecosystem where value is continuously co-created rather than merely delivered.

One of the most significant features of PaaS-driven engagement is its non-linear nature. Actors enter the ecosystem at different points—some as creators, others as integrators, and still others as consumers—but they all have pathways to move from passive interaction to active contribution (Cusumano, 2022). This journey typically begins with discovery: actors are drawn in by the platform's promise of speed, scale, or unique capability.

From there, interaction fuels experimentation, which leads to more sustained co-creation, and ultimately results in loyalty and advocacy.

Behind this progression are three critical enablers: technology, connection, and feedback. Technology—through APIs, SDKs, and robust documentation—lowers the barriers to entry (Ahmed & Kowalkowski, 2025). Connection—through integration frameworks and partnership programmes—fosters ecosystems of trust and shared purpose. Feedback—through real-time analytics and communication channels—ensures the platform remains responsive and aligned with its participants. These enablers work in concert to support a transformative cycle of engagement.

To make sense of how PaaS drives engagement, it is useful to reference two frameworks. **The Engagement Pathway Model** outlines the stages of participation—from initial attraction to eventual loyalty—while the **Value Exchange Framework** highlights the mutual benefits flowing between actors. Platforms provide infrastructure, visibility, and access; developers build functionality; users contribute data, feedback, and advocacy; and all parties benefit from the resulting growth and innovation. When these relationships are balanced and structured, engagement becomes self-sustaining (Jovanovic, Sjödin & Parida, 2021).

For marketers and platform leaders, however, tapping these frameworks requires intentional action. It starts with designing interfaces that invite participation—whether that is through developer onboarding tools, feedback forums, or co-innovative event programmes. All of these must be accompanied by transparent governance, clear value-sharing policies, and mechanisms that reward contribution fairly, be it through visibility, access to beta tools, or direct financial incentives.

PaaS engagements are transforming sectors across the board. In e-commerce, platforms equip merchants with everything from storefronts to marketing CRM systems, making them interdependent, active participants rather than passive tenants. In finance, embedded Banking-as-a-Service (BaaS) platforms enable banks and fintech startups to co-create payment solutions that meet compliance needs without sacrificing innovation (Lee & Shen, 2018). And in healthcare, telemedicine platforms offer integrated portals where providers, patients, and analytics tools converge—improving care outcomes and enriching the patient experience (Agyei-Boapeah et al. 2022).

In each of these examples, success hinges not on technology alone, but on the ecosystems around it—on how well platforms enable actors to participate, to co-create, to own, and to grow. Where PaaS capabilities are combined with transparent value mechanisms and inclusive governance, engagement flourishes and ecosystems thrive.

Marketers and platform leaders have a critical mandate in this context: they must move beyond traditional campaign mindsets and become ecosystem architects. This requires fluency in technology, a knack for community design, and a relentless focus on openness (Boudreau, 2017). They must understand what motivates different actors, design participation pathways that feel rewarding, and ensure contribution is recognised and benefitted. Only then can they transform their platforms from digital marketplaces into collaborative, co-creative growth engines.

PaaS-based engagement is not a marketing feature—it is a paradigm shift. It requires a different mindset, skills, and leadership style. And it brings tangible strategic benefits: platforms that succeed in activating this model grow faster, deepen loyalty, evolve more rapidly, and ultimately sustain value. This is why, in the world of platform economies, mastering engagement is essential for survival and leadership.

Understanding PaaS as a Catalyst for Engagement

PaaS platforms provide the digital foundation for ecosystem interaction. They offer cloud-based environments where actors—from developers and businesses to customers and regulators—can build, integrate, and evolve applications without managing the complexity of back-end infrastructure.

These platforms do more than simplify development—they stimulate engagement by providing shared tools, accessible resources, and the opportunity to contribute to a larger ecosystem (Jovanovic et al. 2021). Their openness and adaptability make them ideal spaces for experimentation, personalisation, and co-creation.

In essence, PaaS platforms function as digital commons—empowering participants to build together and benefit collectively.

How PaaS Drives Actor Engagement

PaaS platforms stimulate engagement through three interlinked drivers:

1. Technology—APIs, SDKs, cloud resources, and plug-ins create the foundation for custom development and seamless integration.

2. Connectivity—Real-time data flow and modular systems ensure that applications, actors, and services interact efficiently.
3. Feedback—Built-in analytics and usage data enable continuous iteration, making the engagement loop responsive and dynamic.

These elements transform engagement from a passive outcome into a strategic input. For example, in a fintech ecosystem, a PaaS platform may allow banks and fintech start-ups to co-develop payment tools that are secure, compliant and user-centric—all within a shared technological framework.

Frameworks for Stimulating PaaS Engagement

Two core frameworks help explain the engagement journey within PaaS environments:

The Engagement Pathway Model

This model outlines the progression of actor involvement:

1. Attraction—actors are drawn to the platform by its tools, reach, or opportunities
2. Interaction—they begin contributing content, applications, or feedback
3. Co-Creation—partnerships form to solve shared problems or innovate together
4. Loyalty—sustained engagement leads to ecosystem investment and advocacy

Engagement within PaaS ecosystems unfolds as a dynamic journey, where actors transition through various stages of involvement (Brodie et al., 2019). Initially, individuals and organisations are attracted to the platform by its tools, reach, or opportunities. This attraction often stems from the platform's ability to address specific needs or offer unique value propositions.

As these actors begin to interact with the platform, they contribute content, applications, or feedback, fostering a collaborative environment. This interaction phase is crucial, as it lays the groundwork for deeper engagement and mutual value creation (Bruce et al., 2019). Progressing further, partnerships form to solve shared problems or innovate together, marking the co-creation stage. Here, the synergy between the platform and its participants leads to the development of novel solutions and enhancements that benefit the entire ecosystem.

Ultimately, sustained engagement leads to ecosystem investment and advocacy, signifying loyalty. Actors become champions of the platform, promoting its benefits and contributing to its continuous growth and improvement.

The Value Exchange Framework

This framework highlights the reciprocal nature of engagement:

1. Platforms offer infrastructure, access, and exposure
2. Developers contribute apps and functionality
3. Customers offer usage data, feedback, and advocacy
4. All actors benefit from shared success and scale

When these exchanges are balanced and transparent, engagement becomes self-reinforcing.

The reciprocal nature of engagement in PaaS ecosystems is underscored by the Value Exchange Framework. Platforms offer infrastructure, access, and exposure, providing the necessary tools and environment for actors to thrive (Nambisan, Zahra & Luo, 2019). In return, developers contribute applications and functionality, enhancing the platform's offerings and appeal. Customers play a pivotal role by offering usage data, feedback, and advocacy. Their insights drive improvements and innovations, ensuring the platform remains responsive to user needs. When these exchanges are balanced and transparent, engagement becomes self-reinforcing, creating a virtuous cycle of continuous value creation and mutual benefit.

Real-World Applications of PaaS Engagement

PaaS models are redefining engagement across multiple sectors:

1. E-commerce: Platforms like **Shopify** offer merchants not just storefronts, but a suite of CRM, inventory, and marketing tools—encouraging active platform participation.

2. Finance: BaaS platform like **Solaris** enable financial institutions to plug in services like KYC, payments, and compliance—fostering collaboration with fintech providers.
3. Healthcare: **Doxy.me** as telemedicine PaaS platform helps connect providers, patients, and data tools in real time—improving care delivery and user experience.

Each case shows how tailored environments stimulate both technical development and human interaction.

Across these sectors, PaaS models move beyond simple infrastructure enablement to become **engagement orchestrators.** In e-commerce, **Shopify's** integrated toolsets embed merchants more deeply into the platform, shaping behaviours as well as operations. In financial services, BaaS platforms such as **Solaris** act as connective tissue, enabling regulated institutions and fintechs to co-create services within shared compliance frameworks (Lee et al. 2018). In healthcare, telemedicine platforms like **Doxy.me** illustrate how PaaS can synchronise human interaction and digital tools in real time, enhancing both clinical workflows and patient experience.

Each case illustrates how tailored environments stimulate both technical development and human interaction, highlighting the versatility and impact of PaaS engagement across industries.

Overcoming Engagement Barriers in PaaS Ecosystems

While the engagement potential is significant, PaaS platforms face several challenges:

1. Integration complexity: Diverse participants must align on standards and protocols. Platforms can address this through robust APIs, documentation, and developer support.
2. Trust and transparency: Data security, ethical governance, and platform neutrality are essential to maintaining credibility with users and contributors.
3. Scalability: As ecosystems grow, performance must remain consistent. This demands continuous investment in infrastructure and monitoring.

Platforms that meet these challenges with transparency and technological agility are better equipped to retain and expand actor engagement.

Despite the significant engagement potential, PaaS platforms face several challenges. Integration complexity arises as diverse participants must align on standards and protocols (Lehmann et al., 2021). Platforms can address this through robust APIs, comprehensive documentation, and dedicated developer support.

Trust and transparency are paramount. Ensuring data security, ethical governance, and platform neutrality is essential to maintaining credibility with users and contributors (Ramezan Zadeh et al., 2025). As ecosystems grow, scalability becomes a concern. Maintaining consistent performance demands continuous investment in infrastructure and monitoring. Platforms that meet these challenges with transparency and technological agility are better equipped to retain and expand actor engagement.

Leadership's Role in Driving PaaS Engagement

Platform leaders—especially orchestrators—must articulate a vision for collaborative value creation. This includes:

1. Setting clear rules of participation
2. Mediating between diverse actor interests
3. Prioritising equitable value distribution

Strong leadership creates a sense of shared purpose and lowers the barriers to participation. It also ensures that engagement is not one-sided, but inclusive and generative.

Marketing Implications of PaaS Engagement

For marketers, PaaS engagement opens a new door of strategic opportunity:

1. Personalised campaigns can be built using real-time behavioural data gathered from PaaS tools.
2. Interactive experiences—such as co-created apps or gamified portals—become touchpoints for deepening relationships.
3. Partner marketing—through developer or contributor campaigns—leverages the network effect of ecosystem actors.

Moreover, marketers become co-creators within the platform. They are no longer just broadcasting value but shaping it with users, developers, and collaborators.

PaaS platforms redefine marketing as a collaborative, continuous, and data-informed practice. Marketers who embrace this shift can move from campaign managers to ecosystem architects—designing strategies that empower actors to engage meaningfully and at scale.

In PaaS ecosystems, leadership is not simply about steering strategy from the top—it is about enabling the conditions for ongoing collaboration, innovation, and mutual value creation (Hendricks et al., 2024). Platform leaders, particularly those in orchestrator roles, are tasked with defining the ecosystem's ethos and direction. Their influence extends beyond technical or operational guidance—it touches on culture, governance, and the facilitation of equitable engagement.

At the core of this role is the articulation of a compelling vision that resonates across a diverse actor base, including developers, users, and enterprise stakeholders. This vision must be clear enough to unify, yet flexible enough to accommodate varied contributions. Leaders must establish transparent rules of participation and ensure that these are consistently upheld. In doing so, they reduce ambiguity and build the trust necessary for actors to invest time, ideas, and resources into the ecosystem.

Furthermore, effective platform leaders mediate between potentially conflicting interests—balancing innovation with risk, openness with security, and commercial ambition with community values. They must proactively resolve tension points, promote inclusivity, and ensure that value distribution reflects the efforts and inputs of all contributors, not just those with the loudest voices or deepest pockets.

In this context, leadership is not static—it is iterative and responsive. It involves creating structures for feedback, listening to diverse ecosystem actors, and adapting the platform model based on evolving needs. Ultimately, strong leadership fosters a participatory environment where actors feel empowered to engage, co-create, and shape the future of the platform together. This is the cornerstone of sustainable engagement in any successful platform ecosystem.

Strategic Opportunities for Ecosystem Marketers

In platform ecosystems, marketing evolves beyond product promotion into a function that shapes relationships and drives collaborative growth. Engagement data, drawn from real-time platform interactions, allows marketers to craft campaigns with unprecedented precision. These campaigns are no longer generic messages broadcast to a wide audience; they are timely, context-aware engagements that respond to how users behave and what they value in the moment. When marketers tap into this data, they gain unprecedented precision in crafting campaigns that speak directly to user needs and motivations at the very moment they arise.

Moreover, collaboration with developers, contributors, and other complementors allows marketers to leverage the reach and credibility of a wider network. Partner marketing campaigns extend the brand's footprint while reinforcing the platform's ecosystem values. Such alliances shift marketing from a linear pipeline to a network effect—where every participant contributes to greater collective impact.

In this context, the marketing leader becomes a narrative architect. Their role is to orchestrate stories that capture not only what the platform offers, but also how it thrives through shared contribution and mutual success. Marketing is no longer peripheral—it becomes the connective tissue that aligns actor intentions, reinforces platform purpose, and strengthens engagement across the ecosystem.

Instead of mass broadcasting, campaigns become agile nudges—micromessages triggered by behaviour, contextual triggers, or milestones. These might manifest as timely prompts to explore new app integrations, notifications celebrating participation in a co-creation initiative, or personalised recommendations that reflect each user's unique journey. These touchpoints reinforce relevance and signal to users that the platform is alive, responsive, and oriented around their experience.

But the opportunity goes deeper than personalisation alone. Interactive experiences—such as co-developed applications, gamified journeys, or collaborative idea challenges—now serve as essential touchpoints that build brand resonance and trust. These engagements aren't superficial add-ons; they structure the user's pathway into becoming an active participant. Whether a developer building solutions for a fintech platform, a merchant integrating new storefront features, or a user contributing feedback in a live forum, these experiences anchor the platform in co-creation. They elevate the platform from technology to community.

At the heart of ecosystem marketing is collaboration—not just between marketer and user, but across the entire chain of participants. By integrating developers, complementors, agencies, and partners into marketing initiatives, the platform extends its influence and credibility (Chen et al., 2022). A joint webinar featuring both brand and complementor voices, or a bundled campaign that promotes an integrated solution, taps into each partner's audience and strengthens collective legitimacy. This network-driven approach transforms marketing from a one-way pipeline into a dynamic web—where every participant's contribution amplifies impact.

With this shift, the modern marketing leader transitions into a narrative architect—someone who weaves stories of joint achievement, highlights shared value, and contextualises diverse contributions within a cohesive ecosystem narrative. It's no longer sufficient to announce what the platform can do; marketers must show how the platform thrives because of its contributors. They must highlight how a new fintech app was born from collaboration, how a user-submitted insight reshaped a feature, or how a shared campaign broke new ground.

By doing so, marketing becomes the connective tissue of platform ecosystems. It aligns disparate actors around shared purpose, provides strategic cadence to co-innovation, and ensures sustained engagement (Nyadzayo et al., 2020). Campaigns transform into collaborative rituals that signal inclusivity, shared success, and mutual benefit. Messages shift from self-promotion to ecosystem purpose, resonating deeply with users who want to belong to something bigger than a transaction.

Ultimately, opportunity lies not in louder marketing—but in deeper marketing. Platform leaders who embrace context-aware campaigns, design participatory experiences, and weave collective narratives will shift marketing from a peripheral expense into a strategic capability. By doing so, they anchor the platform in thriving relationships, co-creative energy, and network-driven resilience. Marketing becomes the ecosystem's orchestrator—ensuring every actor's spark feeds the collective fire.

Visual Framework: The PaaS Engagement Engine

Figure 11.1 introduces a framework that demonstrates how PaaS platforms enable continuous actor engagement through integrated technological and relational drivers within the ecosystem.

This *PaaS Engagement Engine* model illustrates how PaaS platforms integrate multiple enablers to form a self-sustaining engagement cycle that scales value and participation over time.

11 Stimulating Engagement through Platforms as a Service

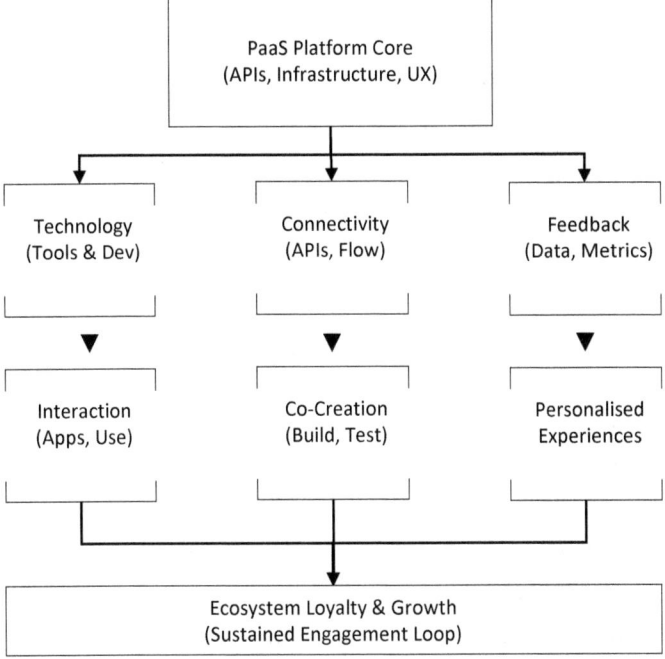

Fig. 11.1 PaaS Engagement Engine Model

Reflective Prompt: Is Your Platform Enabling or Expecting Engagement?

Consider your PaaS or digital service environment:

1. Are you offering tools that actors *want* to use—or just expecting engagement based on access?
2. How do you track and respond to user activity and feedback?
3. Are your APIs, dashboards, and co-creation spaces optimised for ease, trust, and value?
4. What would make your platform irresistible to partners or developers?

Real engagement emerges when your platform becomes a place where actors *want* to return—because they can build, influence, and benefit.

> **Exercise: PaaS Engagement Blueprint**
>
> 1. **Map Your Key Engagement Actors**
>   - Identify the three primary actor groups on your platform (e.g. developers, business clients, end-users).
>   - What tools or services does your PaaS currently offer to each group?
>
> 2. **Audit Your Engagement Enablers**
>   - Rate the strength of your:
>   - *Technology Tools* (ease of build/use)
>   - *Connectivity* (API access, seamlessness)
>   - *Feedback Loops* (user insight, response rates)
>   - What gaps need to be addressed?
>
> 3. **Design a New Engagement Flow**
>   - Choose one actor and define a new or improved journey:
>   - Entry point (e.g. onboarding portal)
>   - Participation step (e.g. submitting app, feedback)
>   - Reward or value returned (e.g. analytics, exposure)
>
> 4. **Implement and Measure**
>   - What data will signal success (e.g. retention, usage, contribution rates)?
>   - Set up mechanisms to capture and respond to that data in real time.

This chapter ensures your PaaS strategy is not just functional—but actively driving engagement through design, clarity, and co-creation.

References

Agyei-Boapeah, H., Evans, R., & Nisar, T. M. (2022). Disruptive innovation: Designing business platforms for new financial services. *Journal of Business Research, 150*, 134–146. https://doi.org/10.1016/j.jbusres.2022.05.066

Ahmed, T., & Kowalkowski, C. (2025). The new industry playbook: Digital service innovation in multi-platform ecosystems. *Journal of Enterprise Information Management. Advance online publication.* https://doi.org/10.1108/JEIM-05-2024-0240

Boudreau, K. J. (2017). Platform boundary choices and governance: Opening up while still coordinating and orchestrating, entrepreneurship, innovation, and platforms. *Advances in Strategic Management, 37*, 227–297. https://doi.org/10.1108/S0742-332220170000037009

Brodie, R. J., Fehrer, J. A., Jaakkola, E., & Conduit, J. (2019). Actor engagement in networks: Defining the conceptual domain. *Journal of Service Research, 22*(2), 173–188. https://doi.org/10.1177/1094670519827385

Bruce, H. L., Wilson, H. N., Macdonald, E. K., & Clarke, B. (2019). Resource integration, value creation and value destruction in collective consumption contexts. *Journal of Business Research, 103*, 173–185. https://doi.org/10.1016/j.jbusres.2019.05.007

Chen, L., Yi, J., Li, S., & Tong, T. W. (2022). Platform governance Design in Platform Ecosystems: Implications for Complementors' multihoming decision. *Journal of Management.* https://doi.org/10.1177/0149206320988337

Cusumano, M. A. (2022). The evolution of research on industry platforms. *Academy of Management Discoveries, 8*(1), 7–14. https://doi.org/10.5465/amd.2020.0091

FA, C., Ramezan Zadeh, M. T., Ozalp, H., & Volberda, H. W. (2025). The role of trust in a platform ecosystem: Exploring the impact of different trust dimensions on complementors' platform revenue. *Research Policy, 54*(8), 104957. https://doi.org/10.2139/ssrn.5180726

Giessmann, A. (2012). Platform as a service—A conjoint study on consumers Preferences. 33rd international conference on information systems (ICIS 2012). -Orlando, FL.

Hendricks, L., Matthyssens, P., & Kowalkowski, C. (2024). The co-evolution of actor engagement and value co-creation on digital platforms: Evidence from the asset management industry. *Journal of Business & Industrial Marketing. (Advance online publication).* https://doi.org/10.1016/j.ijpe.2024.109467

Jovanovic, M., Sjödin, D., & Parida, V. (2021). Co-evolution of platform architecture, platform services, and platform governance: Expanding the platform value of industrial digital platforms. *Technovation.* https://doi.org/10.1016/j.technovation.2020.102218

Lee, I. &. Shin, Y.J. (2018). Fintech: Ecosystem, business models, investment decisions, and challenges, Business Horizons, 61(1), 35–46. doi:https://doi.org/10.1016/j.bushor.2017.09.003.

Lehmann, J., Werder, K., Babar, Y., & Berente, N. (2021). *Establishing and maintaining legitimacy for digital platform innovations.* Proceedings. https://doi.org/10.5465/AMBPP.2021.12602abstract

Nambisan, S., Zahra, S. A., & Luo, Y. (2019). Global platforms and ecosystems: Implications for international business theories. *Journal of International Business Studies, 50*(9), 1464–1486. https://doi.org/10.1057/s41267-019-00262-4

Nyadzayo, M. W., Casidy, R., & Thaichon, P. (2020). B2B purchase engagement: Examining the key drivers and outcomes in professional services. *Industrial Marketing Management, 85*, 197–208. https://doi.org/10.1016/j.indmarman.2019.11.007

12

Community-Building Strategies for Marketers

In the platform economy, communities have evolved from peripheral assets to central pillars of strategic marketing. A well-cultivated community transforms passive audiences into active participants, co-creators, and brand advocates. This shift necessitates a new mindset for marketers—one that prioritises facilitation, belonging, and mutual value creation.

Where traditional marketing focused on delivering messages to segmented audiences, the platform model depends on building continuous interaction among stakeholders. Communities provide the relational infrastructure that enables this interaction. They are the connective tissue between different actors—users, developers, partners, and influencers—who together shape the trajectory of the platform. In this model, marketing's role is no longer just about driving awareness or acquisition; it is about designing and sustaining spaces where participation flourishes.

This reorientation requires marketers to become community architects. Rather than simply curating brand narratives, they must facilitate community-led conversations, surface insights from the edges, and amplify member contributions. The most vibrant platform communities feature multiple forms of value exchange: social capital, shared learning, co-authorship, and product influence (Schüler & Petrik, 2023). Marketers must identify and nurture these loops, ensuring that every member sees clear benefit in staying engaged.

Importantly, community-building in the platform context is not a passive or reactive process. It requires a structured strategy. Communities must be seeded with clear values and purpose, and supported through governance models that ensure psychological safety, diversity of thought, and inclusive participation (Hendricks et al., 2024). These foundational elements determine the community's ability to scale sustainably.

At the heart of community engagement is the experience of belonging. Members return not because they are marketed to, but because they feel seen, heard, and empowered. This emotional resonance is often more powerful than any product feature. Marketers must cultivate rituals—from weekly showcases and live Q&A sessions to collaborative campaigns—that reinforce the community's shared identity and invite deeper participation.

Digital infrastructure also plays a key role. Tools like forums, chat groups, community dashboards, and feedback portals serve as interaction points, but technology alone is not enough. Marketers must embed content strategies, recognition systems, and engagement mechanics that elevate member voices and foster ownership. Co-creation campaigns, gamified contribution systems, and peer learning programmes all increase the community's vitality.

Communities also serve as powerful feedback engines. Because members are embedded in real-time interactions with the platform, their insights offer an ongoing pulse on needs, frustrations, and emerging opportunities (Letaifa, 2014). Marketers can use these insights not only to refine messaging but also to inform product strategy, support operations, and innovation pipelines. The community becomes a strategic asset—a living laboratory where value is co-discovered and co-delivered.

From a growth perspective, communities create network effects. As members invite others, co-produce content, or co-host events, the platform's reach and relevance expand organically. Unlike paid media or traditional advertising, these effects are sustained by trust and shared purpose. Marketers who understand this dynamic invest not just in community acquisition, but in long-term member cultivation.

Community is no longer an add-on to the marketing strategy—it is the strategy. It shifts the marketer's role from message sender to participation enabler, from brand guardian to ecosystem host. Those who master community-building will not only enhance user retention and brand loyalty, but they will also unlock a powerful engine for co-creation, innovation, and sustained platform growth.

The Strategic Role of Communities in Marketing

At its core, a community fosters meaningful connections. Within platform ecosystems, communities act as relational infrastructure, enabling continuous dialogue, shared experiences, and collaborative action, they become essential hubs of strategic value.

Unlike traditional audiences, communities are dynamic entities where members influence one another, establish norms, generate content, and drive innovation. For marketers, this transition means moving from controlling messages to participating in ecosystems—supporting, enabling, and responding rather than merely broadcasting (Nim et al., 2024). Platforms provide fertile ground for community-building by offering digital spaces where individuals with shared interests can interact in real time, ranging from customer forums and private groups to developer networks and branded platforms.

This shift reshapes the marketer's role fundamentally. No longer able to simply control narratives, marketers become active participants in a living ecosystem—supporting, enabling, and responding to community currents. They design environments where voices are amplified, engagement is celebrated, and contributions are woven into the evolving platform narrative.

Platform-based communities thrive on shared purpose, whether solving common challenges, exploring new product ideas, or simply exchanging insights (Nambisan et al., 2019). By creating digital spaces—forums, private groups, hackathons, developer networks, or branded apps—marketers provide the fertile ground for this interaction. These are more than communication tools: they're collaborative canvases where members co-create, network, learn, and innovate.

Crucially, communities foster a sense of belonging that drives deeper commitment. When members recognise their input has influence—be it through beta programmes, peer recognition, or shaping product roadmaps—they become active co-architects rather than consumers. This sense of agency sparks ownership, loyalty, and advocacy, fuelling the organic growth of the ecosystem.

From a strategic viewpoint, marketers leverage this richness to reinforce brand identity, gather real-world insights, and surface authentic stories of user-led innovation. Community-driven content—from tutorials and testimonials to joint campaigns—resonates far more powerfully than top-down messaging. Meanwhile, community moderators, champions, and early adopters become trusted amplifiers and feedback sources.

Perhaps most tellingly, communities enable adaptive marketing. Real-time interaction highlights emerging pain points, unmet needs, and promising ideas before they show up in sales figures or surveys (Hollebeek & Macky, 2019). Marketers can close the loop—listening, validating, iterating content and offers based on live signals—ensuring relevance and resonance at every stage.

The strategic role of communities lies in their capacity to convert passive audiences into proactive, co-creative, and loyal participants. Marketers who embrace this reality—designing structures for two-way communication, recognising contributions, and adapting in partnership with the community—transform their platforms from branded destinations into thriving ecosystems. In doing so, they unlock not just engagement, but collective innovation and sustainable, bottom-up growth.

Core Strategies for Building Strong Communities

Start with Purpose A community without a clear purpose is merely a gathering. Defining a shared purpose attracts the right participants and aligns their engagement (Brodie et al., 2019). Whether the goal is to solve common challenges, facilitate collective learning, or contribute to a cause, a well-articulated purpose anchors the community in meaning.

Foster a Sense of Belonging Belonging serves as the emotional glue of a community (Algesheimer et al., 2005; Moser et al., 2014). Marketers must create inclusive environments where members feel seen, respected, and supported. This can involve facilitating peer mentoring, recognising contributions, or organising virtual and in-person meetups.

Use Storytelling to Strengthen Identity Stories humanise the community's purpose and progress. Sharing member journeys, ecosystem milestones, and collaborative achievements builds pride and reinforces a shared identity (Sergi & Bonneau, 2016). Authentic storytelling transforms participants into protagonists.

Enable Co-Creation and Collaboration Communities thrive when members actively contribute. Platforms should provide avenues for individuals to share content or ideas, collaborate on projects, offer peer support, and influence future features (Peuckert & Kern, 2023). This collaborative energy enhances innovation and deepens investment.

Frameworks for Managing Community Dynamics

The Community Lifecycle Model

This model outlines four stages:

1. **Inception**: Defining purpose and attracting founding members.
2. **Establishment**: Setting structures, roles, and norms.
3. **Growth**: Scaling participation and diversifying content.
4. **Maturity**: Sustaining engagement through renewal and evolution.

Each phase demands distinct leadership approaches, content strategies, and metrics.

The Engagement Pyramid

This framework categorises community members by their level of activity:

1. **Observers**: Consume content passively.
2. **Participants**: Engage through comments, shares, and likes.
3. **Contributors**: Initiate discussions and share insights.
4. **Leaders**: Moderate, shape direction, and recruit new members.

Understanding this distribution enables marketers to tailor experiences that encourage members to ascend to higher engagement tiers.

Technology as an Enabler of Community Strategy

Digital platforms facilitate scalability, personalisation, and insight in community-building efforts (Choudary, 2021). Features such as discussion boards, real-time chats, gamification, and AI-based content suggestions make participation more accessible and rewarding.

Data analytics empower marketers to track engagement patterns, sentiment shifts, topic trends, and churn risks. These insights allow for adaptive content strategies, moderation adjustments, and the design of incentives that keep the community vibrant.

AI can further personalise experiences by recommending groups, connecting like-minded members, or prompting content creation. When used thoughtfully, AI reinforces the feeling that the community recognises and values each individual (Füller et al., 2022).

Common Challenges in Community-Building

Despite the opportunities, marketers must navigate several challenges:

1. **Maintaining Authenticity**: Communities must feel genuine. Overly commercial or inauthentic marketing tactics can alienate members.
2. **Managing Conflict**: Diverse viewpoints enrich a community but can also lead to tension. Clear guidelines and active moderation are essential.
3. **Avoiding Stagnation**: As communities mature, novelty can fade. Regular innovation, content refreshes, and new participation formats are necessary to maintain momentum.

Case Studies in Community Strategy

1. **Financial Platforms**: Often build peer-support communities for investors, like **Etoro** facilitating knowledge sharing and positioning the brand as a trusted advisor (Ng et al., 2022).
2. **Fitness Brands**: Companies like **Peloton** integrate community into their core experience through leaderboards, social recognition, and real-time interaction, driving motivation and loyalty (Davies et al., 2024).
3. **Developer Platforms**: **GitHub** thrives on collaborative contribution, with its community effectively becoming the product, underscoring the importance of ecosystem-first thinking (Lima, Rossi & Musolesi, 2014).

Each example illustrates that successful communities do not merely support a brand—they extend, shape, and sustain it.

Leadership and Community Success

Leadership within communities encompasses both strategic and social dimensions. It includes brand representatives and platform owners, as well as member leaders—moderators, advocates, and contributors (Peng, 2021) who uphold values and inspire others.

Effective community leadership is characterised by:

1. **Empathy**: Prioritising listening over instructing.
2. **Transparency**: Clearly communicating decisions and changes.
3. **Empowerment**: Providing members with the tools and trust to lead.

This distributed leadership model fosters resilience, adaptability, and long-term value within the community.

Marketing in the Age of Community

Community-building has transformed marketing from a series of campaigns into ongoing conversations. It offers a living pulse of customer insight, a source of loyalty, and a multiplier of brand reach.

For marketers, this shift entails:

1. **From Targeting to Welcoming**: Inviting participation rather than directing messages.
2. **From Storytelling to Story-Sharing**: Encouraging members to share their own narratives.
3. **From Message Control to Ecosystem Curation**: Facilitating a dynamic environment where the community shapes the discourse.

Communities are not a mere tactic—they are the infrastructure where meaningful marketing occurs.

Community-building has redefined marketing—instead of running isolated campaigns, brands must now foster ongoing conversations that weave authenticity, insight, and collective energy (Brodie et al., 2019) into the fabric of their ecosystem. This transformation introduces a living pulse, offering real-time customer insight, deepening loyalty, and significantly amplifying brand reach.

The first shift for marketers is to move from targeting to welcoming. Rather than designing campaigns as one-way broadcasts, the aim becomes creating invitation-centric experiences—such as open forums, co-creation workshops, or beta programmes—where individuals feel welcomed to contribute. It transforms marketing from monologue to dialogue, where every voice can shape the narrative and spark new ideas.

Next, marketers move beyond storytelling to story-sharing. Instead of crafting brand-led narratives, they now curate platforms that enable community members to tell their own stories. These might be written guides, video testimonials, or peer-to-peer support expressions. Authentic peer narratives carry emotional weight that traditional marketing cannot match. By elevating member-voiced stories, brands demonstrate humility, celebrate diversity, and harness the genuine experiences that resonate far more deeply than polished ads.

Perhaps the most profound change is shifting from message control to ecosystem curation. Rather than tightly regulating every touchpoint, marketers become stewards of an evolving ecosystem. They create the structures—moderation policies, content templates, reward systems—that enable respectful, open discourse. They then step back, allowing community dynamics to unfold organically. This curation is intentional yet hands-off: it frames the sandbox and supplies the toys but let's participants invent their own games.

In this platform-driven world, communities are no longer promotional tactics—they are strategic infrastructure (Peng, 2021). Well-designed communities generate continuous insight: what's trending, what's challenging, what's valued now. They also build loyalty by giving participants agency, recognition, and a sense of belonging. And their collective scale literally multiplies every marketing message—shared by members, amplified in social networks, and borrowed in adjacent channels.

Ultimately, the energy of community breathes life into marketing. It makes the brand a platform for relationships, a catalyst for innovation, and a hub of shared meaning. For marketers willing to embrace this shift, community-building transforms marketing from periodic outreach to perpetual resonance—an ecosystem where every connection matters and every contribution counts.

Visual Framework: The Community Engagement Flywheel

Figure 12.1 presents a framework outlining the dynamics of community-driven engagement within platform ecosystems. It illustrates how a well-structured community builds engagement through purpose, participation, and value reinforcement—driving continuous growth and loyalty within the platform ecosystem.

This *Community Engagement flywheel* model reflects the self-sustaining nature of healthy communities—where engagement builds identity, and identity reinforces engagement.

12 Community-Building Strategies for Marketers

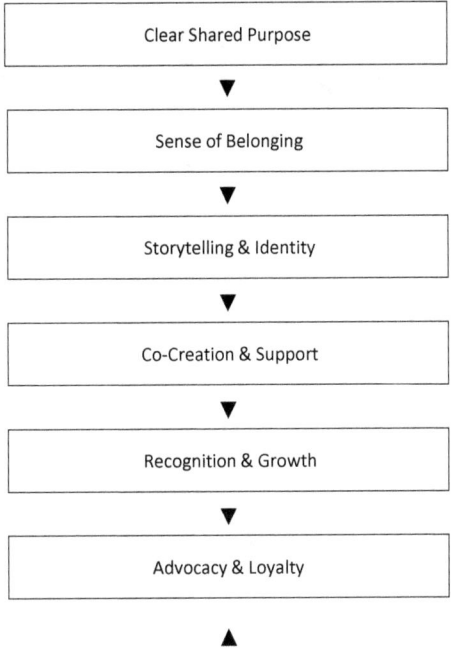

Fig. 12.1 Community Engagement Flywheel Model

Reflective Prompt: Is Your Community Designed for Conversation or Control?

As you evaluate your community strategy:

1. Are you creating space for members to shape the narrative and direction?
2. Do your community guidelines and incentives support openness, contribution, and trust?
3. How are you supporting leadership from within—not just from above?
4. Are you building for long-term participation or short-term visibility?

Community success comes not from control—but from shared meaning and shared value.

Exercise: Community Activation Canvas

1. **Define Your Community's Purpose**
   - What problem does it help solve?
   - What do members gain—emotionally, practically, or socially?

2. **Identify Your Core Member Roles**

   Who are your:
   - Observers
   - Participants
   - Contributors
   - Leaders
   - What does each group need to feel valued and stay engaged?

3. **Design a Participation Ladder**

   How can members:
   - Join easily?
   - Share safely?
   - Collaborate meaningfully?
   - Be recognised publicly?

4. **Create a Community Ritual**
   - What regular moment—newsletter, event, challenge—reinforces identity and connection?
   - How do you celebrate success and bring members together?

5. **Measure Engagement Health**

   Track metrics across:
   - Activity (posts, comments)
   - Retention (logins, participation duration)
   - Sentiment (feedback, satisfaction)
   - Use this insight to adapt tone, tools and touchpoints.

This chapter ensures your community strategy is designed not just for reach—but for relevance, resilience, and relational depth.

References

Ahmed, T., & Kowalkowski, C. (2025). The new industry playbook: Digital service innovation in multi-platform ecosystems. *Journal of Enterprise Information Management. Advance online publication.* https://doi.org/10.1108/JEIM-05-2024-0240

Algesheimer, R., Dholakia, U. M., & Herrmann, A. (2005). The social influence of brand community: Evidence from European car clubs. *Journal of Marketing, 69*(3), 19–34. https://doi.org/10.1509/jmkg.69.3.19.66363

Brodie, R. J., Fehrer, J. A., Jaakkola, E., & Conduit, J. (2019). Actor engagement in networks: Defining the conceptual domain. *Journal of Service Research, 22*(2), 173–188. https://doi.org/10.1177/1094670519827385

Choudary, S. P. (2021). *Platform scale: How an emerging business model helps startups build large empires with minimum investment* (2nd ed.). Platform Thinking Labs.

Davies, M., Hungenberg, E., Aicher, T. J., & Newland, B. L. (2024). Work[out] from home: Examining brand community among connected fitness brand users. *International Journal of Sport Management and Marketing, 24*(2), 113–136. https://doi.org/10.1504/IJSMM.2024.137102

Füller, J., Hutter, K., Wahl, J., Bilgram, V., & Tekic, Z. (2022). How AI revolutionizes innovation management—Perceptions and implementation preferences of AI-based innovators. *Technological Forecasting and Social Change, 178*, 121596. https://doi.org/10.1016/j.techfore.2022.121598

Hendricks, L., Matthyssens, P., & Kowalkowski, C. (2024). The co-evolution of actor engagement and value co-creation on digital platforms: Evidence from the asset management industry. *Journal of Business & Industrial Marketing. (Advance online publication).* https://doi.org/10.1016/j.ijpe.2024.109467

Hollebeek, L. D., & Macky, K. (2019). Digital content marketing's role in fostering consumer engagement, trust, and value: Framework, fundamental propositions, and implications. *Journal of Interactive Marketing, 45*, 27–41. https://doi.org/10.1016/j.intmar.2018.07.003

Letaifa, S. B. (2014). The uneasy transition from supply chains to ecosystems: The value-creation/value-capture dilemma. *Management Decision, 52*(2), 278–295. https://doi.org/10.1108/MD-06-2013-0329

Lima, A., Rossi, L., & Musolesi, M. (2014). Coding together at scale: GitHub as a collaborative social network. doi:https://doi.org/10.48550/arXiv.1407.2535

Moser, C., Deichmann, D., & Groenewegen, P. (2014). The social scaffolding of online communities. *Academy of Management Proceedings, 2014*(1), 11309. https://doi.org/10.5465/AMBPP.2014.11309abstract

Nambisan, S., Zahra, S. A., & Luo, Y. (2019). Global platforms and ecosystems: Implications for international business theories. *Journal of International Business Studies, 50*(9), 1464–1486. https://doi.org/10.1057/s41267-019-00262-4

Ng, E., Tan, B., Sun, Y., & Meng, T. (2022). The strategic options of fintech platforms: An overview and research agenda. *Information Systems Journal, 33*(2), 192–231. https://doi.org/10.1111/isj.12388

Nim, N., Pedada, K., & Hewett, K. (2024). Digital marketing ecosystems and global market expansion: Current state and future research agenda. *International Marketing Review, 41*(5), 872–885. https://doi.org/10.1108/IMR-04-2024-0108

Peng, B. (2021). Digital leadership: State governance in the era of digital technology. *Global Media and China, 5*(4), 365–378. https://doi.org/10.1177/2096608321989835

Peuckert, J., & Kern, F. (2023). How user innovation communities contribute to sustainability transitions: An exploration of three online communities. *Environmental Innovation and Societal Transitions, 49*, 100785. https://doi.org/10.1016/j.eist.2023.100785

Schüler, F., & Petrik, D. (2023). Measuring network effects of digital industrial platforms: Towards a balanced platform performance management. *Information Systems and e-Business Management, 21*, 863–911. https://doi.org/10.1007/s10257-023-00655-x

Sergi, V., & Bonneau, C. (2016). Making mundane work visible on social media: A CMC perspective on community building in professional service firms. *Information and Organization, 26*(3), 142–162. https://doi.org/10.4324/9781351203876-7

13

Using Engagement to Drive Value Co-Creation

Amid a more connected and collaborative economy, the meaning of value is undergoing a profound transformation. Value is no longer a one-way delivery from a brand to a passive consumer. Instead, it is emerging as a dynamic outcome of collective effort—co-created by platforms, customers, partners, and technology layers working in concert. Central to this evolution is engagement: the active participation of diverse actors who bring not just their attention, but their data, ideas, creativity, and energy to the table. When properly structured, engagement becomes much more than a metric—it becomes the engine of value co-creation. And marketers, with their skills in storytelling, community-building, and systems thinking, are uniquely positioned to orchestrate this process.

At its core, meaningful engagement asks two questions: How are we involving stakeholders in shaping experiences, and how do we enable them to elevate those experiences? Engagement begins with invitation. Platforms set the stage by opening channels for users, partners, and developers to share insights, test hypotheses, or propose enhancements (Hendricks et al., 2024). But an invitation is only the start. The real question is: do those contributors feel heard, seen, and rewarded? That requires systems of acknowledgement—feedback loops that show contributors where their input made a difference, data dashboards that illustrate usage trends, and celebration moments that elevate community-driven ideas.

This chapter explores how marketers can activate, sustain, and scale engagement that leads to meaningful co-creation within digital ecosystems.

Next, marketers move from structuring interaction to nurturing contribution. They curate experiences where participants are not just visitors, but active collaborators (Aulkemeier et al., 2019). This could mean community-driven content development, co-authored webinars, or workshops where customers help define new feature sets. It could also mean inviting partners to participate in product sprints or marketing campaigns—turning what might have been a transactional relationship into a collaborative journey.

But engagement must be sustained to generate ongoing co-creation. This calls for intentional habit-forming mechanisms: gamification that rewards progressive contributions; recognition programmes that honour top collaborators; and community governance structures that enable volunteers to manage forums, lead sub-groups or co-lead initiatives (Engert et al., 2025). Each of these touches enhances engagement, elevates ownership, and strengthens the overall ecosystem. They also deepen emotional connection. When contributors see their names attached to features, content, or community events, they move from being consumers to being co-creators and advocates.

Scaling engagement across a platform brings additional challenges—and opportunities. At scale, simple recognition may feel impersonal. That's where co-curation comes into play. Marketers can delegate parts of the ecosystem's narrative architecture to trusted contributors, empowering them to lead regional events, local campaigns, or vertical-specific community cohorts. This not only eases scaling pressures, but also brings variation and relevance to different audience groups.

Scaling participation also requires technology. Community or platform analytics must give real-time insight into who is contributing what, which participants are gaining traction and which contributions are driving usage. AI-driven content tools can help surface emerging trends, translate community sentiment into action items, and flag rising contributors for recognition or networking opportunities (Füller et al., 2022). Chatbots and smart dashboards can guide new entrants, helping them become active members more quickly. In all of this, marketers act as guides—linking behaviour signals with platform design, feedback loops with resource allocation, and community activity with strategic growth goals.

Critically, effective engagement is transparent and reciprocal. Participants should clearly understand how their contributions matter—they help shape roadmap priorities, influence marketing narratives or spark product pivots. And the platform must reward contributions tangibly (Hollebeek & Macky, 2019): early-access privileges, revenue or usage-share programmes, co-branding opportunities, or public acknowledgement. When reciprocal value is visible, engagement becomes trust. When engagement becomes ecosystem trust, platforms gain momentum.

Marketers must also recognise that engagement doesn't happen in a vacuum. It unfolds within a broader ecosystem of regulations, cultural expectations, technical constraints, and competitive forces. Co-created outcomes must align with compliance needs, brand positioning, partner capabilities, and end-user requirements (Füller et al., 2022). Marketers are essential translators here—connecting ecosystem dynamics with strategic alignment, ensuring that co-creation doesn't introduce reputational or operational risk.

At their best, marketers transform engagement into orchestration. They design experiences, systems, and stories that elevate everyday interactions, help communities feel their impact and align contributor activity with business outcomes. They add structure where there was spontaneity—and freedom where there was hierarchy. In doing so, they convert enthusiastic but transactional interactions into deep, ongoing, generative co-creation cycles.

What Is Value Co-Creation—And Why Engagement Matters

Value co-creation is the process through which multiple actors—organisations, users, developers, regulators—jointly create outcomes that none could achieve alone. Rather than being delivered top-down, value emerges through collaboration, iteration, and mutual contribution.

Engagement plays a critical role in this. It is both the signal and the substance of co-creation. Engaged actors:

1. Provide feedback
2. Suggest improvements
3. Co-develop solutions
4. Contribute content
5. Advocate for others

Every touchpoint is an opportunity to generate shared value—but only if the ecosystem supports it.

How Digital Ecosystems Enable Co-Creation

Digital ecosystems are designed for interaction. Platforms, in particular, offer the infrastructure, tools and governance necessary to support distributed collaboration at scale (Choudary, 2021). Consider a fintech platform. By connecting users, start-ups, developers and financial institutions, it creates a collaborative space where new products and services can be shaped by those who use them (Das, 2019). Similarly, in healthcare, digital platforms bring together patients, providers, and researchers to co-design treatments, tools, and experiences that improve outcomes.

Key technologies such as cloud computing, AI and data analytics further amplify co-creation. They make engagement more personalised, more predictive, and more productive—ensuring alignment between actor needs and ecosystem offerings.

Frameworks for Linking Engagement and Co-Creation

Two frameworks provide a lens for understanding this relationship:

1. The Engagement Value Loop:

    (i) **Interaction**: Actors engage with the platform and each other
    (ii) **Integration**: Ideas, data, and resources are combined
    (iii) **Creation**: A shared product, insight, or outcome is generated
    (iv) **Reinforcement**: The value created deepens trust and future engagement

This loop is iterative and generative—the more actors participate, the stronger the ecosystem becomes.

2. The Service-Dominant Logic (SDL) Perspective:

    (i) Value is not embedded in products, but realised through use
    (ii) Every actor is a value creator
    (iii) Resource integration—not just resource delivery—defines success

SDL (Vargo & lusch, 2017) reframes marketing from communication to cooperation.

Strategies for Driving Engagement-Led Co-Creation

1. **Build a Culture of Contribution** Encourage actors to participate through inclusive governance, shared purpose, and visible recognition. Participation should feel invited, not extracted.
2. **Provide Tools That Empower** Platforms should offer APIs, low-code interfaces, data sandboxes, or collaboration portals. These tools lower the barrier to contribution and accelerate innovation.
3. **Design with Incentives** Engagement must be rewarded—through visibility, revenue share, exclusive access, or reputational gain. Incentives signal that contribution is valued and worthwhile.
4. **Use Feedback Loops to Refine and Re-engage** Co-creation is iterative. Feedback systems—surveys, usage analytics, direct conversations—enable platforms to learn, adapt, and evolve offerings in partnership with their users.

Real-World Applications

Across industries, real-world examples illuminate how ecosystems built around active engagement transform into smarter, stronger, and decidedly more human platforms.

Retail: Etsy empowers sellers to co-create the platform experience through storefront customisation, peer reviews, and marketplace innovation. **Etsy** exemplifies co-creation in action. Unlike conventional marketplaces that treat sellers as mere vendors, Etsy empowers them to shape their own presence and contribute to the platform's evolution (Pei & Li, 2023). Customisable storefronts and peer review systems allow artisans to control branding, visual storytelling, and community interaction. Sellers share insights about packaging, product design, and niche trends—Etsy listens, adapts, and scales successful features across the platform. This continuous dialogue turns independent sellers into co-authors of the experience. As artisans innovate—testing new product lines, experimenting with promotions, or adjusting shop layouts—the platform absorbs these iterative changes, refining both UX and seller tools. What emerges is a dynamic marketplace where commerce and creativity merge, each reinforcing the other.

Finance: Digital banking apps like Revolut gather user feedback in real time, shaping everything from UX design to product features. In digital banking, the real-time pulse of user engagement reshapes product development. **Revoluts'** mobile and web banking apps now feature in-app feedback, usage analytics, and rapid-release cycles. When users suggest improvements—simplified onboarding menus, clearer budgeting interfaces, mobile deposit enhancements—those suggestions are quickly evaluated, prioritised, and integrated (Pousttchi & Dehnert, 2018). Rather than treating customers as endpoints, modern fintech platforms engage them as active contributors. They host beta programmes, user forums, and even public feature voting boards. The result: financial services that feel tailor-made, with simplified experiences and practical capabilities that reflect common user needs. These are not retrofitted features—they are built from the ground up by users themselves. The outcome is twofold: adoption accelerates and users feel invested—serving as enthusiastic advocates and recruiting new members through word of mouth.

Healthcare: Patient portals like MyChart is an example of co-developed portals with users that ensure services meet real needs, increasing adherence and satisfaction. **MyChart** is a widely adopted patient portal developed by **Epic Systems**, one of the largest electronic health record (EHR) providers globally. Co-development with Patients & Providers, many health systems using Epic have involved patients in the UX design process, iterating features based on real-world feedback from both patients and clinicians. As such patient co-creation in healthcare illustrates how critical engagement can fundamentally improve service outcomes. Patient portals co-developed with actual users have redefined care experiences. Patients contribute feedback on navigation, messaging clarity, appointment scheduling, medication reminders, and even rated educational content for accessibility (Vanderhout et al., 2025). Medical professionals collaborate with these users, iterating tools until they genuinely satisfy real-world needs. As a result, platforms evolve beyond static medical records into interactive care companions—rich with tailored resources, secure messaging, and shared decision-making functions. Engaged patients are better informed, more compliant, and more willing to participate in care plans. Clinics benefit too—appointment throughput increases, miscommunication falls, and member trust deepens. The result is better adherence, improved outcomes, and co-created health journeys.

In each of these domains, engagement transcends the traditional role of a performance metric—it becomes a foundational mechanism that enhances the intelligence, resilience, and humanity of the ecosystem. When platforms treat engagement as a source of strategic insight, they turn every interaction into an opportunity for learning and evolution.

Across retail, finance, and healthcare, the result is striking: ecosystems that grow not only in size but in depth, adaptability, and trust (FA et al., 2025). The platforms are smarter because they reflect real user needs; they are stronger because they harness continuous feedback; they are more human because they invite participation rather than impose solutions. In each case, engagement is not a metric—it is a mechanism for making the ecosystem smarter, stronger, and more human.

As marketers and ecosystem designers, our task is to cultivate this shift. We must design marketplaces that include storefront customisation, financial services that learn in real-time, and patient care systems that respond to lived experience. Doing so demands a mindset of inclusion, tools that support dialogue, and structures that turn feedback into action.

Ultimately, platforms that prioritise engagement as both philosophy and practice do more than capture attention—they spark collective creativity and elevate shared purpose. In this emerging economy of co-creation, every actor brings something to the table. And every contribution deepens the ecosystem's value, for everyone involved.

Challenges to Address

While engagement is a catalyst for co-creation, it also introduces complexity:

1. **Misaligned goals**: Different actors may value different outcomes. Governance and clarity of purpose are essential.
2. **Participation fatigue**: Actors may disengage if co-creation feels extractive or unrewarding. Sustained motivation is key.
3. **Trust deficits**: If actors fear misuse of data, ideas, or effort, engagement breaks down. Platforms must earn and maintain trust through transparency, fairness, and responsiveness.

Marketing's Role in Enabling Co-Creation

Marketers have a dual role: to *facilitate* co-creation and to *learn* from it.

1. **Facilitation**: Marketers can design engagement journeys, create interactive content, host participatory events, and amplify actor contributions.

2. **Learning**: Co-creation provides real-time insight into preferences, pain points, and priorities—shaping everything from messaging to product strategy.

Campaigns become conversations. Audiences become allies. Marketing becomes a catalyst for growth by design—not just by persuasion.

Co-Creation as Competitive Advantage

In a saturated market, differentiation is not found in louder messages—but in stronger ecosystems. Brands that co-create with their customers and partners build relevance that cannot be replicated. For marketers, the takeaway is clear: engagement is not the end goal. It is the entry point to something more powerful—a shared platform for value, innovation and sustainable growth.

The Strategic Value of Co-Creation

In an era characterised by information saturation and product commoditisation, co-creation stands out as a strategic imperative. It cultivates deeper emotional connections, enhances perceived relevance, boosts innovation capacity, and strengthens trust and loyalty (Adner & Kapoor, 2010). Transitioning from transactional interactions to collaborative relationships, co-creation redefines customers as active contributors to value, positioning it as the new currency in marketing ecosystems.

Visual Framework: The Engagement–Co-Creation Value Loop

Figure 13.1 introduces a framework that outlines the cyclical and compounding relationship between actor engagement and value co-creation within platform ecosystems. It highlights how active participation fuels innovation and shared value, which in turn deepens engagement—creating a continuous loop that strengthens ecosystem resilience and growth (Fig. 13.1).

The *Engagement Co-creation Value Loop* reinforces itself—each cycle of interaction and co-creation deepens the ecosystem's value and resilience.

13 Using Engagement to Drive Value Co-Creation

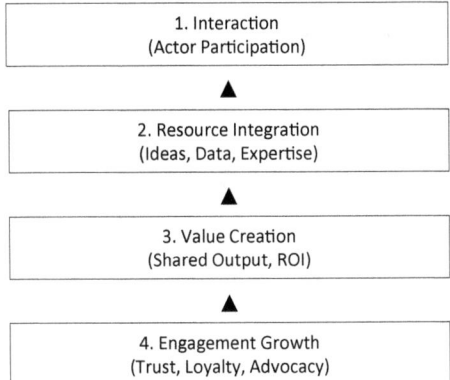

Fig. 13.1 Engagement Co-Creation Value Loop

Reflective Prompt: Are You Creating the Conditions for Shared Value?

As you assess your platform or marketing strategy:

1. Are your engagement touchpoints designed for input or just interaction?
2. Do you have tools in place to integrate user feedback, content, or contribution into your product or service development?
3. How do you demonstrate that actor contributions lead to tangible changes or value?
4. What mechanisms exist to sustain engagement—especially after initial interaction?

Co-creation thrives where engagement is authentic, purposeful, and rewarded.

Exercise: Co-Creation Readiness Canvas

1. **Define Your Ecosystem's Core Actors**
   - Who are your top three actor groups (e.g. users, developers, partners)?
   - What unique value can each contribute?

2. **Map the Co-Creation Loop**
   - How do actors currently interact with the platform?
   - Where can resource integration happen?
   - What shared value is created?
   - How is that value recognised or reinforced?

3. **Identify Friction Points**
   - Where is engagement dropping off?

- Are contributions going unrecognised or under-utilised?
- Is feedback being acted upon?

4. **Design a Co-Creation Activation**

- Choose one actor group
- Define a new or improved journey:
  - Invite participation
  - Enable contribution
  - Recognise and reward outcomes

5. **Establish a Feedback Loop**

- What metrics or tools will help you learn from this initiative?
- How will you show actors their input made an impact?

This chapter ensures your engagement strategy is not just active—but additive, creating real, shared value across your platform.

References

Adner, R., & Kapoor, R. (2010). Value creation in innovation ecosystems: How the structure of technological interdependence affects firm performance in new technology generations. *Strategic Management Journal, 31*(3), 306–333. https://doi.org/10.1002/smj.821

Aulkemeier, F., Iacob, M. E., & van Hillegersberg, J. (2019). Platform-based collaboration in digital ecosystems. *Electronic Markets, 29*, 597–608. https://doi.org/10.1007/s12525-019-00341-2

Breidbach, C., Antons, D., & Salge, O. (2016). Seamless Service? On the Role and Impact of Service Orchestrators in Human-Centered Service Systems. *Journal of Service Research., 19*, 458–476. https://doi.org/10.1177/1094670516666370

Choudary, S. P. (2021). Platform scale: How an emerging business model helps startups build large empires with minimum investment (2nd ed.). Platform Thinking Labs.

Das, S. R. (2019). The future of Fintech. *Financial Management, 48*(4), 981–1007. https://doi.org/10.1111/fima.12297

Engert, M., Farchi, D., & Sayed, M. (2025). Self-organization and governance in digital platform ecosystems: Balancing top-down control and complementor coalitions. *MIS Quarterly, 49*(1), 85–112. https://doi.org/10.25300/MISQ/2024/18413

FA, C., Ramezan Zadeh, M. T., Ozalp, H., & Volberda, H. W. (2025). The role of trust in a platform ecosystem: Exploring the impact of different trust dimensions on complementors' platform revenue. *Research Policy, 54*(8), Article 104957. https://doi.org/10.2139/ssrn.5180726

Füller, J., Hutter, K., Wahl, J., Bilgram, V., & Tekic, Z. (2022). How AI revolutionizes innovation management – Perceptions and implementation preferences of AI-based innovators. *Technological Forecasting and Social Change, 178*, Article 121596. https://doi.org/10.1016/j.techfore.2022.121598

Hendricks, L., Matthyssens, P., & Kowalkowski, C. (2024). The co-evolution of actor engagement and value co-creation on digital platforms: Evidence from the asset management industry. *Journal of Business & Industrial Marketing. (Advance online publication)*. https://doi.org/10.1016/j.ijpe.2024.109467

Hollebeek, L. D., & Macky, K. (2019). Digital content marketing's role in fostering consumer engagement, trust, and value: Framework, fundamental propositions, and implications. *Journal of Interactive Marketing, 45*, 27–41. https://doi.org/10.1016/j.intmar.2018.07.003

Pei, Y., & Li, M. (2023). The effects of information on competition on a hybrid retail platform. International Journal of Production Economics, 260, Article 108843. https://doi.org/10.1016/j.ijpe.2023.108843

Pousttchi, K., & Dehnert, M. (2018). Exploring the digitalization impact on consumer decision-making in retail banking. *Electron Markets, 28*, 265–286. https://doi.org/10.1007/s12525-017-0283-0

Vanderhout, S., Taneja, S., Kalia, K., Wodchis, W. P., & Tang, T. (2025). Patient experiences with MyChart in a large community hospital: A mixed methods study. *Journal of Medical Internet Research, 27*, Article e66353. https://doi.org/10.2196/66353

Vargo, S. L., & Lusch, R. F. (2017). Service-dominant logic 2025. *International Journal of Research in Marketing, 34*(1), 46–67. https://doi.org/10.1016/j.ijresmar.2016.11.001

14

Value Co-Creation—The New Marketing Currency

Value is no longer a static commodity exchanged between businesses and customers. Instead, it has become a dynamic outcome forged through interaction, participation, and co-creation. This shift places marketers in a new and expanded role. They are no longer simply communicators of benefits—they are facilitators of ecosystems, designers of collaborative experiences, and stewards of mutual growth. The strategic imperative of this chapter is to illuminate how value co-creation has emerged as the new currency of marketing—and why it matters now more than ever.

Value co-creation thrives in environments where every stakeholder—customers, partners, developers, internal teams (Aarikka-Stenroos & Jaakkola, 2012)—participates actively in shaping the offerings and the platform itself. For marketers, this means nurturing a mindset that goes beyond message crafting. They must embed themselves within the ecosystem, orchestrating spaces where meaningful collaboration can flourish. This unconventional role includes designing feedback systems, enabling partner portals, and inviting user-generated innovation. By doing so, marketers help stake the claim: value isn't created in isolation—it is built collectively.

The rise of co-creation reflects a deeper cultural and technological shift. Consumers no longer respond to one-way broadcast. They expect to be heard, seen, and involved. They want products that adapt to their lives, services that evolve with their feedback, and experiences that recognise their voice. Platforms like **Etsy**, **GitHub**, and **Peloton** succeeded because they opened the door to participation—not just consumption (Cutolo & Kenney, 2021). Their marketing strategies have embedded this openness into the narrative: "Your contribution shapes the product." This taps into a much stronger emotional connection than any traditional campaign could—because it speaks directly to agency, recognition, and purpose.

Technologies such as AI, cloud services, analytics, and connected devices both enable and accelerate co-creation at scale. AI can personalise outreach—underscoring a user's ideas or behaviour—so that suggested tasks or design tools feel relevant (Füller et al., 2022). Cloud infrastructure gives partners and users access to modular, collaborative spaces. Real-time analytics enable marketers to spot emerging co-creation moments—such as viral user innovation or community insights—and elevate them instantly. These technological enablers make it possible to move from static, episodic campaigns to dynamic, living platforms of shared value.

Marketers must also become proficient in the structures that sustain co-creation. They need to know how to design incentive systems that balance fairness with motivation—whether through recognition, revenue shares, or joint press announcements. They must understand governance frameworks—agreeing on contribution rules, intellectual property terms, or integration standards—that give actors confidence to invest time and creativity. They must nurture community norms that reward collaboration, inclusion, and constructive insight. And they must measure not just reach or conversions, but signs of ecosystem health: contribution rates, partner retention, user innovation frequency, co-designed feature launches, and sentiment around shared success.

The outcome of this approach is profound. Platforms that embrace co-creation gain richer innovation pipelines—ideas surface not from isolated labs but from embedded actors. They gain deeper engagement (Palmié, 2022)—users and partners feel invested, and their loyalty grows. They gain resilience—because solutions evolve in response to real-time input, not top-down forecasts. And they gain differentiation—competition often plays by the rules of scale; co-creation plays by the rules of community, creativity, and continual renewal.

But embracing value co-creation is not easy. It requires a cultural shift away from perfection and control towards openness and iteration. It demands humility from brands—willingness to invite critique and share authority. It calls for new capabilities—community management, ecosystem governance, integration engineering (Gawer & Harracá, 2025). It challenges legacy metrics—demanding new indicators of platform vitality. But perhaps most critically, it calls for leadership—a conviction that co-creation is not a nice-to-have but a business imperative.

As marketers in this platform-centric age, we stand at the intersection of creativity and systems design. Our job is not merely to amplify features—it is to orchestrate frameworks where those features can be imagined, improved, and inherited by thousands of co-creators. We must craft narratives that highlight not just the value we deliver, but the value we build together. We must anchor campaigns not in consumption alone, but in contribution. And we must tell stories not of what we know, but of what we can learn—imagining platforms as living organisms, not static solutions.

Co-creation is the new marketing currency because it aligns purpose with participation, creativity with capability, and growth with goodwill. It shifts metrics from transactions to transformations (Bocconcelli, 2020) collapsing the distance between the maker and the co-creator. In a world saturated with choice and short attention, platforms that enable collaborative value creation to win not just loyalty—but advocacy, innovation, and impact. And at the centre of that transformation stands marketing—not as a storyteller, but as an ecosystem architect.

In the pages ahead, we will unpack the tools, frameworks, and mindsets needed to implement this evolution. You will discover how to design platforms where co-creation thrives, how to measure collaborative value, how to govern ecosystems at scale, and how to lead organisations into this new marketing landscape. Because in platform economies, value isn't given—it's made together. And the marketers who embrace that truth will shape not just products, but the future.

From Delivery to Co-Creation: A Paradigm Shift

Traditionally, marketing operated within a goods-dominant logic. Businesses created value through production, then transferred it to consumers via messaging and distribution. Engagement was largely one-way. Feedback loops were slow. Innovation was centralised.

Digital ecosystems changed that. With the rise of platforms and connected technologies, the service-dominant logic model has taken a foothold. Here, value is not created *for* users but *with* them (Hendricks, Matthyssens & Kowalkowski, 2024)—through interactions, integrations, and shared resource application.

This shift repositions marketing as a relational, not transactional, function. Marketers must now orchestrate participation, not just awareness—and cultivate environments where co-creation is both possible and purposeful.

What Is Value Co-Creation?

Value co-creation occurs when multiple actors—customers, partners, developers, employees—actively contribute to the design, delivery and evolution of a product, service or experience.

It involves:

1. Combining resources (e.g. data, tools, insights)
2. Aligning around shared goals
3. Iterating through feedback and innovation
4. Recognising and distributing shared outcomes

The process is as important as the result. It builds trust, loyalty, and relevance—not just revenue.

Principles of Co-Creation in Marketing Ecosystems

1. **Openness and Inclusivity** Co-creation thrives in environments that welcome diverse perspectives. Brands must open their platforms—structurally and culturally—to stakeholder input.
2. **Reciprocity and Fair Exchange** Contribution must be met with recognition. Whether through visibility, rewards, or influence, actors should feel their participation matters.
3. **Outcome-Orientation** Co-creation is not endless discussion. It is purposeful collaboration, directed towards solving problems, improving experiences, or creating something new.

These principles shape the values of ecosystem brands—and the behaviour of their communities.

Frameworks for Understanding Value Co-Creation

The Co-Creation Spiral

The *Co-Creation Spiral* model illustrates how value in ecosystems is not static but accumulates over time through repeated cycles of contribution, collaboration, and iteration. This model begins with the integration of resources—where stakeholders such as customers, developers, or partners contribute knowledge, tools, insights, or data to a shared platform. These inputs, when combined, form the foundation for meaningful collaboration.

From this foundation, stakeholders engage in joint innovation (Boudreau & Lakhani, 2009). Here, co-created solutions—whether in the form of new products, services, or experiences—emerge through mutual experimentation and creativity. Crucially, this process does not end with the launch of a solution. Instead, feedback becomes the next catalyst. Ecosystem actors provide insight on what works and what needs refinement (Breidbach et al., 2014), which in turn informs the next cycle of development. In this way, value is not only created but amplified through each iteration, making the ecosystem smarter and more responsive over time.

The Actor Engagement Framework

Engagement is not a passive metric—it is the engine of co-creation. *The Actor Engagement* framework highlights how the quality of stakeholder participation drives the success of ecosystem innovation. When actors are deeply engaged, they are more likely to contribute meaningfully—offering ideas, taking ownership of outcomes, and collaborating with others.

Confidence also plays a pivotal role. When stakeholders trust the platform's governance, openness, and responsiveness (Aulkemeier, Iacob, & van Hillegersberg, 2019), their willingness to innovate increases. Likewise, platforms that actively adapt based on feedback foster greater resilience across the ecosystem. This reciprocal relationship between engagement, contribution, and responsiveness forms the structural backbone of effective co-creation.

Together, these two frameworks offer a powerful lens for understanding how platforms move from transaction-based interactions to deeper, value-creating collaborations.

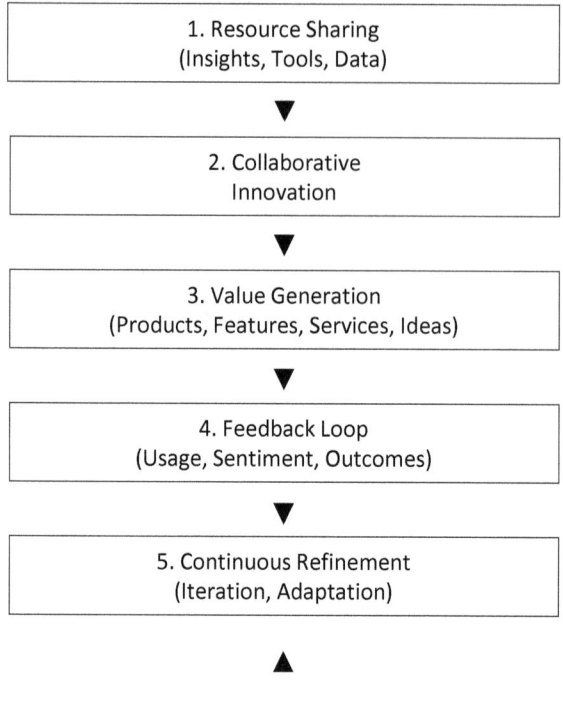

Fig. 14.1 Co-Creation Spiral Model

Visual Framework: The Co-Creation Spiral

Figure 14.1 introduces a framework outlining the iterative and compounding nature of value co-creation in platform ecosystems, highlighting how engagement fuels shared outcomes over time.

The *Co-creation Spiral* model illustrates how each loop generates greater precision, relevance, and stakeholder investment. It turns co-creation from an event into a practice.

> **Reflective Prompt: Are You Inviting Co-Creation—Or Just Expecting It?**
>
> As you assess your marketing strategies and ecosystem structure:
>
> 1. How often do you invite customers or partners into the creation process?
> 2. Are their contributions visible, valued, and acted upon?
> 3. What tools or spaces do you offer to support collaboration?
> 4. How does co-creation inform your product roadmap or brand evolution?

> Genuine co-creation begins with humility—the willingness to build with, not just for.

Exercise: Co-Creation Value Design Canvas

1. **Identify a Key Marketing Initiative or Offering**
   - Product, service, content stream, or campaign
2. **Map Stakeholder Roles**
   - Who can contribute value? (e.g. customers, developers, staff, communities)
   - What kind of contribution is possible? (ideas, data, feedback, content)
3. **Design the Co-Creation Environment**
   - What platforms or tools will facilitate interaction?
   - What incentives or recognition will encourage participation?
4. **Define Success Metrics**
   - What will signal value creation? (retention, satisfaction, UGC, innovation speed)
5. **Create a Reflection Loop**
   - How will you show participants that their input changed the outcome?
   - What will you change, or repeat based on this collaboration?

This chapter helps you harness engagement as a dynamic engine for shared value—revealing how continuous co-creation drives deeper outcomes across the ecosystem.

References

Aarikka-Stenroos, L., & Jaakkola, E. (2012). Value co-creation in knowledge intensive business services: A dyadic perspective on the joint problem-solving process. *Industrial Marketing Management, 41*(1), 15–26. https://doi.org/10.1016/j.indmarman.2011.11.008

Aulkemeier, F., Iacob, M. E., & van Hillegersberg, J. (2019). Platform-based collaboration in digital ecosystems. *Electronic Markets, 29*, 597–608. https://doi.org/10.1007/s12525-019-00341-2

Bocconcelli, R., Carlborg, P., Harrison, D., Hasche, N., Hedvall, K., & Lei, H. (2020). Resource interaction and resource integration: similarities, differences, reflections. *Industrial Marketing Management, 91*, 385–396. https://doi.org/10.1016/j.indmarman.2020.09.016

Boudreau, K., & Lakhani, K. (2009). How to manage outside innovation. *MIT Sloan Management Review., 50*.

Breidbach, C. F., Brodie, R., & Hollebeek, L. (2014). Beyond virtuality: from engagement platforms to engagement ecosystems. *Managing Service Quality, 24*(6), 592–611. https://doi.org/10.1108/MSQ-08-2013-0158

Cutolo, D., & Kenney, M. (2021). Platform-dependent entrepreneurs: Power asymmetries, risks, and strategies in the platform economy. *Academy of Management Perspectives, 35*(4), 584–605. https://doi.org/10.5465/amp.2019.0103

Füller, J., Hutter, K., Wahl, J., Bilgram, V., & Tekic, Z. (2022). How AI revolutionizes innovation management—Perceptions and implementation preferences of AI-based innovators. *Technological Forecasting and Social Change, 178*, 121596. https://doi.org/10.1016/j.techfore.2022.121598

Gawer, A., & Harracá, M. (2025). Inconsistent platform governance and social contagion of misconduct in digital ecosystems: A complementors perspective. *Research Policy, 54(8), Article 104957*. https://doi.org/10.2139/ssrn.5368760

Hendricks, L., Matthyssens, P., & Kowalkowski, C. (2024). The co-evolution of actor engagement and value co-creation on digital platforms: Evidence from the asset management industry. *Journal of Business & Industrial Marketing. (Advance online publication)*. https://doi.org/10.1016/j.ijpe.2024.109467

Palmié, M., Miehé, L., Oghazi, P., Parida, V., & Wincent, J. (2022). The evolution of the digital service ecosystem and digital business model innovation in retail: The emergence of meta-ecosystems and the value of physical interactions. *Technological Forecasting and Social Change, 177*, 121496. https://doi.org/10.1016/j.techfore.2022.121496

Sun, S., Zhang, J., Zhu, Y., Jiang, M., & Chen, S. (2022). Exploring users' willingness to disclose personal information in online healthcare communities: The role of satisfaction. *Technological Forecasting and Social Change, 178*, 121602. https://doi.org/10.1016/j.techfore.2022.121596

15

Reciprocal Resource Integration in Ecosystems

With platforms and partnerships leading the way, success is no longer measured by the resources an organisation controls but by its ability to integrate effectively with others. Reciprocal resource integration has emerged as a fundamental mechanism through which modern ecosystems generate value. It serves as the connective tissue of collaboration, enabling actors to combine their assets, capabilities, and insights to co-create outcomes unattainable by any single entity alone.

This chapter delves into the mechanics of reciprocal integration, explores how marketers can harness its potential, and underscores its foundational role in fostering resilient and innovative ecosystem growth.

At its core, reciprocal integration is about weaving together diverse strengths to form a cohesive whole (Bruce et al., 2019). No longer can companies work in isolation—instead, they must engage in intentional, mutual exchanges—offering their own resources while tapping into others'. Consider a platform that integrates a fintech provider's real-time payments capability, a bank's regulatory expertise, a data analytics firm's insight tools, and a user community's behavioural intelligence (Das, 2019). Individually, each asset has value. But when combined in a unified ecosystem, they produce richer, more adaptive offerings that evolve with user need and context.

For marketers, understanding reciprocal integration means recognising that their role extends far beyond messaging. They become orchestrators of networked collaboration, designing value pathways that activate the unique contributions of platform participants (Hibbert et al., 2012). They think in combinations, not silos—in shared journeys, not solo campaigns. Their work revolves around identifying which resources—technological, intellectual, relational—can be linked together to create something greater than the sum of parts.

This process begins with resource mapping—an exercise in visibility and intention. Marketers must help the organisation visualise every resource under its control: proprietary data sets, user communities, partner capabilities, brand equity, or operational know-how. Simultaneously, they scout for complementary assets available in the ecosystem—perhaps an AI startup with personalisation algorithms, a logistics specialist for faster delivery, or an academic institution with behavioural expertise.

Recognising potential matches sets the stage for meaningful collaboration.

From there, marketers must facilitate the integration itself. This often takes the form of co-development workshops, joint roadmaps, shared innovation challenges, or integrated product feature launches. Marketing becomes a glue agent, connecting product managers with partner teams, aligning value-led messaging across stakeholder groups, and highlighting the benefits of integrated outcomes. For example, a campaign might not just promote "faster delivery"—it might narrate the combined story of a logistics partner, a real-time tracking API, and an end-user app dashboard, showing how these layers work in harmony to create immediate, measurable benefit.

In this role, marketers must also address the often-overlooked dimension of trust and reciprocity. Reciprocal integration only works when participants feel confident that resource exchanges will be fair, transparent, and beneficial (Hilbolling et al., 2019). This requires clear value-sharing agreements, documentation of expected outcomes, mutual visibility into performance metrics, and recognition of contributions—either through branding, shared case studies, or formal "partner spotlight" features. Marketing crafts these narratives, giving visibility to ecosystem partners and signalling that collaboration is more than a business instrument—it's a cultural operating principle.

Beyond trust, marketers also navigate structural and technical complexities. Integration involves aligning APIs, data protocols, UX flows, commercial terms, and joint KPIs. In effect, marketer-led blueprints or playbooks guide this complex dance: How should the partner resource plug in? What data is shared, and how is privacy governed? How is performance measured, and who owns which relationship? By anticipating and clarifying these questions, marketers smooth the path between conceptual integration and operational realisation.

The benefits of strong reciprocal integration are manifold: ecosystems become more resilient (Blasco et al., 2016)—because innovation can occur in partner nodes as well as centrally. Growth becomes more scalable—because each partner brings new users, channels, or cognitive assets. Differentiation deepens—because the platform offers richer, ever-evolving value mixes rather than static features. And importantly, marketing authenticity increases—because it's no longer just broadcasting; it's storytelling about genuine collaboration.

However, reciprocal integration is not a turnkey solution. It demands strategic selectivity—marketers can't integrate with everyone. The key is identifying those partners whose assets both fill critical gaps and align with the platform's long-term vision. It also requires agility—feedback loops must be designed to assess the impact of integrations, surface problems early, and pivot where necessary. And it requires continuity—integrations shouldn't be one-off events; they should evolve into enduring capabilities and relationships.

To embed reciprocal integration at scale, marketers can establish ecosystem calendars—regular cycles that invite partner contributions for new modules, features, or campaigns. They can create integration accelerators—short-term sprints focused on weaving in partner assets. They can build forums—developer communities, advisory councils, co-creation workshops—that foster organic cross-pollination (Derave et al., 2021). And they can measure ecosystem health via composite KPIs: partner retention, integrated feature launches, multi-actor cost savings, or co-developed revenue streams.

Reciprocal resource integration is a strategic superpower in platform ecosystems. It transforms individual assets into collective advantage, turning marketing from brand promotion into ecosystem orchestration. The marketer becomes a convergence artist—seeing the linkages that others miss, translating partner value into shared narratives, and sustaining momentum through governance, measurement, and recognition. When deployed intentionally, reciprocal integration not only amplifies what an organisation can do—it redefines what it can become, together.

Understanding Reciprocal Resource Integration

At its core, reciprocal resource integration is a bidirectional process where actors contribute their unique resources and, in turn, benefit from the resources of others (Breidbach & Brodie, 2017). These resources encompass both tangible assets—such as technology, capital, and infrastructure—and intangible assets, including data, trust, expertise, and community engagement.

Unlike traditional value delivery models, where value is transferred from one party to another, reciprocal integration emphasises co-construction through shared interactions. This approach aligns with the principles of service-dominant logic, which posits that value is realised through collaborative use rather than isolated production.

For instance, consider a fintech platform that integrates:

1. A bank's transaction data to provide financial insights.
2. A start-up's behavioural analytics model to interpret user behaviour.
3. Customer feedback to refine features and enhance user experience.

The culmination of these integrated resources results in a more intelligent and user-centric financial tool, reflecting the collective input and distributed strengths of all participants.

The Dynamics of Ecosystem Integration

Ecosystems thrive on the diversity and complementarity of their actors. The process of integration unfolds through four key stages:

1. **Resource Identification:** Actors assess their capabilities and identify potential partners whose resources complement their own. This stage requires clarity about what each party offers and seeks, laying the groundwork for meaningful collaboration.
2. **Interaction and Exchange:** Platforms facilitate the infrastructure—such as APIs, interfaces, and collaboration tools—that enable efficient and effective integration. These tools support seamless communication and resource sharing among actors.
3. **Transformation:** Through joint efforts, combined resources are transformed into new value propositions, whether in the form of products, services, insights, or experiences. This stage embodies the creative synergy of collaborative innovation.
4. **Feedback and Optimisation:** Outcomes are evaluated, and insights gained are reintegrated into the ecosystem. This iterative process fosters continuous improvement, strengthens relationships, and enhances the ecosystem's adaptability.

This cyclical process not only sustains innovation but also builds relational equity—manifested as trust, loyalty, and a shared sense of purpose among ecosystem participants.

Frameworks for Reciprocal Resource Integration

To navigate the complexities of reciprocal integration, two frameworks offer structured approaches:

1. **The Resource Integration Cycle:**
   - **Mobilisation:** Actors commit resources for sharing.
   - **Interaction:** Structured environments facilitate resource exchange.
   - **Transformation:** Co-created value emerges from combined resources.
   - **Evaluation:** Impact assessments inform adjustments and refinements.

2. **The Value Co-Creation Matrix:**

   This matrix plots integration efforts based on:

- **Resource Intensity**: Ranging from low to high.
- **Interaction Level**: From light coordination to deep collaboration.

It aids marketers in determining the appropriate depth and breadth of partnerships, from simple data sharing arrangements to complex joint ventures.

These frameworks provide marketers with tools to assess, plan, and manage integration efforts strategically, ensuring alignment with organisational goals and ecosystem dynamics.

Technology as an Enabler

Digital technologies are pivotal in scaling and streamlining reciprocal resource integration:

1. **APIs and Cloud Infrastructure:** These technologies simplify collaboration across disparate systems, enabling real-time data sharing and integration.
2. **Artificial Intelligence:** AI algorithms can identify complementary capabilities among actors, predict successful collaboration patterns, and optimise resource allocation.
3. **Blockchain:** By providing transparent and immutable records of transactions, blockchain technology enhances trust and accountability, particularly in ecosystems handling sensitive data.

These technological enablers transform the abstract concept of integration into a practical and scalable process, unlocking new possibilities for innovation and growth.

Real-World Applications

The power of reciprocal resource integration comes to life across various industries, illustrating how interconnected capabilities, shared assets, and mutual value creation drive platform success.

Electric Mobility—Coordinated Infrastructure for Scalable Adoption

In the electric vehicle (EV) industry, collaboration between automakers, battery providers, and charging network operators is essential. For example, **IONITY** is a high-power EV charging network founded by a consortium of major automakers including **BMW Group, Ford, Mercedes-Benz, Hyundai, Kia, and Volkswagen Group (with Audi and Porsche)**. It was created to accelerate the adoption of electric mobility across Europe by building a reliable, fast-charging infrastructure. These actors operate as a coordinated system—not in isolation (Ghosh, 2022). Automakers align vehicle design with emerging battery technologies, while charging networks adapt to accommodate faster or more sustainable power systems. This collaborative alignment ensures that users experience seamless charging access, reliable battery performance, and integrated digital interfaces. Marketers in this space emphasise end-to-end convenience and sustainability, shifting their messaging from product specs to the reliability and interoperability of the entire ecosystem.

Open-Source Software—Collective Innovation at Scale

The open-source community, particularly through platforms like **GitHub**, demonstrates how value emerges from global contribution. This model of communal innovation drives continuous improvement and exemplifies how co-creation can thrive when openness and contribution are structurally enabled (Dabbish et al., 2012). Developers integrate their code, review each other's work, and co-develop features in an environment built on trust and transparency. No single company owns the innovation—it is a community effort that delivers exponential growth in capability. Reciprocal integration here is evident in every pull request, patch, and collaborative sprint. Marketers highlight the platform's openness, the speed of collective innovation, and the inclusive spirit that enables global collaboration.

Retail and E-Commerce—Enabling Sellers Through Embedded Infrastructure

In retail and logistics, large e-commerce platforms have redefined the rules of scale by integrating warehousing services, merchant tools, and advanced customer analytics. These capabilities empower third-party sellers to grow without the burden of building their own logistics infrastructure, effectively allowing them to plug into a much larger system designed for mutual benefit. In e-commerce, platforms like **Amazon** and **Alibaba** have created ecosystems where logistics, data analytics, and marketing support are fully embedded (Zhu & Liu, 2018). Third-party sellers plug into these systems to access warehousing, fulfilment, and customer insight tools that would otherwise require years to build independently. The reciprocal value lies in scale and specialisation—sellers gain reach and infrastructure, while platforms expand their marketplace offerings. Marketers focus on ecosystem enablement, positioning the platform not as a marketplace but as a growth engine for merchants.

Each of these industry examples reveals a common truth: value in platform ecosystems is not delivered unilaterally, not through isolated competition but through ecosystem orchestration (Jovanović et al., 2020). It is co-created through reciprocal resource integration—the thoughtful combination of capabilities, technologies, and relationships that allow everyone in the ecosystem to benefit. For marketers, this changes the narrative. They are no longer selling isolated products. They are shaping networks where every participant adds value, and every engagement creates momentum for mutual success.

In this new landscape, marketers are no longer simply promoters of products; they are ecosystem architects, curating the conditions for shared innovation, scalability, and long-term success.

Challenges in Resource Integration

Despite its advantages, reciprocal integration presents several challenges:

1. **Misalignment:** Disparities in goals or contributions among actors can hinder collaboration. Ensuring strategic fit and mutual understanding is crucial.
2. **Trust Issues:** Concerns about data misuse or intellectual property rights can impede openness. Establishing clear governance structures and ethical guidelines is essential to build and maintain trust.
3. **Coordination Overload:** Managing numerous actors and complex processes can lead to inefficiencies. Streamlined communication and defined protocols are necessary to prevent chaos.

Proactively addressing these challenges is vital, particularly in sectors with stringent regulatory requirements or high sensitivity to data privacy.

The Role of Marketing in Resource Integration

Marketers are uniquely positioned to spearhead reciprocal integration initiatives:

1. **Strategic Insight:** Identifying opportunities where collaboration can enhance brand value and customer experiences.
2. **Narrative Crafting:** Communicating the purpose and benefits of partnerships to stakeholders, fostering buy-in and support.
3. **Stakeholder Engagement:** Facilitating active participation from communities, partners, and users in the integration process.
4. **Impact Measurement:** Evaluating the outcomes of shared resource utilisation on key metrics such as trust, satisfaction, and loyalty.

By transitioning from traditional product promotion to ecosystem curation, marketers can drive meaningful connections and sustained engagement.

Integration as a Strategic Imperative

Reciprocal resource integration has evolved from a strategic advantage into a fundamental necessity. This approach empowers organisations to move beyond siloed capabilities and engage in a more fluid exchange of knowledge, technology, and insight across ecosystem partners (Hein et al., 2019). Through shared innovation, companies harness diverse perspectives and complementary strengths to co-create solutions that none could develop alone.

This collaborative dynamic not only spurs creativity but also accelerates time-to-market, as development processes are streamlined through mutual support and aligned priorities.

Moreover, this model enables a richer understanding of customer needs. By sharing data, analytics, and real-time feedback across the ecosystem, partners are better equipped to design offerings that are tailored, responsive, and relevant. Importantly, reciprocal integration also supports collective risk mitigation. Rather than bearing the weight of uncertainty alone, businesses distribute operational and strategic risks across the network—enhancing adaptability and resilience in the face of market volatility. Ultimately, reciprocal resource integration turns the ecosystem into a living, learning system—one where collaboration fuels value, agility, and sustained innovation.

For marketers, embracing reciprocal integration necessitates the development of new competencies in partnership design, systems thinking, and facilitative leadership. When executed effectively, it fosters not only superior experiences but also robust relationships and sustainable growth.

Visual Framework: The Reciprocal Resource Integration Cycle

Figure 15.1 presents a framework highlighting the dynamic flow of shared resource contribution, collaboration, and ecosystem-level value creation. It outlines the interconnected stages of the cycle and how the cycle then loops back into mobilisation, creating a continuous system of integration, innovation, and ecosystem-wide value enhancement.

Each turn of the cycle within the *Reciprocal Resource Integration Cycle* strengthens trust, sharpens innovation, and embeds a culture of co-ownership across the platform ecosystem.

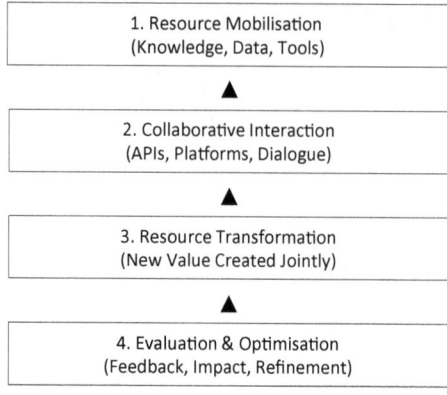

Fig. 15.1 Reciprocal Resource Integration Cycle

Reflective Prompt: Are you Creating a System—or Just Making Connections?

As you evaluate your marketing and partnership approach:

1. Are you identifying resources for collaboration—or just delivering campaigns?
2. What role does your organisation play in integrating external capabilities with internal goals?
3. Are your resource exchanges reciprocal—or one-sided?
4. How transparent are your processes for co-developing outcomes?

Ecosystem value is not extracted—it is constructed, together.

Exercise: Ecosystem Resource Mapping Canvas

1. **Define Your Core Resources**
   - Tangible: Data, tech tools, funding, reach
   - Intangible: Expertise, brand equity, customer trust
2. **Identify Potential Integration Points**
   - Where are current gaps or bottlenecks in your offer?
   - What external actors could complement or extend your capabilities?
3. **Visualise the Value Flow**
   - What will each participant contribute?

- What shared outcome will be created?
- How will this outcome be distributed or accessed?

4. **Develop a Resource Reciprocity Map**

   - Create a table with Table 15.1.

5. **Define Evaluation and Feedback Criteria**

   - What metrics or signals will show that integration is working?
   - How will you adjust contributions over time?

Table 15.1 Resource Reciprocity Map

Actor	Their Contribution	Your Contribution	Shared Outcome	Mechanism for Exchange

This chapter allows marketing leaders to visualise partnerships as living systems of exchange, ensuring that all actors are engaged, empowered, and rewarded through strategic integration.

References

Blasco-Arcas, L., Hernandez-Ortega, B. I., & Jimenez-Martinez, J. (2016). *Engagement platforms: The role of emotions in fostering customer engagement and brand image in interactive media.* https://doi.org/10.1108/JSTP-12-2014-0286

Breidbach, C. F., & Brodie, R. J. (2017). Engagement platforms in the sharing economy: Conceptual foundations and research directions. *Journal of Service Theory and Practice, 27*(4), 761–777. https://doi.org/10.1108/JSTP-04-2016-0071

Bruce, H.L, Wilson, H.N., Macdonald, E.K. & Clarke, B. (2019) Resource integration, value creation and value destruction in collective consumption contexts, Journal of Business Research, 103, 173–185. doi:https://doi.org/10.1016/j.jbusres.2019.05.007.

Dabbish, L., Stuart, C., Tsay, J., & Herbsleb, J. (2012). Social coding in GitHub: Transparency and collaboration in an open software repository. In proceedings of the ACM 2012 conference on computer supported cooperative work (pp. 1277–1286). Association for Computing Machinery. https://doi.org/10.1145/2145204.2145396

Das, S. R. (2019). The future of Fintech. *Financial Management, 48*(4), 981–1007. https://doi.org/10.1111/fima.12297

Derave, T., Prince Sales, T., Gailly, F., & Poels, G. (2021). *Understanding digital marketplace business models: An ontology approach.* PoEM Workshops Computer Science. http://hdl.handle.net/1854/LU-8753007

Frow, P., McColl-Kennedy, J. R., & Payne, A. (2016). Co-creation practices: Their role in shaping a health care ecosystem. *Industrial Marketing Management, 56*, 24–39. https://doi.org/10.1016/j.indmarman.2016.03.007

Ghosh, N., Bhagavathy, S., & Thakur, J. (2022). Accelerating electric vehicle adoption: techno-economic assessment to modify existing fuel stations with fast charging infrastructure. *Clean Technologies and Environmental Policy., 24*, 1–14. https://doi.org/10.1007/s10098-022-02406-x

Hein, A., Weking, J., Schreieck, M., Wiesche, M., Böhm, M., & Krcmar, H. (2019). Value co-creation practices in business-to-business platform ecosystems. *Electronic Markets, 29*, 503–518. https://doi.org/10.1007/s12525-019-00337-y

Hibbert, S., Winklhofer, H., & Sobhy, M. (2012). Customers as resource integrators toward a model of customer learning. *Journal of Service Research, 15*, 247–261. https://doi.org/10.1177/1094670512442805

Hilbolling, S., Berends, H., Deken, F., & Tuertscher, P. (2019). Complementors as connectors: managing open innovation around digital product platforms. *R&D Management.* https://doi.org/10.1111/radm.12371

Jovanović, J. S., Vujadinovic, R., Mitreva, E., Fragassa, C., & Vujovic, A. (2020). The relationship between E-commerce and firm performance: The mediating role of internet Sales channels. *Sustainability., 12.* https://doi.org/10.3390/su12176993

Zhu, F., & Liu, Q. (2018). Competing with complementors: An empirical look at Amazon.com. Strategic Management Journal, 39(10), 2618–2642. doi:https://doi.org/10.1002/smj.2932.

Part IV

Technology as a Catalyst

16

Using Technology to Foster Co-Innovation

Innovation is no longer a solo endeavour. It is a team sport—a shared exercise in imagination, experimentation, and value creation. At the centre of this shift is *co-innovation*: the collaborative process through which businesses, customers, partners, and developers come together to build novel solutions.

Technology plays a pivotal role in enabling this shift. From digital platforms that connect diverse actors to advanced analytics that reveal unmet needs, technology equips ecosystems with the tools, infrastructure, and insight needed to turn collective potential into actual progress. In this chapter, we explore how technology drives co-innovation, what frameworks support its effective use, and how marketers can become active agents in this process.

Technology is the critical enabler that brings co-innovation to life. Digital platforms provide the connective tissue, allowing disparate participants to engage, contribute, and iterate in real time (Jovanovic et al., 2021). These platforms act as shared workspaces where ideas can be submitted, refined, tested, and scaled—often without geographic or organisational boundaries. They host hackathons, ideation forums, beta-testing environments, and collaboration tools that encourage experimentation, feedback, and iteration.

But beyond presence, technology also provides structure. Through advanced analytics and AI, co-innovation platforms gain the capacity to surface insights that human intuition alone would miss. Machines sift through vast streams of usage data, sentiment signals, and engagement patterns to highlight emerging trends, unmet customer needs, or novel patterns of behaviour. These data-driven insights guide participants towards high-impact opportunities and align their efforts with real market demand (Chandler et al., 2019).

Several frameworks make co-innovation processes more structured and effective. The co-creation spiral, for example, outlines a continuous loop where participants integrate resources, innovate together, and refine ideas based on feedback—before looping back to build further. Another useful model emphasises the engagement pyramid, identifying tiers of participants, from lurkers and observers to active contributors and leaders, each requiring different support, recognition, and access.

Technology supports both of these models. It enables tools such as contribution dashboards that track and visualise participation levels and outcomes across the spiral. It enables tiered participation environments where leaders have more privileges, beta users get earlier access, and first-time contributors receive extra encouragement. This combination of platform architecture and behavioural insight transforms abstract ideas into concrete action.

Marketers play a central role in orchestrating co-innovation. They do much more than simply promote new ideas—they design experiences that invite and sustain participation (Boudreau, 2010). They craft communications that signal openness: invitations to submit ideas, opportunities to gain visibility, and clear incentives for contribution. They amplify success stories and build narratives around collaborative breakthroughs. By showcasing how participants shaped outcomes, marketers reinforce that the platform belongs to the collective—not just the brand.

To truly harness technology-driven co-innovation, marketers must think like product managers, data scientists, and experience designers combined. They must understand which collaboration formats work best for different participant groups. Are developers motivated by hackathons and open APIs? Do enterprise customers respond to guided co-design workshops? Are ecosystem partners drawn into beta trials and feedback sessions? The answer shapes platform features, marketing mechanics, and success metrics.

Trust is another crucial dimension. As co-innovation invites external actors deeper into product processes, transparency becomes essential (FA et al., 2025). Technologies like blockchain can help here by recording contribution histories, enabling shared attribution and fair compensation. AI-powered data governance systems can demonstrate that ideas are treated securely, credit is accurately given, and intellectual property is protected. Marketing may not manage these systems directly—but it must understand and communicate them clearly to build confidence among participants.

Scaling co-innovation is also a technological feat (Choudary, 2021). Platforms often start with small cohorts—founders, early adopters, anchor partners. Technology enables these pilots to expand automatically as workflows, moderation rules, and feature templates are refined. An event platform, for instance, can enable external organisers initially and later roll out a partner-as-a-service model once best-practice guidelines are codified. Marketers amplify scale by promoting partner-built extensions, spotlighting community contributions, and inviting further participation—creating a ripple effect that accelerates innovation.

Finally, co-innovation enables continuous renewal. Unlike traditional product cycles, which follow discrete phases of ideation, launch, and sunset, platform innovation never stops (Kumaraswamy et al., 2018). New participant groups emerge, external trends shift, and fresh ideas surface constantly. Technology helps keep up this momentum—supporting ongoing contribution, recording feedback, and triggering updates in near real time. Through well-designed platform flows and marketing support, what starts as a joint project becomes a self-renewing innovation engine.

As you examine the contents of this chapter, the key lesson is clear: technology doesn't simply support co-innovation—it embeds it. It transforms fragmented interactions into structured collaboration, aligns participants with data-driven insight, and scales creativity through design and communication. The modern marketer—acting as co-innovation architect—harnesses this potential to craft platforms that evolve, adapt, and thrive—not because the brand shaped them, but because the ecosystem made them better together.

What Is Co-Innovation?

Co-innovation is more than working together—it is about building something none of the participants could achieve alone. It is characterised by:

1. Shared purpose and aligned incentives
2. Blending of complementary resources and expertise
3. Iterative feedback loops and mutual learning

Unlike traditional innovation models, where a single company controls the process, co-innovation emphasises openness (Jackson et al., 2018). It invites diverse contributions, acknowledges mutual dependence, and uses technology to streamline collaboration and accelerate value creation.

For example, a fintech platform might co-create a digital wallet by combining:

1. A bank's compliance expertise
2. A start-up's mobile UX design
3. A community's feedback on security concerns

The resulting product reflects the collective input of all parties—tailored, secure, and fit for market.

The Role of Digital Platforms

Platforms are the architectural backbone of co-innovation. They provide:

1. **Shared environments** for interaction and experimentation
2. **Standardised tools** like APIs and SDKs for integration
3. **Real-time data infrastructure** for continuous feedback

These platforms do more than facilitate communication—they embed trust, accountability, and alignment. They make contributions visible. They track versioning and updates. They allow co-innovators to test, iterate, and validate ideas before scaling.

The most successful platforms—whether in finance, mobility, or healthcare—actively curate the conditions for co-innovation. They don't just allow participation; they design for it.

Emerging Technologies Driving Co-Innovation

Several breakthrough technologies are transforming how ecosystems approach innovation:

1. **Artificial Intelligence (AI)**: AI analyses vast data sets, identifies trends, and enables personalised offerings. It empowers actors to co-create smarter, more responsive services.
2. **Blockchain**: By creating transparent, immutable records, blockchain builds trust among ecosystem participants. It ensures traceability and accountability in co-developed solutions—essential in regulated or high-stakes contexts.

3. **Internet of Things (IoT)**: IoT connects physical assets to digital interfaces, enabling real-time responsiveness. It allows ecosystems to co-develop solutions based on environmental or behavioural data.
4. **Cloud Computing**: Cloud enables scalable experimentation. It reduces the technical and cost barriers for participation, making co-innovation accessible across actor sizes.

Together, these technologies do more than increase speed—they broaden participation and deepen value.

Frameworks for Understanding Co-Innovation

To operationalise technology-driven co-innovation, two frameworks offer clarity:

1. **The Innovation Ecosystem Framework**

    This model maps the interplay of:

    - **Actors** (who contributes what)
    - **Resources** (what is available to integrate)
    - **Platforms** (how they connect and interact)

    It positions technology as the linchpin—the infrastructure that makes co-creation coherent and scalable.

2. **The Co-Innovation Continuum**

    This spectrum helps leaders assess:

    - Level of collaboration (from consultative to co-creative)
    - Technological complexity (from simple upgrades to transformative breakthroughs)

It reminds marketers and strategists that not all innovation must be radical—and that platforms can house a range of innovation types simultaneously.

Challenges to Navigate

While technology enables co-innovation, it also introduces specific barriers:

1. **Fragmented tech stacks**: Diverse actors often use different systems. Interoperability, standards, and shared APIs are critical for smooth collaboration.
2. **Inequitable access**: Not all ecosystem participants have equal capacity. Smaller players may lack the bandwidth or tools to contribute meaningfully.
3. **Security and privacy concerns**: With co-innovation comes data sharing. Clear protocols, encryption, and compliance frameworks must be in place to maintain trust.

Overcoming these challenges is a design task. It requires inclusive platform governance, robust onboarding, and intentional capability-building.

Co-Innovation in Action: Transforming Industries Through Collaboration

In healthcare, the integration of AI is revolutionising diagnostics (Sun et al., 2022). Collaborative efforts among clinicians, researchers, and technology firms have led to the development of AI-enabled diagnostic tools that enhance accuracy and improve patient outcomes.

The financial services sector is witnessing a transformation through blockchain technology (Haberley et al., 2019). Banks, regulators, and fintech companies are jointly developing blockchain-based payment systems, facilitating faster, more cost-effective, and transparent cross-border transactions.

Retail and e-commerce platforms are empowering merchants, developers, and consumers to co-create modular commerce experiences (Hänninen et al., 2018). This collaborative approach allows businesses to swiftly adapt to changing consumer demands and market trends. These examples illustrate a shift from isolated innovation to collaborative ecosystems, where shared efforts drive adaptability, inclusivity, and resilience.

Marketing's Evolving Role: From Storytelling to Co-Creation

Today, marketing transcends traditional storytelling, embracing co-creation as a core strategy. Marketers are now engaging customers as active contributors, involving them in idea generation, content creation, and product development. This participatory approach fosters deeper emotional connections and enhances brand loyalty.

The utilisation of technologies like AI and analytics enables marketers to refine campaigns in real time, responding swiftly to consumer feedback and behaviour. Platforms serve as infrastructures for customer co-creation, facilitating initiatives such as crowdsourced content and community-driven features. By transforming marketing into a collaborative endeavour, brands not only communicate value but also co-create it, turning messages into movements and customers into co-innovators.

But platforms—whether proprietary brand communities or third-party ecosystems—aren't just channels for delivery. They act as co-creation hubs (Mele et al., 2010). Think of crowdsourced design contests, user-led feature voting, or community forums driving product roadmaps. These are not one-off stunts—they reflect an intentional strategy to build feedback into the lifeblood of innovation.

Consider a consumer goods brand launching a product line extension. Rather than designing in a closed room, marketing teams might crowdsource scent suggestions, gather visual design concepts, or set up public polls to determine features. The result isn't just a product—but a co-created experience where the audience feels ownership (Ekman et al., 2021). The marketing narrative then becomes richer and more authentic—"designed with you," not just "for you."

This collaborative model also amplifies reach and impact. Customers who feel heard become vocal advocates—sharing stories, bringing in peers, and lending credibility that paid ads simply cannot match. Campaigns become living communities, fuelled by authentic voices rather than polished scripts.

Ultimately, co-creation elevates marketing from communication to construction. Brands don't just broadcast value—they build it with their audiences. The result? Messages that turn into movements and customers who step into the role of co-innovators.

As a guiding principle, marketing now becomes a form of co-architectural practice: inviting contribution, fostering reflection, iterating in response, and building together—bit by bit—something greater than what any one party could deliver alone.

Co-Innovation as Strategic Advantage

Using technology to foster co-innovation is not simply a functional choice—it is a strategic imperative. It unlocks:

1. New sources of differentiation
2. Faster learning cycles
3. Shared investment and reduced risk
4. Stronger, stickier relationships with ecosystem actors

It requires marketers to lead beyond the brand—and into the ecosystem. To be facilitators, storytellers, and bridge-builders. To shape not only what is said, but what is made—and how it is made, together.

Visual Framework: The Co-Innovation Technology Stack

Figure 16.1 presents a framework illustrating the layered architecture underpinning co-innovation in platform ecosystems. It highlights four interdependent layers that collectively enable insight-driven collaboration and shared value creation.

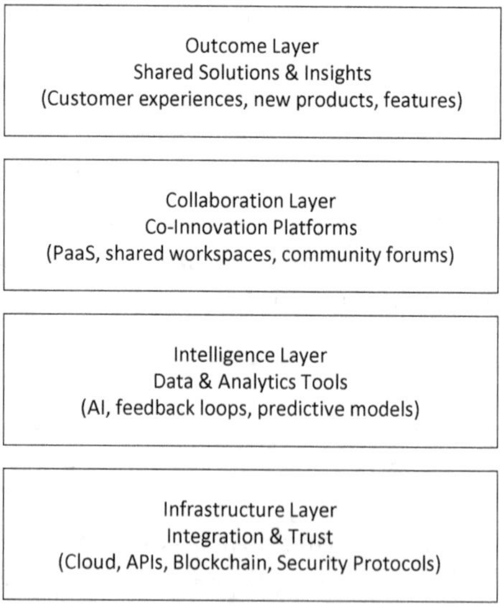

```
┌─────────────────────────────────────────────┐
│              Outcome Layer                  │
│         Shared Solutions & Insights         │
│ (Customer experiences, new products, features) │
└─────────────────────────────────────────────┘

┌─────────────────────────────────────────────┐
│            Collaboration Layer              │
│           Co-Innovation Platforms           │
│   (PaaS, shared workspaces, community forums) │
└─────────────────────────────────────────────┘

┌─────────────────────────────────────────────┐
│            Intelligence Layer               │
│          Data & Analytics Tools             │
│    (AI, feedback loops, predictive models)  │
└─────────────────────────────────────────────┘

┌─────────────────────────────────────────────┐
│           Infrastructure Layer              │
│            Integration & Trust              │
│  (Cloud, APIs, Blockchain, Security Protocols) │
└─────────────────────────────────────────────┘
```

Fig. 16.1 Co-Innovation Technology Stack

Table 16.1 Co-Innovation Opportunity Canvas—Template Grid

Element	Details
Shared goal	
Co-innovators	
Tech enablers	
Trust & Incentives	
Pilot description	
Success measures	

The *Co-Innovation Technology Stack* outlines a layered view of the technology stack enabling co-innovation in ecosystems and illustrates how co-innovation is built upon technical foundations that enable interaction, insight, and shared value creation—from infrastructure to outcomes.

> **Reflective Prompt: Where Does Co-Innovation Live in Your Strategy?**
>
> "Are you building marketing solutions in isolation – or architecting them within a broader ecosystem of shared innovation?"
>
> Reflect on:
>
> 1. How frequently you engage customers or partners in product or service design
> 2. Which technologies your teams are using to invite and scale collaboration
> 3. Where new ideas are coming from—and how they are being shaped
>
> Are your platforms places for transaction—or transformation?

> **Exercise: Co-Innovation Opportunity Canvas (Table 16.1)**
>
> 1. **Define the Shared Goal**
>   - What challenge or opportunity are you solving?
>   - Who else shares this challenge?
> 2. **Identify Potential Co-Innovators**
>   - Internal teams, customers, partners, developers?
>   - What do they know that you don't?
>   - What do you offer that could empower them?
> 3. **Map the Technology Enablers**
>   - What platforms or tools can support co-creation?

- Do you need APIs, data models, digital environments, or community engagement layers?

4. **Design for Trust and Incentives**
   - How will you protect data and intellectual property?
   - How will contributors be recognised or rewarded?

5. **Visualise Your Pilot**
   - Sketch your minimum viable co-innovation initiative.
   - Define success and metrics for participation, output, and mutual value.

This chapter helps leaders identify opportunities to embed co-innovation into their current operations while fostering a culture of experimentation, adaptability, and cross-functional collaboration.

References

Boudreau, K. J. (2010). Open platform strategies and innovation: Granting access vs. devolving control. *Management Science, 56*(10), 1849–1872. https://doi.org/10.1287/mnsc.1100.1215

Chandler, J., Danatzis, I., Wernicke, C., Akaka, M., & Reynolds, D. (2019). How does innovation emerge in a service ecosystem. *Journal of Service Research, 22*(1), 75–89. https://doi.org/10.1177/1094670518797479

Choudary, S. P. (2021). *Platform scale: How an emerging business model helps startups build large empires with minimum investment* (2nd ed.). Platform Thinking Labs.

Ekman, P., Rondell, J. G., & J.G., Anastasiadou, E., Kowalkowski, C., Raggio, R.D. & Thompson, S.M. (2021). Business actor engagement:exploring its antecedents and types. *Industrial Marketing Management, 98*, 179–192. https://doi.org/10.1016/j.indmarman.2021.08.009

FA, C., Ramezan Zadeh, M. T., Ozalp, H., & Volberda, H. W. (2025). The role of trust in a platform ecosystem: Exploring the impact of different trust dimensions on complementors' platform revenue. *Research Policy, 54(8), Article 104957*. https://doi.org/10.2139/ssrn.5180726

Frow, P., McColl-Kennedy, J. R., & Payne, A. (2016). Co-creation practices: Their role in shaping a health care ecosystem. *Industrial Marketing Management, 56*, 24–39. https://doi.org/10.1016/j.indmarman.2016.03.007

Haberly, D., Mcdonald-Korth, D., Urban, M., & Wójcik, D. (2019). Asset management as a digital platform industry: A global financial network perspective. *Geoforum, 106*, 167–181. https://doi.org/10.1016/j.geoforum.2019.08.009

Hänninen, M., Smedlund, A., & Mitronen, L. (2018). Digitalization in retailing: multi-sided platforms as drivers of industry transformation. *Baltic Journal of Management, 13*(2), 152–168. https://doi.org/10.1108/BJM-04-2017-0109

Jackson, K. T., Burgess, S., Toms, F., & Cuthbertson, E. L. (2018). Community engagement: Using feedback loops to empower residents and influence systemic change in culturally diverse communities. *Global Journal of Community Psychology Practice, 9*(2), 1–21. https://doi.org/10.17161/gjcpp.v9i2.20713

Jovanovic, M., Sjödin, D., & Parida, V. (2021). Co-evolution of platform architecture, platform services, and platform governance: Expanding the platform value of industrial digital platforms. *Technovation*. https://doi.org/10.1016/j.technovation.2020.102218

Kumaraswamy, A., Garud, R., & Ansari, S. (2018). Perspectives on disruptive innovations. *Journal of Management Studies, 55*, 1025–1042. https://doi.org/10.1111/joms.12399

Mele, C., Spena, T. R., & Colurcio, M. (2010). Co-creating value innovation through resource integration. *International Journal of Quality and Service Sciences., 2*, 60–78. https://doi.org/10.1108/17566691011026603

Sun, S., Zhang, J., Zhu, Y., Jiang, M., & Chen, S. (2022). Exploring users' willingness to disclose personal information in online healthcare communities: The role of satisfaction. *Technological Forecasting and Social Change, 178*, 121602. https://doi.org/10.1016/j.techfore.2022.121596

17

Case Studies—Successful Value Co-Creation in Fintech

The fintech sector exemplifies how collaborative innovation can redefine financial services. Through strategic partnerships and shared resources, fintech ecosystems have developed solutions that enhance customer experiences and expand market reach. What once was the domain of siloed institutions operating within rigid infrastructures has evolved into an open, dynamic ecosystem driven by shared resources and co-creation. At the heart of this transformation lies the principle of value co-creation—a process by which banks, fintech startups, developers, regulators, and end-users all contribute to building more responsive, inclusive, and engaging financial experiences. This chapter examines case studies that illustrate the principles and practices of effective value co-creation in fintech.

A compelling example of this shift is the rise of embedded finance. Rather than building financial infrastructure from scratch, non-financial platforms—such as e-commerce apps or gig economy services—partner with fintech providers to integrate payment solutions, insurance products, and credit tools directly into the user experience. This collaboration allows each actor to do what they do best: platforms focus on user experience and engagement, while fintechs deliver robust, compliant financial functionality (Hendricks et al., 2024). The result is a seamless experience for users and shared growth for all participants.

Open banking, another transformative force, has demonstrated how structured data sharing and API (Application Programming Interface) connectivity can unlock new possibilities. By exposing secure, standardised data interfaces to third-party developers, traditional banks have enabled a wave of innovation (Ahmed & Kowalkowski, 2025). Fintechs are now building apps that provide real-time spending insights, personalised budgeting tools, and smart credit scoring. These services are made possible not by disruption, but by cooperation—platforms like **Plaid** and **Tink** have emerged to facilitate this flow of data between institutions and innovators, ensuring users are in control while still driving collective benefit.

In lending, co-creation is also redefining how credit is accessed and managed. Marketplace lenders often rely on a hybrid model, where platforms connect borrowers with a network of capital providers and fintech partners handle credit scoring and underwriting algorithms. By working together, they can serve underserved segments, deliver faster approvals, and manage risk more effectively than any single entity operating alone.

Security and identity verification present further opportunities for collaborative value. As onboarding and compliance requirements grow more complex, fintechs increasingly rely on specialist partners to deliver services (Das, 2019). such as digital ID verification, biometric authentication, and fraud detection. These integrations are not merely technical—they signal trust. When users see that a platform has partnered with a known verification provider, confidence increases, onboarding is streamlined, and brand reputation is strengthened.

Co-branded rewards systems further exemplify the power of ecosystem thinking. Fintech platforms collaborate with retail and service partners to offer integrated loyalty programmes that reward users for activity across the network. These systems drive engagement and retention by creating a shared sense of value—every interaction deepens the user's connection to the platform and its partners.

Throughout these examples, a pattern emerges: the most effective fintech innovations are not isolated achievements, but collaborative constructions. Platforms that embrace co-creation cultivate more than features (Haberly et al., 2019)—they nurture relationships, trust, and adaptive learning. For marketers, this means shifting from solitary brand building to ecosystem storytelling. Successful fintech marketing today is about championing shared journeys, highlighting collaborative achievements, and positioning the brand as a connector within a larger web of mutual benefit.

In a sector that depends on trust, clarity, and user empowerment, co-creation is not only a growth lever—it is a competitive necessity. Fintech ecosystems thrive when they prioritise openness, respect user agency, and allow each actor to contribute meaningfully to shared outcomes. This is where marketing and strategy intersect: by curating partnerships, facilitating dialogue, and amplifying ecosystem success stories, marketers ensure that value is not only created—but recognised, shared, and scaled across the network.

Redefining Payments: The Emergence of Digital Wallets

Digital wallets have transformed payment systems by integrating the capabilities of fintech start-ups, traditional banks, and merchants. One notable example is **Mastercard's Track Business Payment Service**, which has been developed in collaboration with several global banks to offer a **B2B digital wallet solution**. This solution enables businesses to securely store, manage, and authenticate payment credentials across a network of trading partners.

In this case, banks contributed financial infrastructure and access to corporate client data, while Mastercard brought expertise in user experience design, payment tokenisation, and data security. Merchants and enterprise platforms further enhanced the ecosystem (Carida et al., 2022) by integrating the solution into ERP and procurement systems, often layering in incentives such as early payment discounts and automated reconciliation features.

The outcome has been a more seamless and secure B2B payment experience—providing convenience for business users, boosting transaction volumes for banks, and giving merchants improved visibility into payment behaviour. This case underscores the role of ecosystem collaboration, reciprocal resource integration, and shared value creation in the evolution of digital wallets for the B2B space.

Enhancing Financial Inclusion: Microfinance Platforms

Fintech has played a pivotal role in promoting financial inclusion, particularly through platforms targeting underserved businesses. One illustrative example is **FlexiPay**, a B2B payment and financing solution developed by **Standard Chartered** in collaboration with fintech partner **Tazapay**. The initiative is designed to provide working capital and facilitate secure payments for small and medium-sized enterprises (SMEs) that often face barriers to accessing traditional credit (Blaschke & Brosius, 2018).

The fintech contributed a streamlined, digital-first platform for invoice financing and payment management. Standard Chartered provided institutional capital and regulatory expertise, while local banks supported the ecosystem by assisting with KYC procedures and onboarding in key emerging markets. Trade networks and digital marketplaces further enriched the solution by integrating **FlexiPay** into SME-facing platforms—helping businesses unlock cash flow and establish transaction histories.

This collaborative model has enabled small businesses to engage more actively in cross-border trade, improving liquidity while offering financial institutions new access points to underserved market segments. The **FlexiPay** case highlights the importance of ecosystem partnerships and co-creation in driving scalable B2B financial inclusion.

Streamlining Compliance: Regulatory Technology (RegTech) Solutions

RegTech has become an essential domain for addressing the increasing complexity of financial compliance through collaborative innovation. One notable example is **ComplyAdvantage**, a RegTech company that developed a platform to automate compliance checks related to AML (anti-money-laundering) and KYC (know-your-customer) regulations. ComplyAdvantage works with global banks that contribute anonymised transaction data and engaged with regulators to ensure alignment with evolving compliance standards.

The resulting platform leverages AI and ML to analyse transaction patterns, flag suspicious activity in real time, and generate dynamic risk scoring—significantly enhancing the efficiency and accuracy of compliance workflows. This collaboration benefited banks by reducing manual compliance costs (Blajer-Gołębiewska et al., 2018), accelerating onboarding processes, and improving risk mitigation. For regulators, it helped standardise reporting and strengthened the industry's capability to proactively detect financial crime.

The case of ComplyAdvantage demonstrates how co-creation in regulated environments can deliver scalable, intelligent compliance solutions that benefit multiple stakeholders across the financial ecosystem.

Democratising Investments: The Rise of Robo-Advisors

Robo-advisors have transformed the investment landscape by using algorithm-driven models to deliver accessible, low-cost financial planning. One illustrative case is **Scalable Capital**, a digital investment platform that was developed through collaboration with institutional asset manager **BlackRock** and real-time data providers. The initiative specifically targeted younger, tech-oriented investors underserved by traditional wealth management (Constantinides et al., 2018).

In this model, Scalable Capital built the digital platform and ML algorithms to personalise investment strategies based on user preferences, financial goals, and changing market conditions. BlackRock contributed deep expertise in portfolio construction, ETF allocation, and risk modelling, while data providers enabled the platform to adapt to real-time market movements—ensuring dynamic and relevant investment guidance.

The result was a scalable robo-advisor solution that lowered barriers to entry for novice investors, offering professional-grade portfolio management with minimal initial capital. At the same time, it provided asset managers like BlackRock with a digital channel to reach new demographics and scale distribution in a cost-effective way.

This case highlights how co-creation in fintech can expand financial inclusion while unlocking new growth pathways for institutional investment firms in the digital era.

Frameworks for Understanding Value Co-Creation in Fintech

The success of these case studies can be analysed through established frameworks:

1. **Ecosystem Co-Creation Framework**: Emphasises resource integration, collaborative governance, and iterative innovation as key elements driving co-creation.
2. **Co-Innovation Matrix**: Categorises co-creation efforts based on collaboration levels and complexity, aiding in strategic planning and execution.

These frameworks provide structured approaches to managing co-creation, ensuring alignment of goals and optimisation of outcomes within fintech ecosystems.

Challenges in Value Co-Creation

Despite its advantages, value co-creation in fintech faces several challenges:

1. **Diverse Objectives**: Aligning the varied goals of different stakeholders requires effective governance and communication.
2. **Trust and Security**: Sharing sensitive data necessitates robust data protection measures to maintain trust among participants.
3. **Scalability**: As ecosystems expand, managing complexity and ensuring equitable value distribution become increasingly challenging.

Addressing these challenges is crucial for sustaining successful co-creation initiatives.

Marketing Through Collaboration: The Strategic Impact of Co-Creation

In the fintech sector, value co-creation is reshaping the way marketing operates. Rather than positioning customers and partners as end recipients, marketers now engage them as active contributors to innovation. This participatory approach enhances engagement by ensuring that solutions reflect real user needs and preferences, deepening resonance with target audiences.

Those who take part in co-creation often evolve into authentic brand advocates. Having played a role in shaping a product or service, they become invested in its success (Gummesson & Mele, 2010) and willingly share their experiences, amplifying reach and credibility through word of mouth.

By actively engaging customers, partners, developers, and even regulators in the innovation process, marketers shift from being storytellers to becoming ecosystem architects. They invite actors to co-design products, provide real-world feedback, and help refine functionalities. This participatory model ensures offerings deeply reflect user needs and market expectations, while fostering a sense of ownership—participants feel personally invested in the solution's success.

When users take part in co-creation—whether through beta-testing, ideation workshops, or early-access programmes—they often evolve into passionate brand advocates. Their endorsement is genuine; they are not merely consumers, but contributors who helped shape the product. This authenticity translates into powerful word-of-mouth promotion. A well-timed social media recommendation from a user who co-developed a feature often carries more weight and credibility than traditional advertising ever could.

Equally important, co-creation provides marketers with compelling narratives. Stories of collaboration, shared problem-solving, and mutual achievement become powerful tools for brand differentiation. These narratives convey more than functionality, they highlight trust, and the human side of innovation. These stories emphasise mutual achievement, transparency, and shared purpose (Van Alstyne et al., 2016). A campaign that showcases how a user's idea led to a new budgeting feature does more than highlight functionality—it communicates innovation as a collective journey and underscores a brand grounded in empathy and trust.

Embracing co-creation also strengthens a brand's relevance. Collaborative development means solutions emerge in response to real-time signals—behavioural data, user sentiment, market trends. Products evolve with the ecosystem rather than lag behind it, keeping the platform agile and adaptive. This alignment boosts loyalty: participants feel heard, valued, and respected.

Ultimately, co-creation moves marketing beyond transactional messaging. It transforms marketers into facilitators of ecosystems that prioritise relationships over rhetoric. They cultivate environments where trust is built not through slogans, but through shared achievements and mutual accountability (Blasco-Arcas et al., 2016). Product launches become collective milestones. Metrics shift towards engagement depth, adoption rates among co-creators, and the volume of user-generated advocacy.

The strategic impact of co-creation in fintech is profound. It enables marketers to build solutions in partnership with stakeholders, generate narratives that resonate at an emotional and intellectual level, and develop ecosystems rooted in trust and shared purpose. This collaborative approach turns marketing into a catalyst for innovation, engagement, and sustained competitive advantage in a rapidly evolving financial landscape.

In summary, these case studies illustrate the transformative potential of value co-creation in fintech. By fostering collaboration among diverse stakeholders, fintech ecosystems can develop innovative solutions that address complex challenges and create shared value.

Visual Framework: The Fintech Value Co-Creation Ecosystem

Figure 17.1 introduces a framework highlighting the multi-actor model that visualises co-creation dynamics within fintech ecosystems. At its core is the Fintech Platform Orchestrator, which plays a pivotal role in in connecting and facilitating reciprocal value exchange between key ecosystem actors—enabling trust, interoperability, and value exchange among diverse actors:

- **Start-ups:** Bring technological innovation and UX capabilities.
- **Banks:** Contribute financial infrastructure and customer bases.
- **Regulators:** Provide stability and trust through oversight.
- **Customers:** Engage as co-creators through feedback and participation.

The *Fintech Value Co-creation Ecosystem* illustrates how together, these actors co-create value through a cyclical, multi-directional flow of resources, insights, and collaboration. The orchestrator ensures strategic alignment, compliance, and iterative innovation.

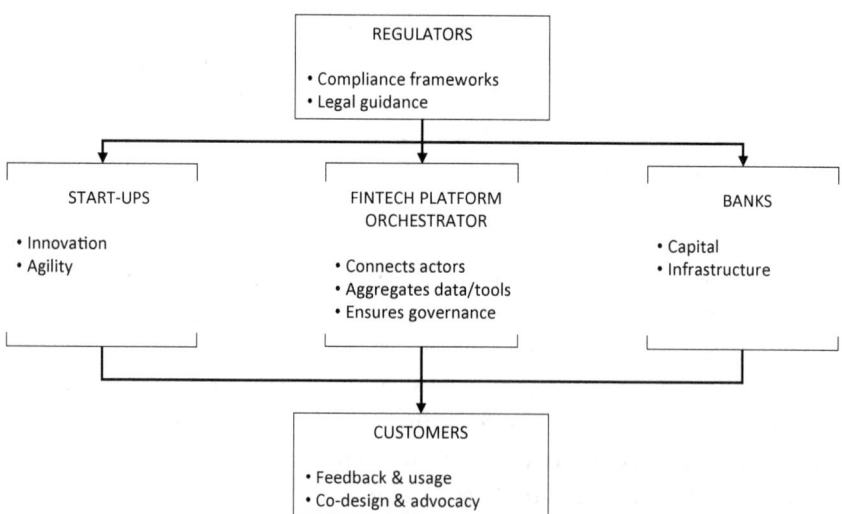

Fig. 17.1 Fintech Value Co-Creation Ecosystem

Reflective Prompt: Where Does Value Co-Creation Exist in Your Ecosystem Strategy?

"Are you collaborating to scale your innovation—or just coordinating for efficiency?"

Reflect on:

1. How actively do your partners contribute to the development of new financial products or services?
2. What mechanisms are in place to incorporate user feedback into platform improvements?
3. Are your compliance processes part of your innovation strategy—or a separate, siloed function?
4. In what ways does your marketing reflect and reinforce the collaborative nature of your ecosystem?
5. Are you positioning your organisation as a facilitator of shared value—or as a single-point solution?

Exercise: Fintech Co-Creation Readiness Canvas

This canvas helps assess your current ecosystem dynamics and prepare for value co-creation at scale.

1. **Define the Shared Value Goal**
   - What customer or market problem are you collectively addressing?
   - How is this need underserved today?

2. **Identify Co-Creation Stakeholders**
   - Which actors are currently involved? (e.g. banks, start-ups, regulators, end-users)
   - Who is missing that could elevate the value of your offering?

3. **Map Resource Contributions**
   - What unique data, infrastructure, or expertise can each stakeholder bring?
   - Where are the dependencies—and where is there overlap?

4. **Establish Governance Foundations**
   - What legal, ethical, and trust protocols need to be in place?
   - How will data be shared? How will value be distributed?

5. **Design and Pilot Your Co-Creation Use Case**
   - Choose one area—compliance automation, financial inclusion, or digital payments.
   - Define the MVP for a co-created solution.
   - Set metrics to measure mutual value and ecosystem participation.

This chapter equips you to lead as a fintech platform orchestrator—connecting diverse actors to enable continuous, compliant, and collaborative value creation at scale.

References

Ahmed, T., & Kowalkowski, C. (2025). The new industry playbook: Digital service innovation in multi-platform ecosystems. *Journal of Enterprise Information Management. Advance online publication.* https://doi.org/10.1108/JEIM-05-2024-0240

Blajer-Gołębiewska, A., Wach, D., & Kos, M. (2018). Financial risk information avoidance. *Economic, Research-Ekonomska Istraživanja, 31*(1), 521–536. https://doi.org/10.1080/1331677X.2018.1439396

Blaschke, M. & Brosius, M. (2018). Digital platforms: Balancing control and generativity.

Blasco-Arcas, L., Hernandez-Ortega, B. I., & Jimenez-Martinez, J. (2016). *Engagement platforms: The role of emotions in fostering customer engagement and brand image in interactive media.* https://doi.org/10.1108/JSTP-12-2014-0286

Block, P. (2016). *The empowered manager positive political skills at work. Business & Economics.* Stanford University Press.

Carida, A., Colurcio, M., Edvardsson, B., & Pastore, A. (2022). *Creating harmony through a plethora of interests, resources, and actors: The challenging task of orchestrating the service ecosystem.* https://doi.org/10.1108/JSTP-06-2021-0110

Constantinides, P., Henfridsson, O., & Parker, G. G. (2018). Platforms and infrastructures in the digital age. *Journal of Information Systems Research, 29*(2), 381–400. https://doi.org/10.1287/isre.2018.0794

Das, S. R. (2019). The future of Fintech. *Financial Management, 48*(4), 981–1007. https://doi.org/10.1111/fima.12297

Gummesson, E., & Mele, C. (2010). Marketing as value co-creation through network interaction and resource integration. *Journal of Business Market Management, 4*(4), 181–198. https://doi.org/10.1007/s12087-010-0044-2

Haberly, D., Mcdonald-Korth, D., Urban, M., & Wójcik, D. (2019). Asset management as a digital platform industry: A global financial network perspective. *Geoforum, 106*, 167–181. https://doi.org/10.1016/j.geoforum.2019.08.009

Hendricks, L., Matthyssens, P., & Kowalkowski, C. (2024). The co-evolution of actor engagement and value co-creation on digital platforms: Evidence from the asset management industry. *Journal of Business & Industrial Marketing.* https://doi.org/10.1016/j.ijpe.2024.109467

Palmié, M., Miehé, L., Oghazi, P., Parida, V., & Wincent, J. (2022). The evolution of the digital service ecosystem and digital business model innovation in retail:

The emergence of meta-ecosystems and the value of physical interactions. *Technological Forecasting and Social Change, 177*, 121496. https://doi.org/10.1016/j.techfore.2022.121496

Van Alstyne, M. W., Parker, G. G., & Choudary, S. P. (2016). Pipelines, platforms, and the new rules of strategy. *Harvard Business Review, 94*(4), 54–62.

18

Challenges and Opportunities for Marketers

Value co-creation has emerged as a transformative approach in modern marketing, enabling businesses to collaborate with customers, partners, and other stakeholders to generate shared value. This collaborative model offers significant benefits, including enhanced innovation, deeper customer engagement, and increased loyalty. However, it also presents unique challenges that marketers must navigate to harness its full potential.

When marketers invite external voices into product design, service development, or storytelling, co-creation ignites innovation rooted in real-world insight. Customers propose functional additions, partners share data that enhances analytics, and users contribute brand stories that enrich campaigns. This collaborative environment accelerates learning, ensuring solutions resonate because they originate from genuine needs, not internal assumptions (Brousseau & Penard, 2007). From a relationship perspective, co-creation elevates engagement well beyond clicks and conversions.

Participants invest emotional and creative capital, becoming active partners rather than passive consumers. This investment leads to attachment—the kind that makes contributors true advocates. Seeing one's input influence outcomes builds a sense of ownership uncommon in traditional marketing models. These advocates amplify brand narratives organically, offering authentic endorsements that resonate deeply across personal and professional networks.

The benefits are powerful and interconnected. Innovation cycles shorten as ideas move quickly from user insight to prototype. Co-developed features often become distinctive, difficult for competitors to replicate. Brands demonstrate transparency by showcasing collaborative roadmaps and crediting contributors, reinforcing consumer trust. Meanwhile, early co-creators evolve into brand ambassadors whose stories extend reach far beyond traditional advertising.

However, co-creation brings unique challenges. Contributors expect their input to matter. Without feedback loops and accountability, engagement diminishes. Marketers must establish transparent governance—setting clear expectations, deadlines, and follow-ups—to build trust. Equitable recognition is also crucial: whether through public acknowledgment, partner features, or access to exclusive content, contributors need to feel valued.

Quality control poses another challenge. Diverse inputs can vary in quality, tone, or technical compatibility (Blaschke & Brosius, 2018). That's why marketing must collaborate with product and engineering teams to define and enforce standards—such as API guidelines, moderation policies, and design templates—to maintain consistency and uphold user experience.

Not every actor wants the same level of participation. To accommodate varying commitment levels, marketers should design tiered engagement paths—from simple surveys and feedback forums to in-depth innovation workshops and advisory panels—ensuring everyone can contribute at the level they prefer.

To succeed, marketers must foster a co-creative culture. This means hosting hackathons, ideation workshops, and pilot programmes that bring together diverse voices. Mapping user journeys helps identify critical moments for contribution—whether early in product development or in shaping marketing content. Systems of feedback and recognition are necessary to close the loop on contributions, with public shout-outs, contributor badges, and story highlights celebrating participants' impact.

Traditional metrics like impressions or downloads fall short in this context (Alaimo & Kallinikos, 2021). Co-creation demands new indicators: frequency of contributions, depth of collaboration, adoption of user-generated features, and sentiment around participation. These metrics reflect the health and momentum of the ecosystem.

In doing this well, marketing becomes more than a function—it becomes a force for collective creativity. Co-creation transforms marketing into meaning-making, moving it from delivering messages to building movements. While demanding in its implementation, the rewards are immense: agile innovation, resilient customer relationships, and a brand ecosystem that thrives in constant dialogue and evolution. In an age where personalisation, authenticity, and community drive customer choice, co-creation isn't just a tactic—it's a strategic advantage. Brands and businesses that embrace it will not just succeed—they will define the future of marketing.

Navigating the Complexities of Co-Creation

One of the primary challenges in value co-creation is managing the complexity of interactions within diverse ecosystems. Co-creation requires integrating resources and perspectives from multiple actors, each with distinct goals and expectations. For instance, in a fintech platform, financial institutions may prioritise regulatory compliance, while startups focus on agility and innovation. Aligning these differing priorities necessitates careful coordination and clear communication to achieve a shared vision.

Maintaining trust among participants is another critical concern. Co-creation often involves sharing sensitive data and intellectual property. Ensuring ethical and secure use of these contributions is essential for building and sustaining trust (FA et al., 2025). Implementing robust governance structures and transparent practices can address concerns around data privacy and equitable value distribution.

Engagement fatigue poses an additional challenge. As co-creation becomes more prevalent, participants may feel overwhelmed by the demands on their time and resources. Customers, in particular, may disengage if they perceive their contributions are undervalued or the process is overly burdensome (Choudary, 2021). Marketers must balance fostering meaningful participation with respecting stakeholders' limits.

Scalability is also a significant hurdle. As ecosystems expand, coordinating interactions and maintaining engagement quality becomes increasingly complex. Investing in technology and processes that support effective scaling is crucial to preserving the integrity of co-creation efforts.

Leveraging Opportunities for Innovation and Growth

Despite these challenges, value co-creation offers unparalleled opportunities for marketers to innovate and build deeper connections with their audiences. Personalisation stands out as a significant benefit. By involving customers directly in the design and development of products and services, marketers can tailor offerings to individual needs and preferences, enhancing satisfaction and fostering loyalty.

Co-creation also enables marketers to tap into the collective creativity and expertise of their stakeholders. Collaborating with partners, customers, and even competitors can lead to innovative solutions that would be unattainable independently (Gummesson & Mele, 2010). For example, in a financial ecosystem, banks and fintech startups might co-develop digital tools that simplify complex financial processes, benefiting all participants.

Additionally, co-creation generates authentic narratives about collaboration and impact. Marketers can highlight stakeholders' contributions, showcasing how their efforts have shaped final outcomes. These stories build trust and differentiate the brand in a crowded marketplace.

Engaging directly with customers and partners also provides real-time insights into their needs and behaviours. These insights inform more effective strategies, enabling businesses to adapt quickly to changing market conditions and customer expectations.

Frameworks for Effective Co-Creation

To navigate the challenges and capitalise on the opportunities of value co-creation, marketers can employ several frameworks:

1. **Ecosystem Alignment Framework**: Emphasises shared goals, clear communication, and collaborative governance to reduce conflicts and foster unity within the ecosystem.
2. **Engagement Continuum Model**: Categorises stakeholders based on their level of participation, helping marketers nurture different types of engagement without overburdening participants.
3. **Trust-Value Matrix**: Focuses on building high levels of trust while ensuring equitable value distribution among participants, fostering long-term commitment and engagement.

The Role of Technology in Enhancing Co-Creation

Technology plays a pivotal role in overcoming co-creation challenges and amplifying its benefits. Digital platforms provide the infrastructure for seamless interaction, offering tools for collaboration, data sharing, and resource integration (Hendricks et al., 2024). For instance, a fintech platform might use APIs to enable real-time data exchange between banks, startups, and customers, facilitating co-creation efforts.

AI and ML further enhance the co-creation process by analysing data, predicting trends, and optimising interactions. These technologies help marketers identify innovation opportunities, tailor strategies to individual needs, and streamline complex processes.

Blockchain technology addresses trust and transparency challenges by providing secure and immutable records of transactions. In ecosystems involving sensitive information, such as healthcare or finance, blockchain fosters confidence among participants, encouraging them to contribute their resources and expertise.

Real-World Applications: Transforming Challenges into Opportunities

Real-world examples illustrate how marketers have successfully navigated co-creation challenges to unlock its opportunities:

1. **Retail Sector: BigCommerce**—Navigating Co-Creation for Personalised Commerce:

   BigCommerce collaborated with merchants and tech partners to co-create personalised shopping experiences. Marketers played a key role in interpreting customer data, aligning partner capabilities, and orchestrating joint go-to-market strategies (Kumaraswamy et al., 2018). By navigating integration and brand consistency challenges, they helped implement AI-driven recommendations that boosted engagement and sales across diverse retail environments.

2. **Financial Industry: CredAble**—Marketing Co-Creation in Digital Lending:

   CredAble partnered with leading banks and compliance providers to build a digital lending platform for underserved SMEs. Marketers were instrumental in shaping a unified value proposition across partners, managing trust in a regulated environment, and driving adoption through education-led campaigns (Oliva & Kallenberg, 2003). Their efforts turned a complex co-creation process into a scalable solution that expanded access to business credit.

Redefining the Marketing Role

Value co-creation is transforming marketers into facilitators of collaboration and drivers of innovation. By embracing co-creation principles, marketers can build ecosystems that deliver superior value, foster loyalty, and create lasting relationships with their audiences.

While managing complexity, maintaining trust, and scaling interactions are significant challenges, the opportunities to innovate, personalise, and differentiate are substantial. Marketers who effectively navigate these challenges will not only succeed in an ecosystem-driven economy but also lay the groundwork for sustainable growth and competitive advantage.

This shift requires a radical transformation of mindset and practice. Marketers must design experiences that enable collaboration: from hackathons and innovation sprints to ideation platforms and peer reviews (Kumaraswamy et al., 2018). Rather than broadcast campaigns, success comes from building interactive environments where stakeholders can contribute—co-designing solutions, producing content, and sharing insights. This emphasis on mutual contribution transforms the brand into a conversation and the marketing function into a community architect and innovation steward.

Yet with opportunity comes complexity. Managing co-creative ecosystems means maintaining trust, ensuring quality, and scaling engagement. Marketing leaders must establish transparent governance processes for vetting contributions, safeguarding data, and equitably recognising participants. They need systems to curate and elevate high-quality inputs, while gently guiding activity to align with platform norms and goals. Scalability depends on designing tiered contribution paths—from simple feedback loops to deeper participation like beta-testing or co-production teams. This creates a structured, yet inclusive, funnel for engagement.

Trust is another cornerstone. In co-creation, it blooms through feedback, acknowledgement, and shared ownership (Palmié et al., 2022). When contributors see their impact—through public credits, feature tags, partner showcases—they become advocates. This not only multiplies reach through word-of-mouth but also strengthens brand authenticity and emotional connection.

The upside is profound. Co-creation accelerates innovation cycles by deriving insights directly from end-users, tapping into diverse perspectives and grounded experience. Marketers gain access to richer narratives—stories of collaboration, problem-solving, and community that resonate far more powerfully than traditional content. These narratives differentiate the brand while reinforcing ecosystem culture and values (Van Alstyne et al., 2016).

The real winners will be those who build and manage these ecosystems well. Metrics shift from impressions and click-rates to measuring depth of interaction: number of contributions, conversion from contributor to advocate, feature adoption rates—indicators of organic momentum and collaborative dynamism.

Redefining the marketing role also means embedding marketing within product, tech, and customer-success teams. The most effective co-creation campaigns stem from cross-functional integration—where marketing co-leads innovation alongside engineers, designers, and community managers.

Ultimately, value co-creation repositions marketing as a mindset, not just a strategy. It marks a move from one-way communication to mutual contribution; from controlling narratives to weaving shared stories; from isolated transactions to interconnected relationships rooted in trust and co-innovation (Liu, Wang, & Su, 2023). Such a shift lays the foundation for more resilient growth and sustainable differentiation—allowing brands to thrive not just in the marketplace, but in ecosystem-driven futures where success is measured by shared progress, not just sales.

In accepting this new role, marketers become more than promoters—they become architects of participation, stewards of collaboration, and leaders of ecosystems that innovate, adapt, and grow together.

Visual Framework: The Co-Creation Challenge-Opportunity Balance

Figure 18.1 introduces a framework highlighting the challenges in ecosystem integration and the engagement potential. It illustrates the dynamic tensions marketers must navigate in ecosystem-driven initiatives. As ecosystems scale, so too does the complexity of collaboration—but this complexity also unlocks greater opportunities for differentiated value creation, innovation, and engagement.

This *Co-Creation Tension* matrix maps four key dimensions of co-creation tension—each presenting both a strategic challenge and a growth opportunity, the model equips marketing leaders to actively balance and harness these tensions to enable effective, high-impact ecosystem strategies.

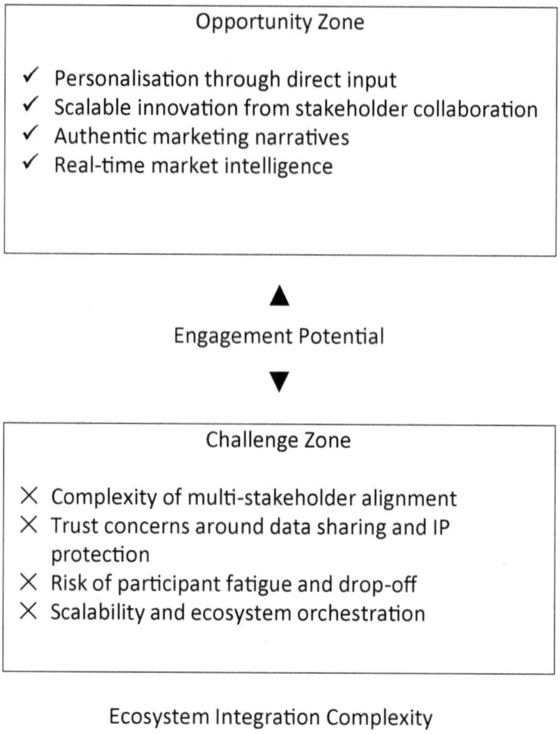

```
┌─────────────────────────────────────────────┐
│              Opportunity Zone               │
│                                             │
│  ✓ Personalisation through direct input     │
│  ✓ Scalable innovation from stakeholder     │
│    collaboration                            │
│  ✓ Authentic marketing narratives           │
│  ✓ Real-time market intelligence            │
│                                             │
└─────────────────────────────────────────────┘
                      ▲
              Engagement Potential
                      ▼
┌─────────────────────────────────────────────┐
│              Challenge Zone                 │
│                                             │
│  ✗ Complexity of multi-stakeholder alignment│
│  ✗ Trust concerns around data sharing and IP│
│    protection                               │
│  ✗ Risk of participant fatigue and drop-off │
│  ✗ Scalability and ecosystem orchestration  │
│                                             │
└─────────────────────────────────────────────┘
            Ecosystem Integration Complexity
```

Fig. 18.1 Co-Creation Challenge-Opportunity Balance

The Co-Creation Tension Matrix

This matrix (Table 18.1) maps the dualities marketers must navigate in value co-creation initiatives:

Reflective Prompt: Balancing the Scales of Co-Creation

"Are your co-creation efforts tipping towards complexity or opportunity?"

Reflect on:

1. How do you align diverse stakeholder objectives within your co-creation initiatives?
2. What measures are in place to ensure data security and build trust among participants?
3. How do you maintain participant engagement without causing fatigue?
4. What strategies do you employ to scale co-creation efforts effectively?

Table 18.1 The Co-Creation Tension Matrix

Dimension	Challenge	Opportunity
Ecosystem complexity	Diverse stakeholder goals and expectations complicate alignment	Diverse perspectives foster innovation and comprehensive solutions
Trust management	Sharing sensitive data raises concerns about misuse and security	Transparent practices build trust and encourage deeper collaboration
Participant engagement	Risk of stakeholder fatigue due to over-involvement	Active engagement leads to personalised offerings and increased loyalty
Scalability	Coordinating growing interactions can dilute engagement quality	Scalable platforms enable broader reach and sustained co-creation efforts

Exercise: Co-Creation Strategy Canvas

This canvas assists in evaluating and enhancing your co-creation strategies by addressing key challenges and leveraging opportunities.

1. **Stakeholder Alignment**
   - List all stakeholders involved in your co-creation initiatives.
   - Identify their primary goals and expectations.
   - Determine areas of alignment and potential conflict.
2. **Trust and Security Measures**
   - Assess the types of sensitive data shared during co-creation.
   - Evaluate existing data protection and privacy measures.
   - Plan enhancements to build and maintain trust.
3. **Engagement Management**
   - Review current participant engagement levels and feedback.
     - Identify signs of engagement fatigue or drop-off.
       - Develop strategies to sustain meaningful participation.
4. **Scalability Planning**
   - Analyse the scalability of current co-creation platforms and processes.
   - Identify bottlenecks or limitations in scaling efforts.
   - Design solutions to enable effective scaling without compromising quality.

This chapter systematically addresses areas where marketers can transform the inherent challenges of value co-creation into strategic opportunities for innovation and growth.

References

Alaimo, C., & Kallinikos, J. (2021). Managing by data: Algorithmic categories and organizing. *Organization Studies, 42*(6), 875–895. https://doi.org/10.1177/0170840620934062

Blaschke, M., & Brosius, M. (2018). Digital platforms: Balancing control and generativity. In Proceedings of the 39th International Conference on Information Systems (ICIS).

Brousseau, E., & Penard, T. (2007). The economics of digital business models: A framework for analyzing the economics of platforms. *Review of Network Economics, 6*(2), 81–110. https://doi.org/10.2202/1446-9022.1112

Choudary, S. P. (2021). *Platform scale: How an emerging business model helps startups build large empires with minimum investment* (2nd ed.). Platform Thinking Labs.

FA, C., Ramezan Zadeh, M. T., Ozalp, H., & Volberda, H. W. (2025). The role of trust in a platform ecosystem: Exploring the impact of different trust dimensions on complementors' platform revenue. *Research Policy, 54*(8), Article 104957. https://doi.org/10.2139/ssrn.5180726

Gummesson, E., & Mele, C. (2010). Marketing as value co-creation through network interaction and resource integration. *Journal of Business Market Management, 4*(4), 181–198. https://doi.org/10.1007/s12087-010-0044-2

Hendricks, L., Matthyssens, P., & Kowalkowski, C. (2024). The co-evolution of actor engagement and value co-creation on digital platforms: Evidence from the asset management industry. *Journal of Business & Industrial Marketing.* https://doi.org/10.1016/j.ijpe.2024.109467

Kumaraswamy, A., Garud, R., & Ansari, S. (2018). Perspectives on disruptive innovations. *Journal of Management Studies, 55*(7), 1025–1042. https://doi.org/10.1111/joms.12399

Liu, X., Wang, W., & Su, Y. (2023). Leveraging complementary resources through relational capital to improve Alliance performance under an uncertain environment: A moderated mediation analysis. *Sustainability, 15*(1), 310. https://doi.org/10.3390/su15010310

Oliva, R., & Kallenberg, R. (2003). Managing the transition from products to services. *International Journal of Service Industry Management, 14*(2), 160–172. https://doi.org/10.1108/09564230310474138

Palmié, M., Miehé, L., Oghazi, P., Parida, V., & Wincent, J. (2022). The evolution of the digital service ecosystem and digital business model innovation in retail: The emergence of meta-ecosystems and the value of physical interactions. *Technological Forecasting and Social Change, 177*, 121496. https://doi.org/10.1016/j.techfore.2022.121496

Van Alstyne, M. W., Parker, G. G., & Choudary, S. P. (2016). Pipelines, platforms, and the new rules of strategy. *Harvard Business Review, 94*(4), 54–62.

19

Understanding Institutional Barriers to Innovation

Institutional barriers are deeply embedded in the frameworks and practices that govern industries. These barriers can take many forms, including regulatory constraints, cultural inertia, and structural inflexibility. In industries such as finance, healthcare, and energy, these barriers are often intended to ensure stability, security, and fairness. While these goals are essential, they can also hinder the adoption of new technologies, business models, and practices.

Cultural factors also contribute to institutional barriers. Organisations with long histories often develop rigid hierarchies and decision-making processes that discourage experimentation. Employees may be reluctant to propose or embrace innovative ideas due to fear of failure or resistance from leadership. This cultural inertia is a common challenge in industries dominated by legacy players.

For instance, in the financial sector, regulations designed to protect consumers and ensure market integrity can slow the deployment of fintech innovations like digital wallets or blockchain solutions (Ahmed & Kowalkowski, 2025). In finance, regulation is essential to protect consumers, prevent fraud, and maintain market balance. However, capital requirements, licensing, and consumer protection rules can slow the rollout of innovations like digital wallets or blockchain-powered services. Start-ups and incumbents alike face lengthy approval processes and demanding compliance standards, which can suppress the agility that financial technology relies on.

A similar rigidity is found in healthcare, compliance requirements for patient privacy and data security may complicate the adoption of telemedicine platforms or AI-driven diagnostics (Cennamo & Santaló, 2019). In healthcare where privacy and data security are paramount. Regulations such as HIPAA in the United States or GDPR in Europe demand rigorous data governance that makes it difficult to deploy telehealth platforms, AI-driven diagnostics, or connected medical devices. Rolling out these tools requires extensive audits, system integrations, and coordination across teams, stretching project timelines and resources well beyond the area of traditional technology deployments.

It isn't just formal rules that slow innovation. Culture and organisational design present equally formidable obstacles. Legacy institutions—like established banks or hospitals—often operate under risk-averse, hierarchical decision-making. Proposals for new ideas are frequently met with hesitation or outright dismissal by leaders focused on stability (Chesbrough, 2020). That resistance stems not from ignorance but from a mindset that equates innovation with disruption, and disruption with risk. Even promising projects stall when champions cannot break through structural inertia.

Further complicating these issues is the rigidity of legacy infrastructures. Siloed departments, outdated systems, and process-heavy workflows make it difficult to introduce agile practices or open architectures (Dhanaraj & Parkhe, 2006). Modern platform thinking demands cross-functional teams, flexible APIs, and data-driven feedback loops—all of which require not just new code, but cultural transformation and operational redesign.

Platform leaders must navigate these tensions carefully. Institutional guardrails are not enemies—they're the reason ecosystems can form with trust and reliability. The challenge lies in engaging with these structures thoughtfully, finding ways to innovate without triggering defensive responses.

Practically, that means partnering with regulators and compliance teams early. It means translating compliance into credibility—using robust data hygiene and transparency as clear values. Piloting projects in safe, controlled environments can build internal buy-in, while sandboxed APIs and compliance-as-code tools allow innovation without compromise. Marketers and ecosystem strategists who understand institutional logic can frame new initiatives in language that resonates with risk-averse stakeholders.

Institutional barriers are more than red tape—they are the foundational framework of mature sectors. Instead of viewing them as obstacles to bypass, ecosystem innovators must learn to shape and operate within them (Faems et al., 2008). By doing so, they can build platforms that are not only transformative, but sustainable, trusted, and ultimately capable of balancing stability with creativity.

Frameworks for Analysing Institutional Barriers

Understanding and addressing institutional barriers requires structured approaches. One such framework is the **Institutional Logic Perspective**, which examines how societal norms, rules, and values shape organisational behaviour. This perspective helps businesses identify the underlying forces that drive resistance to innovation (Fang et al., 2008) and design strategies to align with or transform these forces.

Another useful framework is the **Barrier Mapping Model**, which categorises barriers into three levels: macro, meso, and micro.

1. **Macro-level barriers** include industry-wide regulations and cultural norms.
2. **Meso-level barriers** pertain to organisational structures and policies.
3. **Micro-level barriers** focus on individual behaviours and attitudes.

By mapping barriers at these levels, businesses can develop targeted strategies to overcome them (Galina & Lapina, 2023).

Regulatory Constraints as Barriers

Regulatory constraints are among the most visible and impactful institutional barriers. They are particularly pronounced in industries that prioritise risk management and compliance, such as finance, healthcare, and energy. While regulations are designed to protect consumers and ensure ethical practices, they can also stifle innovation by creating high entry costs and limiting operational flexibility.

For example, AML and KYC requirements in the financial sector demand rigorous compliance processes, which can be resource-intensive and time-consuming. Start-ups in the fintech space often struggle to meet these requirements, delaying the launch of new products or services (Hertwig & Engel, 2016).

In healthcare, regulations such as the Health Insurance Portability and Accountability Act (HIPAA) in the United States impose strict data privacy and security standards. While these regulations protect patients, they also pose challenges for innovators seeking to develop and deploy digital health solutions.

To address regulatory constraints, businesses must engage proactively with policymakers and regulators. Collaborative approaches, such as regulatory sandboxes, allow companies to test innovations in a controlled environment while ensuring compliance. These initiatives foster dialogue between innovators and regulators, creating pathways for change.

Cultural and Organisational Inertia

Cultural and organisational inertia is another significant barrier to innovation. This inertia often arises from a fear of change, a reliance on established practices, and a lack of incentives for experimentation. In traditional industries, leaders and employees may view innovation as a threat to stability, leading to resistance at all levels of the organisation.

For example, in the banking industry, long-established institutions often prioritise risk management over innovation, creating a conservative culture that discourages experimentation. Employees may be hesitant to propose disruptive ideas due to fear of failure or rejection by leadership.

To overcome cultural inertia, organisations must create environments that encourage creativity and experimentation. This involves fostering a culture of psychological safety, where employees feel empowered to share ideas without fear of negative consequences (Mair et al., 2012). Leadership plays a critical role in this transformation by modelling openness to change and rewarding innovative thinking.

Structural Barriers to Innovation

Structural barriers refer to the rigid processes, hierarchies, and resource constraints that limit an organisation's ability to innovate. In industries with complex supply chains or heavily siloed operations, these barriers can prevent the collaboration and agility needed for innovation.

For instance, in the energy sector, large utility companies often operate within highly regulated and capital-intensive environments. This structure can make it difficult to adopt renewable energy technologies or implement smart grid solutions. Similarly, in manufacturing, rigid production processes may inhibit the integration of new technologies like IoT-enabled devices.

Addressing structural barriers requires organisations to adopt more flexible and adaptive models. This may involve restructuring teams to encourage cross-functional collaboration, streamlining decision-making processes, and investing in digital transformation. Agile methodologies and decentralised decision-making are particularly effective in breaking down structural barriers and fostering innovation (Oliva & Kallenberg, 2003).

The Role of Technology in Overcoming Barriers

Technology offers powerful tools for overcoming institutional barriers to innovation. Digital platforms enable businesses to connect with stakeholders, share resources, and streamline operations, reducing the impact of structural and cultural barriers. For example, collaboration tools like **Slack** or **Microsoft Teams** facilitate communication across departments, breaking down silos and fostering teamwork.

Emerging technologies such as AI and blockchain also provide solutions to regulatory and compliance challenges. AI can automate compliance processes, reducing the time and cost associated with regulatory requirements. Blockchain, with its transparent and secure ledger capabilities, enhances trust and accountability, addressing concerns around data integrity and security.

Case Studies: Overcoming Institutional Barriers

Let's unpack some of the real-world examples that illustrate how B2B companies have navigated institutional barriers to drive innovation. In the financial sector, **Revolut Business** partnered with regulators and participated in the United Kingdom's regulatory sandbox to launch its international B2B payments solution (Hendricks & Matthyssens, 2022). By working within a controlled environment, the fintech gained regulatory insight, adjusted its product to meet compliance requirements, and accelerated its path to market. Marketers played a crucial role in translating compliance achievements into trust-building narratives for enterprise clients.

In healthcare, **HealthEdge**, a provider of enterprise software for health insurers, collaborated with payers and regulatory experts to modernise claims and care management systems while aligning with complex compliance mandates. By co-creating solutions that addressed legacy infrastructure and regulatory challenges, HealthEdge enabled insurers to transform core operations (Karplus et al., 2021). Marketing teams were instrumental in simplifying complex value propositions, building institutional trust, and driving adoption among health plans navigating digital transformation.

These examples demonstrate that with the right mix of strategy, regulatory collaboration, and marketing alignment, B2B businesses can overcome even the most entrenched institutional barriers to innovation.

Marketing as a Bridge: Navigating Innovation Within Institutional Boundaries

Institutional barriers permeate every level of a business—they influence much more than product development or operations. They profoundly affect how marketers craft messaging, frame innovation, and engage with audiences. In heavily regulated or traditionally structured sectors, the challenge for marketers is extreme. They must balance creativity with compliance; they are rarely free to speak boldly without institutional guardrails. Yet these barriers also create an opportunity—when marketers learn to navigate them effectively, they become catalysts for meaningful change. Marketers operating in highly regulated or traditional industries must navigate messaging with care, balancing creativity with compliance. When institutional norms resist change, marketing becomes the catalyst for reframing what's possible.

For example, overcoming regulatory constraints allows marketers to frame compliance not as a limitation but as a strength—reassuring stakeholders of the organisation's integrity and alignment with public expectations (Simcoe, 2012). Similarly, dismantling cultural inertia within organisations gives marketers the opportunity to pilot new strategies, experiment with customer engagement formats, and introduce bold ideas.

More than ever, marketers need to act as translators between legacy systems and future-fit innovation. By understanding the underlying logics that drive resistance, marketers can position change as necessary, values-aligned, and ultimately beneficial for all ecosystem actors.

In a world of shifting expectations and accelerating technology, the ability to navigate—and challenge—institutional barriers is a competitive edge.

Consider regulatory constraints. A common mistake is to view them solely as roadblocks. The most savvy marketing leaders do exactly the opposite—they treat compliance as a strategic asset. By framing regulatory alignment as a strength, they send a message of trustworthiness and credibility. Instead of hiding rules, they highlight them: transparent disclosures, easy-to-understand consent mechanisms, and proactive alignment with privacy laws all send signals that the organisation values integrity. In doing so, marketing shifts from being a diffuser of brand messages to a steward of institutional credibility.

Cultural inertia presents a different but equally potent barrier. Large organisations, especially those grounded in legacy practices, can struggle with risk aversion. Marketers in such environments must not simply push messaging—they must refract change through existing mindsets. This often starts with small-scale experimentation: a pilot campaign with customers, an interactive webinar, or a virtual focus group—anything that lets new ideas prove themselves in low-stake environments. Winning early internal champions through targeted success stories makes it easier to scale innovation across the organisation. Marketing leaders who can speak both business and institutional dialects—demonstrating how new tactics align with existing values—build internal bridges for transformation.

At its core, marketing in this context becomes a translation function. Marketers must learn the language of compliance officers and legal teams—knowing what matters to them and why. They must also speak the language of technologists and innovators, helping traditional decision-makers see how new platforms, partnerships, and co-creation initiatives can thrive without disrupting core controls. To succeed, they employ pragmatic reframing, hovering between bold vision and measured feasibility.

Today's stakeholder landscape is unforgiving—regulators, customers, partners and society expect bold innovation but also demand accountability. In this environment, a marketing leader who can simultaneously advocate for experimentation and build trust in established frameworks achieves a rare duality: authority and agility. When marketing becomes that bridge, it transforms from a promotional function into a strategic enabler—ensuring that innovation is not only possible, but rooted in credibility.

In this hybrid role, marketing becomes foundational. To challenge institutional norms effectively requires nuanced positioning—crafting narratives that frame innovation as both progressive and principled. It requires the courage to pilot daring ideas, yet the discipline to ensure processes and compliance are never compromised. When done well, marketing becomes the connective tissue that links legacy systems and future-fit ecosystems—creating both momentum and meaning.

In an age where expectations shift faster than organisational structures, inventiveness is not enough. The greatest opportunity lies in navigating—and preframing—innovation so that it can move seamlessly within institutional boundaries. That is the future of marketing—and the strategic orientation every platform-driven business needs.

Visual Framework: Mapping and Addressing Institutional Barriers

In Figure 19.1 presents a framework on how institutional barriers manifest across three levels-macro, meso, and micro-and provides a structure for identifying and addressing friction within regulated or traditional markets. The

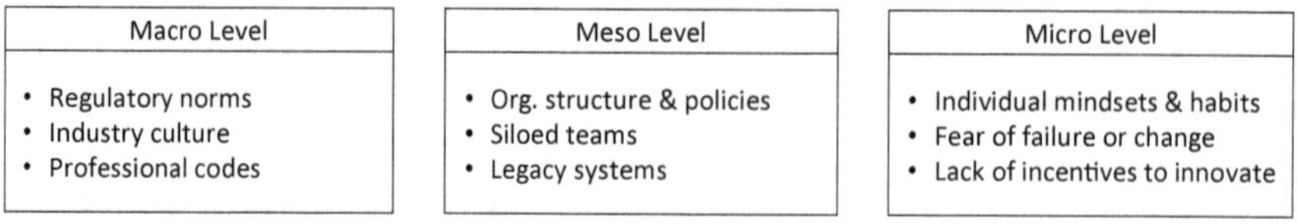

Macro Level	Meso Level	Micro Level
• Regulatory norms • Industry culture • Professional codes	• Org. structure & policies • Siloed teams • Legacy systems	• Individual mindsets & habits • Fear of failure or change • Lack of incentives to innovate

Fig. 19.1 Barrier Mapping Model

Barrier Mapping model, categorises the multi-level obstacles that can inhibit innovation and ecosystem participation. This model enables marketing and strategy leaders to diagnose and proactively respond to layered constraints when driving ecosystem transformation.

> **Reflective Prompt: What's Stopping You from Innovating?**
>
> Ask yourself:
>
> 1. Which institutional logics govern your ecosystem—and how do they reinforce the status quo?
> 2. Where does cultural inertia show up in your marketing, product, or partnership strategies?
> 3. How is your marketing team adapting—or pushing back—against institutional constraints?

> **Exercise: Barrier Transformation Map**
>
> This tool helps marketers and ecosystem leaders diagnose institutional barriers and design actions to address them.
>
> 1. Use Table 19.1 to identify real constraints in your ecosystem.
> 2. Define small, achievable interventions to begin shifting mindsets, behaviours, and structures.
> 3. Revisit quarterly and document the progress of your transformation efforts.

This chapter helps identify where barriers reside—and guides targeted interventions, from industry engagement to internal leadership development and employee empowerment.

Table 19.1 Barrier Transformation Map—Template Grid

Barrier type	Manifestation in ecosystem	Root cause	Action to address
Regulatory	Slow product launch approval	Legacy compliance procedures	Engage with regulators via sandbox
Cultural	Resistance to experimentation	Risk-averse leadership	Run safe-to-fail innovation pilots
Structural	Silos between product and marketing	Organisational hierarchy	Create cross-functional squads
Behavioural	Fear of failure from teams	No incentives for innovation	Reward learning and idea sharing

References

Ahmed, T., & Kowalkowski, C. (2025). The new industry playbook: Digital service innovation in multi-platform ecosystems. *Journal of Enterprise Information Management*. Advance online publication. https://doi.org/10.1108/JEIM-05-2024-0240

Cennamo, C., & Santaló, J. (2019). Generativity tension and value creation in platform ecosystems. *Organization Science, 30*(3), 617–641. https://doi.org/10.1287/orsc.2018.1270

Chesbrough, H. W. (2020). To recover faster from COVID-19, open up: Managerial implications from an open innovation perspective. *Industrial Marketing Management, 88*, 410–413. https://doi.org/10.1016/j.indmarman.2020.04.010

Dhanaraj, C., & Parkhe, A. (2006). Orchestrating innovation networks. *Academy of Management Review, 31*(3), 659–669. https://doi.org/10.5465/amr.2006.21318923

Faems, D., Janssens, M., Madhok, A., & Van Looy, B. (2008). Toward an integrative perspective on alliance governance: Connecting contract design, trust dynamics, and contract application. *Academy of Management Journal, 51*(6), 1053–1078. https://doi.org/10.5465/amj.2008.35732527

Fang, E., Palmatier, R. W., & Evans, K. R. (2008). Influence of customer participation on value creation: A meta-analysis. *Journal of the Academy of Marketing Science, 36*, 169–183. https://doi.org/10.1007/s11747-007-0082-9

Galina, R., & Lapiņa, I. (2023). Digital transformation as a catalyst for sustainability and open innovation. *Journal of Open Innovation: Technology, Market, and Complexity, 9*(1). https://doi.org/10.1016/j.joitmc.2023.100017

Hendricks, L., & Matthyssens, P. (2022). Platform ecosystem development in an institutionalized business market: The case of the asset management industry.

Journal of Business & Industrial Marketing, 38(2), 395–413. https://doi.org/10.1108/JBIM-04-2021-0193

Hertwig, R., & Engel, C. (2016). Homo ignorans: Deliberately choosing not to know. *Perspectives on Psychological Science, 11*(3), 359–372. https://doi.org/10.1177/1745691616635594

Karplus, V. J., Geissmann, T., & Zhang, D. (2021). Institutional complexity, management practices, and firm productivity. *World Development, 142*, Article 105386. https://doi.org/10.1016/j.worlddev.2020.105386

Mair, J., Martí, I., & Ventresca, M. (2012). Building inclusive markets in rural Bangladesh: How intermediaries work institutional voids. *Academy of Management Journal, 55*(4), 819–850. https://doi.org/10.5465/amj.2010.0627

Oliva, R., & Kallenberg, R. (2003). Managing the transition from products to services. *International Journal of Service Industry Management, 14*(2), 160–172. https://doi.org/10.1108/09564230310474138

Simcoe, T. S. (2012). Standard setting committees: Consensus governance for shared technology platforms. *American Economic Review, 102*(1), 305–336. https://doi.org/10.1257/aer.102.1.305

20

Strategies to Overcome Resistance in Marketing for Ecosystems

Marketing for ecosystems means dynamic networks of interconnected actors—including businesses, customers, partners, and regulators—collaborating to create value. Despite their potential for innovation and growth, these ecosystems often encounter resistance stemming from entrenched norms, cultural inertia, and competing interests. Overcoming this resistance is essential for fostering innovation and ensuring the long-term success of the ecosystems.

Resistance in marketing for ecosystems arises from several factors. Structural barriers, such as rigid processes and siloed operations, can limit flexibility and collaboration. Cultural inertia within organisations or industries may discourage actors from embracing change, especially if innovation is perceived as risky or disruptive. Regulatory constraints further complicate the landscape, imposing restrictions that may stifle creativity.

In many cases, resistance also stems from misaligned incentives. Ecosystem participants often prioritise their individual goals over collective objectives, leading to conflicts and a lack of trust. For example, a technology provider in an ecosystem may focus on short-term profitability, while a brand partner prioritises long-term customer engagement. These differing priorities can create friction, slowing the pace of innovation and marketing's job challenging.

One major barrier is structural rigidity. Traditional organisational designs are modular—each department operates in a silo with its own processes and agendas. In such environments, introducing new collaborative efforts often triggers friction (Aarikka-Stenroos & Ritala, 2017). For example, a brand marketing team accustomed to fixed quarterly campaign plans may struggle to integrate influencer-generated content in real time. Supply chain or IT teams may balk at granting data access to partners for fear of compliance concerns. Without agile structure and cross-functional coordination, ecosystems stall at launch.

Cultural inertia presents another challenge. Many industries, especially those steeped in legacy, rely on institutional memories—unwritten rules and standard operating procedures that evolved over decades. When innovation initiatives contradict these norms, stakeholders hesitate. A compliance team may view open API strategies as reckless or risky (Autio et al., 2018). Sales teams may reject new co-marketing channels that have yet to deliver measurable ROI. Without careful change management and internal advocacy, new ecosystem approaches fail in stealth.

Regulatory constraints further complicate matters. Collaboration often requires data sharing, joint promotional campaigns, or evolving technology integrations. But in industries such as finance, healthcare, or energy, even modest shifts can trip red tape. Allocating legal and compliance resources to navigate dynamic ecosystem policies adds cost and slows progress. Marketers must learn to frame collaboration within regulatory guardrails—not only to comply, but to position compliance as a competitive advantage.

A less visible form of resistance is incentive misalignment. Ecosystem participants may talk 'partnership', but act in self-interest. A software vendor might prioritise higher margin enterprise deals over ecosystem collaboration (Dedehayir et al., 2018). A retail brand might want exclusive promotion rather than shared discovery. This divergence erodes trust, especially when ecosystems rely on reciprocity and mutual reward. To achieve true co-creation, platform orchestrators must design governance models, revenue-share agreements, and performance metrics that align incentives across all partners.

All these forms of resistance contribute to ecosystem fragility. Progress becomes episodic rather than continuous. Internal blockers stall pilot programmes; partner distrust slows integrations; regulation blocks data flows. The cumulative effect can be discouraging, causing leadership teams to lose appetite for collaboration.

Yet these same barriers can be reframed as opportunities. Structural fragmentation can drive the creation of cross-functional ecosystem councils (Cennamo, 2021). Cultural inertia can spark internal education programmes to demonstrate ecosystem benefits. Regulatory complexity can be a rallying cry to develop compliance-first platform models. Misaligned incentives can be addressed through clear shared-value agreements and transparent measurement frameworks.

Ultimately, resistance is not inevitable. It is the natural response to change. The real question for ecosystem leaders is not whether resistance exists—but how to design marketing approaches that work with, not against, it. When ecosystems succeed, they do so by identifying pockets of flexibility, aligning early incentives, building trust, and treating regulatory engagement as strategic advantage rather than compliance burden.

That shift—from resisting change to guiding it—is the hallmark of a resilient, adaptive ecosystem. And it is the difference between a failed pilot and a scalable platform that thrives.

Fostering Collaboration Through Shared Vision

One of the most effective strategies for overcoming resistance is to establish a shared vision that aligns the goals of all ecosystem participants. A shared vision provides a sense of purpose and direction, helping actors see how their contributions fit into the larger picture. By articulating clear and compelling objectives, marketers can inspire collaboration and reduce resistance.

For example, in a digital advertising ecosystem, a shared vision might focus on creating personalised and non-intrusive ad experiences that benefit both consumers and businesses. This vision encourages technology providers, advertisers, and content creators to work together, integrating their resources to achieve a common goal.

Collaborative governance structures are essential for supporting this shared vision (Evans & Gawer, 2016). These structures define the rules, roles, and responsibilities of participants, ensuring transparency and fairness. By creating a level playing field, governance mechanisms build trust and facilitate cooperation.

Leveraging Technology to Enable Flexibility

Technology plays a critical role in addressing structural barriers and fostering collaboration within marketing of ecosystems. Digital platforms, for instance, provide the infrastructure for seamless communication and resource sharing. These platforms enable actors to interact, share insights, and coordinate their efforts more effectively.

AI and data analytics further enhance the ecosystem's ability to overcome resistance. AI can identify patterns and opportunities, optimising processes and reducing inefficiencies. For example, in a retail marketing ecosystem,

AI might analyse customer data to recommend personalised promotions, aligning the interests of brands and retailers.

Blockchain technology addresses trust-related barriers by providing secure and transparent records of transactions. This is particularly valuable in ecosystems where data integrity and accountability are critical, such as in programmatic advertising or influencer marketing.

Encouraging Cultural Change Through Leadership

Cultural inertia is one of the most challenging forms of resistance to overcome. Organisations with established practices and hierarchies often struggle to adapt to new ways of thinking. Addressing this requires strong leadership that models openness to innovation and fosters a culture of experimentation.

Leaders play a pivotal role in breaking down resistance by creating an environment where actors feel safe to take risks and propose new ideas. For example, a marketing team leader might encourage cross-functional collaboration, inviting input from technology, sales, and creative teams to develop innovative campaigns. By valuing diverse perspectives and rewarding creativity, leaders can build a culture that embraces change.

Another effective approach is to implement training and development programmes that equip participants with the skills and knowledge needed to navigate the complexities of marketing ecosystems. These programmes help actors understand the benefits of collaboration and innovation, reducing resistance rooted in fear or misunderstanding.

Aligning Incentives to Reduce Friction

Misaligned incentives are a common source of resistance in marketing of ecosystems. To address this, marketers must design incentive structures that align the goals of all participants. This might involve revenue-sharing models, performance-based rewards, or co-branding opportunities that highlight mutual benefits.

For example, in a partnership between a social media platform and a brand, an incentive structure might reward both parties based on engagement metrics such as clicks, shares, and conversions. This alignment ensures that both the platform and the brand are invested in creating compelling and effective content.

Equity-based incentives can also foster collaboration. By providing stakeholders with a share in the ecosystem's success, marketers can create a sense of ownership and commitment that reduces resistance.

Case Studies: Overcoming Resistance in Action

These examples illustrate the effectiveness of these strategies in overcoming resistance within marketing ecosystems. In the financial sector, **Stripe**, a global payments infrastructure provider, partnered with traditional banks to launch embedded finance and digital payment solutions. Despite initial resistance from banks concerned about disintermediation, Stripe established a shared vision centered on customer convenience, developer-friendly integration, and security (Gawer & Cusumano, 2014). By creating collaborative governance models and aligning commercial incentives, Stripe helped financial institutions modernise without losing relevance.

In the retail industry, **Mirakl**, a B2B marketplace platform provider, addressed resistance from traditional retailers and small sellers by offering a white-label, agentic platform that enabled them to launch and operate their own digital marketplaces. As an agentic platform, Mirakl empowers its partners with the tools, autonomy, and infrastructure to build tailored commerce ecosystems (Kretschmer et al., 2022). To reduce adoption barriers, Mirakl also provided onboarding support, flexible business models, and prebuilt integrations with major e-commerce systems. These agentic services allowed ecosystem participants to innovate independently while benefiting from a shared technology backbone—fostering deeper collaboration between Mirakl, retailers, and third-party sellers.

These examples demonstrate that with the right strategies—shared value, co-creation, and partner enablement—marketing ecosystems can overcome resistance and unlock their full potential for innovation and growth.

The Role of Feedback and Adaptation

Feedback loops are essential for overcoming resistance and driving continuous improvement within marketing of ecosystems. By collecting and analysing feedback from participants, marketers can identify pain points, address concerns, and refine their strategies. This iterative process builds trust and ensures that the ecosystem remains responsive to the needs of its participants (Kapoor, 2018). For example, a digital marketing agency might use client feedback to improve its campaign planning process, ensuring that the goals of all stakeholders are met. Similarly, a technology provider might use user feedback to enhance its platform's functionality, reducing friction and encouraging adoption.

These feedback mechanisms not only improve the quality and relevance of solutions but also strengthen relationships across the ecosystem. By demonstrating responsiveness and valuing stakeholder input, marketers can foster a culture of continuous learning and mutual respect—turning resistance into a catalyst for improvement.

Turning Resistance into Resilience: The Strategic Role of Marketers in Ecosystem Transformation

The strategies for overcoming resistance in marketing of ecosystems have profound implications for marketers. By fostering collaboration, leveraging technology, and addressing cultural and structural barriers, marketers can create environments where innovation thrives. These strategies enable marketers to build stronger relationships with their partners, deliver more impactful campaigns, and adapt to the rapidly changing demands of the marketplace.

In the evolving world of platform ecosystems, resistance is inevitable—but it is not immovable. For marketers, it presents not an obstacle, but a strategic inflection point. When approached with clarity and purpose, resistance becomes a signal—highlighting where trust must be built, where incentives misalign, and where culture needs reshaping.

Marketers today sit at the intersection of these tensions. Their role is no longer limited to message distribution or brand management—it is to unlock momentum across the ecosystem. This means creating collaborative structures where actors see clear personal and collective value (Nambisan et al., 2019). It means framing change not as disruption, but as alignment—between what stakeholders fear and what they stand to gain.

The most effective marketers become architects of inclusion. They use co-creation workshops, open data exchanges, and joint campaigns not as tactics, but as tools to dissolve resistance through shared participation (Whalley et al., 2024). By translating ecosystem strategy into emotionally resonant narratives, they help sceptics see themselves in the future—rather than retreat into the comfort of the past.

This isn't about bypassing resistance—it's about transforming it. The resistance that once blocked collaboration becomes the pressure that forges resilience (Perks et al., 2017). And marketers—when bold, intentional, and strategic—are uniquely positioned to lead this transformation. In platform ecosystems, it is not the absence of resistance that marks progress, but the ability to convert friction into fuel. That is marketing leadership redefined.

Ecosystems are fast becoming the foundation of how value is created and scaled. In this environment, resistance is not merely a hurdle—it is a strategic signal. For marketers, overcoming resistance is more than a challenge (Rong et al., 2013)—it is a chance to catalyse alignment, build trust, and accelerate transformation. By decoding the roots of hesitation and applying deliberate, insight-driven strategies, marketers can steer their ecosystems towards deeper collaboration, sustained innovation, and meaningful long-term growth.

Visual Framework: The Ecosystem Resistance Navigation Model

In Figure 20.1 presents a framework, highlighting the circular and reinforcing mechanisms needed to overcome resistance and build sustained alignment in platform ecosystems. Together, these components enable platform leaders to navigate complexity, reduce friction, and foster adaptive, ecosystem-led transformation.

This *Ecosystem Resistance Navigation* model demonstrates the circular and reinforcing nature of ecosystem alignment. Addressing resistance is not linear but iterative, anchored in shared goals, enabled by technology, and sustained by cultural evolution. It emphasises that alignment is not achieved through a single action but through continuous feedback loops across interconnected elements.

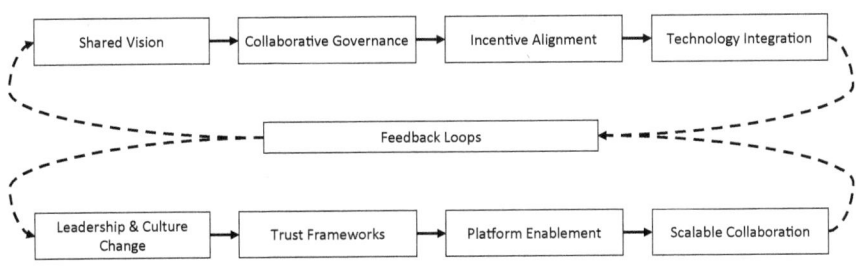

Fig. 20.1 Ecosystem Resistance Navigation Model

> **Reflective Prompt: Where Do You See Resistance—And What Are You Doing About It?**
>
> "Are barriers in your ecosystem signs of misalignment—or invitations to realign for growth?"
>
> Reflect on:
>
> 1. Where resistance typically emerges in your ecosystem (e.g. partners, platforms, internal silos)?
> 2. What incentives (or disincentives) are shaping stakeholder behaviour?
> 3. How your current leadership and cultural models support or hinder innovation
> 4. Whether your feedback processes drive meaningful change—or merely collect data

> **Exercise: The Ecosystem Resistance Audit (Table 20.1)**
>
> **Step 1: Map the Resistance**
>
> - Where is resistance most visible?
> - Who is resisting—and why?
> - What form does the resistance take (cultural, structural, regulatory, behavioural)?
>
> **Step 2: Identify Root Causes**
>
> - Is the resistance based on misaligned goals, fear, or lack of clarity?
> - Are incentives reinforcing the status quo?
> - Is your technology enabling—or inhibiting—collaboration?
>
> **Step 3: Design an Intervention Strategy**
>
> - What leadership behaviours can you model or amplify?
> - Which technological enablers can reduce friction?
> - What narrative or vision can help reframe the opportunity?
>
> **Step 4: Pilot the Shift**
>
> - Start with a small initiative—co-develop a campaign, redesign a process, or simplify collaboration.
> - Track outcomes based on stakeholder engagement, innovation velocity, and sentiment.

This chapter helps you identify the sources of resistance within your marketing ecosystem—and develop targeted strategies to address them.

Table 20.1 The Ecosystem Resistance Audit—Template Grid

Element	Description
Resistance Point	Where and how is resistance manifesting?
Stakeholders Involved	Who is resisting and why?
Root Cause(s)	Misalignment? Lack of trust? Inflexibility?
Strategy to Address	Vision, incentives, tech, leadership, or governance?
Pilot Initiative	What small-scale change can test your strategy?
Metrics for Success	Engagement levels, collaboration frequency, innovation outcomes, trust gain

References

Aarikka-Stenroos, L., & Ritala, P. (2017). Network management in the era of ecosystems: Systematic review and management framework. *Industrial Marketing Management, 67*, 23–36. https://doi.org/10.1016/j.indmarman.2017.08.010

Autio, E., Nambisan, S., Thomas, L. D. W., & Wright, M. (2018). Digital affordances, spatial affordances, and the genesis of entrepreneurial ecosystems. *Strategic Entrepreneurship Journal, 12*(1), 72–95. https://doi.org/10.1002/sej.1266

Cennamo, C. (2021). Competing in digital markets: A platform-based perspective. *Academy of Management Perspectives, 35*(2), 265–291. https://doi.org/10.5465/amp.2016.0048

Dedehayir, O., Mäkinen, S. J., & Ortt, J. R. (2018). Roles during innovation ecosystem genesis: A literature review. *Technological Forecasting and Social Change, 136*, 18–29. https://doi.org/10.1016/j.techfore.2016.11.028

Evans, P., & Gawer, A. (2016). The rise of the platform enterprise: A global survey. *The Center for Global Enterprise.* https://doi.org/10.13140/RG.2.2.35887.05280

Gawer, A., & Cusumano, M. A. (2014). Industry platforms and ecosystem innovation. *Journal of Product Innovation Management, 31*(3), 417–433. https://doi.org/10.1111/jpim.12105

Kapoor, R. (2018). Ecosystems: Broadening the locus of value creation. *Journal of Organizational Design, 7*(1), Article 12. https://doi.org/10.1186/s41469-018-0035-4

Kretschmer, T., Leiponen, A., Schilling, M., & Vasudeva, G. (2022). Platform ecosystems as meta-organizations: Implications for platform strategies. *Strategic Management Journal, 43*(3), 405–424. https://doi.org/10.1002/smj.3250

Nambisan, S., Zahra, S. A., & Luo, Y. (2019). Global platforms and ecosystems: Implications for international business theories. *Journal of International Business Studies, 50*, 1464–1486. https://doi.org/10.1057/s41267-019-00262-4

Perks, H., Kowalkowski, C., Witell, L., & Gustafsson, A. (2017). Network orchestration for value platforms. *Industrial Marketing Management, 67*, 106–121. https://doi.org/10.1016/j.indmarman.2017.08.002

Rong, K., Lin, Y., Shi, Y., & Yu, J. (2013). Linking business ecosystem lifecycle with platform strategy: A triple view of technology, application and organization. *International Journal of Technology Management, 62*(1), 75–93. https://doi.org/10.1504/IJTM.2013.053042

Whalley, J., Stocker, V., & Lutz, C. (2024). A platform for doers? Fiverr and the gig economy. *SSRN*. https://doi.org/10.2139/ssrn.4800456

Part V

Scaling and Structuring for Regional and Global Growth

21

Platforms as a Disruptor: Insights from Asset Management

In sectors traditionally characterised by conservative operations and incremental innovation, Platform-as-a-Service (PaaS) has emerged as a transformative force. Nowhere is this disruption more evident than in asset management—a domain historically defined by manual processes, rigid hierarchies, and cautious, centralised decision-making. PaaS is not merely an upgrade to existing systems; it is an enabler of a more flexible, scalable, and client-centric approach that challenges the very foundations of the industry. While Software-as-a-Service (SaaS) layers intuitive dashboards and tools over the infrastructure and empowers users to self-serve and explore data and make informed decisions.

Understanding how PaaS and SaaS disrupts asset management offers broader insights into the power of digital platforms to break through entrenched rigidities and foster sustainable innovation across industries.

Previously, asset managers have relied on manual workflows for portfolio rebalancing, compliance checks, and client reporting. These processes are often siloed within departments and handled by specialised teams, which slows decision-making and makes adaptation difficult (Avital et al., 2017). PaaS replaces this rigidity with modular, API-driven systems that support automation, real-time data sharing, and scalability. For instance, rebalancing algorithms can trigger pro-rata adjustments automatically based on pre-set client risk profiles, rather than via spreadsheet-driven workflows, significantly speeding up responses to market shifts.

Beyond process improvements, PaaS empowers a shift towards genuinely client-centric service. Instead of delivering generic reports, platforms can create dynamic dashboards that allow clients to drill down into portfolio performance, access predictive analytics powered by AI, or customise investment strategies. Because PaaS supports plug-and-play functionality, providers can offer scalable modularity—adding new compliance tools, risk engines, or ESG scorers on demand. Clients now curate the exact service experience they need, rather than retrofitting their goals to rigid product packages.

Moreover, PaaS dissolves institutional boundaries by enabling service orchestration across multiple firms—custodians, fund managers, analytics vendors, even fintech startups—within a shared ecosystem. This creates collaborative value networks where each partner contributes specialised expertise. Rather than vertically integrated monoliths, asset managers can act as orchestration hubs, offering curated bundles of best-in-class capabilities tailored to client objectives.

PaaS also flips scalability on its head. In legacy models, scaling meant hiring more staff, adding more desks or upgrading internal infrastructure. With PaaS, scaling happens on demand, at near-zero marginal cost. Need to add 10,000 retail investors overnight? The cloud-based platform auto-scales compute, onboarding capacity, reporting feeds, even compliance monitoring—without manual intervention.

Importantly, PaaS doesn't eliminate governance—it makes it smarter. Compliance checkpoints, rules engines, and audit trails are embedded into the platform. Regulators can gain on-demand access to redacted dashboards, while clients can configure notification thresholds for portfolio events. Trust is baked in, not retrofitted.

What emerges from this transformation is a fundamental shift in how asset managers define their value. Instead of being product manufacturers, they become architects of ecosystems—designing service pathways, orchestrating partner integrations, and enabling client-driven customisation. These platforms change the industry's centre of gravity from product to participation. They break rigid workflows, siloed thinking, and uniform service models, replacing them with dynamic, modular, and collaborative systems.

The lessons in asset management are broad. When PaaS enters a conservative industry, it forces a reset: enabling automation over manual workflows; client-led configuration over top-down distribution; ecosystem orchestration over closed systems; and governed flexibility over rigid control. That is why the introduction of PaaS in asset management is far more than a tech upgrade—it is evidence of how digital platforms can break through entrenched industry barriers to spark innovation, client empowerment, and sustained strategic advantage.

The Traditional Asset Management Landscape

For decades, asset management has prioritised stability, regulatory compliance, and careful stewardship of client assets. This risk-averse focus has led to highly structured workflows, with clear divisions of labour among asset managers, financial advisors, and clients. While ensuring accountability, these structures have also created systemic inefficiencies—manual reporting processes, limited personalisation, and operational silos that slow innovation.

Legacy IT systems dominate much of the industry, making the integration of new technologies expensive and complex. These constraints inhibit firms' ability to respond swiftly to market volatility or shifting client expectations, thereby limiting their competitive agility. Regulatory compliance, while necessary, adds yet another layer of complexity, intensifying operational friction and reinforcing conservative mindsets.

How PaaS Disrupts Asset Management

PaaS solutions upend these limitations by offering a flexible, cloud-based infrastructure that reduces the dependency on cumbersome, outdated systems. Rather than being anchored to costly on-premise infrastructure, firms using PaaS can access a dynamic suite of applications, data analytics, and AI-driven tools on demand, significantly lowering barriers to innovation.

Automation represents one of the most transformative impacts of PaaS. Tasks such as portfolio rebalancing, compliance reporting, and risk assessments—once labour-intensive and error-prone—can now be managed seamlessly through ML and AI capabilities embedded in PaaS environments. This operational efficiency liberates human capital to focus on higher-value activities, such as strategic advisory and innovation.

Beyond automation, PaaS facilitates seamless integration with external data providers, client interfaces, and collaborative partner ecosystems. This interconnectedness allows asset managers to offer tailored investment strategies, enhance client communications, and foster stronger engagement. Crucially, PaaS empowers firms to scale their operations flexibly, growing their client base without a proportional increase in complexity or cost.

Frameworks for Understanding PaaS Disruption

Two conceptual models help frame the transformative potential of PaaS.

The **Digital Maturity Model** describes an organisation's progression from isolated digitisation efforts to fully integrated digital ecosystems. PaaS enables firms to leapfrog traditional stages, embedding digital capabilities not as a supplement to business-as-usual, but as the strategic core of their operations.

Complementing this is the **Value Chain Disruption Model**, which highlights how PaaS reconfigures traditional industry roles and relationships. In asset management, PaaS diminishes the need for multiple intermediaries, creating a flatter, more agile network of asset managers, clients, and service providers, all connected via a shared digital backbone.

Case Study: Robo-Advisors Powered by PaaS

A striking example of PaaS-driven disruption in wealth management is the rise of robo-advisors. **Charles Schwab**, a leading asset management firm, leveraged cloud-based Platform-as-a-Service (PaaS) infrastructure to launch **Schwab Intelligent Portfolios**—a fully automated digital advisory solution designed for millennial and tech-savvy investors. Built on scalable cloud architecture, the platform integrates real-time analytics, automated portfolio management, and intuitive client-facing interfaces.

By adopting a PaaS approach, Schwab was able to democratise access to investment advice—enabling clients to start investing with low minimums and receive algorithm-driven, personalised recommendations. Operational efficiency improved significantly, while compliance, tax optimisation, and reporting processes were seamlessly embedded into the platform.

This case illustrates how PaaS enables robo-advisors to scale quickly, reduce costs, enhance user experiences, and unlock access to previously underserved investor segments.

Challenges in Implementing PaaS

Despite its advantages, PaaS adoption presents substantial challenges. The most immediate is the integration of legacy systems, which often requires substantial investment and organisational change. Many firms are deeply reliant on outdated infrastructure that is not easily compatible with modern platforms.

Data security and regulatory compliance are also paramount concerns. Handling sensitive financial data requires strict adherence to evolving legal standards, necessitating close collaboration with PaaS providers to ensure robust protections are in place.

Cultural resistance adds another layer of complexity. Shifting from familiar manual processes to automated, cloud-based operations can generate anxiety among employees. Successful transitions require not just technical solutions but also strong leadership, clear communication, and a strategic focus on the long-term benefits of digital transformation.

Opportunities for Marketing in PaaS-Driven Asset Management

For marketers, PaaS offers a new frontier of opportunity. With data-rich platforms, marketers can deliver unprecedented levels of personalisation, tailoring messaging and offerings to the unique needs and behaviours of individual clients. Automation tools reduce the administrative burden of campaign management, allowing marketing teams to devote more energy to strategic creativity and innovation.

Perhaps most importantly, PaaS facilitates deeper client engagement through integrated collaboration tools, enabling continuous dialogue rather than sporadic campaigns. This shift from transactional interactions to relational engagement strengthens loyalty and drives client lifetime value (Teece, 2018).

Scalability also becomes a powerful advantage. As firms grow and diversify, PaaS ensures that marketing operations can expand accordingly, maintaining consistent quality and relevance across a broader client base.

Marketing Reimagined: PaaS as a Catalyst for Ecosystem Strategy

The impact of PaaS on marketing is profound.

Platform-as-a-Service (PaaS) is more than a technological upgrade—it acts as a catalyst for a cultural and strategic transformation in marketing. Traditional marketing fleets behind product features and ads, but within a PaaS ecosystem, it takes on the role of architecting client-centric experiences that connect continents of users and partners at scale.

First, PaaS enables deeply personalised engagement. With access to real-time analytics, marketing leaders can fine-tune messaging, experiences, and offers based on each actor's context—whether they are a developer integrating APIs, a client exploring product analytics, or a user participating in co-created content (Gawer, 2021). Every interaction becomes an opportunity to learn and iterate, creating a pipeline of continuous improvement rather than isolated campaign bursts. This real-time responsiveness ensures that marketing is never disconnected from the evolving needs of its ecosystem participants.

Second, PaaS reshapes how marketers orchestrate customer journeys. Modular tools and plug-and-play integrations eliminate delays and reduce dependency on IT. New channels, features, or partner solutions can be launched or removed instantly. This speed empowers marketers to test and refine at pace—improving engagement rates, shortening adoption cycles, and refining product-market fit. In effect, marketers transition from campaign managers to platform curators, dynamically assembling engagement paths that cater to segmented ecosystem personas.

Third, PaaS democratises co-creation. By embedding collaboration tools—shared workspaces, community forums, ideation boards—within the platform environment, marketers mobilise contributors across developer networks, brand advocates, and external specialists. Co-created features, user-generated content and joint product experiments become part of marketing's output, not just the product team's roadmap (Evans & Schmalensee, 2013). This collective creativity adds credibility and amplifies reach through authentic stories of collaboration.

Finally, PaaS shifts the culture of marketing from promotion to facilitation. It requires marketers to act as ecosystem integrators—aligning internal teams (sales, support, data science) and external partners to deliver coherent, value-driven journeys. Marketing strategy extends beyond campaigns to include onboarding flows, API-enabled partnerships, certification programmes and performance dashboards—all aimed at strengthening the ecosystem's health and growth. In this context, marketing doesn't just fuel growth—it shapes the structures that sustain it.

In summary, PaaS reimagines marketing as a strategic function deeply embedded in platform dynamics. It empowers marketers to design experiences that are personalised, participatory and adaptive. It transforms marketing from a promotional silo into a connective force that fosters ecosystem resilience, co-creation, and sustained business impact.

Beyond PaaS: The SaaS Synergy

From manual routines to Smart Automation, legacy asset management relies on manual spreadsheets for tasks like portfolio rebalancing, compliance checks, and reporting, leading to slow response times and siloed workflows (Bello et al., 2021). PaaS replaces this with customisable systems that automate processes based on client profiles and real-time triggers. SaaS apps then present this data through intuitive tools, empowering users to self-serve and explore without IT hand-holding.

PaaS provides modular, API-driven infrastructure, ideal for automation, real-time data processing, and seamless integration (Evans & Basole, 2016). **SaaS, layered on top, delivers business-ready applications**, CRM, analytics dashboards, regulatory tools, that clients can use instantly. Together, they transform asset management into a living ecosystem rather than a static service (Choudhury & Sabherwal, 2003).

In the traditional world of asset management, operations have long depended on manual spreadsheets to execute tasks such as portfolio rebalancing, compliance checks, and client reporting. This reliance results in slow response times and siloed workflows that hinder agility. By contrast, a PaaS + SaaS model transforms these manual routines into intelligent, responsive systems. PaaS introduces programmable infrastructure that automates tasks based on real-time triggers and client-specific risk profiles, while SaaS applications layer intuitive dashboards and tools over this infrastructure (Choudhury & Sabherwal, 2003), empowering users to self-serve, explore data, and make informed decisions without IT gatekeeping.

This combination also redefines client service delivery. Rather than a one-size-fits-all model, clients now engage with live dashboards, predictive analytics, and bespoke investment strategies, selecting only the SaaS modules relevant to their goals—be it ESG scoring tools, tax-efficient withdrawal simulators, or advanced portfolio analytics. Behind the scenes, PaaS infrastructure ensures regulatory compliance, data integrity, and seamless scalability, creating a model that is both flexible and robust.

The shift also fosters ecosystem-led collaboration. Asset managers no longer operate in isolation; instead, they function as orchestrators of broader digital environments (Cusumano & Gawer, 2002). PaaS handles the secure integration of custodians, fintech providers, and analytics vendors, while SaaS applications deliver highly specialised workflows to end-users. This architecture enables asset managers to move from being traditional service providers to curators of ecosystem-driven value.

Scalability, once dependent on hiring more staff or upgrading on-premise infrastructure, is also reimagined. With cloud-native PaaS and modular SaaS applications, firms can scale instantly—onboarding thousands of clients with zero incremental overhead (Dedehayir et al., 2019). Auto-scaling ensures performance remains consistent, and SaaS modules can be deployed as needed to meet evolving user expectations.

Finally, governance is embedded by design. Compliance is no longer an afterthought patched onto existing systems; it is integrated through PaaS audit trails, rules engines, and real-time monitoring. Meanwhile, SaaS interfaces enable clients to set their own alert thresholds, configure access controls, and vet integrations—ensuring that trust, transparency, and control are built into every engagement touchpoint.

Visual Framework: The PaaS-Driven Transformation—Disruption in Asset Management

In Figure 21.1 introduces a framework highlighting the evolutionary journey from traditional asset management to digitally enabled, ecosystem-led operations powered by Platform-as-a-Service (PaaS). The model outlines a phased transition from the traditional to the future state.

The *PaaS Transformation Journey* model demonstrates that PaaS is not merely a technological upgrade; it is a catalyst for cultural and strategic transformation. It challenges marketers—and their organisations—to rethink how value is created, delivered, and sustained in an increasingly digital economy.

> **Reflective Prompt: Are You Driving Transformation—Or Just Digitising Old Processes?**
>
> "Are you using platforms to rethink how you create value–or are you simply adding digital tools to legacy workflows?"
>
> Reflect on:
>
> 1. How fully your marketing operations and client engagement models have embraced platform thinking.
> 2. Whether your strategies are built for agility, personalisation, and real-time adaptation—or still rooted in traditional campaign cycles.
> 3. How marketing can play a leading role in orchestrating digital transformation beyond the marketing function itself.

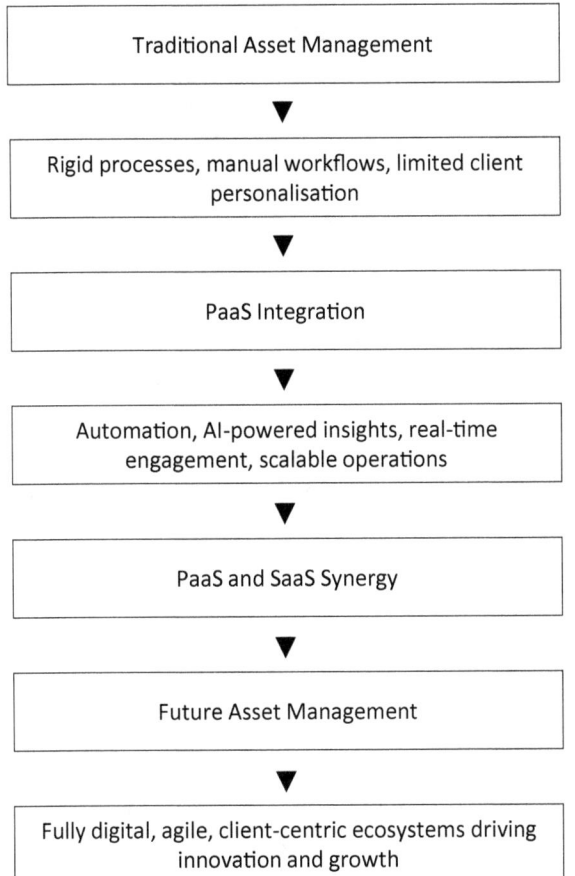

Fig. 21.1 Paas Transformation Journey Model

Exercise: PaaS Transformation Opportunity Canvas (Table 21.1)

Step 1: Audit Your Current Marketing Model

- Where are the rigidities? (e.g. campaign cycles, segmentation methods, reporting processes)

Step 2: Identify Where PaaS Can Disrupt

- Which workflows could be automated?
- Where could data-driven insights enable greater personalisation?

Step 3: Visualise Your Future Ecosystem

- What would a fully PaaS-enabled marketing operation look like?
- How would teams, technologies, and client journeys evolve?

Table 21.1 PaaS Transformation Opportunity Canvas—Template Grid

Element	Description
Current Rigidities	Manual segmentation, delayed reporting, fragmented client insights
Platform Opportunities	AI-driven campaign optimisation, real-time data analytics
New Client Value	Hyper-personalised experiences, continuous engagement
Transformation Steps	Pilot PaaS tools, integrate platforms across teams, upskill marketing
Success Measures	Campaign ROI, client retention rates, innovation adoption speed

This chapter helps you leverage PaaS as a strategic enabler—driving not just digital change, but a fundamental shift in how marketing creates and sustains value.

References

Avital, M., Mathiassen, L., & Schultze, U. (2017). Alternative genres in information systems research. *European Journal of Information Systems, 26*(3), 240–247. https://doi.org/10.1057/s41303-017-0051-4

Bello, S. A., Oyedele, L. O., Akinade, O. O., Bilal, M., Davila Delgado, J. M., Akanbi, L. A., Ajayi, A. O., & Owolabi, H. A. (2021). Cloud computing in construction industry: Use cases, benefits and challenges. *Automation in Construction, 122*, Article 103441. https://doi.org/10.1016/j.autcon.2020.103441

Choudhury, V., & Sabherwal, R. (2003). Portfolios of control in outsourced software development projects. *Information Systems Research, 14*(3), 291–304. https://doi.org/10.1287/isre.14.3.291.16563

Cusumano, M. A., & Gawer, A. (2002). The elements of platform leadership. *MIT Sloan Management Review, 43*(3), 51–58. https://sloanreview.mit.edu/article/the-elements-of-platform-leadership/

Dedehayir, O., Pîrvan, C. I., & Le Fever, H. (2019). Industry platforms as facilitators of disruptive IoT innovations. *Journal of Technology Management & Innovation, 14*(3), 18–28. https://doi.org/10.4067/S0718-27242019000300018

Evans, D. S., & Schmalensee, R. (2013). *The antitrust analysis of multi-sided platform businesses* (NBER Working Paper No. 18783). National Bureau of Economic Research. http://www.nber.org/papers/w18783

Evans, P. C., & Basole, R. C. (2016). Revealing the API ecosystem and enterprise strategy via visual analytics. *Communications of the ACM, 59*(2), 26–28. https://doi.org/10.1145/2856447

Gawer, A. (2021). Digital platforms' boundaries: The interplay of firm scope, platform sides, and digital interfaces. *Long Range Planning, 54*(5), Article 102045. https://doi.org/10.1016/j.lrp.2020.102045

ISG. (2023). PaaS transformation: Managing cloud-native strategies for platform delivery. *ISG White Paper*. https://isg-one.com

Kwon, I.-W. G., Kim, S.-H., & Martin, D. G. (2016). Healthcare supply chain management: Strategic areas for quality and financial improvement. *Technological Forecasting and Social Change, 113*(Part B), 422–428. https://doi.org/10.1016/j.techfore.2016.07.014

Teece, D. J. (2018). Business models and dynamic capabilities. *Long Range Planning, 51*(1), 40–49. https://doi.org/10.1016/j.lrp.2017.06.007

22

Plug-and-Play Solutions for Agility and Scalability

Building on our previous exploration of how PaaS transforms marketing strategy, plug-and-play solutions now emerge as the practical tools that bring this transformation to life. They sit at the intersection of technology and agility—modular, flexible, and swift to deploy—without causing disruption. Plug-and-play solutions enable businesses to deploy new capabilities quickly, seamlessly integrating them into existing infrastructures with minimal technical expertise or system downtime. Far from being a mere operational convenience, these solutions provide the strategic scaffolding that supports experimentation, rapid iteration, and ecosystem scalability.

Organisations are under constant pressure to innovate, respond to market shifts, and meet evolving customer expectations. In this context, plug-and-play solutions have emerged as transformative tools, offering modularity, flexibility, and speed without the disruption traditionally associated with technological change.

As platform ecosystems grow, marketers and product teams are freed from the constraints of monolithic systems. Instead of waiting weeks or months for IT to enable new features, they can integrate new modules within hours. Want to test an advanced analytics tool for customer insights? Plug it in. Need to localise a platform quickly in a new market? Add a multilingual content plug in. These real-time adjustments are driven by user behaviour, not by rigid timelines or internal politics.

This agility carries over into ecosystem partnerships as well. Complementors—developers, agencies, and third-party innovators—can onboard faster when their contributions slot into a plug-and-play framework (Baldwin &

Woodard, 2009). That ease fosters creativity and mutual value: each module enhances the platform, and every partner gains visibility and benefit.

Scalability is another win. As your platform expands—whether by geography, demographic, or domain—new modules can be added on demand. This modular architecture avoids costly tech rewrites or bloated legacy systems. Instead, you adapt incrementally and purposefully, guided by real-world performance and user metrics.

However, the power of plug-and-play depends on thoughtful curation. Without clear API standards, governance protocols, and security oversight, modular growth can lead to fragmentation, performance issues, or inconsistent user experience. Integrations must be vetted, guidelines enforced, and user impact monitored. When done well, plug-and-play becomes an ecosystem advantage; when neglected, it becomes chaos.

Ultimately, plug-and-play solutions deliver more than operational speed—they reinforce the platform-centric mindset we've built throughout this book. They enable marketers to act as ecosystem architects, orchestrate creative collaborations, and prioritise user experience over internal constraints (Constantinides et al., 2018). In a landscape defined by speed, personalisation, and collaboration, these modular building blocks are not optional—they are essential.

Understanding Plug-and-Play Solutions

At their core, plug-and-play solutions are characterised by their interoperability and modularity. Designed to work with existing systems without requiring extensive configuration, they allow organisations to tailor their technology stacks to specific needs, adding or removing components as circumstances dictate. This modularity makes it possible for businesses to remain agile, scaling operations or pivoting strategies without overhauling entire systems.

For instance, the deployment of a plug-and-play payment gateway within a digital commerce platform exemplifies the model's advantage. Within hours, businesses can expand their payment options, improving customer experience and increasing conversion rates without incurring the costs and risks associated with full system reengineering.

The success of plug-and-play models hinges on their ability to ensure interoperability across platforms and ecosystems. This capability empowers businesses to integrate best-in-class tools and services rapidly, creating flexible, responsive infrastructures aligned with organisational goals.

Enhancing Agility Through Plug-and-Play Solutions

Agility, seen as the capacity to respond rapidly to change, is no longer a luxury but a survival requirement in contemporary business (Bharadwaj et al., 2013). Plug-and-play technologies offer a pathway to organisational agility by dramatically reducing the time and effort needed to adopt new tools and processes.

In the financial services sector, for instance, banks and fintech firms have leveraged plug-and-play platforms to roll out digital wallets, fraud detection systems, and customer engagement tools at pace. Rather than embarking on months-long development projects, these organisations can adapt almost instantaneously to technological advancements or regulatory changes (Chesbrough, 2007).

Similarly, in healthcare, real-time diagnostics and monitoring are being revolutionised through plug-and-play devices and data integration systems. Medical institutions can incorporate new technologies without destabilising core operations, improving patient care and enhancing operational efficiency.

This capacity for rapid deployment is particularly critical in regulated industries, where compliance updates often require swift systemic changes (Ghazawneh & Henfridsson, 2013). Plug-and-play solutions enable businesses to maintain compliance proactively, integrating regulatory tools with minimal disruption to their workflows.

Building Scalability Through Modularity

Scalability can be seen as an organisation's ability to grow or pivot without losing effectiveness, which is a natural extension of modular architecture. Plug-and-play solutions allow firms to expand capabilities incrementally, integrating new functionalities as needs evolve.

Retailers, for example, can deploy modular inventory management systems that scale alongside their operations. As product lines expand and logistics grow more complex, additional plug-in features like supply chain analytics or warehouse automation can be integrated seamlessly. This approach avoids the high capital expenditure and risk associated with large, monolithic system replacements.

The cloud has further amplified the scalability advantages of plug-and-play solutions. With cloud-based platforms, organisations can access computing power and services on demand, flexibly scaling their operations to handle everything from seasonal demand spikes to long-term growth.

An e-commerce business, for example, can dynamically increase server capacity during a holiday sales surge by plugging into cloud services, maintaining performance and customer satisfaction without incurring unnecessary permanent costs.

Frameworks for Implementing Plug-and-Play Solutions

Successful adoption of plug-and-play solutions requires a structured and strategic approach. The **Integration Maturity Model** offers a useful framework, guiding organisations through stages from basic, ad hoc integration to full system interoperability. This model underscores the need for technical readiness and change management capabilities as preconditions for successful plug-and-play adoption.

The **Digital Ecosystem Model** provides an additional lens, emphasising the importance of selecting solutions that adhere to open standards and ecosystem norms (Jacobides et al., 2018). Solutions that easily integrate with external partners, customers, and suppliers enable organisations to participate in broader value networks, enhancing their strategic agility.

Both frameworks reinforce the principle that plug-and-play is not merely about ease of deployment—it is about aligning technological innovation with organisational strategy, ensuring that new tools reinforce and amplify business goals.

Navigating Challenges in Adoption

Despite their many advantages, plug-and-play solutions are not without challenges. Compatibility remains a common obstacle, particularly for organisations operating on legacy infrastructure (Kenney & Zysman, 2016). Integrating new components may require updates to existing systems, or even the gradual replacement of outdated technologies.

Vendor lock-in poses another risk. Dependence on proprietary ecosystems can limit future flexibility and escalate costs. To avoid this, businesses should prioritise solutions based on open architecture and standardised protocols, ensuring that they retain control over their technological roadmaps.

Change management also plays a pivotal role in successful implementation. Employees accustomed to traditional systems may resist new tools, fearing disruption or complexity. Clear communication, targeted training, and a focus on the tangible benefits of new technologies are essential strategies for overcoming internal resistance and ensuring smooth transitions.

Real-World Applications of Plug-and-Play Technologies

Across industries, plug-and-play solutions are driving innovation and improving outcomes.

In asset management, modular platforms enable firms to integrate client portals, risk analytics, and compliance tools as needed, streamlining operations and enhancing client service (Selander et al., 2013). By adopting a plug-and-play approach, these firms can respond more effectively to regulatory shifts and client demands without overhauling their entire technology stack.

The energy sector offers another compelling example. Smart grid platforms are using plug-and-play technologies to integrate solar, wind, and battery storage systems into national grids. This modular architecture supports the transition to renewable energy while maintaining reliability and scalability.

Education, too, has embraced the model. Learning Management Systems (LMS) with plug-and-play capabilities allow institutions to integrate a range of third-party applications—virtual labs, adaptive learning modules, and collaboration tools—creating personalised, engaging educational environments without needing to build bespoke systems from scratch.

Plug-and-Play Marketing: Accelerating Agility and Personalisation

The adoption of plug-and-play solutions is fundamentally reshaping marketing functions. Marketing teams can now integrate automation platforms for email, social media, and content management almost instantly, enabling more sophisticated and personalised engagement strategies.

Real-time analytics, powered by plug-and-play integrations, give marketers immediate insights into customer behaviour and campaign effectiveness. This capability supports rapid iteration, allowing teams to refine messaging and tactics on the fly based on real-world feedback.

Thanks to plug-and-play solutions, real-time analytics are no longer aspirational—they are integral to modern marketing execution. As soon as a campaign goes live, teams receive live updates on open rates, clicks, engagement patterns and conversion events. This continuous feedback enables marketers to iterate within hours, not weeks (Wareham et al., 2014). For example, a social ad underperforming with a specific demographic can be paused while the messaging is updated; a landing page seeing low retention can be tweaked and A/B tested within the same day. This rapid exploration mindset shifts marketing from static planning to ongoing optimisation.

Scalability is another critical benefit. As organisations expand—whether geographically, into new verticals, or towards new persona segments—plug-and-play technologies allow marketing teams to "grow sideways" without rebuilding systems. A successful campaign in one country can be localised swiftly by adding multilingual content plug ins. A new product line can be onboarded by integrating feature-focused chatbots or loyalty systems. With these modular components, global consistency and local adaptability coexist effortlessly.

Plug-and-play tools also unlock richer experimentation. Marketers can pilot chat-based support, interactive quizzes, referral engines or community widgets without draining internal resources. If an initiative resonates, it can be institutionalised; if it doesn't, it can be replaced or improved without disrupting the broader stack. This freedom to test and learn becomes a cultural advantage, embedding a mindset of curiosity and iteration into the team.

Critically, plug-and-play marketing also nurtures better collaboration between marketing and other ecosystem actors. Partners, agencies, and complementors can contribute functionality through well-defined modules (Ruutu, Casey, & Kotovirta, 2017). Want a partner to co-manage a campaign or analytics dashboard? They can plug in seamlessly. This reduces friction, aligns contributions with outcomes, and increases shared ownership.

Of course, managing a modular environment requires discipline. API standards must be enforced, data governance protocols kept current, and plug in certifications regularly updated (Tiwana, 2014). Left unchecked, a loosely governed ecosystem can slow performance or create inconsistent customer journeys. Strong oversight ensures that each component integrates smoothly and consistently supports brand experience.

By placing plug-and-play marketing at the centre of their ecosystem strategy, marketers become ecosystem architects. They design experiences, orchestrate functionality, and create feedback-rich environments (Parker et al., 2016)—enabling personalised, emotionally resonant moments at scale. ss era, where speed, relevance and authenticity shape competitive advantage, plug-and-play solutions are no longer optional—they are the engine of modern marketing.

Moreover, scalability becomes far more manageable. As businesses grow, marketing teams can add new channels, audiences, and personalisation layers without undertaking major technological reconfigurations. For example, a brand expanding into international markets can integrate multilingual content management tools into its platform quickly, maintaining consistency and speed.

Visual Framework: Agility and Scalability Through Plug-and-Play

Figure 22.1 presents a framework illustrating how modular solutions enable rapid integration, enhanced agility, and scalable innovation across platform ecosystems. It outlines a progression from Existing Systems requiring minimal disruption to Culminating in Enhanced Innovation and Competitive Advantage.

Utilising *the Plug-and-Play Advantage Cycle* model demonstrates how plug-and-play strategies enable scalable, agile growth—essential for competing in a fast-moving, data-driven landscape.

> **Reflective Prompt: Is Your Organisation Built for Flexibility—Or Fragility?**
>
> "Are you investing in modular platforms that allow for agile innovation–or are you building rigid systems that cannot adapt?"
>
> Reflect on:
>
> 1. Where your current technological limitations are slowing adaptation or innovation.
> 2. How easily your systems can integrate new tools, channels, or data sources.
> 3. Whether your marketing strategies are structured to scale flexibly or risk becoming obsolete.

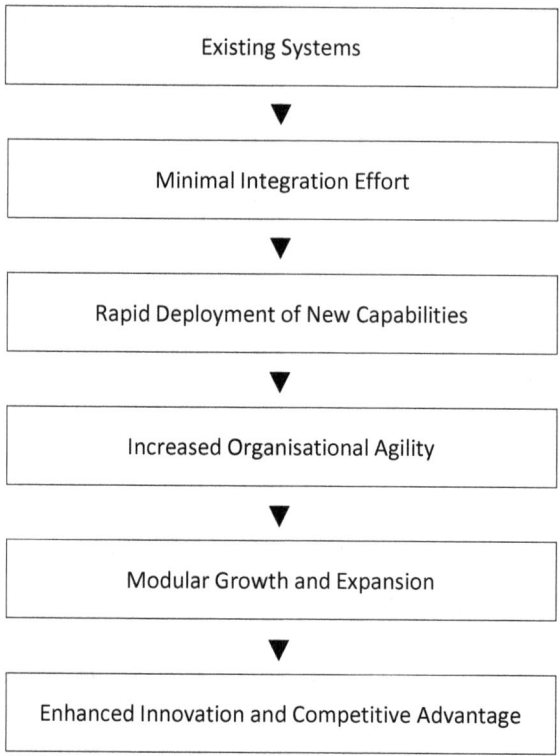

Fig. 22.1 Plug-and-Play Advantage Cycle

> **Exercise: Plug-and-Play Adoption Canvas (Table 22.1)**
>
> **Step 1: Identify Integration Bottlenecks**
>
> - Where are current systems rigid, outdated, or difficult to enhance?
>
> **Step 2: Prioritise Plug-and-Play Opportunities**
>
> - Which marketing functions, operational processes, or customer touchpoints could be improved with modular, integrated solutions?
>
> **Step 3: Visualise a Modular Marketing Ecosystem**
>
> - Imagine a future where systems and teams can adapt effortlessly. What tools, partnerships, or practices would enable that vision?

This chapter helps to drive scalability and agility. In an age where speed, personalisation, and data-driven strategy define competitive advantage, plug-and-play solutions are essential to staying competitive.

Table 22.1 Plug-and-Play Adoption Canvas—Template Grid

Element	Description
Current bottlenecks	Slow integration cycles, limited personalisation
Plug-and-play targets	CRM upgrades, marketing automation, real-time analytics
Ecosystem requirements	Open APIs, cloud compatibility, standards-based interoperability
Change management plan	Communication strategy, training programmes, stakeholder engagement
Success measures	Speed of integration, improved campaign performance, cost savings

References

Baldwin, C. Y., & Woodard, C. J. (2009). The architecture of platforms: A unified view. In A. Gawer (Ed.), *Platforms, markets and innovation* (pp. 19–44). chapter 2,). Edward Elgar Publishing.

Bharadwaj, A., El Sawy, O. A., Pavlou, P. A., & Venkatraman, N. (2013). Digital business strategy: Toward a next generation of insights. *MIS Quarterly, 37*(2), 471–482. https://www.jstor.org/stable/43825919

Chesbrough, H. W. (2007). Why companies should have open business models. *MIT Sloan Management Review, 48*(2), 22–28. https://sloanreview.mit.edu/article/why-companies-should-have-open-business-models/

Constantinides, P., Henfridsson, O., & Parker, G. G. (2018). Platforms and infrastructures in the digital age. *Information Systems Research, 29*(2), 381–400. https://doi.org/10.1287/isre.2018.0794

Ghazawneh, A., & Henfridsson, O. (2013). Balancing platform control and external contribution in third-party development: The boundary resources model. *Information Systems Journal, 23*(2), 173–192. https://doi.org/10.1111/j.1365-2575.2012.00406.x

Jacobides, M. G., Cennamo, C., & Gawer, A. (2018). Towards a theory of ecosystems. *Strategic Management Journal, 39*(8), 2255–2276. https://doi.org/10.1002/smj.2904

Kenney, M., & Zysman, J. (2016). The rise of the platform economy. *Issues in Science and Technology, 32*(3), 61–69.

Parker, G. G., Van Alstyne, M. W., & Choudary, S. P. (2016). *Platform revolution: How networked markets are transforming the economy and how to make them work for you.* Norton & Company.

Ruutu, S., Casey, T., & Kotovirta, V. (2017). Development and competition of digital service platforms: A system dynamics approach. *Technological Forecasting and Social Change, 117*, 119–130. https://doi.org/10.1016/j.techfore.2016.12.011

Selander, L., Henfridsson, O., & Svahn, F. (2013). Capability search and redeem across digital ecosystems. *Journal of Information Technology, 28*(3), 183–197. https://doi.org/10.1057/jit.2013.14

Tiwana, A. (2014). *Platform ecosystems: Aligning architecture, governance, and strategy*. Morgan Kaufmann.

Wareham, J., Fox, P. B., & Cano Giner, J. L. (2014). Technology ecosystem governance. *Organization Science, 25*(4), 1195–1215. https://doi.org/10.2139/ssrn.2201688

23

The Role of Leadership to Drive Change

Leadership today demands more than authority—it requires vision, adaptability, and the courage to navigate a world reshaped by constant change—relentless technological progress, evolving consumer expectations, and global upheavals, leadership is the essential force steering organisational transformation. Today's most effective leaders don't just manage change—they actively drive it. While managers typically focus on optimising stability and processes, change-oriented leaders challenge existing paradigms, inspire teams to envision new possibilities, and guide organisations through the uncertainties of innovation. They serve as catalysts for innovation, empowerment, and strategic renewal, equipping their organisations to thrive in volatility rather than merely survive. Their goal is not simply to maintain stability, but to make the business future-ready.

Leadership focused on change requires a fundamentally different mindset than leadership focused on stability. Where managers refine processes and maximise efficiency, change-oriented leaders challenge norms, inspire ambitious visions, and skilfully guide their teams through uncertainty. They help organisations think systemically—making the leap from incremental improvement to transformative potential.

At its heart, this form of leadership begins with vision. The ability to articulate a bold and meaningful future direction is what moves people from complacency to commitment. Effective leaders translate that vision into strategic priorities (Fairhurst & Grant, 2010), rallying teams to tackle complex challenges, test new ideas, and embrace learning—even when failure is a real possibility. They know that without a meaningful "why", even the most innovative tools or strategies lack traction.

Beyond vision, execution driven by empathy and empowerment is essential. Change-oriented leadership thrives on trust. Rather than relying solely on top-down edicts, these leaders decentralise decision-making, create space for experimentation, and empower frontline teams. They encourage cross-functional collaboration and flatten hierarchies, recognising that insight and creativity often lie beyond the C-suite (Eisenhardt & Brown, 1999). In the context of platform ecosystems, such leaders serve as orchestrators—bringing together marketers, engineers, partners, and regulators to co-create solutions.

Moreover, adaptive leadership requires visible role modelling. When senior leaders themselves embrace experimentation, iteration, and vulnerability, that behaviour cascades throughout the organisation. Teams feel safer to share partial progress, raise concerns, or pivot in the face of new data. In an environment of continuous transformation (Fullan, 2001), leaders who demonstrate humility and curiosity signal that the organisation values exploration—even when direction is not fully clear.

Another hallmark of transformative leadership is relentless learning. These leaders treat disruption not as a threat, but as an invitation to upskill, reskill, and evolve. They invest in organisational learning ecosystems—training programmes, digital sandbox environments, cross-team rotations, and external partnerships—that keep the business agile and capable of adapting at pace.

Accountability is also redefined under this leadership lens. Instead of focusing solely on outputs, change-oriented leaders emphasise adaptability, collaboration, and mutual impact (Battilana & Casciaro, 2012). Performance metrics shift from static KPIs to dynamic indicators—such as time-to-prototype, partner satisfaction, customer co-creation activity, and ecosystem growth. By reshaping organisational incentives, they promote the behaviours needed to realise platform success.

Finally, these leaders are relentlessly inclusive. They know that systemic change cannot happen in echo chambers. They invite voices from diverse functions, disciplines, demographics, and geographies. Building inclusive coalitions across partners, customers, regulatory bodies, and distributors (Ansell & Gash, 2008) ensures that transformation reflects the full spectrum of ecosystem needs and that adoption is meaningful and sustainable.

Leadership in the platform era transcends traditional management. It is, first and foremost, a practice of purposeful transformation. Successful leaders identify and articulate compelling futures, empower collaborators to innovate (Beer & Eisenstat, 2000), create environments of trust and experimentation, elevate continuous learning, and build inclusive coalitions for mutual gain. They are not just stewards of organisational performance—they are architects of strategic renewal, guiding businesses from incremental change to adaptive, scalable ecosystems.

Defining Leadership in the Context of Change

Effective leadership for driving change requires a delicate balance between strategic vision and operational execution. It is not enough to articulate grand ideas; leaders must understand the internal and external dynamics that shape resistance and opportunity. They must recognise barriers such as regulatory constraints, cultural inertia, and limited resources—and design adaptive strategies to overcome them.

Change leaders foster collaboration across traditional silos, build trust through authenticity and transparency, and maintain a relentless focus on aligning the organisation with a shared future-state vision (Denis et al., 2010). They create environments where experimentation is encouraged, failure is reframed as learning, and agility becomes second nature.

These leaders see beyond immediate operational concerns, identifying the long-term implications of industry trends and technological disruptions. They empower teams to take ownership of innovation, thereby ensuring that transformation is not just top-down but participatory and sustainable.

Frameworks for Leadership in Driving Change

Several frameworks offer deep insight into how leadership can drive meaningful change. The **Transformational Leadership Model** outlines four core behaviours that underpin successful leadership (Heifetz et al., 2009) during periods of disruption:

1. **Idealised influence**, where leaders model behaviours that inspire trust and admiration;
2. **Inspirational motivation**, where they articulate an attractive vision for the future;
3. **Intellectual stimulation**, encouraging creativity and challenging norms; and
4. **Individualised consideration**, showing genuine concern for each team member's development and contribution.

Similarly, **Kotter's 8-Step Change Model** provides a practical roadmap for leading transformation. It stresses the importance of creating urgency, building a guiding coalition, forming and communicating a vision, empowering action by removing barriers, and embedding new approaches into the culture (Kotter, 1995). These steps highlight that leadership is not a single intervention but a sustained commitment across all stages of change.

Both frameworks converge on a central insight: successful leadership for change is proactive, people-centred, and deeply strategic.

Building a Vision for Change

The starting point of any successful transformation effort is a compelling and actionable vision. Vision gives direction, meaning, and energy to change initiatives. It acts as a bridge between the present reality and the desired future state, helping stakeholders understand both the "why" and the "how" of transformation.

In industries facing entrenched rigidities, such as financial services or healthcare, visionary leadership can be particularly potent. A fintech company, for instance, might frame its vision around democratising financial access through technology, a message that resonates not only internally but also with customers, partners, and regulators.

A clear vision galvanises collective effort. When leaders connect the vision to the organisation's core mission and values, they inspire alignment, commitment, and purposeful action at all levels.

Empowering Teams to Embrace Change

Empowerment is the cornerstone of successful transformation. Leaders cannot drive change alone; they must equip, enable, and energise their teams to take initiative and innovate.

Creating psychological safety is a critical foundation. When employees feel safe to express ideas, challenge assumptions, and take risks without fear of ridicule or reprisal, creativity flourishes. Leaders foster this environment by encouraging open dialogue, modelling vulnerability, and recognising diverse contributions.

Investing in skills development further strengthens empowerment. Organisations undergoing digital transformation, for instance, benefit from training programmes that build technological fluency and change resilience among employees. When people feel competent, they are more willing to engage with new systems, processes, and paradigms.

Empowered teams are more agile, more innovative, and more committed—qualities essential for thriving in volatile markets.

Overcoming Resistance to Change

Resistance is an inevitable, and often rational, response to change. It stems from fear of the unknown, perceived threats to status or competence, and emotional attachments to existing ways of working. Leaders must approach resistance not as an obstacle to crush but as a signal to engage.

Open, transparent communication is essential. Leaders who proactively explain the rationale behind change, address concerns honestly, and invite stakeholder input create trust and reduce anxiety (Lichtenstein & Plowman, 2009). Collaboration in decision-making, where feasible, increases ownership and diminishes feelings of alienation.

Incentive structures can also shift behaviours. Recognition programmes, career development opportunities, or tangible rewards for embracing new practices signal that change is both valued and personally beneficial.

Ultimately, overcoming resistance requires patience, empathy, and strategic acumen.

The Role of Adaptive Leadership

Adaptive leadership has become particularly salient in the context of digital transformation and systemic disruption. Adaptive leaders embrace uncertainty, viewing complexity as an opportunity for learning and innovation rather than a threat to be eliminated. This leadership style emphasises iterative problem-solving, agile experimentation, and continuous feedback loops (Ospina & Foldy, 2010). Rather than committing prematurely to fixed solutions, adaptive leaders pilot initiatives, gather insights, and refine approaches based on real-world experience.

For instance, an energy sector leader such as **Siemens Energy**, introducing smart grid technology, might launch small-scale pilot programmes in partnership with utilities and municipalities—iteratively refining both the technical backend and customer-facing interfaces before broader rollout. Such adaptive strategies (Schein, 2010) balance boldness with prudence—minimising risk while maximising learning, engagement, and impact.

Adaptive leadership also nurtures resilience, equipping organisations to navigate not only planned transformations but also unexpected disruptions with agility and clarity.

Case Studies: Leadership Driving Change

Across industries, forward-thinking leaders are successfully navigating resistance and accelerating transformation by combining vision with collaboration.

In the financial services sector, **Adyen**, a global payments technology provider, disrupted legacy banking models by leveraging a unified platform to streamline merchant onboarding, compliance, and cross-border payments for enterprise clients. The company's leadership embraced a long-term, product-first strategy—engaging proactively with regulators and enterprise partners, while empowering teams to respond swiftly to evolving market needs.

This clarity of vision enabled Adyen to scale rapidly across industries and geographies.

In healthcare, **Philips HealthSuite** enabled hospitals and care providers to adopt cloud-based patient data and telehealth solutions. Facing resistance from clinical staff and IT administrators, leadership at Philips worked closely with healthcare partners to co-develop use cases, deliver integrated training, and align digital health solutions with real-world workflows. This inclusive leadership approach helped overcome legacy system barriers and regulatory complexity while advancing patient-centric care.

These examples affirm that leadership is not ancillary to change—it is the engine of transformation.

Marketing Leadership in the Age of Ecosystems

Leadership principles extend profoundly into marketing domains. As customer expectations evolve and digital ecosystems become more complex, marketing leaders must model the same adaptive, visionary, and empowering behaviours required for broader organisational change.

Effective marketing leadership aligns campaigns with organisational transformation efforts, ensuring consistent messaging, authentic engagement, and dynamic responsiveness to market signals. Marketing teams that operate under transformational leadership (Fullan, 2001) frameworks are more likely to experiment with new channels, personalise content, and leverage data creatively.

Marketing leadership in the age of ecosystems demands a fundamentally different approach—one where vision, collaboration, and adaptability shape success. As customer expectations become more personalised, immediate, and authentic, marketing leaders must evolve into architects who inspire organisations to embrace experimentation and shared purpose.

First, marketing leadership must align seamlessly with organisational transformations. When executives drive digital or cultural change, marketing should translate strategy into clear, integrated customer initiatives that reinforce the broader mission. Leaders who foster a culture of curiosity and innovation enable teams to experiment (Beer & Eisenstat, 2000), with new channels—such as immersive AR campaigns or voice interfaces—testing and refining content based on live performance.

Second, marketing leaders become bridge-builders across departments. An ecosystem strategy demands coordination among IT, product, legal, finance, and external partners. Those who cultivate relationships with engineers can embed customer feedback into product features. By collaborating with legal and compliance teams, they can launch dynamic and compliant co-creation programmes. Such cross-functional engagement ensures marketing is seen as a unifying force.

Third, adaptive decision-making is essential. In a platform economy, continuous learning is a must. By monitoring engagement metrics, partner activity, and sentiment, leaders can spot new opportunities. Sharing these insights company-wide enables teams to shift from rigid campaign plans to agile, iterative sprints. This approach allows content, channels, offers—even business models—to adapt swiftly to ecosystem signals.

Fourth, inclusivity strengthens marketing strategy. A truly collaborative leader brings diverse voices into the creative process—from customer advocates to regional partners and complementors. Involving these stakeholders early in campaign planning or strategy sessions generates richer ideas and deeper resonance. Inclusivity is essential to ensure that co-created solutions are both relevant and credible.

Moreover, marketing leaders must champion collaboration across traditional boundaries—partnering with IT, product development, legal, and external ecosystem players to deliver integrated, customer-centric experiences.

Leadership in marketing, as in broader organisational contexts, is ultimately about shaping culture, inspiring action, and building enduring value.

Finally, building the right culture makes all the difference. Marketing leaders set the tone by celebrating complementor successes, recognising collaborative achievements, and highlighting each actor's role in the ecosystem. Such behaviours foster internal trust, empower bold ideas, and reinforce co-creation both inside and outside the organisation. This *Leadership-Driven Change Ecosystem* framework outlined, will enable the change needed to transform.

In essence, marketing leadership in platform-driven environments go beyond traditional campaign metrics. It's about crafting ecosystems through visionary guidance, cross-functional orchestration, dynamic responsiveness, stakeholder inclusion, and cultural stewardship. When leaders embrace these dimensions, marketing does more than communicate (Beer & Eisenstat, 2000)—it shapes ecosystems, drives collaboration, and unlocks enduring value for all participants.

Visual Framework: Leadership at the Core of Organisational Transformation

Figure 23.1 presents a framework that charts the leadership journey as a cascading force. It shows the leadership journey as a chain reaction: from vision and strategy, through empowered teams and agile experimentation, to cross-stakeholder collaboration—ultimately driving lasting ecosystem value.

The *Leadership-Driven Change Ecosystem* model, illustrates how marketing leadership evolves into an ecosystem enabler—catalysing transformation

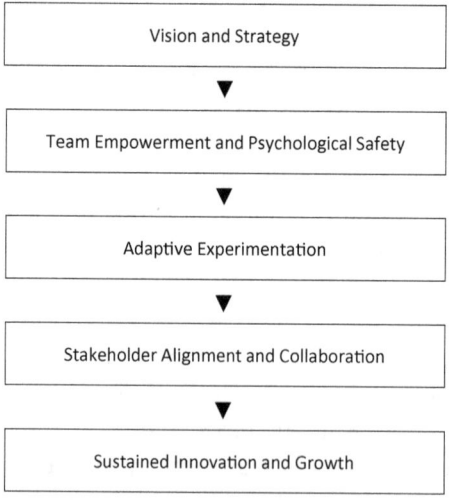

Fig. 23.1 Leadership-Driven Change Ecosystem Model

beyond functional boundaries. It demonstrates how marketing leadership in platform-driven environments becomes a transformative force—not just measuring campaigns, but architecting ecosystems that foster collaboration, adaptability, and sustained innovation.

> **Reflective Prompt: Are You Leading Change—Or Managing Status Quo?**
>
> "Are you actively shaping your organisation's future, or merely optimising its present?"
>
> Reflect on:
>
> 1. How clearly your leadership articulates a vision for transformation.
> 2. How empowered and safe your teams feel to innovate and challenge conventions.
> 3. How well your leadership adapts to uncertainty and learns from feedback.

> **Exercise: Leadership for Change Canvas (Table 23.1)**
>
> **Step 1: Define Your Vision**
>
> - What future state do you envision for your organisation?
> - How will you communicate this vision compellingly?
>
> **Step 2: Empower Teams**
>
> - What structures, behaviours, and support mechanisms foster psychological safety and innovation?
>
> **Step 3: Embed Adaptability**
>
> - Where can you pilot small-scale innovations?
> - How will you collect and apply feedback to refine your approach?

Table 23.1 Leadership for Change Canvas—Template Grid

Element	Description
Vision statement	Articulate future-state goals and alignment with values
Empowerment actions	Training, recognition, transparent communication
Adaptive strategies	Pilot programmes, iterative refinement, continuous learning
Metrics for success	Employee engagement, innovation outputs, stakeholder trust

This chapter gives you a clear blueprint to lead decisively in platform environments, aligning vision, teams, and stakeholders to drive lasting strategic impact.

References

Ansell, C., & Gash, A. (2008). Collaborative governance in theory and practice. *Journal of Public Administration Research and Theory, 18*(4), 543–571. https://doi.org/10.1093/jopart/mum032

Battilana, J., & Casciaro, T. (2012). Change agents, networks, and institutions: A contingency theory of organizational change. *Academy of Management Journal, 55*(2), 381–398. https://doi.org/10.5465/amj.2009.0891

Beer, M., & Eisenstat, R. A. (2000). The silent killers of strategy implementation and learning. *Sloan Management Review, 41*(4), 29–40.

Denis, J. L., Langley, A., & Rouleau, L. (2010). The practice of leadership in the messy world of organizations. *Leadership, 6*(1), 67–88. https://doi.org/10.1177/1742715009354233

Eisenhardt, K. M., & Brown, S. L. (1999). Patching: Restitching business portfolios in dynamic markets. *Harvard Business Review, 77*(3), 72–82.

Fairhurst, G. T., & Grant, D. (2010). The social construction of leadership: A sailing guide. *Management Communication Quarterly, 24*(2), 171–210. https://doi.org/10.1177/0893318909359697

Fullan, M. (2001). *Leading in a culture of change*. Jossey-Bass.

Heifetz, R. A., Grashow, A., & Linsky, M. (2009). The practice of adaptive leadership: Tools and tactics for changing your organization and the world. *Harvard Business Press*. https://doi.org/10.1016/j.lisr.2009.05.001

Kotter, J. P. (1995). Leading change: Why transformation efforts fail. *Harvard Business Review, 73*(2), 59–67. https://hbr.org/1995/05/leading-change-why-transformation-efforts-fail-2

Lichtenstein, B. B., & Plowman, D. A. (2009). The leadership of emergence: A complex systems leadership theory of emergence at successive organizational levels. *The Leadership Quarterly, 20*(4), 617–630. https://doi.org/10.1016/j.leaqua.2009.04.006

Ospina, S. M., & Foldy, E. G. (2010). Building bridges from the margins: The work of leadership in social change organizations. *The Leadership Quarterly, 21*(2), 292–307. https://doi.org/10.1016/j.leaqua.2010.01.008

Schein, E. H. (2010). Organizational culture and leadership (4th ed.). Jossey-Bass. (Schein, 2010).

24

Scaling Platforms with Complementors

In these complex digital ecosystems, scaling a platform is no longer simply about adding new features or attracting more users. It requires building a vibrant, interconnected network where external partners actively contribute to the platform's growth and relevance. At the heart of this network are complementors—independent entities that enhance, extend, and amplify the value created within the platform. Understanding how complementors operate, why they matter, and how to manage these relationships is critical for any organisation seeking to drive sustainable, scalable growth.

Complementors matter because they bring specialised capabilities and fresh perspectives that internal teams may lack. They often focus on niche needs—vertical compliance, domain-specific insights, localised services—allowing platforms to reach new audiences quickly. A fintech platform that integrates fraud prevention tools or identity verification services, for instance, can deliver more robust and compliant offerings than it could alone. Each complementor reinforces platform trust and appeal, helping it resonate with broader user bases.

But integration alone is not enough—complementor relationships must be actively managed. Governing these relationships starts with clear mutual benefit: defining how the platform and its complementors succeed together. This may include revenue sharing, co-marketing opportunities, or priority access to resources. When every party sees returns proportionate to their effort, momentum builds organically—and rapidly.

Establishing structural support is equally vital. This means providing APIs and developer tools that are easy to use, offering dedicated onboarding materials, and designing certification programmes that set quality standards

(Anderson & Tushman, 1990). Platforms also need integration playbooks—guides for technical compatibility—to ensure complementors work consistently and predictably. Regular check-ins and community events, such as hackathons or webinars, provide channels for co-innovation and feedback that foster a stronger sense of shared ownership.

Transparency and trust underpin successful complementor ecosystems. Platforms should openly share metrics—usage stats, revenue contributions, customer feedback—to recognise and guide partners. Acknowledging complementor contributions publicly, through success stories or featured partner profiles, reinforces value and builds momentum across the ecosystem.

Yet challenges abound. Misaligned goals, inconsistent technical standards, or uneven performance from complementors can erode trust. Power imbalances—where dominant complementors may influence platform decisions or block smaller voices (Adner, 2017)—must be consciously avoided. Platforms should therefore cultivate a balanced partner mix, combining marquee partnerships with a healthy base of smaller, agile contributors. Regular governance forums, a neutral advisory council, or a transparent vetting process can help maintain this balance and safeguard smaller participants' interests.

Equally important, complementor ecosystems must evolve strategically. As user needs shift, platforms must keep complementors aligned with emerging priorities—whether through joint roadmap planning or integrating partner-driven feature requests. This ensures that the platform ecosystem remains current and dynamic rather than static or stale. When done right, complementor networks become self-driving engines of innovation and scale. Each partner brings new capabilities, taps into fresh audiences, and strengthens the collective proposition. From there, a virtuous cycle emerges: new capabilities attract new users and partners, which in turn fuels more innovation and growth.

Platforms that integrate, govern, and evolve with complementor ecosystems position themselves not just to grow, but to lead. By collaborating rather than competing alone, these platforms build durable advantage (Boudreau, 2010)—powered by shared insight, diversified capability, and the collective ambition of everyone in the network.

Scaling Smart: Why Complementors Are Your Competitive Edge

Complementors are businesses, developers, service providers, or other actors that offer products, services, or technologies that enrich a platform's core offerings. Unlike competitors, who seek to substitute or replace, complementors create synergies. Their innovations extend the platform's functionality, address user pain points, and unlock new value propositions.

For instance, within a digital advertising platform, complementors might provide advanced analytics tools, creative content integrations, or campaign optimisation engines. In fintech, complementors could include start-ups offering niche services like digital wallets, fraud detection, or robo-advisory platforms. In every case, they transform the platform from a standalone service into a dynamic, evolving ecosystem.

This collaborative structure is central to modern marketing: platforms that succeed in attracting and empowering complementors become richer, more attractive, and more resilient (Ceccagnoli et al., 2012). In turn, complementors gain access to the platform's user base, brand equity, and technical infrastructure, enabling them to scale faster and more efficiently.

The Role of Complementors in Value Creation

Complementors contribute to value creation by diversifying the platform's offerings, addressing unmet needs, and accelerating innovation. They bring specialised expertise and niche capabilities that the core platform provider might lack the resources or strategic focus to develop internally.

By enriching the platform's ecosystem, complementors fuel a virtuous cycle of network effects. As the number and quality of complementors grow, the platform becomes more appealing to users. Greater user engagement, in turn, attracts even more complementors. This feedback loop not only strengthens the platform's competitive advantage but also creates resilience against disruption.

Moreover, complementors drive co-creation dynamics: they are not just service providers but active collaborators. Through APIs, shared data environments, joint marketing initiatives, and integrated user experiences, complementors and platforms co-develop solutions (Cui & Wu, 2016) that neither party could have achieved alone.

Frameworks for Understanding Complementors

Several strategic frameworks shed light on the function of complementors within marketing ecosystems. **The Platform Ecosystem Model** categorises participants into core providers, users, and complementors, showing how each role interrelates and how complementors expand the ecosystem's reach and functionality.

Similarly, **Value Network Analysis** maps the flows of resources, capabilities, and benefits within an ecosystem. This perspective highlights how complementors link into the platform's value chain, often serving as crucial nodes that connect users with enhanced offerings.

Both frameworks emphasise a critical truth: complementors are not peripheral—they are central to the scalability, resilience, and innovation capacity of modern platforms.

Why Complementors Are Critical to Scaling Platforms

Platforms looking to scale effectively must view complementors as strategic partners, not optional extras. Complementors enable platforms to enter new markets, serve diverse user segments, and enrich user experiences without overextending their internal capabilities.

For example, a social media platform that collaborates with third-party developers to offer new content tools or data analytics applications can rapidly broaden its appeal to professional marketers, influencers, and e-commerce brands (Kyriakopoulos & Moorman, 2004). Each successful complementor adds a new reason for users to stay engaged.

Complementors also facilitate network effects—the more valuable services they bring into the platform's ecosystem, the more attractive the platform becomes to future complementors and users alike. This cumulative advantage is a cornerstone of platform dominance in industries like fintech, e-commerce, and mobile applications.

What Makes Complementor Management So Challenging During Scale-Up?

However, managing an ecosystem of complementors is not without complexity. One major challenge is maintaining strategic alignment (Zhu & Liu, 2018). While platforms often prioritise long-term user engagement and ecosystem health, individual complementors may focus narrowly on short-term revenue or market share. These divergent incentives can create friction or conflict if not proactively addressed.

Quality control is another pressing issue. As the number of complementors grows, ensuring consistent user experiences, safeguarding security, and maintaining brand integrity becomes increasingly challenging. Platforms must establish and enforce robust standards—through certification programmes, regular audits, and clear integration guidelines.

Regulatory compliance further complicates matters. Platforms are responsible for ensuring that complementor activities meet legal and ethical standards, particularly in sensitive areas like data privacy, financial transactions, or healthcare services.

Effective complementor management thus requires a balance between openness (to encourage innovation) and governance (to protect users and brand equity).

Case Studies: How Complementors Drive Value

The transformative power of complementors is vividly illustrated across industries. In fintech, platforms like **PayPal** have built thriving ecosystems by partnering with fraud detection services, payment processors, and financial analytics providers. These complementors have enabled PayPal to offer a comprehensive suite of services that extend far beyond basic digital payments.

In retail, **Amazon's** marketplace model hinges on complementors. Third-party sellers, logistics providers, and advertising partners create a multi-layered ecosystem that continually expands Amazon's reach and resilience.

Technology platforms like **Apple's App Store** and **Google Play** similarly showcase the power of complementor ecosystems. By creating vibrant developer communities, these platforms offer an almost limitless range of applications and services, enhancing device value while generating new revenue streams.

These examples underscore that complementors are not auxiliary—they are strategic multipliers of platform success.

Partnering for Scale: How to Engage and Grow with Complementors

Building and sustaining effective relationships with complementors requires intentional strategy and investment. Platforms must foster trust, ensure transparency, and create shared incentives for collaboration.

Providing technical support—such as developer kits, API access, and sandbox environments—makes it easier for complementors to innovate successfully within the ecosystem (Kapoor & Lee, 2013). Offering clear guidelines around integration, security, and user experience helps maintain quality and coherence.

Incentive structures, such as revenue sharing, marketing support, and recognition programmes, can further motivate complementors to prioritise platform-aligned outcomes. Governance mechanisms, including onboarding vetting, periodic reviews, and performance benchmarks, ensure that innovation does not come at the expense of trust and quality.

The most successful platforms act as facilitators and orchestrators, not controllers—curating ecosystems where diverse complementors can thrive and contribute meaningfully.

Marketing with Complementors: Expanding Reach and Relevance

Complementors have transformative implications for marketing. They enable platforms to offer more personalised, comprehensive, and engaging user experiences, enriching the value proposition at every touchpoint.

For marketers, complementors represent an opportunity to co-create campaigns, tap into new audiences, and leverage partner capabilities to amplify reach and impact. Collaborative marketing initiatives that involve complementors—such as joint webinars, bundled promotions, or integrated user experiences—create synergies that no single actor could achieve alone.

Marketing with complementors unlocks powerful avenues for expanding both reach and relevance in meaningful ways. By partnering with external contributors—such as app developers, service integrators, or specialist content creators—platform marketers can deliver far more personalised, comprehensive, and frictionless experiences at every interface with the audience (Fuller et al., 2011). Complementors add dimension and depth to a platform's offering, giving users compelling reasons to stay engaged and explore further.

When marketers co-create campaigns with complementors, the benefits multiply. Imagine hosting joint webinars where partner experts provide deep dives on niche topics that resonate with the shared audience or offering bundled promotions that combine the platform's features with complementary services—such as analytics tools or consulting support—into a unified package. These initiatives not only broaden the platform's appeal, they embed partner value into the experience itself, making marketing efforts feel collaborative rather than purely brand-led.

Beyond creative collaboration, complementors fuel smarter, data-driven marketing. By integrating partner services or tools, platforms gain access to richer insights into user behaviour (Gawer & Cusumano, 2013)—from usage patterns to service preferences and engagement context. When marketers harness this additional layer of intelligence, they can refine audience segmentation, tailor messaging more precisely, and optimise content delivery based on real-world usage. The result is higher conversion rates, better retention, and a stronger sense of individualised engagement. Complementors enhance data-driven marketing by providing deeper insights into user behaviour, preferences, and journeys. This intelligence allows marketers to refine targeting, optimise messaging, and drive higher engagement and conversion rates.

Moreover, marketing efforts with complementors can amplify credibility. When users see trusted third-party brands working alongside the platform (Thomas et al., 2014)—whether through co-branded content, shared case studies, or visible integration—the platform's trustworthiness increases. This collaborative visibility builds reputational equity, reassuring users that the ecosystem is open, robust, and invested in their outcomes.

Operationalising these collaborations demands structure. Platforms benefit from clearly defined frameworks for co-marketing: joint planning sessions, shared KPIs, revenue-share models, and content calendars. Regular alignment meetings encourage transparency, mutual support, and coordinated rollout strategies. Marketers should also provide partners with enablement assets—such as brand guidelines, content templates, and analytics dashboards—to ensure joint initiatives are consistent, effective, and aligned with platform standards.

Finally, ongoing recognition reinforces long-term collaboration. Highlighting successful partner campaigns in newsletters, social channels, or at ecosystem events showcases shared success and inspires others to participate (Rong et al., 2015). Celebrating complementor milestones—whether through awards, spotlights, or community shout-outs—cultivates enthusiasm and loyalty across the network.

Marketing with complementors isn't just a tactic—it's a strategic posture. It broadens audience reach, deepens relevance, enhances precision through data, builds credibility, and fosters a collaborative ecosystem culture. When marketers embrace complementors as active collaborators, marketing evolves into a shared journey of growth, insight, and mutual impact.

In an interconnected landscape, mastering complementor relationships is not a tactical choice—it's a strategic requirement for platform marketing success.

Visual Framework: Complementors and Platform Growth Dynamics

In Figure 24.1 introduces a framework on how complementors fuel platform marketing success by expanding user value, deepening engagement, and driving network growth through collaborative innovation.

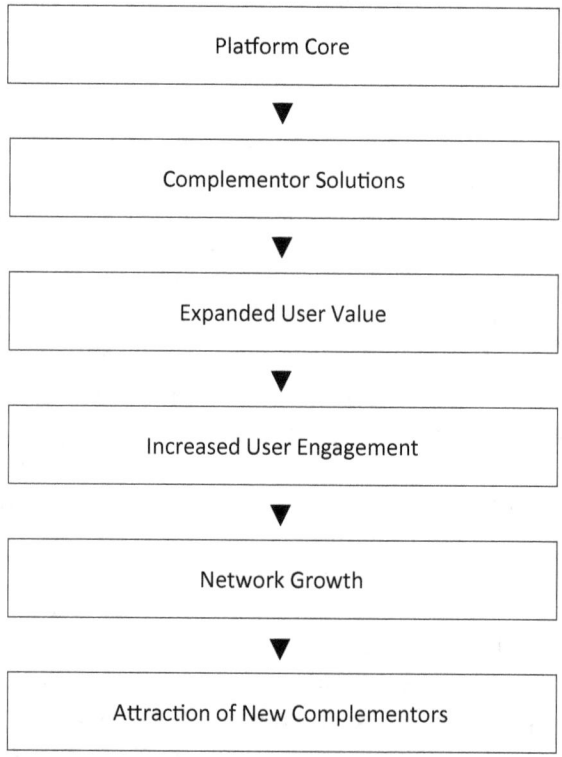

Fig. 24.1 Scaling Platforms Through Complementor Networks

Table 24.1 Complementor Strategy Canvas—Template Grid

Element	Description
Complementor Mapping	Current partners and new opportunity areas
Support Structures	Developer resources, co-marketing programmes, training
Incentives and Rewards	Revenue sharing, brand exposure, ecosystem leadership
Quality and Governance	Integration standards, reviews, performance monitoring

The *Scaling Platforms through Complementor Networks* model highlights the virtuous cycle where strategic partnerships enhance the core offering, attract new users, and draw in more complementors—creating scalable, ecosystem-driven momentum.

> **Reflective Prompt: How Well Are You Leveraging Complementors?**
>
> "Are you treating complementors as peripheral partners–or as core architects of your ecosystem's success?"
>
> Reflect on:
>
> 1. How you identify, attract, and support complementors in your ecosystem.
> 2. Whether you offer the right technical, marketing, and governance frameworks to empower complementors.
> 3. How complementor activities are integrated into your broader marketing and growth strategies.

> **Exercise: Complementor Strategy Canvas (Table 24.1)**
>
> **Step 1: Map Your Complementor Landscape**
>
> - Who are your current complementors? Where are the gaps or opportunities?
>
> **Step 2: Define Collaboration Structures**
>
> - What support (technical, marketing, strategic) do complementors need to succeed?
>
> **Step 3: Align Incentives and Governance**
>
> - How can you align complementor goals with platform growth?
> - What standards and safeguards ensure ecosystem integrity?

This chapter helps you build and sustain ecosystem momentum by showing how to strategically harness partnerships that amplify value, attract users, and scale growth.

References

Adner, R. (2017). Ecosystem as structure: An actionable construct for strategy. *Journal of Management, 43*(1), 39–58. https://doi.org/10.1177/0149206316678451

Anderson, P., & Tushman, M. L. (1990). Technological discontinuities and dominant designs: A cyclical model of technological change. *Administrative Science Quarterly, 35*(4), 604–633. https://doi.org/10.2307/2393511

Boudreau, K. J. (2010). Open platform strategies and innovation: Granting access vs. devolving control. *Management Science, 56*(10), 1849–1872. https://doi.org/10.1287/mnsc.1100.1215

Ceccagnoli, M., Forman, C., Huang, P., & Wu, D. J. (2012). Cocreation of value in a platform ecosystem: The case of enterprise software. *MIS Quarterly, 36*(1), 263–290. https://doi.org/10.2307/41410417

Cui, A. S., & Wu, F. (2016). Utilizing customer knowledge in innovation: Antecedents and impact of customer involvement on new product performance. *Journal of the Academy of Marketing Science, 44*, 516–538. https://doi.org/10.1007/s11747-015-0433-x

Fuller, J., Hutter, K., & Faullant, R. (2011). Why co-creation experience matters: Creative consumers and the differences among them. *Journal of Business Research, 64*(9), 980–988. https://doi.org/10.1111/j.1467-9310.2011.00640.x

Gawer, A., & Cusumano, M. A. (2013). Industry platforms and ecosystem innovation. *Journal of Product Innovation Management, 31*(3), 417–433. https://doi.org/10.1111/jpim.12105

Kapoor, R., & Lee, J. M. (2013). Coordinating and competing in ecosystems: How organizational forms shape new technology investments. *Strategic Management Journal, 34*(3), 274–296. https://doi.org/10.1002/smj.2010

Kyriakopoulos, K., & Moorman, C. (2004). Tradeoffs in marketing exploitation and exploration strategies: The overlooked role of market orientation. *International Journal of Research in Marketing, 21*(3), 219–240. https://doi.org/10.1016/j.ijresmar.2004.01.001

Rong, K., Hu, G., Lin, Y., Shi, Y., & Guo, L. (2015). Understanding business ecosystem using a 6C framework in Internet-of-Things-based sectors. *International Journal of Production Economics, 159*, 41–55. https://doi.org/10.1016/j.ijpe.2014.09.003

Thomas, L. D. W., Autio, E., & Gann, D. M. (2014). Architectural leverage: Putting platforms in context. *Academy of Management Perspectives, 28*(2), 198–219. https://doi.org/10.5465/amp.2011.0105

Zhu, F., & Liu, Q. (2018). Competing with complementors: An empirical look at Amazon.com. *Strategic Management Journal, 39*(10), 2618–2642. https://doi.org/10.1002/smj.2932

25

Collaboration Strategies for Platform Growth

Platforms don't grow in isolation—they scale through purposeful, strategic collaboration in a connected digital economy. Building these alliances enable platforms to access new markets, share resources, and co-create value with partners. By fostering strategic alliances platforms can accelerate growth, enhance innovation and build resilient ecosystems.

Types of Strategic Alliances

1. Joint Ventures: Two or more companies create a new entity, sharing resources, risks, and profits.
2. Equity Alliances: One company invests in another, aligning interests and fostering deeper collaboration.
3. Non-Equity Alliances: Companies collaborate through contractual agreements without equity exchange, focusing on specific projects or objectives.

Selecting the appropriate alliance type depends on factors such as strategic goals, resource availability, and desired level of integration.

Strategic alliances exist along a spectrum of commitment and integration; each suited to different growth objectives and operational contexts. One of the most robust forms is the joint venture (Dussauge et al., 2000; Belderbos et al., 2004). In this model, two or more companies come together to create an entirely new entity, pooling resources, capabilities, and expertise (Ahuja, 2000). They share both the risks and the profits, often entering this arrangement to explore new markets or develop groundbreaking solutions that neither could achieve alone.

Equity alliances take a different shape, where one company acquires a stake in another. This form of partnership signals a deeper alignment of interests and usually reflects a long-term strategic intent (Anand & Khanna, 2000). The equity investment acts as both a financial and symbolic commitment, fostering trust and strengthening collaborative efforts.

On the lighter end of the spectrum are non-equity alliances, where companies form agreements without sharing ownership. These arrangements are often project-based or focused on specific deliverables such as co-marketing campaigns, technology integration, or product development initiatives. Though less formal than joint ventures or equity arrangements, they offer flexibility and speed, particularly valuable in fast-changing markets.

Choosing the right form of alliance requires careful consideration. Strategic goals, desired levels of integration, resource availability, and tolerance for risk all influence the most suitable path forward. The key is alignment, not just on objectives, but on values, expectations, and capabilities.

Fostering Strategic Alliances

Establishing a strategic alliance is more than signing an agreement, it's about building a shared roadmap for sustainable, mutual growth. This process begins with a clear articulation of strategic intent. Platform leaders must define what they seek to accomplish through collaboration (Bamford et al., 2003), whether that's expanding into new geographies, acquiring new technologies, or enhancing user experience through partner capabilities.

The next critical step is partner selection. Here, alignment is everything. Partners must bring complementary strengths and a shared vision for the future. Beyond capability, cultural fit and mutual trust are essential. This stage often involves rigorous due diligence, exploring both the tangible and intangible aspects of potential collaboration.

Once the foundation is laid, effective governance structures must be designed. These frameworks clarify decision-making processes, delineate roles and responsibilities, and establish conflict resolution mechanisms. Without this structure, even the most promising alliance can falter under ambiguity or miscommunication.

Co-creating joint value propositions is another cornerstone. The most successful alliances aren't transactional, they're transformative. By blending resources, expertise, and customer insights, partners can design offerings that are more innovative, differentiated, and aligned with ecosystem needs.

Performance metrics are vital to ensure the alliance remains on track. These should go beyond financial outcomes to include engagement levels, innovation output, customer satisfaction, and ecosystem impact (Hagedoorn, 2002). Transparent reporting against these metrics builds accountability and encourages continuous improvement.

Sustained communication underpins all successful alliances. Regular dialogues help partners anticipate and navigate changes, share lessons, and course-correct when needed. Finally, alliances should be designed with flexibility in mind. As markets evolve, partnerships must evolve with them. Reviewing the relationship periodically and adjusting roles or objectives ensures longevity and relevance (Lavie, 2006).

In essence, fostering strategic alliances is both an art and a discipline, blending vision, structure, and human relationships to drive platform growth through shared success.

Framework for Fostering Strategic Alliances

Successful strategic alliances don't happen by chance—they emerge from intentional design, aligned priorities, and ongoing collaboration. To build and sustain high-performing partnerships, start by understanding the strategic landscape in which your platform operates (Nielsen, 2005). Ask yourself: what gaps are you trying to fill? What strengths are you hoping to amplify? What outcomes would signal success—for your platform, your users, and your ecosystem partners?

This strategic clarity is essential, not just for partner selection, but for maintaining alignment as the relationship evolves. It defines the criteria for evaluating fit, sets the tone for collaboration, and informs how success will be measured (Gulati, 1998). Whether your goals include accelerating product innovation, accessing new customer segments, or expanding geographic reach, being precise about your objectives allows you to approach partnerships with focus and rigor.

Equally important is internal alignment. Before engaging externally, ensure that your own organisation is prepared to support a partnership model. Are internal stakeholders aligned on the value of collaboration? Is there operational bandwidth to support joint initiatives? Are systems in place to track joint performance? Laying this groundwork internally sets the stage for smoother, more productive partnerships.

Ultimately, alliances that thrive are those built on mutual understanding, complementary strengths, and a shared vision for value creation (Inkpen & Tsang, 2005). When these foundations are in place, alliances become more than tactical arrangements—they become strategic growth levers capable of transforming platform potential into ecosystem-wide impact.

To systematically develop and manage strategic alliances, consider the following framework:

1. **Identify Strategic Objectives:** Clearly define what the platform aims to achieve through the alliance, be it market expansion, technology acquisition, or enhanced service offerings.
2. **Partner Selection:** Evaluate potential partners based on complementary strengths, cultural fit, and shared vision. Due diligence is crucial to assess capabilities and align expectations.
3. **Define Governance Structures:** Establish clear roles, responsibilities, and decision-making processes. Effective governance ensures accountability and smooth collaboration.
4. **Develop Joint Value Propositions:** Co-create offerings that leverage each partner's strengths, delivering enhanced value to customers and stakeholders.
5. **Implement Performance Metrics:** Set measurable goals and KPIs to monitor progress, ensuring the alliance remains aligned with strategic objectives.
6. **Foster Open Communication:** Maintain transparent and regular communication channels to address challenges, share insights, and adapt to changing circumstances.
7. **Plan for Evolution:** Recognise that alliances may need to evolve over time. Regularly review and adjust the partnership to respond to new opportunities or challenges.

Visual Framework: The Strategic Alliance Growth Engine

Figure 25.1 presents a framework on how strategic alliances drive platform growth by aligning shared goals, combining capabilities, and enabling value co-creation.

This *Strategic Alliances Driving Platform Growth* model illustrates how alliances move from intention to implementation, driving platform scalability and partner-driven innovation through trust, shared execution, and adaptive alignment.

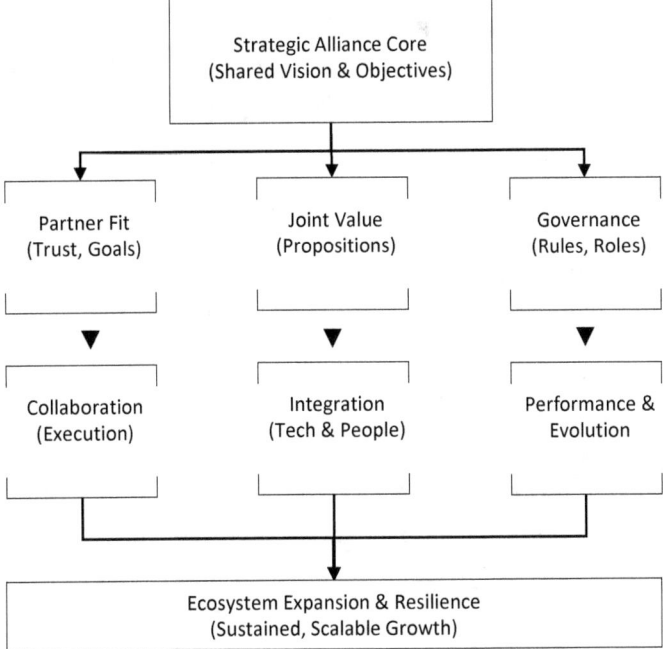

Fig. 25.1 Strategic Alliances Driving Platform Growth Model

> **Reflective Prompt: Are You Building Alliances or Transactions?**
>
> Take a moment to reflect on your current collaborative efforts:
>
> 1. Do your partnerships reflect mutual strategic intent or are they purely functional?
> 2. Have you clearly defined shared outcomes with your partners?
> 3. How robust are your governance structures for collaboration?
> 4. Are you actively co-developing value propositions or simply cross-promoting existing assets?
>
> Strong alliances grow when collaboration is baked into the platform's DNA, not added as an afterthought.

> **Exercise: Strategic Alliance Planning Canvas**
>
> This canvas helps you map, evaluate, and refine strategic collaborations for platform expansion.
>
> 1. **Define Your Strategic Goal**
>   - What specific growth objective does this alliance support (e.g. market entry, product innovation)?
> 2. **Profile Potential Partners**
>   - Who brings the complementary strengths or access you lack?
>   - How do their goals align with yours?
> 3. **Assess Governance and Fit**
>   - What structures will support trust and accountability?
>   - What cultural or operational gaps might exist?
> 4. **Co-Create the Value Proposition**
>   - What combined offering could you deliver that's stronger together than apart?
>   - How does it serve both users and the ecosystem?
> 5. **Plan for Longevity and Adaptability**
>   - What success metrics will you track together?
>   - How will you evolve the alliance over time?

This chapter shows how to turn strategic alliances into scalable action—building trust, alignment, and momentum to power partner-led platform growth.

References

Ahuja, G. (2000). Collaboration networks, structural holes, and innovation: A longitudinal study. *Administrative Science Quarterly, 45*(3), 425–455. https://doi.org/10.2307/2667105

Anand, B. N., & Khanna, T. (2000). Do firms learn to create value? The case of alliances. *Strategic Management Journal, 21*(3), 295–315. https://doi.org/10.1002/(SICI)1097-0266(200003)21:3<295::AID-SMJ91>3.0.CO;2-O

Bamford, J. D., Gomes-Casseres, B., & Robinson, M. S. (2003). *Mastering alliance strategy: A comprehensive guide to design, management, and organization.* Jossey-Bass.

Belderbos, R., Carree, M., & Lokshin, B. (2004). Cooperative R&D and firm performance. *Research Policy, 33*(10), 1477–1492. https://doi.org/10.1016/j.respol.2004.07.003

Dussauge, P., Garrette, B., & Mitchell, W. (2000). Learning from competing partners: Outcomes and durations of scale and link alliances in Europe, North America and Asia. *Strategic Management Journal, 21*(2), 99–126. https://doi.org/10.1002/(SICI)1097-0266(200002)21:2<99::AID-SMJ80>3.0.CO;2-G

Gulati, R. (1998). Alliances and networks. *Strategic Management Journal, 19*(4), 293–317. https://doi.org/10.1002/(SICI)1097-0266(199804)19:4<293::AID-SMJ982>3.0.CO;2-M

Hagedoorn, J. (2002). Inter-firm R&D partnerships: An overview of major trends and patterns since 1960. *Research Policy, 31*(4), 477–492. https://doi.org/10.1016/S0048-7333(01)00120-2

Inkpen, A. C., & Tsang, E. W. K. (2005). Social capital, networks, and knowledge transfer. *Academy of Management Review, 30*(1), 146–165. https://doi.org/10.2307/20159100

Lavie, D. (2006). The competitive advantage of interconnected firms: An extension of the resource-based view. *Academy of Management Review, 31*(3), 638–658. https://www.jstor.org/stable/20159233

Nielsen, B. B. (2005). The role of knowledge embeddedness in the creation of synergies in strategic alliances. *Journal of Business Research, 58*(9), 1194–1204. https://doi.org/10.1016/j.jbusres.2004.05.001

Wassmer, U. (2010). Alliance portfolios: A review and research agenda. *Journal of Management, 36*(1), 141–171. https://doi.org/10.1177/0149206308328484

26

Regional Strategies for Legitimacy and Expansion

Scaling a platform across diverse regions is a strategic and often complex journey. It demands far more than simply replicating a successful model from one market into another. Achieving regional success requires deep sensitivity to local regulations, cultural nuances, and societal expectations. At the heart of successful expansion lies one critical principle: legitimacy. Without it, even the most innovative platforms will struggle to gain traction, attract users, or collaborate effectively with local partners.

It is not simply a matter of translating language or duplicating campaigns—it is a strategic balancing act that weaves together global vision and local authenticity. When moving into new markets, platforms must act with cultural dexterity, respecting not only legal frameworks but also the complex tapestry of local values and societal norms.

Legitimacy starts with rigorous compliance. But it quickly grows beyond paperwork. Consumers want assurance that their data is handled with care, that pricing is transparent, and that the platform aligns with local standards of fairness (Acs et al., 2017). This is especially true in sectors like fintech or healthcare, where mistrust in unfamiliar systems can be a major barrier. A strong regional partner, whether a respected community organisation or a trusted local provider, can help bridge this gap—not only by endorsing legitimacy but by embedding the platform into existing regional trust networks.

Cultural resonance plays an equally vital role. Take customer support, for instance: in some markets, fast and formulaic responses are enough. In others, people expect warm, empathetic engagement—or even personalised outreach from local representatives (Breznitz & Ornston, 2013). Marketing messages, too, must reflect local idioms, success stories, and social norms. A campaign that thrives in one country could be tone-deaf in another, no matter how clever it seems from afar.

Achieving regional legitimacy also confirms the importance of adaptability. From product features to communication styles, platforms that allow for thoughtful customisation signal respect for local identity. Developers may choose different integrations in different regions—think alternative payment methods, local devices, or partnership ecosystems—while the overarching platform architecture remains unified and scalable.

Trustworthy expansion is not a one-time launch—it requires continuous reinforcement. Transparent reporting on compliance milestones, public updates on regional partnerships, and proactive engagement with local user forums help maintain both credibility and momentum. Metrics tied to regional performance—such as Net Promoter Scores, retention rates, or partnership health indicators—offer early warning signs if adjustments are needed.

When platforms invest in regional legitimacy, the payoff is profound. They move from being seen as foreign entrants to becoming local collaborators. They gain user loyalty born of respect, not persuasion. They earn the right to innovate further, unencumbered by suspicion or misunderstanding. In doing so, they transform scale into sustainability—not just growing bigger, but growing deeper and stronger, rooted in trust across every market they enter.

The Importance of Regional Legitimacy

Legitimacy is not simply about legal compliance; it is about being perceived as a trustworthy, responsible, and valued participant within a new regional context. When platforms fail to establish legitimacy, they face regulatory hurdles, user distrust, and partnership challenges that can derail their expansion efforts.

To build legitimacy, platforms must not only meet formal legal and regulatory requirements but also align with the deeper social norms, values, and expectations of each market. For instance, a fintech platform entering a region must address both financial compliance regulations and broader societal concerns around data privacy, financial literacy, and consumer protection.

Cultural alignment is equally vital. A marketing platform expanding into a region where personal relationships drive business decisions must prioritise high-touch customer service, community-building initiatives, and local partnership development—behaviours that signal respect for the local way of doing business.

Frameworks for Regional Strategy Development

Strategic regional expansion requires a structured understanding of local market dynamics. One essential tool is the **Institutional Analysis Framework**, which examines both formal institutions (such as laws and regulatory bodies) and informal institutions (such as customs, traditions, and behavioural norms) (Audretsch et al., 2021). By mapping these factors, platforms can anticipate potential barriers and opportunities.

Another valuable approach is the **CAGE Distance Framework** by Pankaj Ghemawat, which assesses Cultural, Administrative, Geographic, and Economic distances between a platform's home market and the target region (Ghemawat, 2001). Recognising these distances helps platforms design entry strategies that minimise friction and maximise relevance. For example, a platform expanding into a geographically distant but culturally similar region might prioritise digital localisation over product adaptation, while a culturally distant region might require a more profound redesign of both messaging and user experience.

Both frameworks underline the importance of moving beyond superficial market entry tactics to deeply integrated, context-sensitive strategies.

Strategies for Regional Expansion

Regional success starts with listening and learning. Conducting thorough market research—into consumer preferences, local pain points, competitive landscapes, and regulatory environments—is the foundation for designing resonant offerings.

Localisation of services and platforms is crucial. For example, an e-commerce platform expanding into a region with unreliable internet infrastructure might prioritise lightweight mobile apps and offline payment options. Similarly, a SaaS platform targeting new regions might invest heavily in multilingual support and local data hosting solutions to meet both user expectations and regulatory requirements.

Building strategic partnerships with local complementors—such as logistics providers, content creators, or financial institutions—strengthens a platform's credibility and operational efficiency (Alvedalen & Boschma, 2017).

These partners bring regional knowledge, existing networks, and cultural fluency that foreign entrants cannot replicate on their own. Engagement with regulators and policymakers must be proactive and collaborative. Participating in initiatives like regulatory sandboxes allows platforms to test new models while building trust with authorities, aligning innovation with compliance from the outset.

Brand localisation also plays a pivotal role. Successful platforms adapt not just language, but brand tone, aesthetics, and values to reflect regional identities, creating a sense of familiarity and emotional resonance with users.

The Role of Technology in Regional Strategies

Technology serves as both the foundation and the enabler of effective regional expansion. Cloud-based architectures provide the flexibility to localise services while maintaining centralised control and efficiency. Cloud solutions also enable quick deployment of updates, compliance patches, and user-specific adaptations.

AI and advanced analytics offer real-time insights into local user behaviours, enabling platforms to continuously refine their offerings and marketing strategies. Predictive models help identify emerging market needs and guide agile decision-making.

Blockchain technology addresses regional trust deficits by ensuring transparent, tamper-proof records—particularly valuable in markets with weak regulatory enforcement. It enables platforms to guarantee secure transactions and data integrity, building trust from day one.

Case Studies: Regional Expansion in Action

Across industries, successful regional expansions highlight common patterns: local partnerships, cultural adaptation, and technological agility.

In fintech, **Adyen**, a global B2B payments platform, expanded into Asia-Pacific by forming partnerships with local banks and regional payment networks such as **Alipay** and **GrabPay** (Stam & van de Ven, 2021). By integrating regional payment preferences and navigating complex compliance landscapes, Adyen ensured seamless adoption by enterprise merchants across diverse markets.

In retail technology, **VTEX**, a global enterprise digital commerce platform, expanded into Europe and North America by collaborating with local implementation partners, integrating country-specific tax and logistics services, and supporting multi-language, multi-currency storefronts (Brown & Mawson, 2019). This allowed B2B retailers and distributors to rapidly deploy regionally compliant marketplaces tailored to local business practices.

In enterprise technology, **Zendesk** expanded into EMEA and LATAM by establishing regional data centres, partnering with local CX consultants, and tailoring its go-to-market messaging to reflect regional customer service expectations and regulatory requirements (Clarysse et al., 2014). These strategic moves helped Zendesk gain traction with large enterprises seeking scalable, compliant customer support platforms.

Each of these case studies underscores those effective regional strategies hinge on genuine adaptation, not mere replication.

Challenges in Regional Strategies

However, regional expansion is not without its pitfalls. Regulatory fragmentation creates complex compliance landscapes that require significant investment in local expertise and ongoing vigilance.

Cultural missteps can quickly erode brand trust. Over-localising and losing brand consistency—or under-localising and appearing tone-deaf—both carry significant risks. Platforms must find the delicate balance between adaptation and maintaining their core brand promise.

Scalability challenges also loom large. Expanding across multiple, diverse regions strains organisational resources, requiring prioritisation of high-potential markets and phased rollouts.

Successful regional strategies demand patience, nuance, and strategic discipline.

Regional Marketing Strategies: Driving Local Relevance and Global Growth

Regional strategies offer marketers an incredible opportunity. When done thoughtfully, they transform platforms into locally resonant experiences that feel truly personal—while still leveraging the power of a global brand.

Localisation isn't just translation: it's cultural adaptation. What works in one market may fall flat in another. Language must reflect regional idioms, references, and social nuance, but this only scratches the surface. Visual aesthetics—colour palettes, imagery styles, even layout hierarchies—should be chosen based on cultural preference and visual literacy. Brands should understand what imagery evokes trust and relevance in each locale.

Strategically, localisation extends to messaging frameworks and value positioning. A promise of speed and convenience might appeal in urban, tech-forward centres, while more traditional regions may prize local performance or community impact. Marketers must adapt core platform benefits—such as co-creation or innovation—to resonate with region-specific attitudes and pain points, communicating in ways that feel authentic rather than imposed (Qian et al., 2013).

Co-marketing with local complementors further amplifies credibility and presence. Collaborating with regional influencers imbues campaigns with cultural insight (Motoyama & Knowlton, 2017)—whether that means partnering with respected community voices, subject-matter experts, or trendsetters. Joint webinars, regional success stories, or shared content pieces signal that the platform is rooted in local contexts, not merely exporting a brand from afar.

Data plays a vital role in tailoring and iterating regional strategies. Analysing regional behaviour—search trends, feature usage, customer queries—reveals which messaging and channels resonate. Real-time analytics allow campaign refinement on the fly, whether adjusting language tone, shifting channel focus (for example, moving from email to WhatsApp), or optimising content formats to meet regional media habits. Segmentation that accounts for locality, product usage, age demographics, and cultural attitudes boosts personal relevance.

Regional campaigns should feed insights back into the global platform strategy. Lessons learned—about messaging, content performance, compliance preferences, channel adoption—inform global playbooks, improving core offerings for everyone. This creates a virtuous cycle where local insights accelerate global evolution (Spigel, 2017).

When marketers embrace region-first thinking, they do more than drive adoption—they empower deeper loyalty and community. Users feel seen, understood, and appreciated (Kuckertz, 2019). Conversion becomes a by-product of relevance, and durable growth emerges not from mass-market pushes, but from sustained local advocacy and network effects.

Ultimately, the smartest regional marketers don't just replicate centrally defined campaigns—they design with cultural empathy, supported by local partnerships and data-informed decision-making. They ensure every region feels like a customised experience without sacrificing brand consistency or efficiency. In doing so, they position their platforms to scale globally in a way that is genuine, sustainable, and profoundly human.

Marketers who embrace regional strategy thinking position their platforms for stronger customer loyalty, deeper engagement, and more sustainable growth.

Visual Framework: Regional Platform Expansion Playbook

Figure 26.1 introduces a framework outlining a strategic roadmap for regional platform growth—grounded in local insight, regulatory alignment, and adaptive execution.

The *Strategic Pillars for Regional Platform Success* highlights how marketers can scale globally by designing regionally, ensuring relevance, trust, and sustained impact across diverse markets.

> **Reflective Prompt: Are You Designing for Regional Reality?**
>
> "Are you building regional strategies that truly reflect the distinct cultural, regulatory, and economic landscapes of your target markets–or are you exporting a homegrown model and hoping for the best?"
>
> Reflect on:
>
> 1. How deeply you understand each target region's institutions, norms, and user needs.
> 2. Whether you have invested in local partnerships and talent acquisition.
> 3. How your technology stack supports modularity, compliance, and localised innovation.

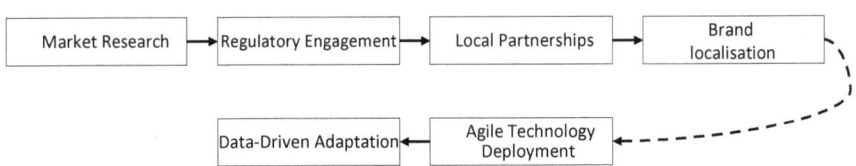

Fig. 26.1 Strategic Pillars for Regional Platform Success

Table 26.1 Regional Strategy Canvas—Template Grid

Element	Description
Market understanding	Cultural, regulatory, and economic landscape analysis
Local partnerships	Identification and engagement of key local actors
Adaptation strategies	Messaging, UX, services tailored to local needs
Scaling plan	Roadmap for testing, learning, and broader regional rollouts

> **Exercise: Regional Strategy Canvas (Table 26.1)**
>
> 1. **Focus on Market Profiling**
>   - What are the key regulatory, cultural, and competitive characteristics of your target region?
> 2. **Outline your Partner Mapping**
>   - Which local complementors could accelerate trust, adoption, or operational efficiency?
> 3. **Enhance Localisation Priorities**
>   - Which aspects of your platform (UX, marketing, compliance) require adaptation?
> 4. **Pilot and Scale**
>   - Define a minimum viable localised strategy. Test, learn, and iterate.

This chapter equips you to drive scalable, regionally attuned platform growth, ensuring your strategy delivers relevance, trust, and results in every market you enter.

References

Acs, Z. J., Stam, E., Audretsch, D. B., & O'Connor, A. (2017). The lineages of the entrepreneurial ecosystem approach. *Small Business Economics, 49*(1), 1–10. https://doi.org/10.1007/s11187-017-9864-8

Alvedalen, J., & Boschma, R. (2017). A critical review of entrepreneurial ecosystems research: Towards a future research agenda. *European Planning Studies, 25*(6), 887–903. https://doi.org/10.1080/09654313.2017.1299694

Audretsch, D. B., Belitski, M., & Caiazza, R. (2021). Start-ups, innovation and knowledge spillovers. *Journal of Technology Transfer, 46*, 1995–2016. https://doi.org/10.1007/s10961-021-09846-5

Breznitz, D., & Ornston, D. (2013). The revolutionary power of peripheral agencies: Explaining radical policy innovation in Finland and Israel. *Comparative Political Studies, 46*(10), 1219–1245. https://doi.org/10.1177/001041401247246

Brown, R., & Mawson, S. (2019). Entrepreneurial ecosystems and public policy in action: A critique of the latest industrial policy blockbuster. *Cambridge Journal of Regions, Economy and Society, 12*(3), 347–368. https://doi.org/10.1093/cjres/rsz011

Clarysse, B., Wright, M., Bruneel, J., & Mahajan, A. (2014). Creating value in ecosystems: Crossing the chasm between knowledge and business ecosystems. *Research Policy, 43*(7), 1164–1176. https://doi.org/10.1016/j.respol.2014.04.014

Ghemawat, P. (2001). Distance still matters: The hard reality of global expansion. *Harvard Business Review, 79*(8), 137–147.

Kuckertz, A. (2019). Let's take the entrepreneurial ecosystem metaphor seriously! *Journal of Business Venturing Insights, 11*, e00124. https://doi.org/10.1016/j.jbvi.2019.e00124

Motoyama, Y., & Knowlton, K. (2017). Examining the connections within the startup ecosystem: A case study of St Louis. *Entrepreneurship Research Journal, 7*(1), 1–19. https://doi.org/10.1515/erj-2016-0011

Qian, H., Acs, Z. J., & Stough, R. R. (2013). Regional systems of entrepreneurship: The nexus of human capital, knowledge and new firm formation. *Journal of Economic Geography, 13*(4), 559–587. https://doi.org/10.1093/jeg/lbs009

Spigel, B. (2017). The relational organization of entrepreneurial ecosystems. *Entrepreneurship Theory and Practice, 41*(1), 49–72. https://doi.org/10.1111/etap.12167

Stam, E., & van de Ven, A. (2021). Entrepreneurial ecosystem elements. *Small Business Economics, 56*, 809–832. https://doi.org/10.1007/s11187-019-00270-6

Part VI

Future-Ready Platform Strategies

27

Using Resource Integration to Amplify Scale

Scaling a marketing platform in a fast-moving digital economy requires more than internal capabilities—it demands collaboration. At the heart of this collaboration lies resource integration: the deliberate combination of technology, expertise, relationships, and insights from multiple actors across the ecosystem. When done well, resource integration enables platforms to expand their capabilities, serve broader audiences, and build ecosystems that are more innovative, resilient, and valuable.

This chapter explores how marketing platforms can strategically harness resource integration to drive scalability and secure lasting competitive advantage.

For marketing leaders, this shift marks a decisive departure from siloed strategies and proprietary development. Instead of building every tool or capability in-house, they are now orchestrating complex networks of partners who collectively enhance the platform's offering. Through this lens, resource integration is not a reactive tactic, but a proactive strategy (Hein et al., 2019)—one that underpins scalability and differentiates brands in an increasingly interconnected marketplace.

The process begins with identifying a platform's core strengths—whether it's a loyal user base, deep industry insights, or robust infrastructure—and then determining what external resources are needed to augment and amplify these assets. Strategic alignment with partners is crucial. The most effective integrations come from collaborations where mutual benefit is embedded from the outset. These are relationships where both platform and partner thrive, with success measured not only by immediate gains but by shared outcomes like user retention, cross-channel engagement, and new market penetration.

Equally important is the seamlessness of the integration itself. Platforms must be designed for modularity and adaptability, with technical infrastructures that support plug-and-play capabilities and operational frameworks that allow for quick onboarding and coordination (Adner & Kapoor, 2010). This means building systems that support interoperability—from open APIs and shared analytics environments to unified user experiences that embed partner functionality directly into the platform journey.

Governance plays a vital role in scaling these collaborative models. As ecosystems grow, consistent standards around data privacy, performance measurement, and service quality ensure that every contributor operates within a trusted and transparent framework. This kind of structured trust is what sustains complex ecosystems over time.

Marketing leaders must also foster a rhythm of co-innovation—whether through pilot projects, joint research, or content collaborations—that continuously renews the value of the ecosystem. These ongoing cycles of experimentation not only deepen engagement but surface new synergies that drive both creative and commercial growth.

Ultimately, resource integration transforms marketing from a closed-loop discipline into a networked capability. Each partner adds a new layer of relevance, a fresh stream of insight, or a novel engagement touchpoint. Together, they enable platforms to evolve from product-centric propositions into dynamic environments of shared innovation and cumulative value. Marketers who master this orchestration position their platforms for long-term resilience—not because they do everything alone, but because they enable others to thrive with them.

The Concept of Resource Integration

Resource integration is the process of assembling complementary assets from a diverse array of ecosystem participants into a cohesive whole that creates greater value than any one actor could achieve independently. In marketing ecosystems, these resources might include technical infrastructure provided by the platform, creative content contributed by users, analytics capabilities offered by complementors, and distribution networks managed by strategic partners.

The act of integration turns isolated capabilities into synergistic offerings, where each actor's strengths amplify the impact of the others. It reflects a broader shift towards value co-creation, where the platform no longer acts as a sole producer of value but as a facilitator of multi-actor collaboration (Breidbach & Maglio, 2016).

For example, consider a digital advertising platform: integration might involve weaving together real-time consumer data from analytics firms, creative assets from advertising agencies, and distribution channels from media partners. The result is a dynamic, highly effective marketing ecosystem that serves advertisers and audiences alike.

Frameworks for Understanding Resource Integration

Resource integration can be understood through the lens of two key frameworks.

The **Service-Dominant Logic (SDL)** framework by Stephen Vargo and Robert Lusch, emphasises that value is always co-created through interactions, not embedded in standalone products or services (Vargo & Lusch, 2016). From this perspective, platforms succeed by orchestrating dynamic exchanges of resources among diverse participants rather than acting as isolated providers.

Complementing this is the **Resource Integration Cycle**, which frames integration as a process with three key stages: mobilisation (identifying and acquiring relevant resources), combination (harmonising them into unified offerings), and leveraging (using the integrated capabilities to generate new value) (Barile et al., 2016).

These frameworks highlight that successful integration is neither accidental nor ad hoc; it is a strategic, deliberate process requiring planning, alignment, and ongoing management.

The Role of Technology in Resource Integration

Technology acts as the critical enabler of resource integration. Without it, connecting, combining, and optimising diverse contributions would be slow, error-prone, and limited in scale.

Cloud-based platforms aggregate and normalise data from multiple sources, enabling real-time insights that drive more precise targeting and decision-making. AI and ML automate the analysis of vast datasets, detect synergies between resources, and even suggest new opportunities for collaboration.

Blockchain technology offers an important foundation of trust, recording interactions securely and transparently. This is particularly vital in ecosystems that handle sensitive information, such as financial transactions or personal data, ensuring that all participants feel confident engaging in resource exchange.

APIs further facilitate seamless integration, allowing third-party complementors to plug into the platform's core systems, extending capabilities without disrupting the underlying infrastructure.

Scaling Through Resource Integration

Resource integration provides platforms with a powerful pathway to scalability. Rather than bearing the full burden of product development, market expansion, or user engagement internally, platforms can leverage the strengths of their ecosystem partners (Ng & Briscoe, 2012).

APIs are a prime example: by offering APIs to third-party developers, a platform can extend its functionalities exponentially. A social media platform might integrate external analytics tools, ad-serving engines, and creative apps—each enriching the core offering without adding strain to internal resources.

Partnerships with complementors also fuel scaling. An e-commerce platform, for example, might partner with logistics providers to enable same-day delivery or integrate with payment gateways to offer localised options across global markets. Each new integration expands the platform's reach, functionality, and user value proposition.

By coordinating the collective strengths of the ecosystem, resource integration allows platforms to scale more rapidly, more sustainably, and with greater strategic agility.

Case Studies: Resource Integration in Practice

Across industries, successful platforms demonstrate the power of resource integration.

In fintech, **Plaid**, a financial data connectivity platform, integrates services such as fraud detection (**e.g. Alloy**), compliance monitoring, and user insights through partnerships with banks, fintechs, and third-party providers.

Rather than building every capability in-house, Plaid enables clients like **Robinhood** and **Chime** to access a secure, modular infrastructure—accelerating product development while ensuring trust and scalability.

In retail, **Amazon Business**, the B2B arm of Amazon, orchestrates a vast network of suppliers, logistics providers, procurement platforms, and data analytics partners to streamline purchasing for enterprises. By integrating services like dynamic pricing, spend analysis, and tailored shipping options, Amazon Business creates a frictionless experience for buyers across verticals—something that would be prohibitively complex for any single supplier to manage alone (Chandler & Lusch, 2015).

In the technology sector, **Salesforce AppExchange** serves as a powerful integration hub. Thousands of developers, ISVs, and marketing technology firms plug into the platform to offer solutions that enhance Salesforce's core CRM capabilities. By enabling customers to assemble tailored tech stacks—from analytics to industry-specific apps—Salesforce fosters a dynamic ecosystem where co-created value and continuous innovation drive long-term platform momentum.

Each of these examples showcases how strategic integration multiplies innovation, scales reach and builds resilience.

Challenges in Resource Integration

Despite its immense potential, resource integration is not without challenges.

One key hurdle is managing complexity. As more actors and resources are brought into the ecosystem, aligning interests, maintaining interoperability, and coordinating contributions becomes exponentially harder.

Ensuring quality and consistency is another critical issue. Platforms must establish rigorous standards and vetting processes to ensure that integrated resources meet user expectations and reinforce the platform's brand promise (Gummesson & Mele, 2010).

Trust remains a foundational concern. Resource integration often requires sharing sensitive information—customer data, proprietary algorithms, strategic insights. Without robust safeguards, legal frameworks, and mutual trust, participants may hesitate to collaborate fully.

Navigating these challenges requires strong governance, technical excellence, and a commitment to ethical, transparent ecosystem management.

Ecosystem-Oriented Marketing Through Resource Integration

For marketers, resource integration offers transformative advantages. By seamlessly connecting data analytics, creative tools, customer relationship platforms, and distribution networks, marketers can orchestrate richer, more personalised, and more effective campaigns.

Integration allows for dynamic targeting—where messaging adapts to user behaviours in real time—and end-to-end measurement, where the impact of marketing activities is tracked seamlessly across touchpoints.

Moreover, as platforms integrate partner capabilities, marketers gain access to broader audiences, deeper insights, and more diverse engagement channels—all without bearing the full cost of development or infrastructure.

Resource integration thus shifts marketing from siloed activities to ecosystem orchestration—driving greater impact, efficiency, and scale.

At the foundation, integrated data analytics provide marketers with real-time intelligence. Instead of relying on de-coupled post-mortem reporting, integrated systems enable immediate understanding of user behaviour—what content resonates, which channels perform best, and where friction points lie. This intelligence feeds directly into dynamic targeting engines that adjust messaging in real time. For example, a user record showing a sudden rise in engagement with sustainability content could trigger personalised offers, eco-focused messaging, or invitations to co-create green initiatives. This approach drives relevance and responsiveness—and it lets marketers shift from broadcast to dialogue.

Creative tools embedded within platform ecosystems further amplify impact. Integration with design applications, video editors, or AR frameworks enables consistent, high-quality content production that leverages user-generated assets, partner contributions, and brand standards (Linde et al., 2021). When creative workflows connect directly with analytics systems, the feedback loop tightens: images, videos, or interactive modules that perform well are highlighted, while underperformers are refined or retired. Marketers therefore evolve from content producers to curators and facilitators—empowering ecosystem participants to co-author campaigns based on what works, rather than pushing fixed narratives.

Customer relationship platforms, when integrated, offer unified views of actor interaction. A marketer can trace a user's journey across touchpoints—initiating behaviour, social engagement, customer support interactions, and referral activity—and craft communication that considers past engagement and future potential (Gummesson & Mele, 2010). These insights support segment-fluid marketing, where users move seamlessly between roles (developer, buyer, advocate), and the platform meets them with tailored experiences at every stage.

Distribution network integration brings external reach into the fold without overhead. By collaborating with partners—whether they are adjacent service providers, regional agencies, or complementary technology stacks—marketers tap into wider audiences through co-branded webinars, joint content packages, or partner-driven referral schemes. These strategies allow marketers to scale efficiently, amplifying reach while sharing costs and leveraging partner credibility.

Furthermore, as platforms integrate partner capabilities—such as fintech compliance modules, health data connectors, or localisation services—marketers can promote bundled offerings that are more compelling than standalone solutions. These bundles enhance value propositions organically and support holistic messaging that highlights ecosystem strengths rather than siloed features (Storbacka et al., 2016). Marketing becomes a vehicle for ecosystem storytelling—illustrating how collaborative resources come together to solve real-world problems.

Equally important, integrated systems support end-to-end measurement. When analytics, creative tools, CRM, and partner performance systems share data, marketers gain visibility into the full marketing ROI—from lead generation to partner-driven sales to long-term engagement. These insights inform budgeting decisions, feature prioritisation, and co-marketing investments—ensuring that resource integration yields measurable value.

Ultimately, resource integration transforms marketing from disconnected campaigns into ecosystem orchestration. It demands new skills—collaboration, systems thinking, relationship management—but rewards marketers with unprecedented impact (Lusch & Nambisan, 2015). Integrated marketing doesn't just amplify brand messages. It elevates the entire platform's relevance, efficiency, and ability to scale—elevating ecosystem marketing as a strategic engine for growth.

Visual Framework: The Resource Integration Flywheel

Figure 27.1 presents a framework that maps out a self-reinforcing cycle. It illustrates how resource integration fuels a self-reinforcing cycle of growth within platform ecosystems.

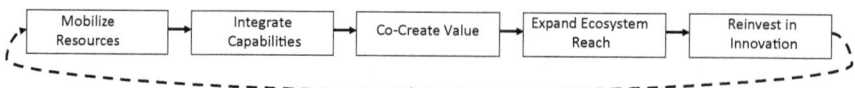

Fig. 27.1 Scaling Through Ecosystem Resource Integration Model

By aligning capabilities and co-creating value, marketers expand reach and accelerate innovation, turning marketing into a strategic engine for scalable ecosystem impact.

The *Scaling Through Ecosystem Resource Integration* model, showcases how aligned resource mobilisation and capability integration drive scalable growth in platform ecosystems.

Reflective Prompt: Are You Integrating to Scale?

"Are you viewing your ecosystem's resources as isolated inputs–or orchestrating them into a dynamic, value-creating system?"

Reflect on:

1. How effectively you are connecting technology, content, data, and partnerships.
2. Whether your integration processes are strategic and scalable—or ad hoc and reactive.
3. What new value could be unlocked if your resource integration became more systematic and dynamic.

Exercise: Resource Integration Strategy Canvas (Table 27.1)

1. **Map Resource Inventory**
   - What internal and external resources are available (technology, expertise, networks, data)?

2. **Identify Integration Opportunities**
   - Where could combining resources create new offerings, improved capabilities, or expanded reach?

3. **Establish Trust and Governance Structures**
   - How will you ensure quality, protect sensitive information, and manage relationships?

4. **Design a Scaling Plan**
   - What partnerships, APIs, or platform extensions will support the next stage of growth?

Table 27.1 Resource Integration Strategy Canvas—Template Grid

Element	Description
Resource inventory	Internal and external assets to integrate
Integration opportunities	Points where resource combinations can drive innovation
Governance structures	Mechanisms for quality assurance and trust management
Scaling plan	Roadmap for ecosystem expansion and value amplification

This chapter helps you transform marketing into a force multiplier, showing how to harness resource integration to drive sustained ecosystem growth and strategic advantage.

References

Adner, R., & Kapoor, R. (2010). Value creation in innovation ecosystems: How the structure of technological interdependence affects firm performance in new technology generations. *Strategic Management Journal, 31*(3), 306–333. https://doi.org/10.1002/smj.821

Barile, S., Lusch, R. F., Reynoso, J., Saviano, M., & Spohrer, J. (2016). Systems, networks, and ecosystems in service research. *Journal of Service Management, 27*(4), 652–674. https://doi.org/10.1108/JOSM-09-2015-0268

Breidbach, C. F., & Maglio, P. P. (2016). Technology-enabled value co-creation: An empirical analysis of actors, resources, and practices. *Industrial Marketing Management, 56*, 73–85. https://doi.org/10.1016/j.indmarman.2016.03.011

Chandler, J. D., & Lusch, R. F. (2015). Service systems: A broadened framework and research agenda on value propositions, engagement, and service experience. *Journal of Service Research, 18*(1), 6–22. https://doi.org/10.1177/1094670514537709

Gummesson, E., & Mele, C. (2010). Marketing as value co-creation through network interaction and resource integration. *Journal of Business Market Management, 4*(4), 181–198. https://doi.org/10.1007/s12087-010-0044-2

Hein, A., Weking, J., Schreieck, M., Wiesche, M., Böhm, M., & Krcmar, H. (2019). Value co-creation practices in business-to-business platform ecosystems. *Electronic Markets, 29*, 503–518. https://doi.org/10.1007/s12525-019-00337-y

Linde, L., Sjödin, D., Parida, V., & Wincent, J. (2021). Dynamic capabilities for ecosystem orchestration: A capability-based framework for smart city innovation initiatives. *Technological Forecasting and Social Change, 166*, 120614. https://doi.org/10.1016/j.techfore.2021.120614

Lusch, R. F., & Nambisan, S. (2015). Service innovation: A service-dominant logic perspective. *MIS Quarterly, 39*(1), 155–175. https://doi.org/10.25300/MISQ/2015/39.1.07

Ng, I. C. L., & Briscoe, G. (2012). Value, variety and viability: New business models for co-creation in outcome-based contracts. *International Journal of Service Science, Management, Engineering, and Technology, 3*(3), 26–48. https://doi.org/10.4018/jssmet.2012070103

Storbacka, K., Brodie, R. J., Böhmann, T., Maglio, P. P., & Nenonen, S. (2016). Actor engagement as a microfoundation for value co-creation. *Journal of Business Research, 69*(8), 3008–3017. https://doi.org/10.1016/j.jbusres.2016.02.034

Vargo, S. L., & Lusch, R. F. (2016). Institutions and axioms: An extension and update of service-dominant logic. *Journal of the Academy of Marketing Science, 44*, 5–23. https://doi.org/10.1007/s11747-015-0456-3

28

Unlocking Future Marketing Potential: The Interplay of Actor Engagement and Co-Creation

In the evolving landscape of marketing, two concepts, actor engagement and co-creation—stand out as the twin engines powering ecosystem success. These interconnected dynamics have shifted the foundations of how marketing platforms operate, moving from transactional value delivery to collaborative value generation. Understanding the rich interplay between actor engagement and co-creation is essential for marketers aiming to unlock future opportunities and secure long-term platform growth.

Actor engagement reflects a move beyond passive consumerism to active, sustained participation. In a platform-based environment, actors are not simply recipients of value but contributors to it. Whether they are customers, developers, influencers, or partners, each plays a role in shaping the platform's direction, offerings, and community. They provide insight, advocate for the brand, and help co-create features, campaigns, and experiences that reflect their needs and aspirations. This depth of involvement transforms engagement into a relational process grounded in trust, reciprocity, and shared purpose.

Co-creation, in turn, evolves naturally from this level of engagement. It is not an additional activity layered onto marketing but a core mechanism through which innovation occurs. When users contribute ideas that are incorporated into products, when partners shape campaigns, or when communities help refine services, co-creation turns marketing into a living, participatory system. It becomes a cycle of input, experimentation, and refinement, wherein value is created not by the brand alone but by the ecosystem surrounding it.

The synergy between these two forces creates a virtuous loop. Engaged actors are more likely to co-create, and those who co-create become more deeply engaged (Brodie et al., 2011). This interaction leads to more adaptive and responsive platforms, where the ecosystem as a whole evolves in step with its contributors. The outcomes are not only more relevant but also more resilient, as they are shaped by diverse perspectives and validated through real-world participation.

For marketers, this shift demands a new approach. It requires designing systems and tools that make participation easy and rewarding, fostering communities where collaboration thrives, and creating feedback loops that show contributors how their input shapes outcomes (Akaka et al., 2013). Recognition, transparency, and shared ownership become crucial levers for sustaining involvement.

Ultimately, marketing leadership in this context is about orchestration rather than control. It is about enabling others to contribute meaningfully, aligning diverse actors around common goals, and cultivating a sense of shared progress. As platforms increasingly rely on ecosystems to innovate and grow, the marketer's ability to manage this interplay between engagement and co-creation will define not just the success of campaigns, but the long-term vitality of the business itself.

How Marketers Can Leverage Actor Engagement and Co-Creation

Actor engagement is more than participation; it's the deep emotional, cognitive, and behavioural investment individuals or organisations make within a marketing ecosystem. Engaged actors contribute time, knowledge, creativity, and enthusiasm—actively shaping the ecosystem's evolution rather than passively consuming its outputs.

Co-creation, meanwhile, is the collaborative process through which value emerges not solely from the platform but from the shared efforts of its participants. It transforms users, partners, and developers from recipients into contributors, fostering a stronger sense of ownership, trust, and shared success.

The relationship between engagement and co-creation is symbiotic: engagement fuels co-creation, and successful co-creation deepens engagement. Without active, motivated actors, co-creation stagnates. Without visible, meaningful opportunities for co-creation, engagement diminishes.

Together, they drive ecosystems from static marketplaces to vibrant, ever-evolving communities.

Frameworks for Understanding the Interplay

Several theoretical frameworks help clarify the intricate relationship between engagement and co-creation.

The **Actor Engagement Framework** dissects engagement into emotional, cognitive, and behavioural dimensions. Emotional engagement captures the attachment and enthusiasm actors feel; cognitive engagement reflects how much attention and thought they invest; behavioural engagement manifests in contributions and participation (Storbacka et al., 2016). By understanding and nurturing all three, platforms can sustain deeper involvement.

The **Value Co-Creation Spiral** illustrates how engagement and co-creation evolve iteratively. As actors contribute resources and ideas, the ecosystem's value proposition improves, attracting even greater engagement. Each cycle strengthens relational bonds and generates new opportunities for innovation, creating a self-reinforcing loop of growth (Vargo & Lusch, 2008).

These frameworks underscore that engagement and co-creation are not linear processes—they are dynamic, interdependent, and iterative.

The Role of Technology in Facilitating Engagement and Co-Creation

Technology acts as the bridge between actors' intentions and tangible co-creation outcomes.

Platforms such as social media hubs, digital marketplaces, and innovation portals leverage advanced personalisation tools to tailor experiences to individual user preferences—fostering deeper emotional and cognitive engagement. Interactive features such as polls, live streams, discussion forums, and content co-creation spaces invite users to actively shape the platform's evolution.

AI elevates this process further by matching actors based on complementary needs and strengths, identifying opportunities for collaboration, and personalising communication at scale. An AI-powered marketing platform, for instance, might intelligently pair advertisers with influencers whose audiences and values align, enhancing both engagement and co-creation potential.

Blockchain technology underpins trust—a critical ingredient for sustained co-creation—by providing transparent, secure records of interactions and contributions, particularly valuable when sensitive data or intellectual property is at stake.

Examples of Engagement and Co-Creation in Practice

Across industries, vibrant examples demonstrate how actor engagement and co-creation fuel ecosystem growth.

In fintech, **Monzo**, a digital banking platform, actively involves users in shaping new features such as bill-splitting tools and saving pots (Jaakkola & Alexander, 2014). Through open forums and customer testing groups, Monzo ensures that its product roadmap reflects real-world user needs—turning customers into collaborators and advocates.

In e-commerce, **Adobe Commerce (formerly Magento)** empowers retailers and developers to co-create through its open-source platform, extension marketplace, and partner community (Frow et al., 2011). By integrating user feedback and enabling third-party contributions, Adobe Commerce drives continuous platform enhancement while deepening engagement with its ecosystem of implementers and merchants.

In technology, **Atlassian's Marketplace** fosters an engaged community of developers by offering extensive APIs, co-marketing support, and revenue-sharing programmes for third-party apps built on products like **Jira** and **Confluence**. This co-creation model has led to a thriving ecosystem of extensions that enrich the core platform and create mutual value (Chandler & Vargo, 2011).

In each case, the line between platform and participant blurs—users and partners become creators, not just consumers.

Challenges in Balancing Engagement and Co-Creation

Despite its promise, nurturing the interplay between engagement and co-creation poses several challenges.

Managing complexity becomes daunting as ecosystems scale. More actors mean more relationships, more expectations, and greater potential for misalignment.

Maintaining trust is critical. Co-creation often demands openness, yet the risks of data breaches, intellectual property misuse, or value misappropriation can dampen willingness to participate.

Preventing engagement fatigue is equally vital. If contributions are undervalued, or if platforms demand too much from their participants without visible reciprocity, enthusiasm can wane.

Platforms must be intentional, transparent, and supportive to sustain momentum over the long term.

Strategies for Enhancing Engagement and Co-Creation

To harness the full potential of these dynamics, platforms should implement deliberate strategies.

Gamification techniques—such as badges, leaderboards, and rewards—can make participation fun and intrinsically motivating, transforming engagement from obligation to excitement.

Open Innovation Frameworks—such as hackathons, open calls for ideas, or co-design programmes—create structured opportunities for actors to contribute meaningfully and visibly.

Recognition and Rewards amplify loyalty. Publicly celebrating contributors, offering revenue-sharing models, or granting early access to new features signals respect and appreciation for actor contributions.

Ultimately, success depends on platforms cultivating a deep sense of mutual investment: actors must believe that their engagement makes a difference—and see tangible proof that it does.

From Messaging to Movement: Marketing in the Age of Co-Creation

For marketers, the implications are profound.

In ecosystems driven by engagement and co-creation, marketing shifts from broadcasting messages to facilitating conversations. Campaigns are no longer designed *for* audiences, but *with* them. Loyalty is built not through repetition, but through participation (Cova & Salle, 2008).

Engaged actors become brand advocates. Co-created products and campaigns generate deeper resonance and broader reach. Data from engaged communities enriches personalisation efforts, creating a virtuous cycle of connection and creativity.

In a world where authenticity, agility, and collaboration are decisive advantages, the interplay of engagement and co-creation is not just a marketing trend—it's the future.

Building on the transformation from messaging to movement, marketers today find themselves at the epicentre of a powerful shift—evolving from craftsperson's of communication to custodians of community and co-creation. In an age defined by collective intelligence, the most compelling campaigns are not those carefully choreographed in boardrooms but those co-authored with the crowd—customers, partners, and creators alike.

When marketing becomes a movement, it moves with purpose. Rather than broadcasting polished narratives, brands spark dialogues—forums that invite participation, feedback loops that shape direction, and challenges that turn passive consumers into active collaborators (Storbacka et al., 2016). Every campaign becomes an open canvas. Themes might emerge from customer forums, feature ideas might originate in co-creation workshops, and content may be crowdsourced from the very people who live with the brand. This authenticity fosters ownership. When someone recognises their idea in a product feature or sees their story reflected in an ad, they don't just respond—they advocate.

Community-sourced innovation naturally builds deeper emotional resonance. A co-created campaign from a financial app, for example, may showcase real user journeys and collective triumphs—not polished corporate messaging (Prahalad & Ramaswamy, 2004). This makes the brand feel more human. Simultaneously, advocates share projects with pride, amplifying reach organically. Word-of-mouth becomes a living, trusted channel rather than a static billboard.

And beyond stories, the feedback itself enhances with precision. When communities test prototypes or vote on features, marketers access real-time insight that fuels personalisation. Recommendations become tailored not by algorithms alone but by community-driven signals. Messaging adapts to micro-moments: a developer receives API updates triggered by their usage patterns, while a small business owner sees case studies featuring peers in their segment (Ramaswamy & Ozcan, 2016).

As this cycle unfolds, marketing morphs into an ecosystem of co-creation, not a one-way funnel. Early participants invite others; feature successes are shared back; iteration becomes communal. Loyalty is no longer built on repetition but on sustained collective contribution. When brands consistently signal "you're part of this," they tap into a far deeper reservoir of connection.

For marketers, then, the challenge and opportunity lie in building the architecture for this movement. That means defining participation channels, social contracts, incentives, recognition systems, and open governance. It means ensuring that the promise of co-creation—visibility, credit, reward—matches the effort required to contribute (Gronroos, 2011). It requires clear alignment between brand values and community ethics. Above all, it means weaving co-creation into the DNA of campaigns so that every message carries the potential for participation.

In essence, this is the growth inflection point: where marketing isn't just about voice—it's about velocity. Velocity of ideas, velocity of contribution, velocity of adaptation. It's a movement where every member becomes a messenger, and every product launch doubles as a celebration of shared ingenuity. At a time where authenticity, agility, and collaboration are not buzzwords but business imperatives, the interplay of engagement and co-creation offers marketers a mission far greater than selling—it invites them to build movements that shape markets, sustain innovation, and cultivate tribe-based loyalty.

Visual Framework: The Engagement—Co-Creation Loop

Figure 28.1 introduces a framework that captures the dynamic loop between engagement and co-creation, where each fuels the other in a continuous cycle of ecosystem growth.

The *Self-Reinforcing Cycle of Actor Engagement and Co-Creation* model outlines how inviting actors to co-create and contribute meaningfully, marketers don't just build campaigns, they build communities that evolve, scale, and sustain innovation together.

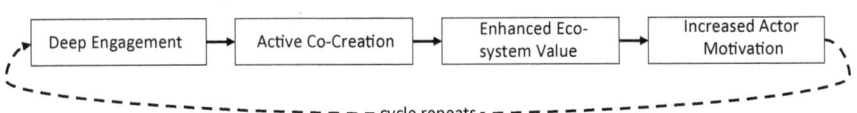

Fig. 28.1 Self-Reinforcing Cycle of Actor Engagement and Co-Creation

> **Reflective Prompt: How Integrated Are Your Engagement and Co-Creation Strategies?**
>
> "Are you treating your users and partners as passive audiences—or as empowered co-creators of your ecosystem's future?"
>
> Reflect on:
>
> 1. Where and how you invite active contributions from your ecosystem actors.
> 2. Whether your engagement strategies truly lead to meaningful opportunities for co-creation.
> 3. How visibly and meaningfully you recognise and reward contributions.

> **Exercise: Engagement—Co-Creation Alignment Map (Table 28.1)**
>
> 1. **Mapping Engagement Inventory**
>   - Where are your users, partners, or developers currently engaging?
> 2. **Discovering Co-Creation Opportunities**
>   - Where could you invite deeper collaboration—idea generation, content creation, solution development?
> 3. **Designing Motivation and Rewards**
>   - What incentives (intrinsic or extrinsic) could fuel more sustained and meaningful contributions?
> 4. **Implementing Feedback and Recognition**
>   - How will you visibly close the loop—showing actors how their contributions matter?

This chapter helps you turn engagement into lasting ecosystem momentum, showing how to co-create with actors to build scalable, evolving, and innovation-driven communities.

Table 28.1 Engagement—Co-Creation Alignment Map—Template Grid

Element	Description
Engagement inventory	Current points of user/partner interaction
Co-creation opportunities	Areas to deepen collaboration
Motivation and rewards	Incentives to sustain participation
Feedback and recognition	Mechanisms to celebrate and reinforce actor contributions

References

Akaka, M. A., Vargo, S. L., & Lusch, R. F. (2013). The complexity of context: A service ecosystems approach for international marketing. *Journal of International Marketing, 21*(4), 1–20. https://doi.org/10.1509/jim.13.0032

Brodie, R. J., Hollebeek, L. D., Juric, B., & Ilic, A. (2011). Customer engagement: Conceptual domain, fundamental propositions, and implications for research. *Journal of Service Research, 14*(3), 252–271. https://doi.org/10.1177/1094670511411703

Chandler, J. D., & Vargo, S. L. (2011). Contextualization and value-in-context: How context frames exchange. *Marketing Theory, 11*(1), 35–49. https://doi.org/10.1177/1470593110393713

Cova, B., & Salle, R. (2008). Marketing solutions in accordance with the SD logic: Co-creating value with customer network actors. *Industrial Marketing Management, 37*, 270–277. https://doi.org/10.1016/j.indmarman.2007.07.005

Frow, P., Payne, A., Wilkinson, I. F., & Young, L. (2011). Customer management and CRM: Addressing the dark side. *Journal of Services Marketing, 25*(2), 79–89. https://doi.org/10.1108/08876041111119804

Gronroos, C. (2011). Value co-creation in service logic: A critical analysis. *Marketing Theory, 11*(3), 279–301. https://doi.org/10.1177/1470593111408177

Jaakkola, E., & Alexander, M. (2014). The role of customer engagement behavior in value co-creation: A service system perspective. *Journal of Service Research, 17*(3), 247–261. https://doi.org/10.1177/1094670514529187

Prahalad, C. K., & Ramaswamy, V. (2004). Co-creating unique value with customers. *Strategy & Leadership, 32*(3), 4–9. https://doi.org/10.1108/10878570410699249

Ramaswamy, V., & Ozcan, K. (2016). Brand value co-creation in a digitalized world: An integrative framework and research implications. *International Journal of Research in Marketing, 33*(1), 93–106. https://doi.org/10.1016/j.ijresmar.2015.07.001

Storbacka, K., Brodie, R. J., Böhmann, T., Maglio, P. P., & Nenonen, S. (2016). Actor engagement as a microfoundation for value co-creation. *Journal of Business Research, 69*(8), 3008–3017. https://doi.org/10.1016/j.jbusres.2016.02.034

Vargo, S. L., & Lusch, R. F. (2008). Service-dominant logic: Continuing the evolution. *Journal of the Academy of Marketing Science, 36*, 1–10. https://doi.org/10.1007/s11747-007-0069-6

29

Advanced Marketing Strategies for Platform Ecosystems

Platform ecosystems represent a seismic shift in how businesses operate, innovate, and connect with their audiences. Moving beyond traditional linear business models, ecosystems thrive on interconnectedness, collaboration, and co-creation, reshaping the expectations of users, partners, and marketers alike. As platforms mature, marketing strategies must also evolve—leveraging the unique dynamics of ecosystems to drive scale, foster innovation, and maintain competitive advantage.

In this chapter, we explore advanced marketing strategies aligned with the complexities and opportunities of platform ecosystems, offering marketers a roadmap to unlock future growth.

No longer confined to traditional linear models where value moves in one direction—platforms are now no longer just channels for promotion or distribution. They become living environments where innovation is not delivered from the centre but emerges at the fringes, shaped by active participants.

As platforms mature, marketing strategies must also evolve—leveraging the unique dynamics of ecosystems to drive scale, foster innovation, and maintain competitive advantage. In this chapter, we explore advanced marketing strategies aligned with the complexities and opportunities of platform ecosystems, offering marketers a roadmap to unlock future growth.

As such, marketing strategies can no longer rely on one-size-fits-all campaigns or static messaging. Instead, they must adapt to dynamic structures where value is created in interactions among producers, consumers, developers, complementors, and institutional stakeholders. This requires a more sophisticated approach—one that integrates strategic orchestration, continuous feedback, and ecosystem awareness.

First, marketers need to embrace strategic orchestration. This means actively designing pathways for collaboration that align with business goals. It requires working closely with product, engineering, legal, and partner teams to embed marketing into the architecture of the platform, ensuring that every feature, interface, and interaction supports broader ecosystem health. For example, launching a public API is not just a technical milestone—it is a marketing moment that signals openness and invites contribution.

Second, marketers must build continuous feedback loops into their strategies. Platforms generate vast amounts of real-time data—from usage patterns and developer behaviour to partner success metrics. Instead of treating data as hindsight, marketers should use it to drive real-time personalisation, adaptive content, and rapid experimentation. A/B tests become evolutionary tools, helping to refine messaging, user journeys, and engagement mechanics in response to actual behaviour within the ecosystem.

Third, ecosystem awareness should guide segmentation and messaging. Traditional demographic or psychographic categories are no longer sufficient. Ecosystem-oriented marketers think in roles—who is contributing, who is consuming, who is influencing, who is governing. Messaging is tailored to each group: developers looking for technical capability, partners seeking co-marketing support, end-users valuing trust and relevance. This role-based approach ensures every actor feels recognised, valued, and connected.

Fourth, marketers need to leverage community and content as core assets. User-generated content, case studies from partner implementations, co-created open-source tools, and community-driven support channels all serve as powerful signals of ecosystem vibrancy. Marketers become stewards of a living narrative—amplifying community voices, highlighting collaboration wins, and recruiting new participants through stories that resonate.

Finally, marketers must adopt long-term ecosystem metrics. Success is not measured in clicks or impressions alone, but in the depth and durability of engagement. Metrics like partner retention, contribution velocity, co-created solutions launched, and network growth become critical. This shift in KPIs encourages investment in areas that nurture the ecosystem—such as partner education, joint innovation events, and governance frameworks.

By aligning marketing strategies with ecosystem dynamics, marketers unlock several advantages. Scale becomes organic as partners introduce their own audiences. Innovation accelerates as external contributors drive feature development. Competitive advantage deepens as the platform evolves in ways no single firm could replicate. And ultimately, the platform becomes resilient—able to withstand disruption through a distributed network of engaged actors.

This alignment transforms marketing into a strategic engine—one that drives not just growth, but ecosystem health and sustainability.

The Evolution of Marketing in Platform Ecosystems

Traditional marketing approaches largely focused on transactional relationships: identifying a need, targeting a customer, and delivering a product or service. In contrast, platform ecosystems demand relational, collaborative, and iterative approaches. Marketers must engage with multiple stakeholders—users, complementors, developers, and even regulators—ensuring that interactions create mutual, evolving value.

Network effects dominate these environments: the more users and partners participate, the greater the platform's value. Advanced marketing strategies must not only attract participants but also amplify their contributions, catalysing vibrant, self-sustaining ecosystems.

Leveraging Data for Precision Marketing

Data is the foundation of advanced marketing strategies within platform ecosystems. Every interaction—whether a user browsing a product, a partner integrating an API, or a developer launching a tool—generates valuable data points.

Harnessing this data enables marketers to move beyond broad segmentation towards precision marketing. Predictive analytics models allow platforms to anticipate user behaviours and preferences, enabling proactive engagement. For instance, a fintech platform might predict which users are most likely to adopt a new budgeting tool and deliver personalised onboarding experiences tailored to their needs.

AI-driven recommendation engines push personalisation even further. By dynamically curating product suggestions, content feeds, or service bundles based on behavioural patterns, platforms can deliver hyper-relevant experiences that foster loyalty and deepen engagement.

Building Ecosystem Loyalty Through Co-Branding

Co-branding within ecosystems is not simply a partnership tactic—it is a strategic lever for loyalty and growth.

When platforms and complementors collaborate to create joint value propositions, they signal trust, innovation, and community to users. For instance, a social media platform might partner with influential content creators to highlight new creative tools, showcasing the ecosystem's versatility while expanding its reach.

Effective co-branding demands alignment on vision, values, and user expectations. Misaligned partnerships risk diluting brand equity, while well-orchestrated collaborations can deepen emotional resonance with users and strengthen the platform's positioning as a facilitator of success.

Fostering Engagement Through Gamification

Gamification transforms engagement from passive interaction into dynamic participation.

By integrating points, leaderboards, rewards, or challenges, platforms can create motivating structures that drive user contributions, loyalty, and advocacy. For example, a marketing platform might gamify feedback collection, rewarding users for submitting ideas that improve products or services.

Gamification is equally potent for complementors. Recognising partner contributions—such as awarding badges for innovation milestones or offering incentives for ecosystem-enriching initiatives—keeps collaborators energised and invested in mutual success (Amit & Zott, 2012).

Properly designed gamification strategies sustain momentum, encourage exploration, and elevate the entire ecosystem's vibrancy.

Expanding Reach Through Multichannel Strategies

In platform ecosystems, multichannel strategies are essential to maintain visibility, drive adoption, and support engagement across diverse audiences.

Social media remains a critical tool for real-time storytelling, community building, and viral amplification. Platforms can use social channels not just for broadcasting messages, but for sparking dialogues, showcasing co-creation stories, and celebrating ecosystem wins.

Email marketing offers a parallel path to personalised, permission-based engagement—particularly effective when segmented by behavioural insights. Meanwhile, thought leadership via whitepapers, webinars, and conference sponsorships helps establish authority and credibility, positioning platforms as trusted ecosystem leaders.

By weaving together digital and traditional channels, marketers ensure a cohesive narrative that resonates across touchpoints.

Aligning Marketing with Ecosystem Governance

Governance structures shape the rules, norms, and expectations within a platform ecosystem—and advanced marketing strategies must reflect these frameworks.

Platforms that champion transparency, equity, and inclusivity must ensure that their marketing campaigns mirror these values. Communications should emphasise data privacy, ethical standards, and support for diverse communities, reinforcing the platform's integrity.

Moreover, marketing strategies should advocate for fair value distribution across the ecosystem. Highlighting success stories of partners, celebrating user innovations, and demonstrating commitment to mutual growth strengthens credibility and loyalty.

Governance is not a backstage function; it must be woven into the brand narrative and ecosystem experience.

Frameworks for Advanced Marketing Strategies

Several strategic frameworks illuminate the path forward.

The **Ecosystem Value Proposition (EVP) Framework** encourages platforms to articulate a clear, differentiated promise to each ecosystem actor—users, complementors, partners (Zollo & Winter, 2002). A robust EVP clarifies why stakeholders should engage, contribute, and remain loyal over time.

The **Platform Growth Loop** framework maps how acquisition, engagement, and retention fuel each other. Advanced strategies must design for each loop stage: attracting actors, enabling valuable contributions (Teece et al., 1997), and ensuring ongoing motivation.

Mastering these frameworks helps marketers synchronise their efforts with the ecosystem's natural dynamics, creating compounding advantages over time.

Case Studies: Advanced Strategies in Action

Across sectors, leading platforms demonstrate how advanced marketing strategies unlock scalable growth and strengthen ecosystem dynamics.

In fintech, **Marqeta**, a modern card issuing platform, partnered with **J.P. Morgan** to co-develop branded payment experiences for enterprise clients. Joint marketing efforts positioned the solution as a flexible, embedded finance offering—accelerating B2B adoption and expanding reach into new verticals (Autio & Thomas, 2022).

In technology, **ServiceNow's Store** incentivised ecosystem developers by promoting top-performing apps through curated collections and enterprise customer showcases. This visibility acted as both a reward and a growth engine, driving partner engagement and improving the overall quality of offerings available to enterprise IT teams.

In B2B retail, **Algonomy** (formerly Manthan), an AI-driven merchandising and personalisation platform, enabled enterprise retailers to use real-time behavioural data for tailored promotions. By integrating marketing automation with commerce workflows, clients increased average order values and improved campaign ROI through contextual relevance.

Each example illustrates how precision, collaboration, and ecosystem-aligned marketing create tangible competitive advantage.

Marketing as Ecosystem Architecture

Advanced strategies reposition marketers not as content pushers but as ecosystem architects—curating collaborations, nurturing network effects, and continuously optimising actor experiences.

By leveraging data-driven insights, activating multichannel narratives, celebrating complementor success, and aligning with governance principles, marketers amplify the vitality and resilience of their ecosystems.

The most progressive marketing strategies position marketers not merely as content producers but as ecosystem architects—carefully designing collaboration pathways, activating network effects, and continually fine-tuning actor experiences. This architectural approach signals a pivotal shift: marketing is not a final layer piled on top of strategy, but the connective tissue that shapes, sustains, and amplifies the entire ecosystem.

At its core, marketing as ecosystem architecture requires a mindset change. Instead of asking "What content do we publish this quarter?" marketers must lead with questions like "How do we structure partner journeys so that contributions flow organically?" and "How can we tune user prompts or incentives to spark engagement and innovation?" Tactical activities become parts of strategic engineering (Teece, 2007)—each blog post, campaign, or event must serve an ecosystem-building purpose.

One of the key levers in this transformation is data-driven insight. Ecosystem architects use real-time analytics to map how actors—developers, sellers, influencers, end-users—move through the system, where drop-off or friction occurs, and which interactions yield new ideas or co-created products (Demil & Lecocq, 2010). Armed with this insight, marketers can pinpoint opportunities to surface cross-actor introductions, suggest partnership collaborations, or highlight emerging developer solutions. The job becomes less about pushing brand messages and more about orchestrating meaningful introductions, momentum and trust.

Multichannel narratives are another hallmark of this architectural approach. Instead of siloed email, social, or event campaigns, marketers curate story arcs that move fluidly across touchpoints. A new partner integration might be introduced via a developer webinar, highlighted through a customer case study, amplified on social media, and supported with tracking links in the platform itself. Each channel reinforces the others and serves to anchor the integration into the ecosystem's collective memory (Barney, 1991).

Crucially, ecosystem architects don't just celebrate their brand; they celebrate the ecosystem itself. Complementor success becomes a marketing asset—each partner story is showcased, each developer extension is promoted, each user-generated innovation is elevated. This approach shifts the narrative from "look at what we built" to "look at what we enable together"—reinforcing the sense of shared ownership and discovery.

Effective ecosystem marketing also requires attention to governance principles. Transparency, fairness, and shared rules must be woven into campaigns and engagement mechanics (Reeves & Deimler, 2011). When marketers highlight the clarity of API terms, the simplicity of onboarding processes, or the openness of feedback forums, they aren't just promoting features—they are reinforcing norms that build trust. This governance-led narrative reassures both large institutional applicants and small independent innovators that the platform is stable and open.

Over time, this architectural approach compounds. As engagement deepens, network effects emerge—more partners, more users, more discovery (Felin & Powell, 2016). Each added actor increases the odds of new interactions, creating a virtuous cycle of growth. Instead of chasing campaigns, ecosystem architects invest in systems that invite contributions, reveal value, celebrate success, and guide participants towards greater impact.

In the future of platform ecosystems, marketing ceases to be peripheral—it becomes foundational. Those who master ecosystem architecture will not only grow faster; they will build platforms that adapt, renew, and thrive long after competitors have faded.

Visual Framework: The Advanced Marketing Flywheel for Ecosystems

Figure 29.1 presents a framework that illustrates advanced marketing functions as the engine of continuous platform growth—where insights drive engagement, engagement fuels contribution, and contribution amplifies co-creation and network effects.

The *Self-Perpetuating Growth* model demonstrates how in an era of ecosystems, marketing is not a support role but a strategic force, building, scaling, and sustaining platforms through iterative, data-informed collaboration.

> **Reflective Prompt: Are You Marketing *With* Your Ecosystem or *To* It?**
>
> "Are your strategies designed to amplify the ecosystem" strengths–or are they merely pushing content into it?"
>
> Reflect on:
>
> 1. How you collaborate with users, complementors, and partners in campaign design.
> 2. Whether your messaging reflects the ecosystem's governance values.
> 3. How data is informing (or limiting) your personalisation efforts.
> 4. How you celebrate and scale success stories within your ecosystem.

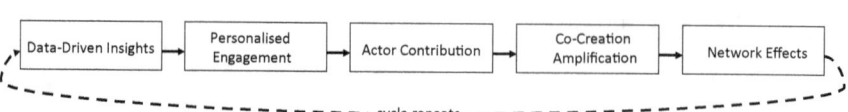

Fig. 29.1 Self-Perpetuating Growth Model

Table 29.1 Platform Marketing Strategy Alignment Grid—Template Grid

Element	Description
Stakeholder Touchpoints	Current actor engagement moments
Amplification Opportunities	New strategies to deepen engagement
Governance Alignment	Values and fairness principles integration
Feedback Loop	Post-campaign data gathering and response plan

Exercise: Platform Marketing Strategy Alignment Grid (Table 29.1)

1. **Map Stakeholder Touchpoints**
   - Where are users, complementors, and partners currently engaging with the platform?
2. **Identify Amplification Opportunities**
   - Where can co-branding, gamification, or multichannel campaigns strengthen engagement?
3. **Ensure Governance Alignment**
   - Do your campaigns reflect your platform's values, fairness principles, and ethical standards?
4. **Create a Feedback Loop**
   - How will you gather insights post-campaign—and how will you act on them?

This chapter equips you to lead platform growth through marketing that is insight-driven, co-creative, and built to scale with the ecosystem.

References

Amit, R., & Zott, C. (2012). Creating value through business model innovation. *MIT Sloan Management Review, 53*(3), 41–49. https://sloanreview.mit.edu/article/creating-value-through-business-model-innovation/

Autio, E., & Thomas, L. D. W. (2022). Value creation in digital platform ecosystems: A dynamic capability perspective. *Strategic Management Journal, 43*(5), 899–923. https://doi.org/10.4337/9781788119986.00017

Barney, J. B. (1991). Firm resources and sustained competitive advantage. *Journal of Management, 17*(1), 99–120. https://doi.org/10.1177/014920639101700108

Demil, B., & Lecocq, X. (2010). Business model evolution: In search of dynamic consistency. *Long Range Planning, 43*(2–3), 227–246. https://doi.org/10.1016/j.lrp.2010.02.004

Eisenhardt, K. M., & Martin, J. A. (2000). Dynamic capabilities: What are they? *Strategic Management Journal, 21*(10–11), 1105–1121. https://doi.org/10.1002/1097-0266(200010/11)21:10/11%3c1105::AID-SMJ133%3e3.0.CO;2-E

Felin, T., & Powell, T. C. (2016). Designing organizations for dynamic capabilities. *California Management Review, 58*(4), 78–96. https://doi.org/10.1525/cmr.2016.58.4.78

Reeves, M., & Deimler, M. (2011). Adaptability: The new competitive advantage. *Harvard Business Review, 89*(7/8), 134–141. https://hbr.org/2011/07/adaptability-the-new-competitive-advantage

Teece, D. J. (2007). Explicating dynamic capabilities: The nature and microfoundations of (sustainable) enterprise performance. *Strategic Management Journal, 28*(13), 1319–1350. https://doi.org/10.1002/smj.640

Teece, D. J., Pisano, G., & Shuen, A. (1997). Dynamic capabilities and strategic management. *Strategic Management Journal, 18*(7), 509–533. https://doi.org/10.1002/(SICI)1097-0266(199708)18:7%3c509::AID-SMJ882%3e3.0.CO;2-Z

Turner, R., & Miterev, M. (2019). The Organizational design of the project-based organization. *Project Management Journal*. https://doi.org/10.1177/8756972819859074

Zollo, M., & Winter, S. G. (2002). Deliberate learning and the evolution of dynamic capabilities. *Organization Science, 13*(3), 339–351. https://doi.org/10.1287/orsc.13.3.339.2780

30

Emerging Trends in AI, IoT, and Cloud Computing for Marketers

As technology accelerates beyond anything we've known before, marketers are no longer just users of tools—they are architects of transformation. Three technologies stand out for their ability to reshape marketing ecosystems in profound ways: AI and IoT, and cloud computing. Each offers unique possibilities, but together they form a powerful, integrated foundation for sustained growth, engagement, and innovation. This chapter explores the role these technologies play individually and collectively, offering actionable insights into how marketing ecosystems can harness them for future growth.

AI has moved from concept to strategic asset. It enables marketers to make data-driven decisions in real time by analysing user behaviour, detecting emerging trends, and tailoring messaging precisely to individuals. Predictive modelling can trigger personalised offers based on customer intent, while sentiment analysis adjusts brand tone across channels. In ecosystem terms, AI acts as the interpreter—transforming raw engagement metrics into actionable marketing signals and enabling platforms to evolve dynamically with stakeholder needs.

Meanwhile, IoT connects the digital and physical worlds, offering relentless streams of usage data and behavioural insight. Smart speakers, wearables, and connected appliances become nodes in a vast network that provide marketers with contextual information about how products are used, when, and why. With this insight, marketing becomes predictive—suggesting product upgrades when usage patterns change, optimising service triggers in real time, and enabling personalised experiences that resonate with life as it happens.

Underlying both AI and IoT, cloud computing provides the technical scaffolding for seamless integration. Cloud environments offer scalability, flexibility, and shared access—precisely the infrastructure modern marketing ecosystems require. They host analytics engines, co-creation portals, and API frameworks that empower partners to build alongside your platform. With cloud-native systems, marketers can quickly launch new features, onboard collaborators, and iterate without major tech investment.

Individually each technology is powerful. Together, they become transformative. When IoT devices collect real-world interaction data into the cloud, AI uses that data to uncover patterns and generate insights. These insights then trigger personalised actions—such as dynamic app notifications or targeted recommendations—while API-enabled partners build additional extensions around them. The result is not just marketing—it is a responsive, living organism woven into the very fabric of the platform.

To use this triad effectively, marketers must think holistically. AI, IoT, and cloud must be integrated into unified user journeys, decision frameworks, and co-creation loops. That means aligning teams around shared data infrastructures, setting transparent governance standards, and building feedback mechanisms that recognise and refine partner contributions. It also requires investing in upskilling marketing professionals to understand AI dashboards, interpret sensor data, and collaborate productively with engineers.

Some key starting points include mapping your ecosystem's data flow from device to insight; testing IoT-based personalisation triggers; and opening cloud-native collaboration spaces—like hackathons, analytics portals, or shared campaign environments—for external partners. Measurement must evolve too. Beyond open rates and click-throughs, marketers should track engagement signals such as API usage, referral conversions, and sensor-triggered interactions.

In this convergent technological era, maintaining competitive advantage means turning disruption into innovation. AI supplies foresight, IoT delivers context, and cloud enables scale. When integrated thoughtfully, these forces allow marketers to design ecosystems that are adaptive, deeply engaging, and capable of co-creating value at every level (Miah et al., 2023). This is the future of marketing—not merely a campaign engine, but an intelligent, responsive platform where strategy, technology, and collaboration unite.

The Role of AI in Transforming Marketing

AI has moved beyond buzzword status into a foundational pillar of modern marketing practice. By analysing vast datasets, identifying patterns, and making real-time predictions, AI empowers marketers to refine targeting, personalise experiences, and optimise resource allocation like never before.

One of AI's most impactful applications is predictive analytics. By examining historical behaviours and real-time inputs, predictive models forecast customer actions, enabling marketers to intervene proactively (Chatterjee et al., 2021). A retail platform, for instance, might use AI to identify customers at risk of abandoning shopping carts, triggering personalised incentives to nudge them towards completion.

Recommendation engines further showcase AI's transformative power. E-commerce sites use AI to suggest complementary products, driving upsell opportunities while enhancing customer satisfaction. These systems learn continuously, refining suggestions to match evolving user preferences.

In customer service, chatbots and virtual assistants have revolutionised interaction management. Equipped with natural language processing, these tools deliver instant, context-aware support—enhancing user experience while reducing operational overhead.

The Expanding Influence of IoT

The IoT bridges the physical and digital worlds, connecting devices and enabling new data-driven touchpoints.

For marketers, IoT opens unprecedented windows into consumer behaviour. Devices like fitness trackers, smart home appliances, and connected vehicles generate rich data streams, providing insights into daily routines, preferences, and unmet needs (Brynjolfsson & McAfee, 2017).

IoT also powers real-time engagement. A connected refrigerator might detect low inventory and prompt users with personalised grocery discounts. Retail stores use beacons to deliver location-specific promotions directly to shoppers' smartphones, blending convenience with relevance.

By embedding marketing within the fabric of everyday life, IoT enables experiences that are timely, contextual, and deeply personal.

Cloud Computing as the Backbone of Marketing Innovation

Cloud computing underpins the flexibility, scalability, and speed necessary for modern marketing operations.

Cloud platforms allow teams to integrate diverse datasets—from CRM systems to social listening tools—creating unified, real-time customer profiles (Evans & Gawer, 2016). This integrated view enables more strategic, insight-driven decisions.

Cloud infrastructure also enhances collaboration, allowing global teams to work synchronously, regardless of geography. Creative assets, campaign data, and analytics dashboards are accessible on-demand, supporting agility and coherence in multichannel strategies.

Moreover, cloud ecosystems support experimentation and scaling. Whether deploying AI models, running IoT applications, or testing new marketing technologies, cloud solutions provide the elasticity marketers need to innovate without the burden of heavy upfront investment.

The Convergence of AI, IoT, and Cloud Computing

The real magic happens when AI, IoT, and cloud computing converge—creating dynamic, self-learning ecosystems that amplify each technology's impact.

Imagine a wearable device tracking a user's fitness goals. The data flows into the cloud, where AI models analyse patterns and generate personalised wellness recommendations. These recommendations are then delivered seamlessly through a mobile app, fostering ongoing engagement and brand loyalty (Kraus et al., 2021).

This convergence enables real-time marketing—where platforms can adapt instantly to changes in user behaviour, external conditions, or market opportunities. Whether it's dynamically adjusting offers based on IoT signals or optimising customer journeys through AI insights, the possibilities are both expansive and deeply interconnected.

Frameworks for Integrating Emerging Technologies

To harness these technologies effectively, marketers can adopt structured frameworks.

The **Technology Integration Model** emphasises assessing organisational readiness, aligning technological capabilities with business goals, and iterating based on real-world feedback. Successful integration requires not just technology, but strategy, governance, and cultural buy-in.

Similarly, the **Data-Driven Marketing Framework** focuses on systematic data collection, integration, and application. By embedding AI, IoT, and cloud computing into this framework, marketers unlock higher precision, deeper insights, and more agile execution (Atzori et al., 2010).

Both models stress that technology is not a silver bullet—it must be purposefully woven into the marketing fabric to unlock real value.

Challenges and Considerations

While these technologies promise immense benefits, they also introduce critical challenges.

Data privacy and security are paramount, particularly as IoT expands the volume and sensitivity of personal data collected. Regulatory compliance with GDPR, CCPA, and emerging standards is non-negotiable, demanding robust data governance.

Integration complexity poses another hurdle. Successfully combining AI, IoT, and cloud solutions requires technical expertise and seamless interoperability (Lee & Lee, 2015). Organisations must invest in talent and foster collaboration across IT, marketing, and data science teams.

Finally, cost considerations must be managed carefully. Although cloud solutions offer scalability, initial investments in infrastructure, tools, and training can be substantial. Clear ROI frameworks and phased implementation plans help mitigate these risks.

From Digital to Predictive: Marketing in the Age of Intelligent Ecosystem

The convergence of AI, IoT, and cloud computing is redefining the marketing function—from isolated campaign execution to real-time, ecosystem-driven value creation.

Marketers now have the tools to deliver hyper-personalised experiences, optimise every touchpoint, and pivot strategies instantaneously based on real-world signals. Marketing is transformed into a living, intelligent ecosystem that continually creates value through real-world responsiveness and meaningful connection. Rather than executing discrete programmes, marketing professionals are now tasked with designing adaptive systems that learn, predict, and evolve alongside customer behaviour and ecosystem dynamics.

As these technologies continue to evolve, those who proactively embrace their convergence will be better positioned to lead in creativity, agility, and customer connection. The future of marketing is not just digital—it is predictive, adaptive, and deeply interconnected.

AI sits at the core of this transformation, enabling predictive personalisation that goes far beyond traditional segmentation. ML models can analyse vast streams of data—from click patterns to purchase history to sensor signals—and anticipate what each individual needs before they even know it themselves (Davenport et al., 2020). Whether it's surfacing the next best offer, adjusting messaging based on tone, or adapting content recommendations in real time, AI turns marketing into a proactive, rather than reactive, endeavour.

IoT contributes a deeper sense of context. Connected devices—from wearables and smart appliances to in-store beacons—provide continuous feedback about how, when, and where customers interact with products and services. This contextual layer allows marketers to serve moments that matter: a reminder to reorder a consumable product when supplies run low, an offer to upgrade a subscription after a surge in usage, or a digital coupon triggered by proximity within a store. These real-world touchpoints combine with AI insights to increase relevance while preserving user trust.

Cloud computing underpins the entire infrastructure, offering scale and flexibility without compromising performance. By centralising data storage, analytics engines, and API collaboration frameworks, the cloud enables marketers to deploy sophisticated solutions across geographies, channels, and partners (Vargo & Lusch, 2008). Collaboration becomes easier and faster: internal teams, complementors, and developers can access shared toolsets to experiment, iterate, and build new capabilities—without waiting for long development cycles.

This triad enables a new type of marketing—one that is predictive, adaptive, and deeply interconnected. When AI signals an emerging trend, IoT confirms it through usage data, and cloud orchestration activates the right response (Wamba-Taguimdje et al., 2020)—like adjusting product suggestions, running a campaign in select markets, or offering a partner-built extension—the system moves in concert. The result is a seamless experience that feels human, helpful, and intelligent.

The strategic advantage belongs to those who embrace this convergence. Marketers must deepen their fluency across technology and analytics, collaborating closely with data scientists, engineers, and ecosystem partners. It's no longer sufficient to know your buyer's persona—you must also understand their sensor-generated data and algorithm-derived triggers.

Measurement evolves accordingly. Beyond impressions, clicks, and conversions, leaders now track predictive accuracy, real-time engagement rates, and ecosystem contribution metrics (Ng et al., 2009). Success looks like fewer manual campaigns and more autonomous, intelligent systems that respond to behaviour with speed and precision.

Within this intelligent ecosystem, marketing is radically different. It isn't just about being digital—it's about being predictive: anticipating customer needs; adaptive: altering experiences on the fly; and interconnected: building through collaboration across technology and audience layers. Those who can master this future-facing model won't merely lead in their categories—they'll define them.

Visual Framework: The Connected Future of Marketing

Figure 30.1 introduces a framework that captures the future-facing blueprint of marketing, where IoT, cloud, and AI converge to deliver predictive, adaptive, and hyper-connected experiences.

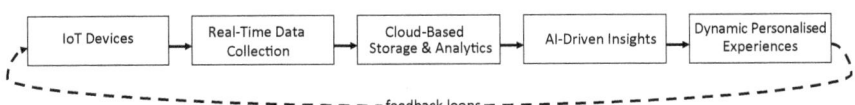

Fig. 30.1 AI-IoT-Cloud Integration Model for Marketers

Table 30.1 Emerging Technology Adoption Readiness Audit—Template Grid

Element	Description
Current Capabilities	Technologies already in place and their uses
Opportunity Areas	New initiatives enabled by AI, IoT, or cloud
Readiness Assessment	Skills, resources, and infrastructure gaps
Pilot Plan	Targeted test project with defined outcomes

The *AI-IoT-Cloud Integration Model for Marketers* outlines how in this intelligent ecosystem, marketers don't follow trends, they anticipate them, shaping categories through seamless data flow, real-time responsiveness, and ecosystem-wide collaboration.

Reflective Prompt: Is Your Marketing Infrastructure Ready for the Future?

"Are you piecing together isolated solutions—or building a connected ecosystem that anticipates, adapts, and evolves with your customers?"

Reflect on:

1. How your organisation currently integrates AI, IoT, and cloud platforms.
2. Where gaps exist in real-time data collection or predictive decision-making.
3. What new touchpoints or channels IoT could enable.
4. How your governance model supports—or limits—innovation with emerging technologies.

Exercise: Emerging Technology Adoption Readiness Audit (Table 30.1)

1. **Map Current Capabilities**
   - Which AI, IoT, and cloud technologies are already in use?
   - What are their integration points?

2. **Identify Opportunity Areas**
   - Where could real-time data, AI insights, or IoT engagement improve customer experiences?

3. **Assess Readiness**
   - What infrastructure, skills, or partnerships are needed to advance integration?

4. **Create a Pilot Plan**
   - Select one emerging technology initiative.

- Define success metrics (e.g. engagement lift, conversion rate improvements, operational efficiency gains).

This chapter helps you unlock strategic advantage by turning emerging technologies into interconnected marketing capabilities that drive foresight, agility, and value across the ecosystem.

References

Atzori, L., Iera, A., & Morabito, G. (2010). The internet of things: A survey. *Computer Networks, 54*(15), 2787–2805. https://doi.org/10.1016/j.comnet.2010.05.010

Brynjolfsson, E., & McAfee, A. (2017). Machine, platform, crowd: Harnessing our digital future. W. W. Norton

Chatterjee, S., Rana, N., Tamilmani, K., & Sharma, A. (2021). The effect of AI-based CRM on organization performance and competitive advantage: An empirical analysis in the B2B context. *Industrial Marketing Management*. https://doi.org/10.1016/j.indmarman.2021.07.013

Davenport, T. H., Guha, A., Grewal, D., & Bressgott, T. (2020). How artificial intelligence will change the future of marketing. *Journal of the Academy of Marketing Science, 48*, 24–42. https://doi.org/10.1007/s11747-019-00696-0

Evans, P., & Gawer, A. (2016). *The rise of the platform enterprise*. https://doi.org/10.13140/RG.2.2.35887.05280.

Kraus, S., Schiavone, F., Pluzhnikova, A., & Invernizzi, A. C. (2021). Digital transformation in healthcare: Analyzing the current state-of-research. *Journal of Business Research, 123*, 557–567. https://doi.org/10.1016/j.jbusres.2020.10.030

Lee, I., & Lee, K. (2015). The Internet of Things (IoT): Applications, investments, and challenges for enterprises. *Business Horizons, 58*(4), 431–440. https://doi.org/10.1016/j.bushor.2015.03.008

Miah, M., Akter, M., Samid, D., & Siam, M. (2023). AI in decision making: Transforming business strategies. *ABC Research Alert, 11*(3), 14–23. https://doi.org/10.18034/ra.v11i3.667

Ng, I. C. L., Maull, R., & Yip, N. (2009). Outcome-based contracts as a driver for systems thinking and service-dominant logic in service science: Evidence from the defense industry. *European Management Journal, 27*(6), 377–387. https://doi.org/10.1016/j.emj.2009.05.002

Vargo, S. L., & Lusch, R. F. (2008). Service-dominant logic: Continuing the evolution. *Journal of the Academy of Marketing Science, 36*, 1–10. https://doi.org/10.1007/s11747-007-0069-6

Wamba-Taguimdje, S. L., Fosso Wamba, S., Kala Kamdjoug, J. R., & Tchatchouang Wanko, C. E. (2020). Influence of artificial intelligence (AI) on firm performance: The business value of AI-based transformation projects. *Business Process Management Journal, 26*(7), 1893–1924. https://doi.org/10.1108/BPMJ-10-2019-0411

31

Designing a Scalable Platform-Driven Marketing Strategy

This is the marketer's guide to designing, scaling, and leading platform growth. In an economy where digital ecosystems define both opportunity and advantage, marketing is no longer a peripheral function—it is the strategic core. Platforms have emerged as a foundational element in the next wave of marketing evolution. Offering flexibility, scalability, and seamless integration, platforms enable marketers to craft dynamic strategies that adapt in real-time, scale effortlessly, and deliver deeply personalised experiences. This closing chapter unpacks how marketers can lead and strategically leverage platforms to architect future-ready marketing ecosystems that drive sustainable growth and innovation.

As digital ecosystems become more complex and customer expectations continue to rise, developing a scalable platform-driven marketing strategy is not just an opportunity—it's a necessity. Platform-driven marketing isn't a passing phase—it's the foundation upon which tomorrow's market leaders will be built. These platforms are not static structures but adaptive, real-time environments where value is co-created continuously by users, partners, and algorithms working in unison.

Marketing within these environments requires a radical shift in mindset. Rather than crafting isolated campaigns, marketers must engineer living systems—interconnected, data-informed, and user-empowered. This means designing feedback loops that refine experiences in real time, integrating APIs that evolve with audience needs, and scaling strategies through ecosystem partnerships that expand reach and capability.

Critically, marketers must become ecosystem architects. They build the conditions for collaboration, ensure the health of actor relationships, and curate narratives that resonate across a complex network of contributors. Their role transcends communication—it shapes trust, mobilises innovation, and aligns internal capabilities with external expectations.

When executed effectively, platform marketing delivers unmatched agility. A new feature can be deployed across global markets overnight. A shift in sentiment can trigger dynamic content personalisation. A strategic partner can be activated through plug-and-play integrations that require minimal downtime.

Equally, platform marketing fosters resilience. Ecosystems thrive through redundancy and diversity. When user engagement dips in one segment, community insights or complementor-driven campaigns can reignite participation (Benediktova & Nevosad, 2021). When external disruptions arise, platform-based networks offer alternative growth paths and faster pivots.

Success here requires clarity of purpose, disciplined governance, and a deep understanding of how value circulates across interconnected actors. Marketers must champion transparency, encourage open innovation, and use data not just to report but to adapt, anticipate, and lead (Chaffey & Ellis-Chadwick, 2019).

In sum, platform strategy is not simply about adopting new tools—it's about adopting a new way of thinking. And marketers are uniquely equipped to lead this charge. With their instinct for connection, their command of narrative, and their access to insight, they can turn platforms into engines of engagement, trust, and growth.

This isn't just a call to action—it's a blueprint. The future of marketing will be built by those who can design for complexity, scale through collaboration, and lead with clarity across the platform frontier.

Understanding the Role of Platforms in Marketing

At its core, platforms provide a cloud-based environment where businesses can develop, deploy, and manage applications without the burden of maintaining their own infrastructure. For marketers, this opens new horizons: platforms serve as unified environments where CRM systems, analytics tools, content management systems, and emerging technologies converge to power integrated, data-driven strategies.

The modular architecture of platforms allows marketers to pick and choose best-in-class components, stitching them together into an ecosystem tailored to their needs (Day, 2011). Whether adding a new AI-powered recommendation engine or scaling content delivery networks to support global campaigns, marketers can adapt and evolve without major disruptions. Platforms don't just simplify operations—it fuels agility, collaboration, and innovation.

Building a Scalable Platform-Driven Framework

A robust platform-driven marketing strategy rests on three key pillars: Resource Integration, Automation, and Adaptability.

Resource Integration brings together internal assets (e.g. CRM databases) and external capabilities (e.g. social listening APIs) into a seamless whole. Imagine a campaign that automatically pulls real-time sentiment analysis from social media feeds while syncing it with personalised email marketing—this is the power of integration.

Automation lies at the heart of efficiency and scale. Through platforms, marketers can automate customer segmentation, lead scoring, multichannel campaign deployment, and real-time performance reporting (Edelman & Singer, 2015). Freed from repetitive tasks, teams can focus on creativity, strategy, and experimentation.

Adaptability ensures that marketing strategies can pivot swiftly. As market dynamics shift or new technologies emerge, platforms enable instant reconfiguration, whether by integrating AI chatbots into customer service workflows or deploying new campaign features across global regions.

Leveraging Data for Precision and Personalisation

Data is the driving force of a platform-driven marketing strategy. Platforms aggregate data from myriad touchpoints—social media, web traffic, CRM systems, IoT devices—creating a 360-degree view of customers in real-time (Lamberton & Stephen, 2016).

Predictive analytics enable marketers to anticipate customer needs, offering products and content before customers even articulate them. For instance, a customer browsing fitness gear could be automatically segmented into a "health-focused" persona group, triggering personalised product recommendations or loyalty offers.

Real-time dashboards allow adaptive campaign management, enabling teams to adjust creatives, targeting, or budgets on the fly based on performance insights. In an era where customer preferences change rapidly, such precision is invaluable.

Fostering Collaboration and Innovation

Platforms are inherently collaborative spaces, empowering cross-functional teams to work in sync regardless of location.

Marketing, sales, IT, and product teams can co-create campaigns, share assets, and manage workflows transparently within a single environment. Project management tools, shared analytics dashboards, and integrated content libraries become hubs of collective innovation.

Moreover, platforms foster an experimental culture. Testing new customer experiences—such as a gamified loyalty app or a dynamic social media campaign—becomes faster, safer, and more scalable (Kannan & Li, 2017). Pilot projects can be launched, refined through user feedback, and scaled seamlessly.

Collaborative governance structures within platforms ensure that innovation doesn't happen in silos but is embedded across the ecosystem.

Overcoming Challenges in Platform Adoption

Despite its advantages, adopting a platform-driven strategy presents hurdles.

Legacy system integration can be a barrier. Organisations must thoughtfully plan migrations, sometimes running hybrid models as they transition critical functions onto the platform environment. Data privacy and compliance challenges are heightened in the cloud. Marketers must ensure strict adherence to GDPR, CCPA, and industry-specific regulations, working closely with IT and legal teams (Lamberton & Stephen, 2016).

Cost management requires vigilance. While platform solutions reduce capital expenditures, operational expenses can grow as teams add more services. Clear usage governance and ROI tracking are essential to avoid cost creep.

Case Studies: Platform-Driven Marketing in Action

In fintech, **Temenos**, a B2B digital banking platform, enabled banks to integrate CRM, core banking, mobile app development, and analytics into a unified ecosystem (Hollebeek & Macky, 2019). One regional bank used Temenos to launch a personalised financial planning service targeting millennials, resulting in a 25% increase in customer retention through tailored insights and marketing automation.

In retail, **Algolia**, a B2B AI-powered search and discovery platform, helped enterprise retailers personalise product discovery, content targeting, and marketing automation across digital storefronts. By integrating with platforms like Salesforce Commerce Cloud and Adobe, clients achieved a 30% uplift in average order value through faster, more relevant user journey (Verhoef et al., 2021).

In healthcare, **Innovaccer**, a B2B healthcare data platform, enabled provider networks to unify patient engagement, appointment coordination, and follow-up outreach through its integrated platform (Harrigan et al., 2017). By leveraging real-time data and intelligent automation, healthcare organisations improved patient retention and operational efficiency across care journeys.

Each example illustrates how resource integration, automation, and adaptability drive scale and impact.

The Role of Emerging Technologies in Platform Strategies

Emerging technologies supercharge platforms.

1. **AI** enables hyper-personalisation through predictive modelling.
2. **IoT** devices feed real-time engagement data into marketing campaigns.
3. **Blockchain** fosters trust by securing transactions and protecting user data across ecosystems.

For example, a smart home energy platform could integrate IoT device data, AI energy optimisation models, and blockchain-secured billing into a seamless customer experience—all orchestrated through a Platform infrastructure.

Platforms are not just a back-end infrastructure decision—it is redefining marketing strategy at its core.

It empowers marketing teams to move from isolated campaigns to always-on, customer-centric ecosystems. It allows personalisation at scale, agile experimentation, and faster iteration cycles (Stephen, 2016). It integrates creativity, data science, and operations into one connected environment.

Ultimately, platform-driven marketing strategies unlock a new paradigm: marketing as an adaptive, collaborative, and scalable platform for value creation.

As we conclude this journey through the evolving landscape of platform-driven marketing, one truth becomes clear: platforms are not merely enablers of scale or efficiency—they are the blueprint for a new era of growth (Benediktova & Nevosad, 2021). In a world where agility, collaboration, and co-creation define competitive advantage, marketers stand at the centre of a powerful shift. No longer confined to campaign management or brand messaging, they are now architects of ecosystems, stewards of trust, and orchestrators of continuous innovation.

This book has unpacked how platform strategies transform not only how we market, but how we build, connect, grow and lead. The challenge ahead is not just to adopt these strategies, but to lead with them—with clarity, creativity, and conviction. Marketing's future will be shaped by those who design for integration, act with intent, and embrace platforms not as tools, but as foundations for enduring, scalable, human-centered value. The playbook has changed—and it's time to lead the next chapter.

Visual Framework: Building a Scalable Platform-Driven Marketing Strategy

Figure 31.1 presents a framework that maps a strategic progression and illustrates how marketing within platform ecosystems drives sustainable growth through intentional integration, automation, and continuous innovation built around human-centered value.

The *Scalable Platform Marketing* model, demonstrates how intentional alignment between human-centred value and technology-led capabilities enables marketing to scale impact, accelerate innovation, and drive long-term ecosystem advantage.

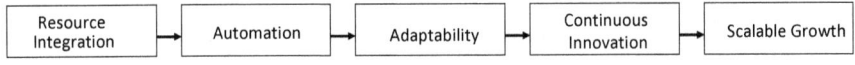

Fig. 31.1 Scalable Platform Marketing Model

> **Reflective Prompt: Are You Architecting for Scalability?**
>
> "Is your marketing strategy built for short-term campaigns–or for a scalable, adaptive future?"
>
> Reflect on:
>
> 1. How modular your current marketing technology stack is.
> 2. Whether your team can launch new initiatives without major infrastructure changes.
> 3. How quickly your campaigns can pivot in response to customer or market shifts.
> 4. What emerging technologies could be layered into your ecosystem through Platform.

> **Exercise: Platform-Driven Marketing Readiness Blueprint (Table 31.1)**
>
> 1. **Assess Current Stack**
>   - What marketing platforms and tools are currently in use?
>   - How integrated and modular are they?
> 2. **Identify Gaps**
>   - Where does a lack of flexibility, automation, or integration create friction?
> 3. **Map Future Capabilities**
>   - What capabilities (e.g. real-time personalisation, predictive insights) could be enabled through Platform?
> 4. **Design a Pilot Initiative**
>   - Choose one marketing function to migrate to or launch via a platform.
>   - Define success metrics: speed to market, customer engagement uplift, cost efficiency, etc.

This chapter enables you to architect marketing for scale, combining integration, automation, and innovation to create sustained growth rooted in real human impact.

Table 31.1 Platform-Driven Marketing Readiness Blueprint—Template Grid

Element	Description
Current Tech Stack	Platforms and tools in use
Gaps Identified	Flexibility, automation, or integration issues
Future Capabilities	New functionality enabled by platform
Pilot Initiative	Small-scale platform-driven project

References

Benediktova, L., & Nevosad, L. (2021). Strategic marketing in digital platform ecosystems. *Marketing Science & Inspirations, 16*(2), 2–11. https://doi.org/10.15240/tul/001/2021-2-001

Chaffey, D., & Ellis-Chadwick, F. (2019). *Digital marketing* (7th ed.). Pearson Education

Day, G. S. (2011). Closing the marketing capabilities gap. *Journal of Marketing, 75*(4), 183–195. https://doi.org/10.1509/jmkg.75.4.183

Edelman, D. C., & Singer, M. (2015). Competing on customer journeys. *Harvard Business Review, 93*(11), 88–100. https://doi.org/10.13140/RG.2.2.34634.95688

Harrigan, P., Evers, U., Miles, M., & Daly, T. (2017). Customer engagement and the relationship between involvement, engagement, and loyalty. *Journal of Marketing Management, 33*(5–6), 378–409. https://doi.org/10.1016/j.jbusres.2017.11.046

Hollebeek, L. D., & Macky, K. (2019). Digital content marketing's role in fostering consumer engagement, trust, and value: Framework, fundamental propositions, and implications. *Journal of Interactive Marketing, 45*, 27–41. https://doi.org/10.1016/j.intmar.2018.07.003

Kannan, P. K., & Li, H. (2017). Digital marketing: A framework, review and research agenda. *International Journal of Research in Marketing, 34*(1), 22–45. https://doi.org/10.1016/j.ijresmar.2016.11.006

Lamberton, C., & Stephen, A. T. (2016). A thematic exploration of digital, social media, and mobile marketing: Research evolution from 2000 to 2015 and an agenda for future inquiry. *Journal of Marketing, 80*(6), 146–172. https://doi.org/10.1509/jm.15.0415

Rust, R. T., & Huang, M.-H. (2014). The service revolution and the transformation of marketing science. *Marketing Science, 33*(2), 206–221. https://doi.org/10.1287/mksc.2013.0836

Stephen, A. T. (2016). The role of digital and social media marketing in consumer behavior. *Current Opinion in Psychology, 10*, 17–21. https://doi.org/10.1016/j.copsyc.2015.10.016

Verhoef, P. C., Broekhuizen, T., Bart, Y., Bhattacharya, A., Qi Dong, J., Fabian, N., & Haenlein, M. (2021). Digital transformation: A multidisciplinary reflection and research agenda. *Journal of Business Research, 122*, 889–901. https://doi.org/10.1016/j.jbusres.2019.09.022

Conclusion

The Future Is Collaborative

We began this journey by exploring the profound transformation underway in how businesses create, deliver, and sustain value. The shift is no longer speculative or emerging, it is here. We have moved from ownership to access, from one-way communication to multi-directional dialogue, from products as endpoints to platforms as enablers of ongoing interaction. Value creation is no longer confined within the walls of individual firms, it now flows through dynamic, interconnected ecosystems. Throughout these chapters, one central insight has held true: platforms are not just technological constructs. They are social systems, organised constellations of people, processes, and technologies. Their power lies not simply in scale, but in their ability to orchestrate diverse contributions, activate co-creation, and build durable trust across a wide range of actors.

As AI, IoT, cloud computing, and other digital innovations redefine what is possible, and as societal expectations around transparency, inclusion, and sustainability evolve, platform leaders face a new mandate. Tomorrow's successful marketers will not be those who shout the loudest or move the fastest. They will be those who master a fundamentally different form of leadership:

1. **Marketing that invites, not dictates**—that creates space for others to contribute, collaborate, and co-own the outcome.
2. **Marketing that facilitates, not controls**—that builds frameworks, scaffolds engagement, and empowers creativity across the ecosystem.

3. **Marketing that co-creates, not just sells**—that aligns innovation with shared purpose and ensures every actor finds value in the collective journey.

The Platform Playbook has outlined how marketers can step into this role. From building co-creative campaigns and unlocking actor engagement, to overcoming institutional resistance and scaling through regional legitimacy, the book has offered a strategic roadmap for navigating this new terrain.

But platform ecosystems are never static. They evolve continuously, with every new participant, every new insight, every shift in technology or regulation. Success will not come from rigidly adhering to a single model, but from embracing adaptability as a core competency. The most impactful marketers will be those who remain open, listening to signals, iterating on value, and evolving their strategies alongside their communities.

Ultimately, the future of marketing, and of business itself, will be collaborative. It will belong to those who design not just for profit, but for participation. To those who build not just products, but platforms that empower others. To those who see their role not as owners of value, but as architects of ecosystems where everyone has a stake—and everyone can win.

This is more than a strategic marketing playbook. It is an invitation.

An invitation to lead differently. To market boldly. To build together.

This is your ***Platform Playbook***. Step into it.

Consolidated References

Aanestad, M., Vassilakopoulou, P., & Øvrelid, E. (2019). *Collaborative innovation in healthcare: Boundary resources for peripheral actors*. https://aisel.aisnet.org/icis2019/is_health/is_health/24

Aarikka-Stenroos, L., & Jaakkola, E. (2012). Value co-creation in knowledge intensive business services: A dyadic perspective on the joint problem-solving process. *Industrial Marketing Management, 41*(1), 15–26. https://doi.org/10.1016/j.indmarman.2011.11.008

Aarikka-Stenroos, L., & Ritala, P. (2017). Network management in the era of ecosystems: Systematic review and management framework. *Industrial Marketing Management, 67*, 23–36. https://doi.org/10.1016/j.indmarman.2017.08.010

Acs, Z. J., Stam, E., Audretsch, D. B., & O'Connor, A. (2017). The lineages of the entrepreneurial ecosystem approach. *Small Business Economics, 49*(1), 1–10. https://doi.org/10.1007/s11187-017-9864-8

Adner, R., & Kapoor, R. (2010). Value creation in innovation ecosystems: How the structure of technological interdependence affects firm performance in new technology generations. *Strategic Management Journal, 31*(3), 306–333. https://doi.org/10.1002/smj.821

Adner, R., & Lieberman, M. B. (2021). Disruption through complements. *Strategy Science, 6*(1), 91–109. https://doi.org/10.1287/stsc.2021.0125

Agarwal, S., & Kapoor, R. (2019). *Two faces of value creation in business ecosystems: Leveraging complementarities and managing interdependencies* [Working paper]. The Wharton School, University of Pennsylvania.

Agyei-Boapeah, H., Evans, R., & Nisar, T. M. (2022). Disruptive innovation: Designing business platforms for new financial services. *Journal of Business Research, 150*, 134–146. https://doi.org/10.1016/j.jbusres.2022.05.066

Ahmed, T., & Kowalkowski, C. (2025). The new industry playbook: Digital service innovation in multi-platform ecosystems. *Journal of Enterprise Information Management*. Advance online publication. https://doi.org/10.1108/JEIM-05-2024-0240

Ahuja, G. (2000). Collaboration networks, structural holes, and innovation: A longitudinal study. *Administrative Science Quarterly, 45*(3), 425–455. https://doi.org/10.2307/2667105

Ajimati, M. O., Carroll, N., & Maher, M. (2024). Adoption of low-code and no-code development: A systematic literature review and future research agenda. *Journal of Systems and Software, 222*, Article 112300. https://doi.org/10.1016/j.jss.2024.112300

Akaka, M. A., Vargo, S. L., & Lusch, R. F. (2013). The complexity of context: A service ecosystems approach for international marketing. *Journal of International Marketing, 21*(4), 1–20. https://doi.org/10.1509/jim.13.0032

Alaimo, C., & Kallinikos, J. (2021). Managing by data: Algorithmic categories and organizing. *Organization Studies, 42*(6), 875–895. https://doi.org/10.1177/0170840620934062

Algesheimer, R., Dholakia, U. M., & Herrmann, A. (2005). The social influence of brand community: Evidence from European car clubs. *Journal of Marketing, 69*(3), 19–34. https://doi.org/10.1509/jmkg.69.3.19.66363

Altschwager, T., Drennan, J., Winklhofer, H., & Jarvis, W. (2016). Actor engagement in the sharing economy: A life-cycle perspective. *Proceedings of ANZMAC Conference Turning Visions into Reality*.

Alvedalen, J., & Boschma, R. (2017). A critical review of entrepreneurial ecosystems research: Towards a future research agenda. *European Planning Studies, 25*(6), 887–903. https://doi.org/10.1080/09654313.2017.1299694

Amit, R., & Zott, C. (2012). Creating value through business model innovation. *MIT Sloan Management Review, 53*(3), 41–49. https://sloanreview.mit.edu/article/creating-value-through-business-model-innovation/

Anand, B. N., & Khanna, T. (2000). Do firms learn to create value? The case of alliances. *Strategic Management Journal, 21*(3), 295–315. https://doi.org/10.1002/(SICI)1097-0266(200003)21:3%3c295::AID-SMJ91%3e3.0.CO;2-O

Anderson, P., & Tushman, M. L. (1990). Technological discontinuities and dominant designs: A cyclical model of technological change. *Administrative Science Quarterly, 35*(4), 604–633. https://doi.org/10.2307/2393511

Ansell, C., & Gash, A. (2008). Collaborative governance in theory and practice. *Journal of Public Administration Research and Theory, 18*(4), 543–571. https://doi.org/10.1093/jopart/mum032

Atzori, L., Iera, A., & Morabito, G. (2010). The internet of things: A survey. *Computer Networks, 54*(15), 2787–2805. https://doi.org/10.1016/j.comnet.2010.05.010

Audretsch, D. B., Belitski, M., & Caiazza, R. (2021). Start-ups, innovation and knowledge spillovers. *Journal of Technology Transfer, 46*, 1995–2016. https://doi.org/10.1007/s10961-021-09846-5

Aulkemeier, F., Iacob, M. E., & van Hillegersberg, J. (2019). Platform-based collaboration in digital ecosystems. *Electronic Markets, 29*, 597–608. https://doi.org/10.1007/s12525-019-00341-2

Autio, E., Nambisan, S., Thomas, L. D. W., & Wright, M. (2018). Digital affordances, spatial affordances, and the genesis of entrepreneurial ecosystems. *Strategic Entrepreneurship Journal, 12*(1), 72–95. https://doi.org/10.1002/sej.1266

Avital, M., Mathiassen, L., & Schultze, U. (2017). Alternative genres in information systems research. *European Journal of Information Systems, 26*(3), 240–247. https://doi.org/10.1057/s41303-017-0051-4

Baldwin, C. Y., & Woodard, C. J. (2009). The architecture of platforms: A unified view. In A. Gawer (Ed.), *Platforms, markets and innovation* (chapter 2, pp. 19–44). Edward Elgar Publishing.

Bamford, J. D., Gomes-Casseres, B., & Robinson, M. S. (2003). *Mastering alliance strategy: A comprehensive guide to design, management, and organization.* Jossey-Bass.

Barile, S., Lusch, R. F., Reynoso, J., Saviano, M., & Spohrer, J. (2016). Systems, networks, and ecosystems in service research. *Journal of Service Management, 27*(4), 652–674. https://doi.org/10.1108/JOSM-09-2015-0268

Barney, J. B. (1991). Firm resources and sustained competitive advantage. *Journal of Management, 17*(1), 99–120. https://doi.org/10.1177/014920639101700108

Battilana, J., & Casciaro, T. (2012). Change agents, networks, and institutions: A contingency theory of organizational change. *Academy of Management Journal, 55*(2), 381–398. https://doi.org/10.5465/amj.2009.0891

Beer, M., & Eisenstat, R. A. (2000). The silent killers of strategy implementation and learning. *Sloan Management Review, 41*(4), 29–40.

Belderbos, R., Carree, M., & Lokshin, B. (2004). Cooperative R&D and firm performance. *Research Policy, 33*(10), 1477–1492. https://doi.org/10.1016/j.respol.2004.07.003

Bello, S. A., Oyedele, L. O., Akinade, O. O., Bilal, M., Davila Delgado, J. M., Akanbi, L. A., Ajayi, A. O., & Owolabi, H. A. (2021). Cloud computing in construction industry: Use cases, benefits and challenges. *Automation in Construction, 122*, Article 103441. https://doi.org/10.1016/j.autcon.2020.103441

Benediktova, L., & Nevosad, L. (2021). Strategic marketing in digital platform ecosystems. *Marketing Science & Inspirations, 16*(2), 2–11. https://doi.org/10.15240/tul/001/2021-2-001

Bharadwaj, A., El Sawy, O. A., Pavlou, P. A., & Venkatraman, N. (2013). Digital business strategy: Toward a next generation of insights. *MIS Quarterly, 37*(2), 471–482. https://www.jstor.org/stable/43825919

Blajer-Gołębiewska, A., Wach, D., & Kos, M. (2018). Financial risk information avoidance. *Economic Research-Ekonomska Istraživanja, 31*(1), 521–536. https://doi.org/10.1080/1331677X.2018.1439396

Blaschke, M., & Brosius, M. (2018). Digital platforms: Balancing control and generativity.

Blasco-Arcas, L., Hernandez-Ortega, B. I., & Jimenez-Martinez, J. (2016). Engagement platforms: The role of emotions in fostering customer engagement and brand image in interactive media. https://doi.org/10.1108/JSTP-12-2014-0286

Block, P. (2016). *The empowered manager positive political skills at work Business & Economics.* Stanford University Press.

Bocconcelli, R., Carlborg, P., Harrison, D., Hasche, N., Hedvall, K., & Lei, H. (2020). Resource interaction and resource integration: Similarities, differences, reflections. *Industrial Marketing Management, 91*, 385–396. https://doi.org/10.1016/j.indmarman.2020.09.016

Boudreau, K., & Lakhani, K. (2009). How to manage outside innovation. *MIT Sloan Management Review, 50*.

Boudreau, K. J. (2010). Open platform strategies and innovation: Granting access vs. devolving control. *Management Science, 56*(10), 1849–1872. https://doi.org/10.1287/mnsc.1100.1215

Boudreau, K. J. (2017). Platform boundary choices and governance: Opening up while still coordinating and orchestrating, entrepreneurship, innovation, and platforms. *Advances in Strategic Management, 37*, 227–297. https://doi.org/10.1108/S0742-332220170000037009

Breidbach, C., Antons, D., & Salge, O. (2016). Seamless service? On the role and impact of service orchestrators in human-centered service systems. *Journal of Service Research., 19*, 458–476. https://doi.org/10.1177/1094670516666370

Breidbach, C. F., & Brodie, R. J. (2017). Engagement platforms in the sharing economy: Conceptual foundations and research directions. *Journal of Service Theory and Practice, 27*(4), 761–777. https://doi.org/10.1108/JSTP-04-2016-0071

Breidbach, C. F., & Maglio, P. P. (2016). Technology-enabled value co-creation: An empirical analysis of actors, resources, and practices. *Industrial Marketing Management, 56*, 73–85. https://doi.org/10.1016/j.indmarman.2016.03.011

Breidbach, C. F., Brodie, R., & Hollebeek, L. (2014). Beyond virtuality: From engagement platforms to engagement ecosystems. *Managing Service Quality, 24*(6), 592–611. https://doi.org/10.1108/MSQ-08-2013-0158

Breznitz, D., & Ornston, D. (2013). The revolutionary power of peripheral agencies: Explaining radical policy innovation in Finland and Israel. *Comparative Political Studies, 46*(10), 1219–1245. https://doi.org/10.1177/001041401247246

Brinker, S. (2020). The rise of the platform ecosystem: Martech's shift toward composability. *Chiefmartec Blog.* https://chiefmartec.com

Brodie, R. J., Fehrer, J. A., Jaakkola, E., & Conduit, J. (2019). Actor engagement in networks: Defining the conceptual domain. *Journal of Service Research, 22*(2), 173–188. https://doi.org/10.1177/1094670519827385

Brodie, R. J., Hollebeek, L. D., Juric, B., & Ilic, A. (2011). Customer engagement: Conceptual domain, fundamental propositions, and implications for research. *Journal of Service Research, 14*(3), 252–271. https://doi.org/10.1177/1094670511411703

Brousseau, E., & Penard, T. (2007). The economics of digital business models: A framework for analyzing the economics of platforms. *Review of Network Economics, 6*(2), 81–110. https://doi.org/10.2202/1446-9022.1112

Brown, R., & Mawson, S. (2019). Entrepreneurial ecosystems and public policy in action: A critique of the latest industrial policy blockbuster. *Cambridge Journal of Regions, Economy and Society, 12*(3), 347–368. https://doi.org/10.1093/cjres/rsz011

Bruce, H. L., Wilson, H. N., Macdonald, E. K., & Clarke, B. (2019). Resource integration, value creation and value destruction in collective consumption contexts. *Journal of Business Research, 103*, 173–185. https://doi.org/10.1016/j.jbusres.2019.05.007

Bruce, H. L., Wilson, H. N., Macdonald, E. K., & Clarke, B. (2019). Resource integration, value creation and value destruction in collective consumption contexts. *Journal of Business Research, 103*, 173–185. https://doi.org/10.1016/j.jbusres.2019.05.007

Brynjolfsson, E., & McAfee, A. (2017). *Machine, platform, crowd: Harnessing our digital future*. W. W. Norton & Company.

Budde, L., Haenggi, R., Laglia, L., & Friedli, T. (2024). Leading the transition to multi-sided platforms (MSPs) in a B2B context–the case of a recycling SME. *Industrial Marketing Management, 116*, 106–119. https://doi.org/10.1016/j.indmarman.2023.12.002

Carida, A., Colurcio, M., Edvardsson, B., & Pastore, A. (2022). *Creating harmony through a plethora of interests, resources, and actors: The challenging task of orchestrating the service ecosystem*. https://doi.org/10.1108/JSTP-06-2021-0110

Carst, A. E., & Hu, Y. (2023). Complementors as ecosystem actors: A systematic review. *Management Review Quarterly, 73*, 123–150. https://doi.org/10.1007/s11301-023-00368-y

Ceccagnoli, M., Forman, C., Huang, P., & Wu, D. J. (2012). Cocreation of value in a platform ecosystem: The case of enterprise software. *MIS Quarterly, 36*(1), 263–290. https://www.jstor.org/stable/41410417

Cennamo, C. (2021). Competing in digital markets: A platform-based perspective. *Academy of Management Perspectives, 35*(2), 265–291. https://doi.org/10.5465/amp.2016.0048

Cennamo, C., & Santalo, J. (2019). Generativity tension and value creation in platform ecosystems. *Organization Science, 30*(3), 617–641. https://doi.org/10.1287/orsc.2018.1270

Chaffey, D., & Ellis-Chadwick, F. (2019). *Digital marketing* (7th ed.). Pearson Education

Chandler, J. D., & Lusch, R. F. (2015). Service systems: A broadened framework and research agenda on value propositions, engagement, and service experience. *Journal of Service Research, 18*(1), 6–22. https://doi.org/10.1177/1094670514537

Chandler, J. D., & Vargo, S. L. (2011). Contextualization and value-in-context: How context frames exchange. *Marketing Theory, 11*(1), 35–49. https://doi.org/10.1177/1470593110393713

Chandler, J., Danatzis, I., Wernicke, C., Akaka, M., & Reynolds, D. (2019). How does innovation emerge in a service ecosystem. *Journal of Service Research, 22*(1), 75–89. https://doi.org/10.1177/1094670518797479

Chatterjee, S., Rana, N., Tamilmani, K., & Sharma, A. (2021). The effect of AI-based CRM on organization performance and competitive advantage: An empirical analysis in the B2B context. *Industrial Marketing Management.* https://doi.org/10.1016/j.indmarman.2021.07.013

Chen, L., Yi, J., Li, S., & Tong, T. W. (2022). Platform governance design in platform ecosystems: Implications for complementors' multihoming decision. *Journal of Management, 48*(3), 630–656. https://doi.org/10.1177/0149206320988337

Cheong, B. C. (2025). Leveraging blockchain for enhanced transparency and traceability in sustainable supply chains. *Discover Analytics, 3,* 6. https://doi.org/10.1007/s44257-025-00032-7

Chesbrough, H. W. (2007). Why companies should have open business models. *MIT Sloan Management Review, 48*(2), 22–28. https://sloanreview.mit.edu/article/why-companies-should-have-open-business-models/

Chesbrough, H. W. (2020). To recover faster from COVID-19, open up: Managerial implications from an open innovation perspective. *Industrial Marketing Management, 88,* 410–413. https://doi.org/10.1016/j.indmarman.2020.04.010

Choudary, S. P. (2021). *Platform scale: How an emerging business model helps startups build large empires with minimum investment.* (2nd ed.). Platform Thinking Labs.

Choudhury, V., & Sabherwal, R. (2003). Portfolios of control in outsourced software development projects. *Information Systems Research, 14*(3), 291–304. https://doi.org/10.1287/isre.14.3.291.16563

Clarysse, B., Wright, M., Bruneel, J., & Mahajan, A. (2014). Creating value in ecosystems: Crossing the chasm between knowledge and business ecosystems. *Research Policy, 43*(7), 1164–1176. https://doi.org/10.1016/j.respol.2014.04.014

Constantinides, P., Henfridsson, O., & Parker, G. G. (2018). Introduction—Platforms and infrastructures in the digital age. *Information Systems Research, 29*(2), 381–400. https://doi.org/10.1287/isre.2018.0794

Cova, B., & Salle, R. (2008). Marketing solutions in accordance with the SD logic: Co-creating value with customer network actors. *Industrial Marketing Management, 37,* 270–277. https://doi.org/10.1016/j.indmarman.2007.07.005

Cui, A. S., & Wu, F. (2016). Utilizing customer knowledge in innovation: Antecedents and impact of customer involvement on new product performance. *Journal of the Academy of Marketing Science, 44,* 516–538. https://doi.org/10.1007/s11747-015-0433-x

Cusumano, M. A., & Gawer, A. (2002). The elements of platform leadership. *MIT Sloan Management Review, 43*(3), 51–58. https://sloanreview.mit.edu/article/the-elements-of-platform-leadership/

Cusumano, M. A. (2022). The evolution of research on industry platforms. *Academy of Management Discoveries, 8*(1), 7–14. https://doi.org/10.5465/amd.2020.0091

Cutolo, D., & Kenney, M. (2021). Platform-dependent entrepreneurs: Power asymmetries, risks, and strategies in the platform economy. *Academy of Management Perspectives, 35*(4), 584–605. https://doi.org/10.5465/amp.2019.0103

Dabbish, L., Stuart, C., Tsay, J., & Herbsleb, J. (2012). Social coding in GitHub: Transparency and collaboration in an open software repository. In *Proceedings of the ACM 2012 conference on computer supported cooperative work* (pp. 1277–1286). Association for Computing Machinery. https://doi.org/10.1145/2145204.2145396

Das, S. R. (2019). The future of Fintech. *Financial Management, 48*(4), 981–1007. https://doi.org/10.1111/fima.12297

Davenport, T. H., Guha, A., Grewal, D., & Bressgott, T. (2020). How artificial intelligence will change the future of marketing. *Journal of the Academy of Marketing Science, 48,* 24–42. https://doi.org/10.1007/s11747-019-00696-0

Davies, M., Hungenberg, E., Aicher, T. J., & Newland, B. L. (2024). Work[out] from home: Examining brand community among connected fitness brand users. *International Journal of Sport Management and Marketing, 24*(2), 113–136. https://doi.org/10.1504/IJSMM.2024.137102

Day, G. S. (2011). Closing the marketing capabilities gap. *Journal of Marketing, 75*(4), 183–195. https://doi.org/10.1509/jmkg.75.4.183

Day, G. S. (2020). Closing the marketing capabilities gap. *Journal of Marketing, 84*(4), 45–66.

de Reuver, M., Sørensen, C., & Basole, R. C. (2018). The digital platform: A research agenda. *Journal of Information Technology, 33*(2), 124–135. https://doi.org/10.1057/s41265-016-0033-3

Dedehayir, O., Mäkinen, S. J., & Ortt, J. R. (2018). Roles during innovation ecosystem genesis: A literature review. *Technological Forecasting and Social Change, 136,* 18–29. https://doi.org/10.1016/j.techfore.2016.11.028

Dedehayir, O., Pîrvan, C. I., & Le Fever, H. (2019). Industry platforms as facilitators of disruptive IoT innovations. *Journal of Technology Management & Innovation, 14*(3), 18–28. https://doi.org/10.4067/S0718-27242019000300018

Demil, B., & Lecocq, X. (2010). Business model evolution: In search of dynamic consistency. *Long Range Planning, 43*(2–3), 227–246. https://doi.org/10.1016/j.lrp.2010.02.004

Denis, J. L., Langley, A., & Rouleau, L. (2010). The practice of leadership in the messy world of organizations. *Leadership, 6*(1), 67–88. https://doi.org/10.1177/1742715009354233

Derave, T., Prince Sales, T., Gailly, F., & Poels, G. (2021). Understanding digital marketplace business models: An ontology approach. In *PoEM workshops computer science*. http://hdl.handle.net/1854/LU-8753007

Dhanaraj, C., & Parkhe, A. (2006). Orchestrating innovation networks. *Academy of Management Review, 31*(3), 659–669. https://doi.org/10.5465/amr.2006.21318923

Dremel, C., Haskamp, T., Marx, C., & Uebernickel, F. (2021). Understanding inertia in digital transformation: A literature review and multilevel research framework. *Proceedings of the 42nd International Conference on Information Systems*.

Dussauge, P., Garrette, B., & Mitchell, W. (2000). Learning from competing partners: Outcomes and durations of scale and link alliances in Europe, North America and Asia. *Strategic Management Journal, 21*(2), 99–126. https://doi.org/10.1002/(SICI)1097-0266(200002)21:2%3c99::AID-SMJ80%3e3.0.CO;2-G

Edelman, D. C., & Singer, M. (2015). Competing on customer journeys. *Harvard Business Review, 93*(11), 88–100. https://doi.org/10.13140/RG.2.2.34634.95688

Eisenhardt, K. M., & Brown, S. L. (1999). Patching: Restitching business portfolios in dynamic markets. *Harvard Business Review, 77*(3), 72–82.

Eisenhardt, K. M., & Martin, J. A. (2000). Dynamic capabilities: What are they? *Strategic Management Journal, 21*(10–11), 1105–1121. https://doi.org/10.1002/1097-0266(200010/11)21:10/11%3c1105::AID-SMJ133%3e3.0.CO;2-E

Ekman, P., Rondell, J. G., Anastasiadou, E., Kowalkowski, C., Raggio, R. D., & Thompson, S. M. (2021). Business actor engagement: Exploring its antecedents and types. *Industrial Marketing Management, 98*, 179–192. https://doi.org/10.1016/j.indmarman.2021.08.009

Engert, M., Evers, J., Hein, A., & Krcmar, H. (2021). The engagement of complementors and the role of platform boundary resources in e-commerce platform ecosystems. *Information Systems Frontiers, 23*(3), 667–685. https://doi.org/10.1007/s10796-021-10236-3

Engert, M., Farchi, D., & Sayed, M. (2025). Self-organization and governance in digital platform ecosystems: Balancing top-down control and complementor coalitions. *MIS Quarterly, 49*(1), 85–112. https://doi.org/10.25300/MISQ/2024/18413

Evans, D. S., & Schmalensee, R. (2013). *The antitrust analysis of multi-sided platform businesses* (NBER Working Paper No. 18783). National Bureau of Economic Research. http://www.nber.org/papers/w18783

Evans, D. S., & Schmalensee, R. (2016). *Matchmakers: The new economics of multisided platforms*. Harvard Business Review Press.

Evans, P. C., & Basole, R. C. (2016). Revealing the API ecosystem and enterprise strategy via visual analytics. *Communications of the ACM, 59*(2), 26–28. https://doi.org/10.1145/2856447

Evans, P., & Gawer, A. (2016). *The rise of the platform enterprise: A global survey*. The Center for Global Enterprise. https://doi.org/10.13140/RG.2.2.35887.05280

FA, C., Ramezan Zadeh, M. T., Ozalp, H., & Volberda, H. W. (2025). The role of trust in a platform ecosystem: Exploring the impact of different trust dimensions on complementors' platform revenue. *Research Policy, 54*(8), Article 104957. https://doi.org/10.2139/ssrn.5180726

Faems, D., Janssens, M., Madhok, A., & Van Looy, B. (2008). Toward an integrative perspective on alliance governance: Connecting contract design, trust dynamics, and contract application. *Academy of Management Journal, 51*(6), 1053–1078. https://doi.org/10.5465/amj.2008.35732527

Fairhurst, G. T., & Grant, D. (2010). The social construction of leadership: A sailing guide. *Management Communication Quarterly, 24*(2), 171–210. https://doi.org/10.1177/0893318909359697

Fang, E., Palmatier, R. W., & Evans, K. R. (2008). Influence of customer participation on value creation: A meta-analysis. *Journal of the Academy of Marketing Science, 36*, 169–183. https://doi.org/10.1007/s11747-007-0082-9

Felin, T., & Powell, T. C. (2016). Designing organizations for dynamic capabilities. *California Management Review, 58*(4), 78–96. https://doi.org/10.1525/cmr.2016.58.4.78

Foss, N. J., Schmidt, J., & Teece, D. J. (2022). Ecosystem leadership as a dynamic capability. *Long Range Planning, 56*(6), Article 102270. https://doi.org/10.1016/j.lrp.2022.102270

Frow, P., McColl-Kennedy, J. R., & Payne, A. (2016). Co-creation practices: Their role in shaping a health care ecosystem. *Industrial Marketing Management, 56*, 24–39. https://doi.org/10.1016/j.indmarman.2016.03.007

Frow, P., Payne, A., Wilkinson, I. F., & Young, L. (2011). Customer management and CRM: Addressing the dark side. *Journal of Services Marketing, 25*(2), 79–89. https://doi.org/10.1108/08876041111119804

Fullan, M. (2001). *Leading in a culture of change*. Jossey-Bass.

Fuller, J., Hutter, K., & Faullant, R. (2011). Why co-creation experience matters: Creative consumers and the differences among them. *Journal of Business Research, 64*(9), 980–988. https://doi.org/10.1111/j.1467-9310.2011.00640.x

Füller, J., Hutter, K., Wahl, J., Bilgram, V., & Tekic, Z. (2022). How AI revolutionizes innovation management—Perceptions and implementation preferences of AI-based innovators. *Technological Forecasting and Social Change, 178*, 121596. https://doi.org/10.1016/j.techfore.2022.121598

Fürstenau, D., Baiyere, A., Schewina, K., Schulte-Althoff, M., & Rothe, H. (2023). Extended generativity theory on digital platforms. *Information Systems Research, 34*(4), 1686–1710. https://doi.org/10.1287/isre.2023.1209

Galina, R., & Lapiņa, I. (2023). Digital transformation as a catalyst for sustainability and open innovation. *Journal of Open Innovation: Technology, Market, and Complexity, 9*(1). https://doi.org/10.1016/j.joitmc.2023.100017

Gawer, A. (2021). Digital platforms' boundaries: The interplay of firm scope, platform sides, and digital interfaces. *Long Range Planning, 54*(5), Article 102045. https://doi.org/10.1016/j.lrp.2020.102045

Gawer, A., & Cusumano, M. A. (2014). Industry platforms and ecosystem innovation. *Journal of Product Innovation Management, 31*(3), 417–433. https://onlinelibrary.wiley.com/doi/10.1111/jpim.12105

Gawer, A., & Harracá, M. (2025). Inconsistent platform governance and social contagion of misconduct in digital ecosystems: A complementors perspective. *Research Policy, 54*(8), Article 104957. https://doi.org/10.2139/ssrn.5368760

Ghazawneh, A., & Henfridsson, O. (2013). Balancing platform control and external contribution in third-party development: The boundary resources model. *Information Systems Journal, 23*(2), 173–192. https://doi.org/10.1111/j.1365-2575.2012.00406.x

Ghemawat, P. (2001). Distance still matters: The hard reality of global expansion. *Harvard Business Review, 79*(8), 137–147.

Ghosh, N., Bhagavathy, S., & Thakur, J. (2022). Accelerating electric vehicle adoption: Techno-economic assessment to modify existing fuel stations with fast charging infrastructure. *Clean Technologies and Environmental Policy., 24*, 1–14. https://doi.org/10.1007/s10098-022-02406-x

Giessmann, A. (2012). *Platform as a service—A conjoint study on consumers' preferences*. 33rd International Conference on Information Systems (ICIS 2012). Orlando, FL.

Grewal, D., Guha, A., Satornino, C. B., & Schweiger, E. B. (2021). Artificial intelligence: The light and the darkness. *Journal of Business Research, 136*, 229–236. https://doi.org/10.1016/j.jbusres.2021.07.043

Gronroos, C. (2011). Value co-creation in service logic: A critical analysis. *Marketing Theory, 11*(3), 279–301. https://doi.org/10.1177/1470593111408177

Gu, G., & Li, Z. (2022). Technology fragmentation, platform investment, and complementary innovation. *SSRN*. https://doi.org/10.2139/ssrn.4061870

Gulati, R. (1998). Alliances and networks. *Strategic Management Journal, 19*(4), 293–317. https://doi.org/10.1002/(SICI)1097-0266(199804)19:4%3c293::AID-SMJ982%3e3.0.CO;2-M

Gummesson, E., & Mele, C. (2010). Marketing as value co-creation through network interaction and resource integration. *Journal of Business Market Management, 4*(4), 181–198. https://doi.org/10.1007/s12087-010-0044-2

Haberly, D., Mcdonald-Korth, D., Urban, M., & Wójcik, D. (2019). Asset management as a digital platform industry: A global financial network perspective. *Geoforum, 106*, 167–181. https://doi.org/10.1016/j.geoforum.2019.08.009

Hagedoorn, J. (2002). Inter-firm R&D partnerships: An overview of major trends and patterns since 1960. *Research Policy, 31*(4), 477–492. https://doi.org/10.1016/S0048-7333(01)00120-2

Hagiu, A., & Wright, J. (2020). Data-enabled learning in digital platforms. *American Economic Review, 110*(3), 889–917. https://doi.org/10.1111/1756-2171.12453

Hanafizadeh, P. (2025). Governance system design model in platform ecosystems by a socio-technical systems theory. *Digital Policy, Regulation and Governance*. Advance online publication. https://doi.org/10.1108/DPRG-04-2025-0105

Hänninen, M., Smedlund, A., & Mitronen, L. (2018). Digitalization in retailing: Multi-sided platforms as drivers of industry transformation. *Baltic Journal of Management, 13*(2), 152–168. https://doi.org/10.1108/BJM-04-2017-0109

Harrigan, P., Evers, U., Miles, M., & Daly, T. (2017). Customer engagement and the relationship between involvement, engagement, and loyalty. *Journal of Marketing Management, 33*(5–6), 378–409. https://doi.org/10.1016/j.jbusres.2017.11.046

Heifetz, R. A., Grashow, A., & Linsky, M. (2009). The practice of adaptive leadership: Tools and tactics for changing your organization and the world. *Harvard Business Press*. https://doi.org/10.1016/j.lisr.2009.05.001

Heimburg, V., & Wiesche, M. (2022). Relations between actors in digital platform ecosystems: A literature review. In *ECIS 2022 Research Papers* (Paper 93). Association for Information Systems. https://aisel.aisnet.org/ecis2022_rp/93

Hein, A., Weking, J., Schreieck, M., Wiesche, M., Böhm, M., & Krcmar, H. (2023). Value co-creation in platform ecosystems: A structured literature review and future research directions. *Electronic Markets, 33*, 369–388. https://doi.org/10.1007/s12525-021-00473-9

Hein, A., Weking, J., Schreieck, M., Wiesche, M., Böhm, M., & Krcmar, H. (2019). Value co-creation practices in business-to-business platform ecosystems. *Electronic Markets, 29*, 503–518. https://doi.org/10.1007/s12525-019-00337-y

Hendrickx, L., & Matthyssens, P. (2022). Platform ecosystem development in an institutionalized business market: The case of the asset management industry. *Journal of Business & Industrial Marketing, 38*(2), 395–413. https://doi.org/10.1108/JBIM-04-2021-0193

Hendrickx, L., Matthyssens, P., & Kowalkowski, C. (2024). The co-evolution of actor engagement and value co-creation on digital platforms: Evidence from the asset management industry. *Journal of Business & Industrial Marketing*. (Advance online publication) https://doi.org/10.1016/j.ijpe.2024.109467

Hertwig, R., & Engel, C. (2016). Homo ignorans: Deliberately choosing not to know. *Perspectives on Psychological Science, 11*(3), 359–372. https://doi.org/10.1177/1745691616635594

Hibbert, S., Winklhofer, H., & Sobhy, M. (2012). Customers as resource integrators toward a model of customer learning. *Journal of Service Research, 15*, 247–261. https://doi.org/10.1177/1094670512442805

Hilbolling, S., Berends, H., Deken, F., & Tuertscher, P. (2019). Complementors as connectors: Managing open innovation around digital product platforms. *R&D Management*. https://doi.org/10.1111/radm.12371

Hirt, M., & Willmott, P. (2020). The CEO moment: Leadership for a new era. *McKinsey Quarterly*. https://www.mckinsey.com/featured-insights/leadership/the-ceo-moment-leadership-for-a-new-era

Hollebeek, L. D., & Macky, K. (2019). Digital content marketing's role in fostering consumer engagement, trust, and value: Framework, fundamental propositions, and implications. *Journal of Interactive Marketing, 45*, 27–41. https://doi.org/10.1016/j.intmar.2018.07.003

Iglesias, O., Landgraf, P., Ind, N., Markovic, S., & Koporcic, N. (2020). Corporate brand identity co-creation in business-to-business contexts. *Industrial Marketing Management, 85*, 32–43. https://doi.org/10.1016/j.indmarman.2019.09.008

Inkpen, A. C., & Tsang, E. W. K. (2005). Social capital, networks, and knowledge transfer. *Academy of Management Review, 30*(1), 146–165. https://doi.org/10.2307/20159100

ISG. (2023). PaaS transformation: Managing cloud-native strategies for platform delivery. *ISG White Paper*. https://isg-one.com

Jaakkola, E., & Alexander, M. (2014). The role of customer engagement behavior in value co-creation: A service system perspective. *Journal of Service Research, 17*(3), 247–261. https://doi.org/10.1177/1094670514529187

Jackson, K. T., Burgess, S., Toms, F., & Cuthbertson, E. L. (2018). Community engagement: Using feedback loops to empower residents and influence systemic change in culturally diverse communities. *Global Journal of Community Psychology Practice, 9*(2), 1–21. https://doi.org/10.17161/gjcpp.v9i2.20713

Jacobides, M. G., Cennamo, C., & Gawer, A. (2018). Towards a theory of ecosystems. *Strategic Management Journal, 39*(8), 2255–2276. https://doi.org/10.1002/smj.2904

Jacobides, M. G., Cennamo, C., & Gawer, A. (2018). Towards a theory of ecosystems. *Strategic Management Journal, 39*(8), 2255–2276. https://doi.org/10.1002/smj.2904

Jacobides, M. G., Cennamo, C., & Gawer, A. (2024). Externalities and complementarities in platforms and ecosystems: From structural solutions to endogenous failures. *Research Policy, 53*(1). https://doi.org/10.1016/j.respol.2023.104845

Jovanović, J. S., Vujadinovic, R., Mitreva, E., Fragassa, C., & Vujovic, A. (2020). The relationship between E-commerce and firm performance: The mediating role of internet sales channels. *Sustainability. 12*. https://doi.org/10.3390/su12176993

Jovanovic, M., Sjödin, D., & Parida, V. (2022). Co-evolution of platform architecture, platform services, and platform governance: Expanding the platform value of industrial digital platforms. *Technovation, 118*, Article 102218. https://doi.org/10.1016/j.technovation.2020.102218

Kannan, P. K., & Li, H. (2017). Digital marketing: A framework, review and research agenda. *International Journal of Research in Marketing, 34*(1), 22–45. https://doi.org/10.1016/j.ijresmar.2016.11.006

Kapoor, R. (2018). Ecosystems: Broadening the locus of value creation. *Journal of Organizational Design, 7*(1), Article 12. https://doi.org/10.1186/s41469-018-0035-4

Kapoor, R., & Lee, J. M. (2013). Coordinating and competing in ecosystems: How organizational forms shape new technology investments. *Strategic Management Journal, 34*(3), 274–296. https://doi.org/10.1002/smj.2010

Kari, A., Bellin, P., Matzner, M., & Gersch, M. (2025). Governing the emergence of network-driven platform ecosystems. *Electronic Markets, 35*. https://doi.org/10.1007/s12525-024-00745-9

Karplus, V. J., Geissmann, T., & Zhang, D. (2021). Institutional complexity, management practices, and firm productivity. *World Development, 142*, Article 105386. https://doi.org/10.1016/j.worlddev.2020.105386

Kartika, L. (2023). The role of strategic leadership and dynamic capabilities in the new reality of today's business world. https://doi.org/10.2991/978-94-6463-244-6_32

Katz, M. L., & Shapiro, C. (1985). Network externalities, competition, and compatibility. *The American Economic Review, 75*(3), 424–440. https://www.jstor.org/stable/1814809

Kenney, M., & Zysman, J. (2016). The rise of the platform economy. *Issues in Science and Technology, 32*(3), 61–69.

Kim, J. Y., & Parker, G. G. (2020). Platform strategy. *Harvard Business Review, 98*(1), 94–101.

Kotter, J. P. (1995). Leading change: Why transformation efforts fail. *Harvard Business Review, 73*(2), 59–67. https://hbr.org/1995/05/leading-change-why-transformation-efforts-fail-2

Kowalkowski, C., Persson Ridell, O., Röndell, J., & Sörhammar, D. (2012). The co-creative practice of forming a value proposition. *Journal of Marketing Management, 28*(13–14), 1553–1570. https://doi.org/10.1080/0267257X.2012.736875

Kraus, S., Schiavone, F., Pluzhnikova, A., & Invernizzi, A. C. (2021). Digital transformation in healthcare: Analyzing the current state-of-research. *Journal of Business Research, 123*, 557–567. https://doi.org/10.1016/j.jbusres.2020.10.030

Kretschmer, T., Leiponen, A., Schilling, M., & Vasudeva, G. (2022). Platform ecosystems as meta-organizations: Implications for platform strategies. *Strategic Management Journal, 43*(3), 405–424. https://doi.org/10.1002/smj.3250

Kuckertz, A. (2019). Let's take the entrepreneurial ecosystem metaphor seriously! *Journal of Business Venturing Insights, 11*, Article e00124. https://doi.org/10.1016/j.jbvi.2019.e00124

Kumar, V., Dixit, A., Javalgi, R. G., & Dass, M. (2021a). Digital transformation of business-to-business marketing: Framework and research agenda. *Journal of Business & Industrial Marketing, 36*(5), 849–867. https://doi.org/10.1016/j.indmarman.2021.03.008

Kumar, V., Ramachandran, D., & Kumar, B. (2021b). Influence of new-age technologies on marketing: A research agenda. *Journal of Business Research, 125*, 864–877. https://doi.org/10.1016/j.jbusres.2020.01.007

Kumaraswamy, A., Garud, R., & Ansari, S. (2018). Perspectives on disruptive innovations. *Journal of Management Studies, 55*, 1025–1042. https://doi.org/10.1111/joms.12399

Kwon, I.-W. G., Kim, S.-H., & Martin, D. G. (2016). Healthcare supply chain management: Strategic areas for quality and financial improvement. *Technological Forecasting and Social Change, 113*(Part B), 422–428. https://doi.org/10.1016/j.techfore.2016.07.014

Kyriakopoulos, K., & Moorman, C. (2004). Tradeoffs in marketing exploitation and exploration strategies: The overlooked role of market orientation. *International Journal of Research in Marketing, 21*(3), 219–240. https://doi.org/10.1016/j.ijresmar.2004.01.001

Laczko, C., Hullova, D., Needham, A., Ross, A., & Battisti, M. (2023). Building innovation ecosystems: Navigating tensions between trust and control. *California*

Management Review, 65(4), 101–122. https://doi.org/10.1177/00081256231183209

Lamberton, C., & Stephen, A. T. (2016). A thematic exploration of digital, social media, and mobile marketing: Research evolution from 2000 to 2015 and an agenda for future inquiry. *Journal of Marketing, 80*(6), 146–172. https://doi.org/10.1509/jm.15.0415

Lavie, D. (2006). The competitive advantage of interconnected firms: An extension of the resource-based view. *Academy of Management Review, 31*(3), 638–658. https://www.jstor.org/stable/20159233

Lee, I., &. Shin, Y. J. (2018). Fintech: Ecosystem, business models, investment decisions, and challenges. *Business Horizons, 61*(1), 35–46. https://doi.org/10.1016/j.bushor.2017.09.003

Lee, I., & Lee, K. (2015). The internet of things (IoT): Applications, investments, and challenges for enterprises. *Business Horizons, 58*(4), 431–440. https://doi.org/10.1016/j.bushor.2015.03.008

Lehmann, J., Werder, K., Babar, Y., & Berente, N. (2021). Establishing and maintaining legitimacy for digital platform innovations. In *Academy of management proceedings.* https://doi.org/10.5465/AMBPP.2021.12602abstract

Lemon, K. N., & Verhoef, P. C. (2016). Understanding customer experience throughout the customer journey. *Journal of Marketing, 80*(6), 69–96. https://doi.org/10.1509/jm.15.0420

Letaifa, S. B. (2014). The uneasy transition from supply chains to ecosystems: The value-creation/value-capture dilemma. *Management Decision, 52*(2), 278–295. https://doi.org/10.1108/MD-06-2013-0329

Liang, L., Tian, L., Xie, J., Xu, J., & Zhang, W. (2021). Optimal pricing model of car-sharing: Market pricing or platform pricing. *Industrial Management & Data Systems, 121*(3), 594–612. https://doi.org/10.1108/IMDS-04-2020-0230

Lichtenstein, B. B., & Plowman, D. A. (2009). The leadership of emergence: A complex systems leadership theory of emergence at successive organizational levels. *The Leadership Quarterly, 20*(4), 617–630. https://doi.org/10.1016/j.leaqua.2009.04.006

Lima, A., Rossi, L., & Musolesi, M. (2014). *Coding together at scale: GitHub as a collaborative social network.* https://doi.org/10.48550/arXiv.1407.2535

Linde, L., Sjödin, D., Parida, V., & Wincent, J. (2021). Dynamic capabilities for ecosystem orchestration: A capability-based framework for smart city innovation initiatives. *Technological Forecasting and Social Change, 166*, Article 120614. https://doi.org/10.1016/j.techfore.2021.120614

Liu, X., Wang, W., & Su, Y. (2023). Leveraging complementary resources through relational capital to improve alliance performance under an uncertain environment: A moderated mediation analysis. *Sustainability, 15*(1), 310. https://doi.org/10.3390/su15010310

Liu, Z., Li, Z., Zhang, Y., Mutukumira, A. N., Feng, Y., Cui, Y., Wang, S., Wang, J., & Wang, S. (2024). Comparing business, innovation, and platform ecosystems: A systematic review of the literature. *Biomimetics, 9*(4), Article 216. https://doi.org/10.3390/biomimetics9040216

Lusch, R. F., & Nambisan, S. (2015). Service innovation: A service-dominant logic perspective. *MIS Quarterly, 39*(1), 155–175. https://doi.org/10.25300/MISQ/2015/39.1.07

Mair, J., Martí, I., & Ventresca, M. (2012). Building inclusive markets in rural Bangladesh: How intermediaries work institutional voids. *Academy of Management Journal, 55*(4), 819–850. https://doi.org/10.5465/amj.2010.0627

Mancuso, I., Petruzzelli, A. M., & Panniello, U. (2024). Value creation in data-centric B2B platforms: A model based on multiple case studies. *Industrial Marketing Management, 119*, 1–14. https://doi.org/10.1016/j.indmarman.2024.04.001

Martin, K. D., & Murphy, P. E. (2017). The role of data privacy in marketing. *Journal of the Academy of Marketing Science, 45*(2), 135–155. https://doi.org/10.1007/s11747-016-0495-4

McIntyre, D. P., & Srinivasan, A. (2017). Networks, platforms, and strategy: Emerging views and next steps. *Strategic Management Journal, 38*(1), 141–160. https://doi.org/10.1002/smj.2596

McKinsey Digital. (2024, September 13). Technology alone is never enough for true productivity. *McKinsey & Company.* https://www.mckinsey.com/capabilities/mckinsey-digital/our-insights/technology-alone-is-never-enough-for-true-productivity

Meadows, D. H. (2008). *Thinking in systems: A primer.* Chelsea Green Publishing.

Mele, C., Spena, T. R., & Colurcio, M. (2010). Co-creating value innovation through resource integration. *International Journal of Quality and Service Sciences., 2*, 60–78. https://doi.org/10.1108/17566691011026603

Miah, M., Akter, M., Samid, D., & Siam, M. (2023). AI in decision making: Transforming business strategies. *ABC Research Alert, 11*(3), 14–23. https://doi.org/10.18034/ra.v11i3.667

Mintz, O. (2023). Metrics for marketing decisions: Drivers and implications for performance. *NIM Marketing Intelligence Review., 15*, 18–23. https://doi.org/10.2478/nimmir-2023-0003

Möller, K., Nenonen, S., & Storbacka, K. (2020). Networks, ecosystems, fields, market systems? Making sense of the business environment. *Industrial Marketing Management, 90*, 380–399. https://doi.org/10.1016/j.indmarman.2020.07.013

Moser, C., Deichmann, D., & Groenewegen, P. (2014). The social scaffolding of online communities. *Academy of Management Proceedings, 2014*(1), 11309. https://doi.org/10.5465/AMBPP.2014.11309abstract

Motoyama, Y., & Knowlton, K. (2017). Examining the connections within the startup ecosystem: A case study of St. Louis. *Entrepreneurship Research Journal, 7*(1), 1–19. https://doi.org/10.1515/erj-2016-0011

Nambisan, S., & Baron, R. A. (2009). Virtual customer environments: Testing a model of voluntary participation in value co-creation activities. *Journal of Product Innovation Management, 26*(4), 388–406. https://doi.org/10.1111/j.1540-5885.2009.00667.x

Nambisan, S., Zahra, S. A., & Luo, Y. (2019). Global platforms and ecosystems: Implications for international business theories. *Journal of International Business Studies, 50*(9), 1464–1486. https://doi.org/10.1057/s41267-019-00262-4

Narvaiza, L., Campos, J. A., Martín-Peña, M. L., & Díaz-Garrido, E. (2024). Characterizing digital service innovation: Phases, actors, functions and interactions in the context of a digital service platform. *Journal of Service Management, 35*(2), 253–279. https://doi.org/10.1108/JOSM-12-2022-0401

Ng, I. C. L., & Briscoe, G. (2012). Value, variety and viability: New business models for co-creation in outcome-based contracts. *International Journal of Service Science, Management, Engineering, and Technology, 3*(3), 26–48. https://doi.org/10.4018/jssmet.2012070103

Ng, I. C. L., & Wakenshaw, S. Y. L. (2017). The Internet-of-Things: Review and research directions. *International Journal of Research in Marketing, 34*(1), 3–21. https://doi.org/10.1016/j.ijresmar.2016.11.003

Ng, I. C. L., Maull, R., & Yip, N. (2009). Outcome-based contracts as a driver for systems thinking and service-dominant logic in service science: Evidence from the defense industry. *European Management Journal, 27*(6), 377–387. https://doi.org/10.1016/j.emj.2009.05.002

Nielsen, B. B. (2005). The role of knowledge embeddedness in the creation of synergies in strategic alliances. *Journal of Business Research, 58*(9), 1194–1204. https://doi.org/10.1016/j.jbusres.2004.05.001

Nim, N., Pedada, K., & Hewett, K. (2024). Digital marketing ecosystems and global market expansion: Current state and future research agenda. *International Marketing Review, 41*(5), 872–885. https://doi.org/10.1108/IMR-04-2024-0108

Nyadzayo, M. W., Casidy, R., & Thaichon, P. (2020). B2B purchase engagement: Examining the key drivers and outcomes in professional services. *Industrial Marketing Management, 85*, 197–208. https://doi.org/10.1016/j.indmarman.2019.11.007

Oliva, R., & Kallenberg, R. (2003). Managing the transition from products to services. *International Journal of Service Industry Management, 14*(2), 160–172. https://doi.org/10.1108/09564230310474138

Ospina, S. M., & Foldy, E. G. (2010). Building bridges from the margins: The work of leadership in social change organizations. *The Leadership Quarterly, 21*(2), 292–307. https://doi.org/10.1016/j.leaqua.2010.01.008

Palmié, M., Miehé, L., Oghazi, P., Parida, V., & Wincent, J. (2022). The evolution of the digital service ecosystem and digital business model innovation in retail: The emergence of meta-ecosystems and the value of physical interactions. *Technological Forecasting and Social Change, 177*, Article 121496. https://doi.org/10.1016/j.techfore.2021.121496

Parker, G. G., Van Alstyne, M. W., & Choudary, S. P. (2016). *Platform revolution: How networked markets are transforming the economy and how to make them work for you*. W. W. Norton & Company.

Parker, G., & Van Alstyne, M. (2023). Platforms: Their structure, benefits, and challenges. In *handbook of digital enterprise* (pp. 763–780). Springer. https://doi.org/10.1007/978-3-031-45304-5_33

Paul, M., Maglaras, L., Ferrag, M. A., & Almomani, I. (2023). Digitization of healthcare sector: A study on privacy and security concerns. *ICT Express, 9*(4), 571–588. https://doi.org/10.1016/j.icte.2023.02.007

Pei, Y., & Li, M. (2023). The effects of information on competition on a hybrid retail platform. *International Journal of Production Economics, 260*, Article 108843. https://doi.org/10.1016/j.ijpe.2023.108843

Peng, B. (2021). Digital leadership: State governance in the era of digital technology. *Global Media and China, 5*(4), 365–378. https://doi.org/10.1177/2096608321989835

Peng, H., Lu, Y., & Gupta, S. (2023). Promoting value emergence through digital platform ecosystems: Perspectives on resource integration in China. *Technological Forecasting and Social Change, 189*, Article 122338. https://doi.org/10.1016/j.techfore.2022.122338

Perks, H., Kowalkowski, C., Witell, L., & Gustafsson, A. (2017). Network orchestration for value platforms. *Industrial Marketing Management, 67*, 106–121. https://doi.org/10.1016/j.indmarman.2017.08.002

Peuckert, J., & Kern, F. (2023). How user innovation communities contribute to sustainability transitions: An exploration of three online communities. *Environmental Innovation and Societal Transitions, 49*, Article 100785. https://doi.org/10.1016/j.eist.2023.100785

Pousttchi, K., & Dehnert, M. (2018). Exploring the digitalization impact on consumer decision-making in retail banking. *Electron Markets, 28*, 265–286. https://doi.org/10.1007/s12525-017-0283-0

Prahalad, C. K., & Ramaswamy, V. (2004). Co-creating unique value with customers. *Strategy & Leadership, 32*(3), 4–9. https://doi.org/10.1108/10878570410699249

Qian, H., Acs, Z. J., & Stough, R. R. (2013). Regional systems of entrepreneurship: The nexus of human capital, knowledge and new firm formation. *Journal of Economic Geography, 13*(4), 559–587. https://doi.org/10.1093/jeg/lbs009

Ramaswamy, V., & Ozcan, K. (2016). Brand value co-creation in a digitalized world: An integrative framework and research implications. *International Journal of Research in Marketing, 33*(1), 93–106. https://doi.org/10.1016/j.ijresmar.2015.07.001

Ramaswamy, V., & Ozcan, K. (2018). *The co-creation paradigm*. Stanford University Press.

Rawlins, J. M., De Lange, W. J., & Fraser, G. C. G. (2018). An Ecosystem service value chain analysis framework: A conceptual paper. *Ecological Economics, 147*, 84–95. https://doi.org/10.1016/j.ecolecon.2017.12.023

Reeves, M., & Deimler, M. (2011). Adaptability: The new competitive advantage. *Harvard Business Review, 89*(7/8), 134–141. https://hbr.org/2011/07/adaptability-the-new-competitive-advantage

Reiners, S. (2022). Trust and its extensions in digital platform ecosystems: Key concepts and issues for future research. https://doi.org/10.1109/CBI54897.2022.10042.

Ritala, P., Keränen, J., Fishburn, J., & Ruokonen, M. (2024). Selling and monetizing data in B2B markets: Four data-driven value propositions. *Technovation, 130*, Article 102935. https://doi.org/10.1016/j.technovation.2023.102935

Rong, K., Hu, G., Lin, Y., Shi, Y., & Guo, L. (2015). Understanding business ecosystem using a 6C framework in Internet-of-Things-based sectors. *International Journal of Production Economics, 159*, 41–55. https://doi.org/10.1016/j.ijpe.2014.09.003

Rong, K., Lin, Y., Shi, Y., & Yu, J. (2013). Linking business ecosystem lifecycle with platform strategy: A triple view of technology, application and organization. *International Journal of Technology Management, 62*(1), 75–93. https://doi.org/10.1504/IJTM.2013.053042

Roundy, P. T., & Fayard, A.-L. (2021). Narratives in entrepreneurial ecosystems: Drivers of effectuation. *Small Business Economics, 57*(2), 467–483. https://doi.org/10.1007/s11187-021-00531-3

Rust, R. T., & Huang, M.-H. (2014). The service revolution and the transformation of marketing science. *Marketing Science, 33*(2), 206–221. https://doi.org/10.1287/mksc.2013.0836

Ruutu, S., Casey, T., & Kotovirta, V. (2017). Development and competition of digital service platforms: A system dynamics approach. *Technological Forecasting and Social Change, 117*, 119–130. https://doi.org/10.1016/j.techfore.2016.12.011

Schein, E. H. (2010). *Organizational culture and leadership* (4th ed.). Jossey-Bass.

Schivinski, B., Christodoulides, G., & Dabrowski, D. (2016). Measuring consumers' engagement with brand-related social-media content: Development and validation of the COBRAs scale. *Journal of Advertising Research, 56*(1), 64–80. https://doi.org/10.2501/JAR-2016-000

Schüler, F., & Petrik, D. (2023). Measuring network effects of digital industrial platforms: Towards a balanced platform performance management. *Information Systems and e-Business Management, 21*, 863–911. https://doi.org/10.1007/s10257-023-00655-x

Selander, L., Henfridsson, O., & Svahn, F. (2013). Capability search and redeem across digital ecosystems. *Journal of Information Technology, 28*(3), 183–197. https://doi.org/10.1057/jit.2013.14

Sergi, V., & Bonneau, C. (2016). Making mundane work visible on social media: A CMC perspective on community building in professional service firms. *Information and Organization, 26*(3), 142–162. https://doi.org/10.4324/9781351203876-7

Shen, L., Shi, Q., Parida, V., & Jovanovic, M. (2024). Ecosystem orchestration practices for industrial firms: A qualitative meta-analysis, framework development and research agenda. *Technological Forecasting and Social Change, 198*, Article 122171. https://doi.org/10.1016/j.jbusres.2023.114463

Simcoe, T. S. (2012). Standard setting committees: Consensus governance for shared technology platforms. *American Economic Review, 102*(1), 305–336. https://doi.org/10.1257/aer.102.1.305

Spigel, B. (2017). The relational organization of entrepreneurial ecosystems. *Entrepreneurship Theory and Practice, 41*(1), 49–72. https://doi.org/10.1111/etap.12167

Stam, E., & van de Ven, A. (2021). Entrepreneurial ecosystem elements. *Small Business Economics, 56*, 809–832. https://doi.org/10.1007/s11187-019-00270-6

Stephen, A. T. (2016). The role of digital and social media marketing in consumer behavior. *Current Opinion in Psychology, 10*, 17–21. https://doi.org/10.1016/j.copsyc.2015.10.016

Storbacka, K., Brodie, R. J., Böhmann, T., Maglio, P. P., & Nenonen, S. (2016). Actor engagement as a microfoundation for value co-creation. *Journal of Business Research, 69*(8), 3008–3017. https://doi.org/10.1016/j.jbusres.2016.02.034

Sun, S., Zhang, J., Zhu, Y., Jiang, M., & Chen, S. (2022). Exploring users' willingness to disclose personal information in online healthcare communities: The role of satisfaction. *Technological Forecasting and Social Change, 178*, 121602. https://doi.org/10.1016/j.techfore.2022.121596

Teece, D. J. (2007). Explicating dynamic capabilities: The nature and microfoundations of (sustainable) enterprise performance. *Strategic Management Journal, 28*(13), 1319–1350. https://doi.org/10.1002/smj.640

Teece, D. J. (2018). Business models and dynamic capabilities. *Long Range Planning, 51*(1), 40–49. https://doi.org/10.1016/j.lrp.2017.06.007

Teece, D. J., Pisano, G., & Shuen, A. (1997). Dynamic capabilities and strategic management. *Strategic Management Journal, 18*(7), 509–533. https://doi.org/10.1002/(SICI)1097-0266(199708)18:7%3c509::AID-SMJ882%3e3.0.CO;2-Z

Thomas, L. D. W., & Autio, E. (2019). Innovation ecosystems. *SSRN Electronic Journal*. https://doi.org/10.2139/ssrn.3476925

Thomas, L. D. W., Autio, E., & Gann, D. M. (2014). Architectural leverage: Putting platforms in context. *Academy of Management Perspectives, 28*(2), 198–219. https://doi.org/10.5465/amp.2011.0105

Thomas, L. D. W., Ritala, P., Karhu, K., & Heiskala, M. (2024). Vertical, horizontal, and collective complementarities in platform ecosystems. *Growth and Change, 55*(2), 350–371. https://doi.org/10.1080/14479338.2024.2303593

Thomke, S. (2020). *Experimentation works: The surprising power of business experiments*. Harvard Business Review Press.

Thornton, P. H., Ocasio, W., & Lounsbury, M. (2012). *The institutional logics perspective: A new approach to culture, structure, and process*. Oxford University Press.

Tiwana, A. (2014). *Platform ecosystems: Aligning architecture, governance, and strategy.* Morgan Kaufmann.

Tiwana, A. (2014). *Platform ecosystems: Aligning architecture, governance, and strategy.* Morgan Kaufmann.

Tiwana, A., Konsynski, B., & Bush, A. A. (2010). Research commentary—Platform evolution: Coevolution of platform architecture, governance, and environmental dynamics. *Information Systems Research, 21*(4), 675–687. https://doi.org/10.1287/isre.1100.0323

Torres Pena, M. V., & Breidbach, C. F. (2021). On emergence in service platforms: An application to P2P lending. *Journal of Business Research, 135*, 337–347. https://doi.org/10.1016/j.jbusres.2021.06.057

Treiblmaier, H. (2018). The impact of blockchain on the supply chain: A theory-based research framework and a call for action. *Supply Chain Management: An International Journal, 23*(6), 545–559. https://doi.org/10.1108/SCM-01-2018-0029

Tsytsyna, E., & Valminen, T. (2024). How are actor dynamics balanced in ecosystems? An in-depth case study of an autonomous maritime transportation ecosystem. *Review of Managerial Science, 18*, 2547–2582. https://doi.org/10.1007/s11846-023-00688-z

Turner, R., & Miterev, M. (2019). The organizational design of the project-based organization. *Project Management Journal.* https://doi.org/10.1177/8756972819985974

Van Alstyne, M. W., Parker, G. G., & Choudary, S. P. (2016). Pipelines, platforms, and the new rules of strategy. *Harvard Business Review, 94*(4), 54–62.

Van Dyck, M., Lüttgens, D., Diener, K., Piller, F. T., & Pollok, P. (2024). From product to platform: How incumbents' assumptions and choices shape their platform strategy. *Research Policy, 53*(1), Article 104904. https://doi.org/10.1016/j.respol.2023.104904

Vanderhout, S., Taneja, S., Kalia, K., Wodchis, W. P., & Tang, T. (2025). Patient experiences with MyChart in a large community hospital: A mixed methods study. *Journal of Medical Internet Research, 27*, Article e66353. https://doi.org/10.2196/66353

Vargo, S. L., & Lusch, R. F. (2004). Evolving to a new dominant logic for marketing. *Journal of Marketing, 68*(1), 1–17. https://doi.org/10.1509/jmkg.68.1.1.24036

Vargo, S. L., & Lusch, R. F. (2008). Service-dominant logic: Continuing the evolution. *Journal of the Academy of Marketing Science, 36*, 1–10. https://doi.org/10.1007/s11747-007-0069-6

Vargo, S. L., & Lusch, R. F. (2016). Institutions and axioms: An extension and update of service-dominant logic. *Journal of the Academy of Marketing Science, 44*(1), 5–23. https://doi.org/10.1007/s11747-015-0456-3

Vargo, S. L., & Lusch, R. F. (2017). Service-dominant logic 2025. *International Journal of Research in Marketing, 34*(1), 46–67. https://doi.org/10.1016/j.ijresmar.2016.11.001

Vaska, S., Massaro, M., Bagarotto, E. M., & Dal Mas, F. (2021). The digital transformation of business model innovation: A structured literature review. *Frontiers in Psychology, 11*, Article 539363. https://doi.org/10.3389/fpsyg.2020.539363

Verhoef, P. C., Broekhuizen, T., Bart, Y., Bhattacharya, A., Qi Dong, J., Fabian, N., & Haenlein, M. (2021). Digital transformation: A multidisciplinary reflection and research agenda. *Journal of Business Research, 122*, 889–901. https://doi.org/10.1016/j.jbusres.2019.09.022

Wamba-Taguimdje, S. L., Fosso Wamba, S., Kala Kamdjoug, J. R., & Tchatchouang Wanko, C. E. (2020). Influence of artificial intelligence (AI) on firm performance: The business value of AI-based transformation projects. *Business Process Management Journal, 26*(7), 1893–1924. https://doi.org/10.1108/BPMJ-10-2019-0411

Wang, C., Zhao, X., & Hong, J. (2024). A meta-analysis of the effects of interaction on value co-creation in online collaborative innovation communities based on the service ecosystem framework. *Behavioral Sciences, 14*(12), 1177. https://doi.org/10.3390/bs14121177

Wang, Yu & Jin, Xiu. (2023). Exploring the role of shared leadership on job performance in IT industries: Testing the moderated mediation model. *Sustainability*. https://doi.org/10.3390/su152416767

Wareham, J., Fox, P. B., & Cano Giner, J. L. (2014). Technology ecosystem governance. *Organization Science, 25*(4), 1195–1215. https://doi.org/10.1287/orsc.2014.0895

Wassmer, U. (2010). Alliance portfolios: A review and research agenda. *Journal of Management, 36*(1), 141–171. https://doi.org/10.1177/0149206308328484

Whalley, J., Stocker, V., & Lutz, C. (2024). A platform for doers? Fiverr and the gig economy. *SSRN*. https://doi.org/10.2139/ssrn.4800456

Wiersema, F. (2013). The B2B agenda: The current state of B2B marketing and a look ahead. *Journal of Business & Industrial Marketing, 28*(8), 638–642. https://doi.org/10.1016/j.indmarman.2013.02.015

Wilden, R., Devinney, T., & Dowling, G. (2016). The architecture of dynamic capability research identifying the building blocks of a configurational approach. *Academy of Management Annals., 10*, 997–1076. https://doi.org/10.5465/19416520.2016.1161966

Wirtz, J., & Lovelock, C. (2022). *Services marketing: People, technology, strategy* (9th ed.). https://doi.org/10.1142/y0024

Yi, J., He, J., & Yang, L. (2019). Platform heterogeneity, platform governance and complementors' product performance: An empirical study of the mobile application industry. *Frontiers of Business Research in China, 13*(1), 13. https://doi.org/10.1186/s11782-019-0060-3

Zhu, F., & Liu, Q. (2018). Competing with complementors: An empirical look at Amazon.com. *Strategic Management Journal, 39*(10), 2618–2642. https://doi.org/10.1002/smj.2932

Zollo, M., & Winter, S. G. (2002). Deliberate learning and the evolution of dynamic capabilities. *Organization Science, 13*(3), 339–351. https://doi.org/10.1287/orsc.13.3.339.2780

Index

A

actor engagement x, xii, 4, 89–91, 94, 95, 118, 119, 122, 146, 303, 306, 321, 342
adaptive governance 16
adaptive leadership 252
Adaptive Marketing 15
Adobe 306, 337
Adyen 256, 284
Agile 15, 210
AI 5, 7, 14, 24, 26, 45, 66, 70, 80, 93, 100, 103, 104, 106, 131, 140, 142, 152, 160, 163, 173, 174, 176, 178, 179, 188, 201, 207, 211, 219, 230, 231, 238, 284, 295, 305, 315, 318, 323–330, 335, 337, 341
Algolia 337
Algonomy 318
Alibaba 3, 46, 165
Alipay 284
Alloy 296
Amazon 3, 21, 46, 94, 105, 106, 165, 265, 297
Amwell 70

API 29, 57, 66, 68, 124, 160, 185, 198, 218, 229, 234, 235, 242, 246, 266, 308, 314, 315, 319, 324, 328
Apple's App Store 265
Artificial intelligence
 AI 5
asset management 21, 229–232, 235, 245
Atlassian 306
Audi 164
automation 7, 67, 94, 192, 229–231, 235, 243, 245, 248, 318, 337–340

B

B2B x–xii, xviii, 36, 67, 187, 188, 211, 221, 284, 285, 297, 318, 337
Banking-as-a-Service 114
BigCommerce 201
BlackRock 189
Blockchain 6, 45, 80, 163, 176, 201, 211, 220, 284, 296, 306, 337

BMW Group 164
brand equity 160, 168, 263, 265, 316
build trust 24, 78, 89, 102, 104, 105, 108, 198, 200, 204, 205, 213, 219, 223, 253, 319

C

CAC 31, 32
Chime 297
Cloud computing 23, 45, 326, 328
cloud infrastructure 5
co-innovation 122, 173–178, 180–182, 203, 262, 294
Collaborative Innovation 45, 68
Community 14, 104, 128, 129, 131–136, 140, 308
community engagement 128, 161, 182
complementors 10, 13, 16, 34, 57–59, 61, 62, 65–73, 82, 83, 100, 121, 246, 257, 261–269, 283, 286, 288, 294, 296, 313, 315–317, 320, 321, 328
Compliance-as-a-Service 81
Confluence 306
Conga 69
CredAble 201
Cross River Bank 46
customer engagement 197, 212, 217, 243, 339
customer experience 72, 242, 337

D

data-driven xvii, 32, 173, 175, 208, 237, 247, 248, 267, 318, 319, 323, 325, 334
data governance 83, 94, 174, 208, 246, 327
digital banking 144, 306, 337
digital ecosystems 57, 93, 99, 101, 107, 139, 232, 256, 261, 333

Digital platforms 131, 173, 200, 211, 219
digital transformation v, x, 210, 211, 233, 236, 254, 255
distributed leadership 83, 133
Doxy.me 118

E

ecosystem design 18, 32, 79, 80, 102
ecosystem orchestration 161, 165, 230, 298, 299
ecosystem thinking x, xviii, 186
energy sector 210, 245, 255
Engagement loops 31
Epic Systems 81, 144
Equity Alliances 273
ethical 78, 106, 108, 118, 119, 166, 193, 199, 209, 265, 297, 317, 321
Etoro 132
Etsy 143, 151

F

feedback loops 5, 7, 27, 43, 80, 90, 91, 139, 140, 161, 175, 198, 202, 208, 255, 304, 308, 314, 333
Feedzai 69
finance 22, 69, 70, 78, 81, 83, 94, 101, 114, 145, 176, 185, 201, 207, 209, 218, 221, 257, 318
financial platforms 26, 185
financial services 46, 77, 144, 145, 178, 185, 243, 254, 256
fintech ecosystems 185, 190, 191
fintech platforms 144
FlexiPay 187, 188
Ford 164
fostering collaboration 118, 191, 219, 222

G

GDPR 81, 105, 208, 327, 336
GitHub 43, 132, 151, 164
Google Play 265
governance models 41, 58, 79, 81, 128, 218, 221
GrabPay 284

H

healthcare 9, 23, 69, 70, 78, 81, 83, 105, 114, 142, 144, 145, 176, 178, 201, 207, 209, 211, 218, 243, 254, 256, 265, 281, 337
HealthEdge 211
HIPAA 81, 105, 208, 209
human-centered 338
Hyundai 164

I

Innovaccer 337
Institutional Logic 79, 209
institutional resistance 79, 85, 342
interoperability 77, 164, 242, 244, 249, 294, 297, 327
IONITY 164
IoT 5, 6, 177, 210, 323–330, 335, 337, 341
iTranslate 69

J

Jira 306
Joint Ventures 273

K

Kia 164
KYC 69, 118, 188, 209

L

legitimacy 58, 78, 81–83, 85, 87, 122, 281, 282, 342

Lifecycle 95, 131
low inter-organisational trust 79

M

marketing leadership 16, 38, 60, 90, 223, 256–259, 304
marketing strategy 108, 128, 147, 241, 257, 333, 335, 338, 339
Marqeta 318
Mastercard's 187
Mercedes-Benz 164
Mirakl 221
modern marketing 27, 89, 122, 197, 246, 247, 263, 324–326
modularity 230, 241, 242, 287, 294
Monzo 94, 306
MyChart 81, 144

N

Netflix 94
network effects 4, 25, 27, 28, 35, 36, 57, 103, 128, 263, 264, 286, 318, 320
networks v, 9, 14, 21, 27, 41, 55, 60, 66, 67, 72, 99, 129, 134, 164, 165, 188, 197, 217, 230, 234, 244, 262, 281, 284, 293, 294, 298, 300, 334, 335, 337
Non-Equity 273
Nova Credit 69

O

Onfido 69
operational efficiency 231, 243, 283, 288, 331, 337
orchestration 7, 16, 17, 48, 90, 141, 230, 258, 294, 304, 313, 314, 329
orchestrators 4, 5, 17, 56–59, 61, 82, 83, 119, 159, 218, 235, 252, 266, 338

P

Partner marketing 119, 121
PayPal 104, 105, 265
Peloton 132, 151
personalisation 4, 5, 22, 24, 46, 94, 96, 115, 121, 231, 233, 236, 237, 242, 247–249, 308, 318
Philips 256
Plaid 186, 296
platform architecture 174, 282
platform-driven marketing 333, 335, 338
platform engagement 6, 37
platform growth 6, 9, 31, 33, 66, 91, 128, 269, 275, 276, 278, 287, 288, 303, 320, 321, 333
platform marketer 6
platform models xii, 218
platform strategy xviii, 15, 48, 286, 334
plug-and-play 113, 230, 234, 241–248, 294, 334
Porsche 164
Press Ganey 81

R

real-time analytics 24, 114, 232, 234, 246, 249, 319
reciprocal integration 159–161, 163, 166, 167
regional strategy 287
regulatory constraints 207, 209, 212, 253
resilience 23, 56, 60, 77, 82, 99, 101, 122, 133, 136, 144, 146, 152, 155, 167, 178, 223, 234, 254, 256, 263–265, 294, 297, 318, 334
resource integration 4, 147, 159, 161, 163–165, 167, 187, 189, 200, 293–301, 337

retail 43, 145, 165, 186, 201, 218, 219, 221, 230, 265, 285, 297, 318, 325, 337
retention 34, 36, 70, 91, 124, 128, 152, 157, 161, 186, 238, 246, 267, 282, 294, 314, 317, 337
Revolut 143, 211
Robinhood 297
Robo-advisors 189

S

SaaS 57, 229, 235, 236, 283
Salesforce 3, 43, 69, 297, 337
scalability 4, 24, 26, 32, 60, 65, 119, 131, 165, 205, 229, 230, 235, 241, 243, 245, 247, 248, 264, 276, 293, 296, 297, 324, 326, 327, 333
SDL 45, 142, 295
ServiceNow 318
shared value x, 28, 41, 55, 108, 122, 135, 141, 147, 148, 152, 157, 181, 187, 191, 193, 197, 221
shared vision 34, 46, 67, 199, 219, 221, 274, 276
Shopify 117
Slack or Microsoft Teams 211
Socure 69
software 9, 43, 53, 57, 211, 218
Solaris 118
Spotify 94
Standard Chartered 187
Starling Bank 81
strategic alliances 273, 275, 276, 278
strategic vision xvii, 36, 253
Stripe 221
structural inertia 78, 208
systemic xvii, 16, 46, 77, 83, 103, 231, 243, 252, 255
systems thinking 9, 139, 167, 299

T

Tazapay 187
technology stack 23, 181, 245, 287, 339
Teladoc Health 105
Telehealth 70
TeleTracking 46
Temenos 337
Tink 186
transformational leadership 256
Transparency and trust 262
trustworthiness 212, 267

U

user-generated 4, 26, 36, 151, 191, 198, 234, 298, 319
user journeys 35, 198, 308, 314, 324

V

value co-creation v, x, 41, 42, 44, 59, 60, 89, 139, 146, 151, 152, 156, 185, 190, 191, 193, 199, 200, 203–205, 276, 295
value exchange 6, 34, 95, 113, 127, 192
velocity 8, 32, 33, 224, 309, 314
visual frameworks 9
Volkswagen Group 164
VTEX 285

W

Withings 70
Woebot Health 70

Z

Zendesk 285

GPSR Compliance

The European Union's (EU) General Product Safety Regulation (GPSR) is a set of rules that requires consumer products to be safe and our obligations to ensure this.

If you have any concerns about our products, you can contact us on

ProductSafety@springernature.com

In case Publisher is established outside the EU, the EU authorized representative is:

Springer Nature Customer Service Center GmbH
Europaplatz 3
69115 Heidelberg, Germany